Surrealism in North Africa and Western Asia: Crossings and Encounters

Edited by

Monique Bellan
Julia Drost

BEIRUTER TEXTE UND STUDIEN

HERAUSGEGEBEN VOM
ORIENT-INSTITUT BEIRUT

BAND 141

Surrealism in North Africa and Western Asia: Crossings and Encounters

Edited by

Monique Bellan
Julia Drost

OIB

DEUTSCHES FORUM
FÜR KUNSTGESCHICHTE
CENTRE ALLEMAND
D'HISTOIRE DE L'ART
PARIS

BEIRUT 2021

ERGON VERLAG
IN KOMMISSION

Umschlaggestaltung: Taline Yozgatian

Cover illustration:
The "Mousquetaires". Antoine Tabet, Georges Schehadé, Antoine Mourani, and Alexandre Abouchaar, at the café du Phare, Beirut, 1929. Archives Georges Schehadé / IMEC.

Bibliografische Information der Deutschen Nationalbibliothek
Die Deutsche Nationalbibliothek verzeichnet diese Publikation in der Deutschen Nationalbibliografie; detaillierte bibliografische Daten sind im Internet über http://dnb.d-nb.de abrufbar.

Bibliographic information published by the Deutsche Nationalbibliothek
The Deutsche Nationalbibliothek lists this publication in the Deutsche Nationalbibliografie; detailed bibliographic data are available in the Internet at http://dnb.d-nb.de.

ISBN 978-3-95650-858-5 (Print)
ISBN 978-3-95650-859-2 (ePDF)
ISSN 0067-4931

 Gedruckt mit Unterstützung des Orient-Instituts Beirut, gegründet von der Deutschen Morgenländischen Gesellschaft, aus Mitteln des Bundesministeriums für Bildung und Forschung.

Die Beiruter Texte und Studien werden herausgegeben unter der Mitarbeit von Lale Behzadi, Birgit Krawietz, Sonja Mejcher-Atassi, Birgit Schäbler und Henning Sievert.

Wissenschaftlich betreut von Christopher Bahl und Abdallah Soufan.

Ergon – ein Verlag in der Nomos Verlagsgesellschaft, Baden-Baden

Gedruckt auf alterungsbeständigem Papier

Table of contents

Acknowledgements

This volume has its origins in the joint workshop "The Avant-Garde and its Networks: Surrealism in Paris, North Africa and the Middle East since the 1930s", held by the Orient-Institut Beirut and the Deutsches Forum für Kunstgeschichte Paris (German Forum for Art History in Paris) from 14–15 November 2016 in Beirut. The initial idea for it arose out of a chance encounter between us, the editors, in autumn 2015. Monique was working on surrealism in Egypt within the context of her research project on aesthetic reflection, while Julia had, for several years, been investigating surrealism's international networks with a special focus on the art market. This led to the idea of a joint workshop examining the connections between Paris, as the place of origin of the surrealist movement, and North Africa and Western Asia. We were interested in both the North–South and South–South relationships and the possible connections between artists, writers and groups. In this, we were guided by the assumption that all kinds of reciprocal relationships – of both a direct and indirect nature – existed between Paris and the regions of North Africa and Western Asia that were not necessarily linear, but which took place through third parties, and it was our intention to investigate these relationships.

With their specific research into individual protagonists in various countries of the region, the ten essays in this volume contribute to a deeper knowledge of surrealism and foster a better understanding of why surrealism, as a revolutionary and accessible artistic movement, had the potential to stimulate and enrich artistic production in a historical and cultural region so different to Paris, London and New York.

This volume is the fruit of numerous colleagues' work. The editors would like to express their sincere thanks to Sam Bardaouil, Judith Bihr, Cléa Daridan, Fabrice Flahutez, Catherine Hansen, Megan C. MacDonald, Arturo Monaco, Eyüp Özveren and Jad Tabet, all of whom took part in the workshop, as well as to the authors Ambra D'Antone and Alfred el-Khoury, who joined the project later. We also thank Nadia Bou Ali and Sonja Mejcher-Atassi for participating as discussants in the workshop and contributing to the debates. The Orient-Institut Beirut and the Deutsches Forum für Kunstgeschichte Paris, namely their directors Stefan Leder and Birgit Schäbler in Beirut, and Thomas Kirchner in Paris, have supported the project with great interest and commitment right from the start. Our thanks go as well to the interns of both institutions for their editorial assistance and picture research, namely Ida Forbriger, Hans Magne Jaatun, Maxime Kuhlmey, Michael Rauch, Alexander Reindl, Lena Syen and Manzi Tanna-Händel. We would also like to offer our sincere gratitude to Christopher Bahl and Abdallah Soufan for coordinating this publication, to the BTS Advisory Board for its critical input, to the peer-reviewers for their constructive feedback and to Tim Curnow (English) and Françoise Joly (French) for their expert copy-editing.

Berlin and Los Angeles, May 2020

Monique Bellan and Julia Drost

Note on transliteration

This book uses the transliteration system of the *International Journal of Middle East Studies* (*IJMES*) to convert Arabic into English. This applies for citations and titles of books, articles and journals. For artists' and authors' names, the chapters generally adhere to the spelling that these persons used themselves or under which they are commonly known to facilitate recognition. However, some authors use full transliteration throughout their entire chapter.

Note on contributors

Monique Bellan is a researcher who focuses on art, aesthetics and their political dimensions. She holds a PhD in Arabic Studies from the Free University of Berlin and an MA from the University of Bonn. She has worked as a researcher at the collaborative research centre on Aesthetic Experience and the Dissolution of Artistic Limits, and, from 2013 to 2019, as a research associate at the Orient-Institut Beirut with a project on aesthetic reflection and art critique in Lebanon. She is the author of *Dismember Remember: Das anatomische Theater von Lina Saneh und Rabih Mroué* (Reichert, 2013). Among her recent publications is *The Art Salon in the Arab Region: Politics of Taste Making* (BTS, 2018), co-edited with Nadia von Maltzahn.

Ambra D'Antone is a collaborative doctoral candidate at The Courtauld Institute of Art and Tate Modern, supervised by Prof. Gavin Parkinson and Dr Matthew Gale. Her thesis provides a historical and methodological reconfiguration of the international surrealist presence by analyzing the artistic and literary expressions of surrealism in the Levant region as instances of translation. She is the editor-in-chief of immediations no. 17, the 2020 issue of The Courtauld Institute of Art's academic journal.

Cléa Daridan is an art historian, critic and curator. She is shortly to submit her PhD thesis entitled "Histoire de la conscience du patrimoine Alexandrin, de Nasser à nos jours" at the Sorbonne University from which she holds an MA in Art History. Recently, she won a residency at the Villa Médicis, Académie de France in Rome. She is a regular lecturer and guest speaker at international universities and institutions, including ENSAD, Parsons School and the CESE in Paris, ESAD in Reims, NYU in New York and UNIGE in Geneva. She has regularly contributed to international publications such as *Intramuros*, *Diptyk* and *La Tribune de l'Art*. To be published: "Almagia/Ambron: Itinéraire d'une famille de mécènes et collectionneurs juifs au croisement de l'Italie fasciste et de l'Égypte nassérienne", *Mélanges*, Rome, EFR.

Julia Drost is a director of research at the German Center for Art History in Paris where she has been responsible for the Young Academics Department since 2013. Her research focuses on German–French art relations and the international networks and the history of ideas of surrealism. She co-curated numerous exhibitions, including "Max Ernst: Le jardin de la France" in Tours (2009–2010) and a "Max Ernst Retrospective" at the Albertina in Vienna and at the Fondation Beyeler in Basel (2012–2013). She has been a member of the Editorial Board of the *Journal for Art Market Studies* since 2017. She was a scholar in residence for the 2019–2020 academic year at the Getty Research Institute. She is currently working on a new book project "Utopias and Dystopias of Nature: Ecological Thought in Surrealism".

Fabrice Flahutez is an art historian, filmmaker, publisher, curator and professor at the University of Lyon-Saint-Étienne. He is the author of a history of lettrism titled *Le Lettrisme historique était une avant-garde 1945–1953* (Les Presses du réel, 2011) and of *Isidore Isou's Library: A Certain Look on Lettrism* (Artvenir, 2014), together with Camille Morando. With Fabien Danesi and Emmanuel Guy he co-authored *La Fabrique du cinéma de Guy Debord* (Actes-Sud, 2013) and *Undercover Guy Debord* (Artvenir, 2013). He is also a specialist in surrealism and artist groups after 1945 in Europe. He is currently working on a monograph on Slavko Kopač, to be published in 2021.

Alfred el-Khoury studied Arabic language and literature at the Lebanese University and the American University of Beirut. He is currently a doctoral candidate in the Department of Arabic Studies at the University of Bamberg. Beside Arabic surrealism and avant-gardist projects in Arabic literature, el-Khoury's research interests include old Arabic poetry, metaphor, literary theory and philology. His doctoral project investigates metaphor in corpora of Arabic poetry between the pre-Islamic and early Abbasid periods and proposes a re-examination of questions of tradition, meaning production and poetical innovation. El-Khoury has taught courses on Arabic poetry and literature at the American University of Beirut, the University of Bamberg and the University of Erlangen-Nuremberg.

Megan C. MacDonald is affiliated with the viticulture/oenologie programme at the CFPPA Montmorot, France. Her research focuses on contemporary francophone and Mediterranean literary and visual cultures, and her work has appeared in journals such as *Sites/Contemporary French and Francophone Studies*, *Francosphères*, the *International Journal of Francophone Studies*, *Feminist Media Studies* and *Expressions Maghrébines*. She is the co-editor with Claire Launchbury of *Urban Bridges, Global Capitals: Trans-Mediterranean Francosphères* (Liverpool University Press, 2020) and her forthcoming book is titled *Monsters without Borders: Literary Precarity and the Postcolonial Navette*. She was in residence for the 2018–2019 academic year as a EURIAS fellow at IMéRA, Institute of Advanced Studies, Université Aix-Marseille working on the project "The Way Back: Mediterranean Wakes and Urban Archival Futures".

Arturo Monaco is a postdoctoral fellow at Sapienza University of Rome/Istituto per l'Oriente "C.A. Nallino" with a project on the reception of Greek mythology in Arabic literature. He holds a PhD in Civilizations, Cultures and Societies of Asia and Africa, Sapienza University of Rome (2016). His PhD dissertation explores the surrealist trend in modern Arabic literature, with a special focus on the surrealist manifestations in Egypt, Syria and Lebanon between the 1930s and 1960s. He also holds an MA in Oriental Languages and Civilizations from

Sapienza University of Rome (2012). Currently, he is a lecturer of Arabic language and literature at the University of Catania. His research interests include modern Arabic poetry, Arab literary press and intercultural exchanges between Arabic and foreign literatures.

Eyüp Özveren is an independent scholar based in Istanbul. Before his retirement in 2018, he served as a professor at the Faculty of Economic and Administrative Sciences of the Middle East Technical University in Ankara. His primary specialization was in teaching institutional political economy, economic history and economic thought in the Department of Economics, as well as cinema and literature in the Media and Cultural Studies programme of his university. He has published extensively in disparate domains such as Mediterranean studies, economics, literature and visual arts. He is currently working on a series of publications, intended as constitutive parts of a book project, about the advent of surrealism across the Mediterranean.

Jad Tabet is an architect and planner working between Beirut and Paris. He is currently president of the Lebanese Order of Engineers and Architects and president of the Arab Union of Architects, a member of the UNESCO High Level Reflection Group for Strategic Transformation and a former member of the UNESCO World Heritage Committee (2001–2005 and 2013–2017). Tabet is the author of several academic publications on war and reconstruction, and on the relationship between heritage and modernity. He taught architecture at the National Institute of Fine Arts at the Lebanese University, the Faculty of Engineering and Architecture at the American University of Beirut and the Belleville School of Architecture in Paris and served as distinguished faculty member at the Paris School of International Affairs (PSIA, Sciences Po Paris).

Introduction
Surrealism in North Africa and Western Asia: Crossings and encounters

Monique Bellan / Julia Drost

When, where and what was surrealism? These questions appear obsolete when looking at Paris, London or New York, for example, where research into surrealism has been abundant and well documented. When turning our gaze to other regions, especially outside the Western realm, things seem to be much less obvious and barely studied.

The recent exhibition on the group Art et Liberté (1938–1948) in Paris, curated by Sam Bardaouil and Till Fellrath, along with the comprehensive scholarly study by Sam Bardaouil on this very group, can be considered a turning point in the exploration of surrealism in the Arab region.[1] For the first time, the group was exhibited in its historical context and at the former centre of surrealism itself, namely in Paris. The shift of centre and periphery implied here is the prelude to a paradigmatic global turn, which considers surrealism outside Paris not as peripheral phenomena but as equal avant-gardes.

Surrealism's distinct moral dimension and its political and aesthetic radicalism were fundamental for its international appeal. Its ability to adapt, engage and merge with local conditions makes it an interesting phenomenon to study, especially in the light of today's modernism approaches in regions outside Europe and North America. The present volume sets out to investigate surrealism since the 1930s in a geographic area – Syria, Lebanon, Egypt, Turkey and Algeria – which has largely been neglected in terms of modern art historical studies, but which has fortunately gained rising scholarly attention during the past two decades.

1 *Art et Liberté: Rupture, War and Surrealism in Egypt (1938–1948)*, Centre Pompidou, Paris, 19 October 2016–16 January 2017, curated by Sam Bardaouil and Till Fellrath. After Paris, the exhibition was shown at the Museo Nacional Centro de Arte Reina Sofía in Madrid (14 February–28 May 2017), Kunstsammlung Nordrhein-Westfalen K20 in Düsseldorf (15 July–15 October 2017), Tate Liverpool (17 November 2017–17 March 2018) and finally at the Moderna Museet in Stockholm (21 April–19 August 2018). Shortly before, another exhibition was paying tribute to the Egyptian surrealist movement at the Ministry of Culture's Palace of Arts in Cairo: *When Art becomes Liberty: The Egyptian Surrealists (1938–1965)*, Palace of Arts, Cairo, 28 September–28 October 2016, curated by Hoor Al-Qasimi, Salah M. Hassan, Ehab Ellaban and Nagla Samir. Also see the publications by Sam Bardaouil, *Surrealism in Egypt: Modernism and the Art and Liberty Group*, London: I.B. Tauris 2017; and by Sam Bardaouil and Till Fellrath, eds., *Art et Liberté: Rupture, War and Surrealism in Egypt (1938–1948)*, Paris: Skira/Centre Georges Pompidou 2016.

One aspect we were interested in when we first started this project was to analyze how Parisian surrealism spread throughout the world, and specifically to North Africa and Western Asia. As we gained deeper insight into the relations we became aware that the matter was far more complex. From the 1930s onwards, surrealism did not simply emerge in different cultural contexts from French surrealism. In fact, it developed its own characteristics and was – although always related to Breton's surrealism – never subordinated to a French "leadership". Michael Richardson emphasizes that the adherence to surrealism "represented a confirmation of what writers and artists had already been looking for either individually or collectively".[2] Hence, it was more the approach to life in general, the strong critical component and the fierce and often provocative rejection of the hegemony of the bourgeoisie or the ruling class that made artists, writers and intellectuals in other cultural contexts receptive to surrealism.

For our context and for the following discussion of concepts of modernism, it is therefore interesting to keep in mind the model of "communicating vessels" that Richardson brings to the fore in the context of the relation between surrealism and the Caribbean:

> [...] it is a question neither of surrealism "in" the Caribbean nor of "Caribbean surrealism", but rather about what happened when surrealism and the Caribbean came into interrelation. It is thus the story of an encounter that forged a dynamic by which surrealism and the Caribbean were reciprocally energized.[3]

Linking surrealism to a specific nation or region does not give it an identity that helps in differentiating it from other surrealisms; nor is it necessary or in any way meaningful. What is more significant is to look at the outcome of these relations in terms of individual encounters and projects and how cross-fertilizing processes may have shaped or informed local specificities.

How did André Breton envision surrealism's relation with the world? Despite its very beginnings as a local, Paris-confined movement, it soon spread to many countries, not least due to various journals to which Breton, the writer, was a main contributor: "The international distribution of surrealism occurred [...] when various non-affiliated avant-garde journals produced special issues on surrealism [...]."[4] The dissemination of surrealim was backed by travelling artists and writers who planted the seeds of surrealism in their home or host countries. This is what Martin Puchner describes as the "decentering of surrealism".[5] In 1935, Benjamin

---

2 Michael Richardson, "Surrealism Faced with Cultural Difference", in: *Cosmopolitan Modernisms*, Kobena Mercer, ed., Cambridge, MA: MIT Press 2005, 74.

3 Richardson, "Surrealism Faced with Cultural Difference", 74.

4 Martin Puchner, *Poetry of the Revolution: Marx, Manifestos and the Avant-Gardes*, Princeton: Princeton University Press 2006, 187.

5 "Increasingly, however, Breton's authority over surrealism, and thus his monopoly over its manifestos, was challenged by a process that could be described as the decentering of surrealism." Puchner, *Poetry of the Revolution*, 187.

Péret wrote that "to avoid its own desiccation", surrealism had to "bypass the narrow borders of France and adopt an international presence".[6] By the time surrealism had irreversibly spread, André Breton proclaimed the "limits not frontiers of surrealism" in the *Nouvelle Revue française* (1937) and thereby the wide-spreading character of his movement: "[...] surrealism now tends to unify in one name the aspirations of the inventive writers and artists of all countries".[7] Many years later, in 1970, the former member of the Belgian wing of surrealism Marcel Mariën (1920–1993) retrospectively expressed a similar view: "To the extent that surrealism could have any connection with geography, one couldn't think of it as other than international, or, better still, and once and for all – stateless."[8]

The pronounced desire to question and overcome traditional geographies was demonstrated by the geopolitical world map *Le Monde au temps des surréalistes* that reflected its ideological convictions (fig. 1).

However, the scholarly analysis through a geographical lens, as pursued in the case studies of the present volume, can be a helpful tool to understand surrealism as an international or global phenomenon.

Surrealism in global and local perspective

The discussion of surrealism and its relation to Egyptian, Lebanese, Syrian, Turkish and Algerian artists, writers and intellectuals must be embedded in the context of broader discussions about modernism in regions outside Western Europe and North America. An increasing number of recent publications have been looking critically at modernism in Africa, South America and Asia, which had hitherto largely been regarded as "belated", "missing", "not yet", "not quite" and basically copying Western models. The centre–periphery model, although still quite common, is more and more being pushed off the pedestal by concepts such as "global modernism", "transnational modernism" and "world art", while Eric Hayot and Rebecca Walkowitz argue for a new vocabulary for global modernism.[9]

---

6 "[...] pour ne pas se dessécher" surrealism had to "sortir du cadre étroit des frontières de ce pays et prendre une figure internationale". Benjamin Péret, "Le Surréalisme international", *Cahiers d'art* 5–6 (1935), 138.

7 André Breton, "Limits Not Frontiers of Surrealism", in: *Surrealism*, ed. Herbert Read, New York: Praeger Publishers 1971, 99. Original French: "limites non-frontières du surréalisme [...] le surréalisme tend à unifier aujourd'hui sur son nom les aspirations des écrivains et des artistes novateurs de tous les pays." "Limites non-frontières du surréalisme", dans André Breton, *Œuvres complètes*, dir. Marguerite Bonnet, Paris : Gallimard/Pléiade 1988–2008, 3:661.

8 Marcel Mariën interviewed by Christian Bussy, *Surrealist Transformaction* 2 (1970); cited in Michael Richardson, "'Other' Surrealisms: Center and Periphery in International Perspective", in: *A Companion to Dada and Surrealism*, David Hopkins, ed., Chichester: Wiley Blackwell 2016, 131.

9 The latter depart from the premise that modernism was a world phenomenon and that "global modernism" therefore is a tautology. Nevertheless, Hayot and Walkowitz point out

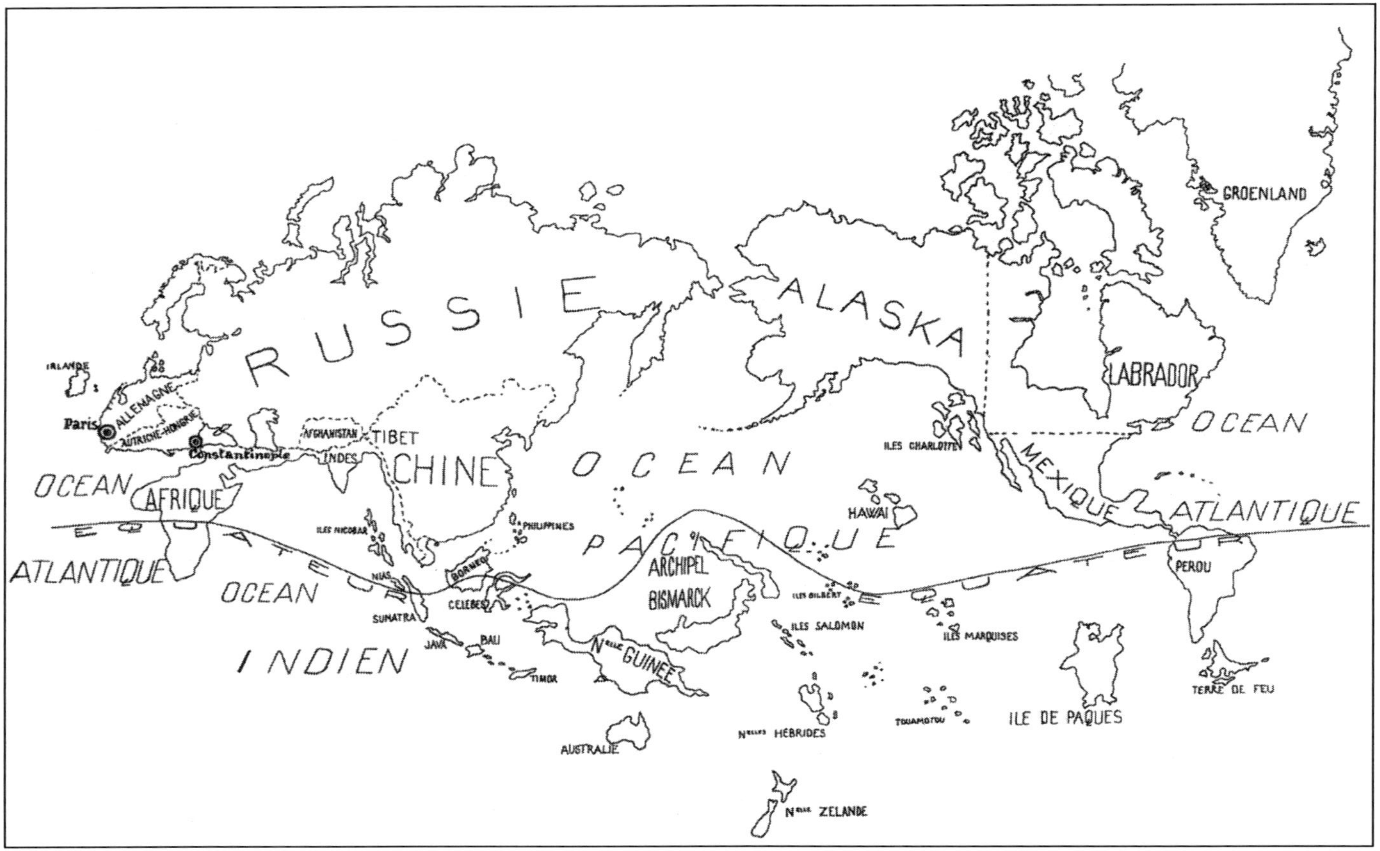

Figure 1: Anonymous, *Surrealist Map of the World* (Le monde au temps des surréalistes), in *Le surréalisme en 1929*, special issue of *Variétés* (Brussels), June 1929.

Recent initiatives have been aiming at decentring and decolonizing arts and culture, and knowledge more broadly, by remodelling university curricula as well as curatorial and scholarly practices. Regarding the Arab world, this implies a comprehensive, long-needed revision of institutionalized and deeply rooted perspectives on non-Western art and on official narratives that are being deconstructed. This goes hand in hand with a diversification of cultural and academic fields in order to overcome the monolithic narrative of the West's monopoly over modernism in favour of a more inclusive artistic canon and art history. A very important and long-awaited initiative is the recent publication of primary documents on modern art in the Arab world by Anneka Lenssen, Sarah Rogers and Nada Shabout.[10] It is important as it shows the discourses on modern art in other parts of the world – outside the "centres" – which were often taking place in parallel. One such discovery is the poet and essayist May Ziadeh's (1886–1941) statement from 1912, which strongly resonates with the surrealists' credo of the power of imagination: "Imagination is a lost guest roving the earth; it is the strongest cultural force. Its movement never ceases throughout our lives."[11] Cairo-based Ziadeh belonged to a network of thinkers known as the Mahjar (a literary movement of Arabic speaking writers who had emigrated to America from the Levant at the turn of the twentieth century) "whose writing often cast the arts as a cross-medium field – encompassing poetry, the visual arts, dance and more – of spiritual feeling not beholden to modern rationalism".[12] The value of undertakings such as the publishing of primary documents on Arab modern art can therefore not be overestimated as it brings together the shattered voices of some of the most important contributors to the discourse on Arab modern art. It provides the material on the grounds of which the rereading, and possibly rewriting, of art history can take place.

This change in perspective is necessarily connected to a shift of power, and constitutes a significant step in starting to recognize modernist artistic expressions from these regions as equally authentic and valuable. Most importantly, this perspective jettisons the idea that the West stands for innovation and modernization whereas the rest merely provides raw material, but otherwise stays rooted in traditions and at best excels in craft rather than in the arts. However, the retrospective inclusion of previously excluded art histories has some pitfalls. Kobena Mercer

that they transitionally stick to this terminology only "[…] to indicate that the force of the adjective is still needed as a contrast for some other more local or 'normal' modernism imagined to be not so, or not all, global. […] We are not asking, was modernism global? It was and is, in theory and in practice." Eric Hayot and Rebecca L. Walkowitz, *A New Vocabulary for Global Modernism*, New York: Columbia University Press 2016, 7.

10 Anneka Lenssen, Sarah Rogers and Nada Shabout, eds., *Modern Art in the Arab World: Primary Documents*, New York: Museum of Modern Art 2018.

11 May Ziadeh, "Something about Art", in: *Modern Art in the Arab World: Primary Documents*, Anneka Lenssen, Sarah Rogers and Nada Shabout, eds., New York: Museum of Modern Art 2018, 45.

12 Ziadeh, "Something about Art", 45.

points out that it risks being merely additive and not paying tribute to the many encounters, collaborations and exchanges that took place between artists and institutions from the West and the so-called global South.[13] Therefore, inclusive research into surrealism needs to point out these connections and cross-fertilization processes to avoid falling into the trap of a superficial retroactive construction, which risks merely adding an exotic flavour to the predominant narrative. It needs to provide detailed accounts of the respective artistic and literary developments and their discourses to unveil the possible connections.

Christian Kravagna's concept of a postcolonial art history of contact argues in a similar direction although the author is sceptical about big concepts such as global art history or world art studies. Kravagna underlines that the retrospective application of concepts such as transculturality, hybridity and syncretism are not suitable tools to expand Western art history – which has been exclusive for a long time – beyond its traditional regional confines.[14] The claim of an all-encompassing history of world art or global art seems not only theoretically impossible but also politically disputable as it risks feeding a neo-imperialistic knowledge project.[15] Instead, Kravagna advocates for a history of contact which brings the historical transcultural encounters of actors in the artistic field to the fore. This approach examines the conditions under which the transcultural, hybrid and syncretistic approach of specific non-Western thinkers and artists played a role in shaping new identity concepts in society, science and the arts.[16] Applied to the present volume's concern of uncovering what have until now been largely hidden histories of surrealism in the regions of North Africa and Western Asia, this means that research has to take the various local contexts and conditions into consideration to a much greater extent than has happened previously.

The concept of "constellational modernism" which has recently been introduced by Alex Dika Seggerman to describe the multinational connections of Egyptian modernism from 1879 to 1967 is a new compelling approach.[17] Based on the form of an astrological constellation, it implies a specific and finite number of

---

13 "Like the additive model before it, the contemporary ideology now surrounding the notion of 'inclusion' creates a pressure to pursue this goal as an end in itself, as if 'inclusion' was the end of the story." Kobena Mercer, "Introduction", in: *Cosmopolitan Modernisms*, Kobena Mercer, ed., Cambridge, MA: MIT Press 2015, 13.

14 Christian Kravagna, *Transmoderne: Eine Kunstgeschichte des Kontakts*, Berlin: b_books 2017, 13.

15 Kravagna, *Transmoderne*, 14.

16 "Vielmehr steht die Frage im Mittelpunkt, unter welchen Bedingungen und mit welchen Agenden bestimmte das Transkulturelle/Hybride/Synkretistische von bestimmten Denker/innen und Künstler/innen dem Reich der kolonialen Verachtung entrissen wurde und im Rahmen von neuen, selbstbestimmten Identitätskonzepten und diversen Projekten der befreiungspolitischen Transformation kolonialer bzw. rassistischer Grenzregime in Gesellschaft, Wissenschaft und Künsten eine Aufwertung erfuhr." Kravagna, *Transmoderne*, 14.

17 Alex Dika Seggerman, *Modernism on the Nile: Art in Egypt between the Islamic and the Contemporary*, Cairo: American University in Cairo Press 2019.

connections evoked through travels, exhibitions, degrees and circulated textual and visual materials.[18] The author relies on this concept as it provides more accuracy than global or transnational approaches to modernism and allows for more individualism regarding each artist's specific trajectory and encounters. In addition, constellational modernism refers not only to the circulation of art objects and artists, but also takes the aesthetic into account, "in that a constellation is not only a set of stars but also an image drawn from linking them".[19] Another advantage of the constellational perspective on modernism is that it rejects a central core or narrative thereby flattening hierarchies. It "rather frames modernism as a series of overlapping and intersecting units as opposed to concentric circles emanating from the metropole".[20] Together with Kravagna's art history of contact, Seggerman's constellational modernism comes closest to the methodological approach underlying the present volume: it seeks to explore connections, encounters and exchanges on individual, institutional and also spiritual levels.

While it is imperative to find meaningful research concepts and tools through which to approach and reassess multiple artistic and literary developments and interrelations, it is no less important to look at certain modernist phenomena in more depth and to differentiate between discourse and practice. The findings will often reveal that while a specific artistic technique was applied and mastered, the accompanying aesthetic discourse that led to the development, evolution or dismissal of certain artistic approaches, movements and currents was often missing. For example, in her study on Ottoman painting, Wendy Shaw points out that cultures around the world have amalgamated Western and modern practices with local ones, which eventually led to differential modernities.[21] In the case of Turkey, painting in the Western modality was not the same as Western painting "because it does not contain the legacy of its discourse".[22] Shaw emphasizes that although Ottoman art in the Western modality appeared during the modern era, it is "distinctly not modernist".[23] The author explicitly hints at an understanding of modernism as a critical movement that radically questioned artistic traditions and hitherto prevailing perceptions and representations. This was not the case with Ottoman painting as it did not – and could not – refer to any such traditions in its own culture.

This strongly resonates with what Lebanese poet and journalist Abbas Baydoun says on the relation between culture and arts in contemporary Lebanon. Baydoun criticizes the lack of self-awareness and the superficiality in the way that artistic

18 Seggerman, *Modernism on the Nile*, 6.
19 Seggerman, *Modernism on the Nile*, 7.
20 Seggerman, *Modernism on the Nile*, 8.
21 Wendy M.K. Shaw, *Ottoman Painting: Reflections of Western Art from the Ottoman Empire to the Turkish Republic*, London: I.B. Tauris 2011, 1.
22 Shaw, *Ottoman Painting*, 1.
23 Shaw, *Ottoman Painting*, 1.

concepts have been taken over from the West, namely as pure techniques and styles and without the philosophical and historical background.[24] "If we acknowledge that the philosophy of art is an inseparable part of modern art", he says, "then we would understand that we produce an art which is cut off from its culture, thus transforming the international trademark into an art without culture."[25] Baydoun critically remarks that the artists' main preoccupation is to please and therefore to create an art that "bedazzles" with elegance and symmetry, but does not expose ideas and questions or create disharmony and friction. This is one of the reasons that surrealism did not find fertile ground in Lebanon, he states with a certain sarcasm: "We did not celebrate Surrealism because it dealt with expression and ideas; and expression and thought disrupt the balance and fluidity of our paintings."[26] The reception of modernist art, and surrealism more specifically, was selective and depended on the general attitude towards art and its (aesthetic and societal) function. The underpinning of artistic techniques with relevant theoretical questions and considerations that led to specific choices is often missing in contexts where the historical developments of art and art institutions followed different paths. And here we come to another specificity of the region studied in this volume: while poetry was deeply anchored in local literary traditions, fine art followed a different trajectory as it was basically injected from outside, with young artists from North Africa and Western Asia being sent abroad for apprenticeships during the late nineteenth and early twentieth centuries, mainly to Paris and Rome. Art academies and other institutions were only established in the first half of the twentieth century (e.g. the School of Fine Arts was founded in Cairo in 1908 and the Académie Libanaise des Beaux-Arts in Beirut in 1943). Accordingly – with the notable exception of Egypt – there were hardly any anti-academic and avant-garde movements. This may explain why surrealism was more widespread in poetry than in visual art.

Undoubtedly, this volume aims to situate itself within the broader field of global modernism in the sense that we understand modernism as a phenomenon that spread globally. Nevertheless, as has been stated by several authors mentioned above, this is too broad a concept and does not help in understanding the local particularities of each case. Moreover, rhizomatic connections that are not necessarily visible on the surface create new nodes and points of exchange which need to be uncovered in a first step in order to enrich the history of surrealism. In many cases, a lack of surrealist groups does not necessarily imply the absence of the discussion of surrealist ideas. A lack of manifestos and journals – representative of

24 Abbas Baydoun, "Culture and Arts; Re: The Actual", in: *Home Works: A Forum on Cultural Practices in the Region; Egypt, Iran, Iraq, Lebanon, Palestine and Syria*, Christine Tohme and Mona Abu Rayyan, eds., Beirut: Lebanese Association for Plastic Arts – Ashkal Alwan 2002, 24.

25 Baydoun, "Culture and Arts", 24–25.

26 Baydoun, "Culture and Arts", 25.

a group's identity and political or artistic stance and claims – does not, of course, mean that surrealism cannot be found in other, more subtle, expressions. Often, the political climate does not allow for overt criticism or mocking. There are many reasons that either favour or prevent the development and circulation of subversive ideas, one of these being the structure of the respective cultural fields and their openness to receive such ideas.

The spread of surrealism was also sparked by chance encounters with international key figures of the cultural and artistic life of the time who acted as "messengers". Such actors were sometimes on cultural missions and occupied influential positions, disposed of rich cultural backgrounds and were highly interested in arts, literature, architecture, music and so on. Other times, they were artists who had been closely connected with surrealist circles in Paris and elsewhere, and through their work they introduced new audiences, fellow artists and writers to these ideas. The importance of individual actors for the intellectual and artistic exchange and for the circulation of ideas must not be underestimated. The present volume aims at drawing a clearer picture of the "sporadic resonance"[27] of surrealism in Western Asia and North Africa, thereby contributing to the history of both transmodernism and surrealism.

Outline of the book

The ten case studies in the present volume range thematically, chronologically and geographically from the 1930s to the 1980s, extending from Egypt, Lebanon and Turkey to Syria and Algeria, and bring to light untold stories of encounters and contacts that form the building blocks of a history of "transmodernity". By presenting and analyzing new sources, they open up new historical, cultural and artistic contexts and add to our knowledge of surrealism as an international – both global and local – phenomenon. There is a fundamental methodological challenge which affects research more generally, but which poses particular problems in the areas covered here because of practical difficulties such as the accessibility of archives. Archives in the region are often incomplete, scattered or missing, imposing strict limits on the writing of history. This is why, far from thinking that we could give a final insight into the existence of surrealist ideas in these regions, we instead hope to contribute some pieces of a larger puzzle.

The ten contributions are arranged in two main thematic parts: one that focuses on surrealism – or its absence – in its multiple variations and genealogies, and one that examines the different encounters and perceptions of surrealism.

---

27 Dawn Ades, Krzysztof Fijałkowski, Steven Harris, Michael Richardson and Georges Sebbag, eds., *The International Encyclopedia of Surrealism*, vol. 1, *Movements*, London: Bloomsbury 2019, xv.

Multiple surrealisms

Classically, the avant-garde defines itself through a manifesto. So did surrealism, but with the peculiarity that multiple surrealisms gave birth to multiple manifestos, as Monique Bellan demonstrates in her contribution focusing on the manifestos of Art et Liberté, Arab Surrealism in Exile and Habib Tengour as "eccentric" expressions of surrealism. They relate to the various centres of surrealism from a satellite position only to become centres themselves and eventually to create new genealogies of surrealism. The notion of the centre itself is relativized; the eccentric can therefore also be described as a way of expressing the anti-Eurocentrism of the initiatives debated here.

In their contributions dedicated to the question of surrealism in Turkey, Eyüp Özveren and Ambra D'Antone engage in an unspoken dialogue. Eyüp Özveren interprets Turkey in the interwar period as a world apart from the rest of the Balkans, the Middle East and North Africa. After the collapse of the tricontinental, multi-ethnic and multireligious Ottoman Empire, the young Turkish republic was interested in links with Europe, especially with Paris, in a spirit of modernization. Numerous artists, such as Nurullah Berk (1906–1982), Bedri Rahmi Eyüboğlu (1911–1975) and Hale Asaf (1905–1938), studied at the Académie Lhote in Paris. However, this opportunity to deal with Parisian surrealism does not seem to have been seized. Özveren nevertheless counts on future research that might bring to light surrealist evidence in Hale Asaf's work.

Ambra D'Antone, on the other hand, identifies a specific Turkish surrealism from the 1940s onwards. The author's argumentation is embedded in the concept of global surrealism which questions the uniqueness of Parisian surrealism. Referring to Wendy Shaw's "differential modernism", D'Antone develops her thesis of a differential surrealism through two examples: one is the group of poets consisting of Oktay Rifat, Melih Cevdet Anday and Orhan Veli and their publication *Garip* (published in Istanbul in 1941); and the other is the exhibition *Phallisme* at the Turkish–German Cultural Centre in Istanbul in 1958. Despite the distance in time between them, both developed similar aesthetic approaches representative of Turkish surrealism, in which the encounters of the artists with one another and their individual works played a major role.

As for Syria, Arturo Monaco identifies the year 1947 as the official beginning of the surrealist experience, and he connects this to the release of the poetry collection *Suryāl* by Ūrkhān Muyassar (1911?–1965). This cosmopolitan poet and journalist from Aleppo, who spoke numerous languages, had become familiar with surrealism through his travels. He published numerous writings on Parisian surrealism and art events and developed a "para-surrealism" in his own poetry, which Monaco sees as situated between surrealism and symbolism.

Surrealist encounters

Jad Tabet, son of the architect Antoine Tabet (1907–1964), deals with the intellectual scene in Lebanon between 1920 and 1960 from a personal perspective. The friendship of the young Lebanese Antoine Tabet, Nehmé Eddé (1902–1992), Alexandre Abouchaar (1905–?), Georges Schehadé (1905?–1989), and Antoine Mourani (1907–1967) – the "five musketeers" (*les cinq mousquetaires*) as they called themselves – is part of the history of the radical cultural, political and social upheavals which the region went through in the first half of the twentieth century, from the fall of the Ottoman Empire to the rise of national movements in the 1950s. Together, they discussed surrealist ideas and met Gabriel Bounoure, an important cultural figure of the time who had contacts with the surrealist circles in Paris.

The Lebanese poet Georges Schehadé also engaged in a dialogue with Parisian intellectuals, as Julia Drost shows. Commuting all his life between Beirut and Paris, he was a traveller between worlds and cultures, calling himself a "son of surrealism" (*fils du surréalisme*). André Breton, for his part, welcomed the Lebanese poet and dramaturge as a new member of the surrealist movement which was reconstituting itself after the Second World War.

The importance of individual personal contacts and relationships between poets and artists in Lebanon and the surrealist movement in Paris is addressed in the contribution by Alfred el-Khoury. The Lebanese poet Unsī al-Ḥājj (1937–2014) translated texts by Jacques Prévert (1900–1977), Antonin Artaud (1896–1948) and André Breton (1896–1966) into Arabic in the magazines *Shiʿr* and *al-Mulḥaq*. El-Khoury examines how Unsī al-Ḥājj made these writers known in the Arabic context and further demonstrates that al-Ḥājj's own poetry is strongly influenced by these authors.

Cléa Daridan places surrealism in Egypt in the wider political and social context of the Francophonie and examines, through the archives of magazines, how French journalists in Egypt reported on surrealism in Egypt. Thus, with Art et Liberté, the Cairo art scene placed itself for the first time on a par with Paris in the Eurocentric discourse of the French press. The revolution of 1952 with its nationalistic project led to the end of the Francophonie and put the question of an "authentic Egyptian art" in the foreground.

Fabrice Flahutez's case study deals with the Egyptian poet Joyce Mansour (1928–1986), who, like Georges Schehadé, not only wrote in French but was held up by André Breton after the Second World War as a representative of international surrealism. The contribution does not pose the question of an Egyptian surrealism, but introduces the principle of an "internationalist will of surrealism" (*volonté internationaliste du surréalisme*), which makes it "stateless".

Megan C. MacDonald connects Antonin Artaud (1896–1948) and Habib Tengour (b. 1947) in a spiritual encounter. The author uses the metaphor of "germination" to describe alternative kinships and genealogies of surrealism across the

Mediterranean. Her reading of surrealism as trans-Mediterranean dreaming via plague logic allows for a transhistorical perspective, thereby expanding the understanding of surrealism.

Conclusion

So, when, where and what was surrealism, and was the attraction towards it necessarily linked to the desire to found a group or become a member of one? As we can learn from examples such as that of Unsī al-Ḥājj presented in Alfred el-Khoury's chapter, not every artist or poet with a surrealist leaning was inclined to obey the identity and rules of a movement or a group:

> I often wonder: If I had the chance to be in Paris in the twenties, and, consequently, to meet Breton, Aragon, Soupault, Artaud, Éluard and Char, would I be attracted to surrealism to the extent of joining it? And if we suppose that I joined it, would I remain committed for a long time? I do not think so. I have several contradictions in my character that make me uncomfortable and uncomforting inside any movement.[28]

It is well known that André Breton, the "pope of surrealism" as his opponents called him, headed the movement with the strictness of a religious sect that often led to the exclusion of those who did not strictly abide by surrealist techniques or fully embrace their visions.[29] This led many, such as Antonin Artaud or the group around the journal *Documents* – Georges Bataille, Michel Leiris and Robert Desnos, to name only a few – to distance themselves from Breton and his movement.[30] Alfred el-Khoury, in his analysis of al-Ḥājj's relation to Breton, points out that only when al-Ḥājj distanced himself from Breton, the leader, could he discover Breton, the poet. It seems therefore necessary to clearly distinguish between Breton's movement and surrealism as a way of thinking or viewing the world, a sort of philosophy, whose main ideas have been adapted in many ways to different historical, political, cultural and aesthetic contexts.

---

28 Unsī al-Ḥājj, "Ayna al-mutahawwirūn ḥāriqū l-ḥayāt: Ajmal al-ḥarīq wa-dhurwat al-jiddiyyah fī muntahā l-ḥubb wa-l-ʿabath", interview with ʿAbduh Wāzin, *al-Nahār*, 23 January 1983, 9.

29 Pierre Taminiaux, in his article on the relation between Breton and Trotsky, or between surrealism and communism, points out that their concepts were essentially different: whereas communism was targeting the individual's relation to society with the ultimate aim of a total inclusion, surrealism was focusing on the individual's relation to community. "In many ways, it [the surrealist community] operated and defined itself as a secret entity, with all its peculiar rituals and norms of behavior, and claimed its deliberate marginality as an existential necessity. [...] The surrealist subject was not a universal one, as was the communist revolutionary. He recognized himself as other and did not pretend to reach the whole of humanity. A form of self-exclusion was at the source of his creative power and of his unique character. In this sense, to belong to the community did not mean to belong to the world but instead to a group that could always contradict it." Pierre Taminiaux, "Breton and Trotsky: The Revolutionary Memory of Surrealism", *Yale French Studies* 109 (2006), 61.

30 See "Un cadavre", in *Tracts surréalistes et déclarations collectives*, vol. 1, *1922–1939*, José Pierre, ed., Paris: Terrain vague 1980.

It seems that individualism played a major role, not only in al-Ḥājj's approach to surrealism but in that of many others as well. Subordination to a leader and to specific rules were not always desired, and thus the need for a group with a specific – political and/or artistic – agenda did not always manifest. The formation of a group also largely depended on the historical circumstances and the social and political context, as was the case when the French surrealist movement was founded in 1924 in reaction to the First World War. Nevertheless, individualism and collectivism do not necessarily exclude each other, as pointed out by Ambra D'Antone in her chapter on Turkish surrealism. The author convincingly argues for a non-binary approach, fleshed out by André Massons's statement from 1938 that surrealism is "the collective experience of individualism".[31]

Hence, surrealism has many ways of manifesting itself, most of which are individual, often blended with other influences, and this takes place most often in poetry (at least in the region we are looking at). A new look at global surrealism therefore needs to take these micro-level manifestations into consideration when addressing questions such as when, where and what surrealism was. The answer might reveal that surrealism was far more widespread than presumed until now.

[31] Robert S. Short, "The Politics of Surrealism, 1920–1936", *Journal of Contemporary History* 1 (1966), 21.

Part I:
Multiple surrealisms

Chapter 1

Three eccentric manifestos: Art et Liberté, the Arab Surrealist Movement in Exile and Habib Tengour's "non-message"

Monique Bellan

Eccentricity and the "manifest" are in principle two opposite modes of thought and motions: the eccentric breaks out whereas the manifesto tries to grasp, concentrate and give form to specific thoughts and claims.[1] The present chapter aims at rereading the manifestos of Art et Liberté,[2] the Arab Surrealist Movement in Exile,[3] and Habib Tengour's "non-message"[4] in the light of their respective contexts of emergence and their (spiritual or discursive) connectedness to earlier surrealist manifestos such as André Breton's surrealist manifesto from 1924. Although they have been subject to examination in previous studies on surrealism, this has happened – at least to my knowledge – neither extensively nor synoptically. This chapter by no means claims to provide a comprehensive reading of these manifestos, but tries to carve out both their radical singularities as well as their comparability.

The manifestos can be described as "eccentric" insofar as they relate to the various centres of surrealism from a satellite position only to become centres themselves and eventually to create new genealogies of surrealism. One important centre is the surrealist movement in Paris, represented through the persona of André Breton (1896–1966). But there are other centres: the group Art et Liberté and its spokesperson Georges Henein (1914–1973); or Ibn Arabi (1165–1240),[5] who is referred to as a surrealist *avant la lettre* by Tengour. The eccentric here is used both as a spatial (in relation to the centre) and a normative approach (as deviant from whichever norm) which finds its expression in the manifestos. It can also be described as a way of expressing the anti-Eurocentrism of the initiatives debated here.

---

1 I am grateful to Ralf Osman Hajjar for sharing some eccentric ideas.
2 Art et Liberté was a group of artists, poets and writers with a strong affinity to surrealism; the spokesperson was Georges Henein, and the manifesto was released in 1938.
3 Abdul Kader El Janabi released the manifesto of this Paris-based group in 1973.
4 Habib Tengour wrote the manifesto on Maghrebian surrealism in 1981.
5 Ibn Arabi was a Muslim philosopher, scholar, poet, and mystic with a comprehensive body of work most of which remains untranslated up until now. For further information see: Chittick, William, "Ibn 'Arabî", *The Stanford Encyclopedia of Philosophy* (Spring 2020 Edition), Edward N. Zalta (ed.), https://plato.stanford.edu/archives/spr2020/entries/ibn-arabi/.

The manifesto as political manifestation

A manifesto is usually considered an indicator for the existence of a surrealist group. Yet, there are large differences in concept, vision and approach, which justifies the idea of eccentricity or deviations from previous surrealist manifestos.

The release of a manifesto was not only central for Parisian surrealism: this practice was adopted and adapted in many regions of the world, among them North Africa and Western Asia. However, a manifesto is not a precondition per se for adherence to the idea of surrealism. Surrealism was taken up in many ways and forms, most often on an individual level. The reason for a lack of more such manifestations may be the fact that political conditions were often not favourable for these provocative expressions of dissent. At the same time, many poets and artists preferred a more individualistic approach.[6]

A manifesto is generally related to the political or artistic status quo, which it seeks to protest against or to overcome. Manifestos have their origin in the political realm. From the nineteenth century, they progressively serve politically oppositional groups, articulating their claims, as with the manifesto of the Communist Party (1848) written by Karl Marx and Friedrich Engels.[7] From the beginning of the twentieth century onwards, a shift takes place as the artistic avant-gardes increasingly use this genre to convey their different programmes and positions, thereby adopting the role of the ones who signal the future. It is characteristic for twentieth-century avant-garde movements such as futurism, Dada, symbolism and surrealism, amongst others – whose leitmotif was the dissolution of the boundaries of art and life – to have a manifesto that served as a catalyst for their claims, provocative attitudes and often accusations. At the same time, the manifesto is generally an indicator for a programme, and it is explicit, addresses a specific public and has a group character.[8] An additional criterion is the self-designation of the text as a manifesto.[9]

However, the manifesto allows for variations. There are single-authored and signed manifestos where the group character is missing, as well as manifestos where all other, aforementioned criteria, are absent.[10] The latter applies to Habib Tengour's manifesto, which is neither signed by a group nor conveys an explicit message, but belongs more to the poetic realm. Sometimes, manifestos do not have a genre label in their title, as for example with Art et Liberté's manifesto "Long Live

---

6 See introduction, pp. 26–27.

7 Hubert van den Berg and Walter Fähnders, eds., *Avantgarde*, Stuttgart: J.B. Metzler 2009, 202–203.

8 Walter Fähnders, "'Vielleicht ein Manifest': Zur Entwicklung des avantgardistischen Manifestes", in: *"Die ganze Welt ist eine Manifestation": Die europäische Avantgarde und ihre Manifeste*, Wolfgang Asholt and Walter Fähnders, eds., Darmstadt: Wissenschaftliche Buchgesellschaft 1997, 21.

9 Fähnders, "'Vielleicht ein Manifest'", 21.

10 Fähnders, "'Vielleicht ein Manifest'", 21.

Degenerate Art", where the title itself hints at certain inherent claims without having to add the word *manifesto*.

The function of the manifesto is twofold. On the one hand, it aims at delineating the group from the exterior and its structures and values, such as family, nation and religion. At the same time, it has an important function targeting the cohesion of the group,[11] thereby creating exclusiveness and an identity. It also establishes the rules and sets the standards which the members are expected to follow and apply to secure their *appartenance* to the group. There are many examples of members, for example in the surrealist group around André Breton, who were excluded due to misconduct or lack of compliance with certain literary or artistic principles.[12]

Another important point is the internationalism of surrealism, both in the composition of its groups and its spread. The members belonged to a great number of different nationalities (thereby performing a *de facto* non-national approach as claimed by surrealism), the manifestos were sometimes penned and often distributed in different languages and signed by an international group of individuals who were not necessarily congruent with the actual members but sometimes included other people as well. Surrealism is the only avant-garde movement that continuously managed to "regenerate itself from its original impulses and ideas",[13] not least due to its internationalism. What makes it compatible with different cultural and temporal contexts is its quality as an approach to life, which existed long before surrealism was labelled as such and classified as an artistic, literary and political movement. It is an approach that seeks to think, feel and conceptualize life and art beyond any given boundaries and therefore considers the imagination as its strongest tool to overcome the limitations imposed by the capitalist system and its credo of the rationalization of life.

The following three examples of surrealist initiatives focus on the historical, intellectual, artistic, political, social and philosophical contexts of their respective emergence while at the same time trying to show the connections and spiritual filiations to previous figures of surrealism, most prominently André Breton and Georges Henein.

Art et Liberté/al-Fann wa-l-ḥurriyyah, *1938*

Art et Liberté (1938–1948) was the only official surrealist group that appeared in Cairo, and it emerged shortly after Breton's first and second surrealist manifestos in 1924 and 1930. The label "surrealist" was applied to the group from outside, as

11 Karlheinz Barck, "Latenter Surrealismus manifest: Manifeste des Surrealismus als Medien seiner Internationalisierung", in: *"Die ganze Welt ist eine Manifestation": Die europäische Avantgarde und ihre Manifeste*, Wolfgang Asholt and Walter Fähnders, eds., Darmstadt: Wissenschaftliche Buchgesellschaft 1997, 303.

12 See introduction, 26.

13 Barck, "Latenter Surrealismus manifest", 305.

the group itself never referred to its own practices as surrealist, but as "free" or "independent" art (*al-fann al-ḥurr*). More important than strictly abiding by surrealist techniques in poetry or art was to subvert the hegemony of the bourgeoisie and the prevailing order and morals. The group's heterogenous composition also allowed for artists and writers whose approach was not surrealist. The group's spokesperson was the poet Georges Henein, who had met André Breton in Paris in 1936. That same year, Henein contributed to *Un effort*, the organ of the francophone literary group Les Essayistes in Cairo of which he was a member from 1935, as well as to *Les Humbles*, a Marxist–Leninist periodical published in Paris.[14] On 4 February 1937, Henein gave a lecture on surrealism at Les Essayistes, which was broadcast by Egyptian State Broadcasting.[15] Marie-Francine Desvaux-Mansour points out that, through this radio broadcast, the Egyptians were for the first time acquainted with Lautréamont (1846–1870), Jacques Prévert (1900–1977), Jacques Vaché (1895–1919) and Henri Michaux (1899–1984), who all had a major influence on the surrealists: "It is at this moment that the influence of surrealism reaches visual art and poetry, in spite of the incomprehension of a public still attached to nineteenth-century values and to the former poetic tradition."[16] Desvaux-Mansour also emphasizes that both Georges Henein and Edmond Jabès (1912–1991), who was another important Egyptian poet of the time, were more influenced by Max Jacob (1876–1944), Yves Bonnefoy (1923–2016) and Paul Éluard (1895–1952) than by André Breton.[17] This relativizes the position of Breton as the most influential representative of surrealism, which applies probably first and foremost to his position as the leader of the movement.

Art et Liberté was born in the tense political climate between World War I and World War II, amidst huge social and political tensions in Egypt and an overall dire and oppressive situation. Patrick M. Kane in his insightful study on mid-twentieth-century aesthetics in Egypt, delineates the political situation in 1938 as deeply marked by the agrarian crisis in Egypt, the Depression, food shortages, low wages,

---

14 Sam Bardaouil, *Surrealism in Egypt: Modernism and the Art and Liberty Group*, London: I.B. Tauris 2017, 5.

15 Georges Henein, "Bilan du movement surréaliste", in: *Œuvres: Poèmes, récits, essais, articles et pamphlets*, Paris: Denoël 2006. The transcription of Henein's lecture was also published in *Revue des conférences françaises en Orient* (October 1937) and in *Pleine marge* 24 (November 1996).

16 Marie-Francine Desvaux-Mansour, "Le Surréalisme à travers Joyce Mansour: Peinture et poésie, le miroir du désir", PhD thesis, University of Paris 1 Panthéon-Sorbonne 2014, 90, https://www.theses.fr/2014PA010520. Translation by the author. Original French: "C'est à ce moment que l'influence du surréalisme atteint à la fois l'art plastique et la poésie, malgré l'incompréhension d'un public encore attaché aux valeurs littéraires du XIXe siècle et à la tradition poétique ancienne." Patrick M. Kane confirms the importance of this lecture and its "immediate political relevance" for the young generation of artists and writers in *The Politics of Art in Modern Egypt: Aesthetics, Ideology and Nation-Building*, London: I.B. Tauris 2013, 56.

17 Desvaux-Mansour, "Le Surréalisme", 90.

expropriations of crops and forced rents, which "opened a polemic among Egyptian intellectuals over the role of the state and the looming threat of fascism".[18] This is framed by the rise and the political and institutional struggle of new intellectuals, especially art teachers and artists, who vehemently opposed the hegemony of academic art and "advocated the discourse of a broader aesthetic experience based on the inclusion of all classes and members of society".[19] The non-conformist artists and intellectuals encompassed the role of subversive elements with the aim of dismantling the dominant official discourse and its authorities, embodied by the politician and art collector Muhammad Mahmud Khalil (1877–1953) and propelled by the Society of the Lovers of Fine Art and the Cairo Art Salon, both of which he headed in an autocratic manner until 1951.[20] Khalil had a distinguished taste for French impressionist and post-impressionist art and an important collection thereof. His taste also dominated the Cairo Art Salon and the selection process, which prompted groups such as Art et Liberté to raise their critical voices.[21]

The founding of Art et Liberté took place on 22 December 1938, with the publication of its manifesto "Vive l'art dégénéré" (Long Live Degenerate Art/ *Yaḥya al-fann al-munḥatt*).[22] The statutes were released a few weeks later, on 9 January 1939,[23] with the following three aims: to defend the freedom of art and culture; to circulate new publications, to organize lectures and to write on the prominent thinkers of the modern era; and to connect Egyptian youth to the literary, artistic and social movements in the world.[24] The members included Georges Henein, the painter and later film director Kamel El Telmisany (1905–1972), the author Anwar Kamel (1913–1991), the painter Fouad Kamel (1919–1973) and the painter and theoretician Ramses Younan (1913–1966), although the latter was not among the signatories of the manifesto.[25] The manifesto represented a statement of solidarity with artists and writers suffering under fascism in Europe:

---

18 Kane, *Politics of Art*, 53.

19 Kane, *Politics of Art*, 2.

20 Nadia Radwan, "How a Ceramic Vase in the Art Salon Changed Artistic Discourse in Egypt", in: *The Art Salon in the Arab Region: Politics of Taste Making*, Nadia von Maltzahn and Monique Bellan, eds., Beirut: Orient-Institut Beirut 2018, 120.

21 Radwan, "Ceramic Vase", 120–121. Before Art et Liberté came into being, others had already paved the way for institutional and aesthetic critique, such as La Chimère, which was founded in 1924 by Mahmud Mukhtar (1891–1934) and the French painter Roger Bréval (dates unknown), or Huda Sharawi (1879–1947) and her initiative to validate arts and crafts and thereby the role of women in art. In 1924, she succeeded in getting a ceramic piece of her artisanal school admitted to the Cairo Art Salon. Radwan, "Ceramic Vase", 122–126.

22 For further information on the foundation of the group and the manifesto, refer also to Cléa Daridan's chapter in the present volume.

23 Several readings circulate concerning the exact date. In *al-Taṭawwur*, we read 9 January 1939; Sam Bardaouil retrieves from a letter of Henein to Breton that it was 6 January 1939. See Hisham Qishta, ed., *al-Taṭawwur*, 2nd ed., Cairo: Elias Publishing 2016, 89; and Bardaouil, *Surrealism in Egypt*, 54.

24 Hisham Qishta, *al-Taṭawwur*, 89.

25 Bardaouil, *Surrealism in Egypt*, 3 and 245-246 for the signatories.

> We know how hostile our society is towards any new literary or artistic creation that threatens, directly or indirectly, the moral values upon which it relies for its continued existence – or even survival.
> This hostility can be seen today in totalitarian countries – especially Hitler's Germany – in despicable aggression towards an art that uniformed brutes promoted to the rank of all-powerful arbitrators classify as "degenerate".
> From Cézanne to Picasso (and in literary terms, from Henri Heine to Thomas Mann) the very finest contemporary artistic genius, the freest and most preciously human modern art, is insulted, trampled underfoot, forbidden.
> We find absurd, and deserving of total disdain, the religious, racist and nationalist prejudices that make up the tyranny of certain individuals who, drunk on their own temporary omniscience, seek to subjugate the destiny of the work of art.
> We refuse to see in these regressive myths anything but real concentration camps of thought.
> Art – as a permanent spiritual and emotional exchange between all of humanity – can no longer be bound by such arbitrary limits.
> In Vienna, which is in the hands of the barbarians, canvases by Renoir are lacerated and Freud's work are burned in public squares. The most brilliant triumphs of great German artists such as Max Ernst, Paul Klee, Kokoschka, George Grosz, Kandinsky and Karl Hofer (winner of the 1938 Carnegie Prize) are blacklisted and must cede to the inept platitudes of nationalist-socialist art.
> In Rome, a so-called "literary improvement" commission has just completed its unsavory task, concluding that "anything that is anti-Italian, anti-racist, immoral or depressive" must be removed from circulation.
> Intellectuals, writers, artists! Let us take on the challenge together. We are totally united with the degenerate art. It represents any chance we have of a future. Let us work for its victory over the new Middle Age that is rising up in the very midst of the West.[26]

The manifesto was penned by Georges Henein and signed by thirty-one artists, writers, journalists and lawyers. Interestingly, the manifesto does not refer to the situation in Egypt, at least not explicitly; nevertheless, it "launched a polemic against the elitist and autocratic nature of Egyptian cultural institutions and civil society at large".[27] This sustains the idea of it being primarily an expression of solidarity under the banner of internationalism prior to the formal founding of the group a few weeks later, during which the "Surrealists emerged as followers of Henein's initiative".[28]

The similarity of the manifesto with the "Manifesto for an Independent Revolutionary Art"[29] of the International Federation of Independent Revolutionary Art (FIARI) from 25 July 1938, and the debate about whether Art et Liberté was or was not aligned with FIARI remains contested. The FIARI manifesto was co-signed by André Breton and Diego Rivera (1886–1957) in Mexico and in large parts

---

26 For the manifesto and the names of the signees, refer to Bardaouil, *Surrealism in Egypt*, 245–246.

27 Kane, *Politics of Art*, 56.

28 Kane, *Politics of Art*, 56.

29 For the text of that manifesto, see e.g. https://www.marxists.org/subject/art/lit_crit/works/rivera/manifesto.htm.

penned by Breton and Leon Trotsky (1879–1940). Sam Bardaouil advocates for the group's independence and emphasizes that Art et Liberté "was not an Egyptian chapter of the Trotskyite FIARI" and "in 1939 was not compelled to align itself with Trotskyism, as did Breton, for it still relied on support from the Stalinist Communists in Egypt to disseminate its message".[30] Regardless of this debate, the political climate in which both manifestos emerged – with its all-encompassing, spreading totalitarianism – was the same. Hence, the external similarity comes as no surprise. However, the underlying statement of the Egyptian document is a different one: it is not only about solidarity with degenerate art, but the concept of Europe as the centre of modernity is deconstructed. The inherent message of the manifesto is: "We are the avant-garde and you can learn something from us!" Art et Liberté does not *follow* an international movement but is *itself* a source of inspiration. The eccentricity here lies in the fact that support and, at the same time, new inspiration are offered from a movement outside the "centre", thereby reversing the Eurocentrism of surrealism. Art et Liberté stages this "message" in its manifesto and presents itself as a collective of individual voices, thereby situating itself at the centre of revolutionary and free art.

Dissolution of borders and comprehensive collaboration

One of the characteristics of avant-garde groups in general is for artists, writers, poets, photographers, directors and others to work together under one roof. Transcending the boundaries of individual genres, such groups pursued the aim of propounding a particular conception of art and life – frequently coupled with political demands, in this case of an anti-fascist nature. Alongside other means of diffusion, surrealist groups generally publicized their convictions, essays and literary texts in their own journals. The organ of the group Art et Liberté was called *al-Taṭawwur* (Evolution), and a total of seven issues were published between January and September 1940.[31]

In their journal, the members of Art et Liberté, particularly Georges Henein, Kamel El Telmisany, Ramses Younan and Anwar Kamel, criticized the desolate political and social situation and advocated for the emancipation of the most deprived: women, peasants and workers. The first issue begins with Anwar Kamel's editorial "A New Direction" (*Ittijāh jadīd*) and the group's credo: "We believe in constant progress and continuous change. We oppose myths and fairy tales and fight against inherited values which exploit the power of the individual in his material and spiritual life."[32] The article continues by defining Egyptian society in its

30 For further information on this debate, see Bardaouil, *Surrealism in Egypt*, 48–59, 53.

31 In 2016, the journal was reissued by Hisham Qishta.

32 Anwar Kamel, "Ittijāh jadīd", *al-Taṭawwur* 1 (January 1940), reprinted in Qishta, ed., *al-Taṭawwur*, 26. Translation by the author.

current state as sick and out of balance, its moral standards and social and economic situation in disorder. The journal's aim is to instigate the youth to introduce a new phase of intellectual struggle to overcome the status quo.[33]

In the years 1940 to 1945, the group held five exhibitions under the banner *Expositions de l'art indépendant* (Exhibitions of Independent Art).[34] Its aim was

> [...] to integrate the activity of the young artists in Egypt into the grand circuits of modern, passionate and tumultuous art that rebels against any police, religious or commercial rules, an art whose pulse we can feel in New York, London and Mexico, everywhere where the Diego Riveras, the Paalens, the Tanguys and the Henry Moores are carrying on the struggle.[35]

The group wanted to connect young artists in and from Egypt with the new centres of international revolutionary art – New York, London, Mexico – integrating them into an international network. Here, specific regional and superordinate global interests came together to help surrealism in Cairo to develop. It is a recalcitrant art that is advocated, one that is coupled with militancy to overcome the political order. The outlined spiritual proximity to famous artists such as Diego Rivera, Paalen, Tanguy and Henry Moore sets the direction and at the same time gives credibility to the group's own positions.

We can conclude with the following: The manifesto preluded the founding of the group and embedded it in a global intellectual and artistic movement. It also set the tone for the group's more local political, social and artistic challenges, namely to combat fascist tendencies inside Egypt, injustice, poverty, discrimination and art institutions that were closely related to the political elite and their tastes. The publication of the manifesto also launched a long debate on Art et Liberté and the term "degenerate art" in the weekly journal *al-Risālah* initiated by the critic Aziz Ahmad Fahmi with the aim of defaming the group.[36] This debate between Fahmi and members of the group bears witness to the reception of this initiative and its clash with the values then in place. Art et Liberté's alignment

---

33 Kamel, "Ittijāh jadīd", 26. The desperate situation of the youth (including the members of Art et Liberté) is vividly expressed in Henein's words (translation by the author): "All is closed in front of them. The youth, they're in a mousetrap. They cannot go back, nor ahead. In fact, they can. They can go backward, but only through suicide. They can go forward, but through revolution. Suicide is useless and condemned by morality. Revolution is useful and punished by law." Georges Henein, "La Grande Pitié de la jeunesse du monde", in: *Œuvres: Poèmes, récits, essais, articles et pamphlets*, Paris: Denoël 2006, 314.

34 For further information on the exhibitions, see Sam Bardaouil, "'Dirty Dark Loud and Hysteric': The London and Paris Surrealist Exhibitions of the 1930s and the Exhibition Practices of the Art and Liberty Group in Cairo", *Dada/Surrealism* 19 (2013); Monique Bellan, "Defying the Order from Within: Art et Liberté and its Reordering of Visual Codes", in: *The Art Salon in the Arab Region: Politics of Taste Making*, Nadia von Maltzahn and Monique Bellan, eds., Beirut: Orient-Institut Beirut 2018.

35 Sarane Alexandrian, *Georges Henein, 1914–73*, Paris: Seghers 1981, 34.

36 For this debate, see Don LaCoss, "Egyptian Surrealism and 'Degenerate Art' in 1939", *Arab Studies Journal* 18, no. 1 (Spring 2010).

with a global movement also helped in defining a direction of its own. It resembled international surrealism, but introduced a new aspect: namely the paradox that universality can only be achieved through "situatedness":

> Rather, on the periphery artists experience being modern and its antipodes as a matter of localized struggle, even if the outcomes and implications are part of a global totality of struggles. Situatedness is absolutely crucial, therefore, to the agency of the avant-garde in a context where the older institutional arrangements and private and public forms of provisions no longer apply.[37]

The claim of being universal therefore only works as a conjunction of individual context-related struggles that may largely differ in the way things are conceptualized and implemented.

Arab Surrealist Movement in Exile, 1973

Abdul Kader El Janabi (b. 1944 in Baghdad) founded the Arab Surrealist Movement in Exile and its journal *Le Désir libertaire/al-Raghbah al-ibāḥiyyah* in Paris on 25 December 1973 together with a group of exiles from different Arab countries. This coincides almost to the day with the release of Art et Liberté's manifesto thirty-five years earlier (22 December 1938).[38] In addition to Abdul Kader El Janabi, the members of the group included Maroine Dib (Syria), Farid Lariby (Algeria), Ghazi Younes (Lebanon), Ali Fenjan (Iraq) and Mohammad Awad (Iraq), who all contributed either by writing, poetry or drawing.

Another interesting parallel is El Janabi's meeting with Georges Henein in Paris in 1973 (in 1937, Georges Henein had met André Breton in Paris). El Janabi's meeting with Henein was brief, but apparently influenced his adoption of surrealism. In his autobiographical work *Tarbiyat ʿAbdul Qādir al-Janābī* (The education of Abdul Kader El Janabi), El Janabi writes: "I never met André Breton but I had the feeling that he was embodied in Georges Henein".[39] After meeting Henein shortly before his death in 1973, he started to regard himself as the elder artist's heir considering it his duty to spread the knowledge about Art et Liberté as the only "organized manifestation of surrealism"[40] that Arab societies have witnessed.

As El Janabi explains in his autobiographical survey, which begins in Baghdad and leads us to London and Paris amongst other places, he only learned of the

---

37 John Roberts, *Revolutionary Time and the Avant-Garde*, London: Verso 2015, 46.

38 For further reading on Abdel Kader El Janabi, see Sibylla Krainick, *Arabischer Surrealismus im Exil: Der irakische Dichter und Publizist ʿAbd al-Qādir al-Ǧanābī*, Wiesbaden: Reichert 2001.

39 ʿAbdul Qādir al-Janābī, *Tarbiyat ʿAbdul Qādir al-Janābī*, Beirut: Dār al-Jadīd 1995, 90. Original Arabic: "*Lam arā Brūtūn fī ḥayātī, lakinnanī shaʿirtu wa kaʾanna Jūrj Ḥneyn Brūtūn nafsuhu*". English translation by the author.

40 Abdul Kader El Janabi, "Ces années de tous les rêves ou les ombres passaient en murmurant", in: *Le Désir libertaire: Le Surréalisme arabe à Paris 1973–1975*, Abdul Kader El Janabi, ed., Toulouse: Éditions de l'Asymétrie 2018, 30-37, 32.

existence of Art et Liberté in London in 1970 while doing research on surrealism.[41] At the British Library he came across some issues of the *London Bulletin*,[42] which also contained Art et Liberté's manifesto "Long Live Degenerate Art" in French and Arabic.[43] There, he discovered Georges Henein's name, whose "Message from Cairo to the American Poets" he had read previously in the magazine *View*, along with a few poems here and there. At the time, El Janabi had not been aware of Henein's connection to surrealism in Cairo.[44] Back in Paris, El Janabi asked friends about Henein and found out that he was working for the magazine *L'Express*.[45] He contacted and met Henein. At the first meeting between the two men, El Janabi asked him about the manifesto "Long Live Degenerate Art" and the group Art et Liberté. El Janabi also showed him a statement that he had written in London ending with the following sentence: "Let the parties fall, the organizations, the trees, I will not fall."[46] El Janabi had published it along with some Dadaist poems. Apparently, Henein was impressed by his radical tone.

What was the political situation when the Arab Surrealist Movement in Exile was founded? The founding took place in the aftermath of the worldwide protests of 1968 and fell in a decade, the 1970s, which can be characterized as a "period of generalized subversion".[47] The so-called Arab defeat of 1967, which was a turning point in Arab history and marked a shift towards a pronounced political commitment in literature and art, was still tangible and with the beginning of the 1970s, the Israeli–Palestinian conflict had entered a new violent phase. *Le Désir libertaire* positioned itself clearly against this conflict and in an internationalist perspective advocated for the union of the proletarians against the war.[48]

As with the previous Paris-based surrealist movement and Art et Liberté, the founding of the group was followed by the publication of a manifesto and a journal – *Le Désir libertaire/al-Raghbah al-ibāḥiyyah* – whose provocative tone was met with vehement criticism in the Arab countries,[49] with the result that it could only

41 Al-Janābī, *Tarbiyat ʿAbdul Qādir al-Janābī*, 89.

42 The *London Bulletin* was edited by the Belgian artist and writer E.L.T. Mesens (1903–1971), who was associated with the surrealist movement. A total of twenty numbers was published by the London Gallery between April 1938 and June 1940. For more information, see: https://monoskop.org/London_Bulletin.

43 Al-Janābī, *Tarbiyat ʿAbdul Qādir al-Janābī*, 89.

44 Al-Janābī, *Tarbiyat ʿAbdul Qādir al-Janābī*, 89.

45 In his autobiographical text, El Janabi classifies it as "*majallah yamīniyyah*" (a conservative magazine); see al-Janābī, *Tarbiyat ʿAbdul Qādir al-Janābī*, 89.

46 Al-Janābī, *Tarbiyat ʿAbdul Qādir al-Janābī*, 89–90.

47 Marc Kober, "Introduction", in: *Le Désir libertaire: Le Surréalisme arabe à Paris 1973–1975*, Abdul Kader El Janabi, ed., Toulouse: Éditions de l'Asymétrie 2018, 14.

48 Marc Kober, "Introduction", 10.

49 El Janabi reports that the only well-disposed critics were a number of Lebanese journalists on the daily newspaper *al-Nahār*, such as Nazih Khater and Issam Mahfouz. In most cases, the members of the group were described as Zionists and CIA agents. See Abdul Kader El Janabi, ed., *Le Désir libertaire: Le Surréalisme arabe à Paris 1973–1975*, Toulouse: Éditions de l'Asymétrie 2018, 34.

be sold unofficially (mainly in Beirut).[50] For El Janabi too, surrealism was linked to a moral concern: "*Le Désir libertaire*, the journal of the Arab surrealists, was born from within this search for a clear vision of life and daily conduct [...] for a moral position in a world without morality, in order to reconquer the power of international imagination."[51]

Whereas French surrealism mainly advocated an anti-moral standpoint, Arab surrealists struggled to find a moral position in the first place. This did not mean that they were living in a world without morality, but that it had become implausible and unsustainable. To classify imagination as "international" (*al-khayāl al-umamiyy*) raises some questions: Is imagination not per se beyond any boundaries? If so, why does El Janabi make it a point to emphasize its internationalism? The only explanation seems to be his intention to embed this initiative in a broader array of struggles against oppression of all kinds and thereby link it to an international movement, or as John Roberts says: "The manifesto speaks to a native anti-imperialist and Arabo-Muslim audience and an international avant-garde alike."[52]

The journal's main targets were the language of the Koran, religion and the Arab nation (*al-ummah al-ʿarabiyyah*): "Our surrealism is to destroy the Arab fatherland!"[53] Marc Kober determines that "for the first time the Arabs use the word *surrealist* to define themselves".[54] Neither Georges Henein, nor Ramses Younan, nor Unsi al-Hajj founded any surrealist group, he says. It is therefore the "first declaration of an Arab surrealism".[55] This clearly addresses the question "What is surrealism and who is a surrealist?". Is it because others say so, or because groups or individuals define themselves as surrealist?

At the beginning of the 1980s, El Janabi produced the second series of *Le Désir libertaire*, which was no longer predominantly surrealist, but instead open to various positions which were juxtaposed in an eclectic mix.[56] It brought together numerous texts from various contexts of a subversive and critical bent, such as surrealism, the Frankfurt School, lettrism and situationism, and its supreme aim was to attack the notion of homeland and religion (Islam).[57] The journal published texts by André Breton, Karl Marx, Georges Henein, Ramses Younan, Karl Kraus, Theodor Adorno, the situationists and Benjamin Péret, amongst others, while El

---

50 El Janabi, *Le Désir libertaire*, 35.

51 El Janabi, *Tarbiyat ʿAbdul Qādir al-Janābī*, 95. Original Arabic: "*Min ṣulb hādhā al-baḥth ʿan ru'yah wāḍiḥah fī al-ḥayāt wa sulūk yaumiyyi [...], ʿan mawqif akhlāqiyy fī ʿālam bilā akhlāq, wulidat al-raghbah al-ibāḥiyyah, lisān ḥal al-suriyaliyyin al-ʿarab, min ajli istirdād sulṭat al-khayāl al-umamiyy.*" English translation by the author.

52 Roberts, *Revolutionary Time*, 41.

53 Kober, "Introduction", 9.

54 "Pour la première fois, les Arabes utilisent le mot *surréaliste* pour se définir." Kober, "Introduction", 10.

55 "C'est la première déclaration d'un surréalisme arabe". Kober, "Introduction", 10.

56 Kober, "Introduction", 18.

57 Kober, "Introduction", 16.

Janabi criticized the stagnation of the Arab region, which in his eyes affected every area of society and culture. This he declared to be the "arch-enemy".[58] Included in the journal were also poems by Unsi al-Hajj, Serge Tzvetkov, Paul Celan, Joyce Mansour and others in French and in Arabic.

The poet Édouard Jaguer (1924-2006), founder of the group *Phases*, who had been close to the Paris surrealists in his youth, described *Le Désir libertaire* as "one of the most beautiful surprises surrealism has sprung on itself":[59] what he most likely meant by this was the surprise of discovering that an Arab surrealist group had been founded in the place where surrealism had originated almost five decades before. The geographical collage "Arabie-sur-Seine" in the subtitle of the journal, *Publication de l'Association Arabie-sur-Seine*, reflects the exile status of the group and at the same time represents a repurposing in the surrealist manner.

Preceded by a contextualizing foreword, the manifesto of the Arab Surrealist Movement was reprinted in issue 3 of the magazine *Arsenal: Surrealist Subversion*,[60] published in Chicago under the editorship of Franklin Rosemont.[61] Interestingly, the movement is positioned in a direct line with the Egyptian group Art et Liberté and described as its continuation:

> The Arab Surrealist Movement was reconstituted in the early 1970s, but its origins extend back to the mid-30s, when the Egyptian poet and theorist Georges Henein (who adhered to the movement in 1934 as a student in Paris) and the Egyptian painter Ramses Younan introduced Surrealism to Cairo. [...] Henein's sensitiveness to the many and wide-ranging problems of human expression in the postwar period, and his profound revolutionary integrity, give his entire work a special significance today to the surrealists of all countries, and most especially, of course, to A.K. El Janaby and his comrades, who are in the truest sense the continuators of the effort begun by Georges Henein and Ramses Younan.[62]

Rosemont combined the two groups into a single historical narrative despite the relationship between them being more coincidental. As El Janabi himself claimed, he had not heard of the existence of the group Art et Liberté until the beginning of the 1970s. To represent his group explicitly as a successor to Art et Liberté can be interpreted as an idea of Rosemont's, however it was reinforced by El Janabi's expressed spiritual closeness to Henein, and through him, to Breton. Interestingly, even the idea of the manifesto itself seems to have sprung up retroactively: in the introductory paragraph of the 1975 manifesto, reprinted in his 2018 publication, El Janabi writes: "In Spring 1975, Franklin Rosemont (1943–2009), founder of the

58 "Avant-propos" in El Janabi, *Le Désir libertaire*, 34.

59 Kober, "Introduction", 13. Original French: "l'une des plus belles surprises que le surréalisme se soit faite à lui-même". Translation by the author.

60 In total, four issues were published between 1970 and 1989.

61 Franklin Rosemont (1943–2009) was, among other things, a poet and artist, and co-founder of the Chicago Surrealist Group.

62 The text of this article, including the manifesto, is available at https://theanarchistlibrary.org/library/various-authors-Surrealism-in-the-arab-world.

surrealist group in Chicago, asked us for a text to illustrate the approach of *Le Désir libertaire* for issue number 3 of *Arsenal*. The text below is based on the editorial article of issue number 5 of our journal."[63] The "manifesto" is thus a retroactive construction of an identity and a programme, intended to fit into the narrative as a group with a clear beginning, an "ancestry" and specific aims. To a certain extent, the surrealist identity of *Le Désir libertaire* and its ties to Art et Liberté can be regarded as a projection from outside. The image of surrealism in the Arab world as it is drawn by Franklin Rosemont is a distorted one: "The current resurgence of Surrealism in the Arab world is a revolutionary development of the greatest significance, demonstrating once more that the strategy of the unfettered imagination is always and necessarily global."[64] The Arab Surrealist Movement is neither a direct successor of Art et Liberté nor is it based in the Arab world, but in Paris.

The tone – that is the outrage – and style of the manifesto of the Arab surrealist movement from 1975 is reminiscent of Art et Liberté's writings, such as in their journal *al-Taṭawwur*. However, the older group's vocabulary had been much less provocative than the wording found in the Paris-based manifesto.

> With disgust we shove aside the dregs of survival and the impoverished rational ideas which stuff the ash-can-heads of intellectuals.
>
> 1. We incite individuals and the masses to unleash their instincts against all forms of repression – including the repressive "reason" of the bourgeois order.
> 2. The great values of the ruling class (the fatherland, family, religion, school, barracks, churches, mosques and other rottenness) make us laugh. Joyously we piss on their tombs.
> 3. We spit on the fatherland to drown in it the fumes of death. We combat and ridicule the very idea of the fatherland. To affirm one's fatherland is to insult the totality of man.
> 4. We practice subversion 24 hours a day. We excite sadistic urges against all that is established, not only because we are the enemies of this new stone age that is imposed on us, but above all because it is through our subversive activity that we discover new dimensions.
> 5. We poison the intellectual atmosphere with the elixir of the imagination, so that the poet will realize himself in realizing the historical transformation of poetry:
>   a. from form into matter;
>   b. from simple words hanging on coat racks of paper into the desirable flesh of the imagination that we shall absorb until everything separating dream from reality is dissolved.
>
> Surrealism is nothing but the actualization of this surreality.

63 El Janabi, *Le Désir libertaire*, 45.
64 El Janabi, *Le Désir libertaire*, 45.

6. We explode the mosques and the streets with the scandal of sex returning to its body, bursting into flames at each encounter – secret until then.
7. We liberate language from the prisons and stock markets of capitalist confusion.[65]

The key words and targets of surrealist subversion are all present in this manifesto: fatherland, religion, family, the bourgeois order and the transformative power of imagination. Although they seem old-fashioned in the 1970s, they show that in fact not much has changed compared to the 1920s and 1930s. Whereas Art et Liberté's manifesto was much more descriptive of a specific situation, the present manifesto is characterized by action and violence: "we spit", "we poison", "we practice subversion", "we excite sadistic urges", "we explode", "we liberate" and so on. As such, the manifesto is highly performative. The anti-nationalistic, iconoclastic imagination that it evokes is shaped into an image.

As was mentioned before, it would be reductive to tie El Janabi's group exclusively to surrealism – or rather, to an understanding of surrealism such as represented by Art et Liberté and other earlier surrealist groups – especially from the 1980s onwards. This testifies to the chronological distance between Art et Liberté and El Janabi's group, during which the later surrealist developments had, to some extent, merged into other movements. Thus, the Arab Surrealist Movement in Exile can be seen as a melting pot of subversive trends from different epochs and contexts that were eclectically united under the banner of surrealism. It gains momentum from the collage-like juxtaposition of highly diverse and subversive perspectives that can be observed in their journal *Le Désir libertaire*. As such, it is quite realistic even though it is labelled surrealistic. Reality is not transcended in a surrealist manner, but rather looked at from a very realistic point of view.

Habib Tengour on Maghrebian surrealism, 1981

Habib Tengour (born 1947 in Mostaganem, Algeria) is a French-Algerian poet, sociologist and anthropologist. He wrote the manifesto on Maghrebian surrealism in Constantine, Algeria, and it is dated 7 March 1981. Unlike the previous manifestos, it comprises no declaration of political solidarity or appeal for resistance nor does it announce a programmatic position. Instead it meanderingly and humorously brings to light surrealistic elements in Maghrebian culture and tradition.[66] In this sense, Tengour's manifesto is a "non-message". Nevertheless, it carries an implicit message through the manifesto's composition as a dialogue with Breton.

---

65 El Janabi, http://theanarchistlibrary.org/library/various-authors-surrealism-in-the-arab-world; for the French original see El Janabi, *Le Désir libertaire*, 45-47.

66 Habib Tengour, "Maghrebian Surrealism [Essay & Manifesto]", trans. Pierre Joris, 2017, https://jacket2.org/commentary/habib-tengour-maghrebian-Surrealism-essay-manifesto.

The time of its creation falls into a period of turmoil in France, when French youth of North African backgrounds were fighting for their rights.[67] By addressing Maghrebians and their relationship to France, the manifesto indirectly reflects this struggle for identity and recognition and the critical engagement with the other. In his opening statement the author connects surrealism with the Maghreb in various ways and with an increasing sense of the absurd:

MAGHREBIAN SURREALISM
SURREALISM IN THE MAGHREB
SURREALIST MAGHREB
THE MAGHREBIAN SURREALISTS
MAGHREBIAN SURREALITY
THE SURREALIST REVOLUTION IN THE MAGHREB
SURREALIST MAGHREB PRESS SERVICE
SURREALISM IN THE SERVICE OF THE MAGHREB
Etc.

The author cites all the constituent elements of a surrealist aesthetic – dreams, madness, subversion and the marvellous – all of which he finds in Maghrebian culture. The Maghrebian has, for a long time, been a surrealist "without knowing it" he writes.[68] Tengour cites the example of the Arab Andalusian scholar, poet, philosopher and mystic Ibn Arabi to illustrate this:

> In what I have written I have never had a deliberate purpose, like other writers. Glimmers of divine inspiration illuminated me and nearly overcame me, so that I couldn't free my mind of them except by writing down what they revealed to me. If my works show any kind of formal composition, this form is not intentional. I have written some of my works on the behest of Allah, sent to me during my sleep or through revelation.[69]

Tengour shows with this that automatic writing and the unconscious played a role long before it was termed "surrealist". In so doing, Tengour relieves Parisian surrealism of its pioneering role and deprives it of the groundbreaking role that Breton claimed for it.

Unlike El Janabi, he sees himself not as an heir or continuator but as a writer putting what was a pre-existing Maghrebian surrealism into words. His essay/manifesto contains citations from Breton's text, which are set in italics and consist mainly of half-sentences while occasionally incorporating an entire section. Even the style is reminiscent of Breton's. By juxtaposing and interweaving pieces of Breton's manifesto with his own, Tengour creates a dialogic text where two voices are merged into one but are still distinguishable. At some point, Tengour conveys

67 In her contribution to this volume, Megan C. MacDonald further addresses the political circumstances in France at the beginning of the 1980s.
68 Tengour, "Maghrebian Surrealism".
69 Tengour, "Maghrebian Surrealism".

an implicit criticism of Breton's encyclopaedic definition of surrealism, with which he sought to fix surrealism "once and for all".[70] André Breton:

> Those who might dispute our right to employ the term SURREALISM in the very special sense that we understand it are being extremely dishonest, for there can be no doubt that this word had no currency before we came along. Therefore, I am defining it once and for all: SURREALISM, *n.* Psychic automatism in its pure state, by which one proposes to express – verbally, by means of the written word, or in any other manner – the actual functioning of thought. Dictated by the thought, in the absence of any control exercised by reason, exempt from any aesthetic or moral concern.
>
> ENCYCLOPEDIA. *Philosophy.* Surrealism is based on the belief in the superior reality of certain forms of previously neglected associations, in the omnipotence of dream, in the disinterested play of thought. It tends to ruin once and for all other psychic mechanisms and to substitute itself for them in solving all the principal problems of life. The following have performed acts of ABSOLUTE SURREALISM: Messrs. Aragon, Baron, Boiffard, Breton, Carrive, Crevel, Delteil, Desnos, Éluard, Gérard, Limbour, Malkine, Morise, Naville, Noll, Péret, Picon, Soupault, Vitrac.[71]

By entirely capitalizing the terms "surrealism" and "absolute surrealism", and by giving its definition the form of an encyclopaedia entry, Breton makes use of this format as an authority of knowledge to claim absolute validity. In addition, he names several well-known poets to add credibility and to give concrete and ideal examples. Tengour uses Breton's definition and gives it a different twist. Given their conflicted identity, he defines the Maghrebians as predestined for surrealistic thinking: "Indeed there does exist a divided space called the Maghreb but the Maghrebian is always elsewhere. And that is where he realizes himself."[72] Breton's examples of "acts of absolute surrealism" are juxtaposed by "acts of relative surrealism" in Tengour's manifesto, another term that originates from Breton:

> During the twenties, some Maghrebians in exile "*performed acts of Relative SURREALISM.*" It was difficult for them to do otherwise: the family was a lack they wept over in front of a post office window, the fatherland a confiscated identity and religion a recognition.[73]

As a result of the alienation and yearning for home experienced by Maghrebians during their exile in France, their attitude toward the institutions of family, nation and religion can be seen as ambivalent and deficient with regard to the three main targets of surrealist subversion: family, homeland and religion. Faced with a lack of absolute surrealism, Tengour qualifies this attitude as relative surrealism. He does not accompany his reference to relative surrealism with specific names, unlike

70 "But Breton has defined Surrealism '*once and for all*'" (italics in the original). Tengour, "Maghrebian Surrealism".

71 André Breton, "Manifesto of Surrealism" [1924], 1999, http://www.exquisitecorpse.com/assets/manifesto_of_Surrealism.pdf. For the French version, see André Breton, *Manifestes du surréalisme*, Paris: Gallimard 1981, 36–37.

72 Tengour, "Maghrebian Surrealism".

73 Tengour, "Maghrebian Surrealism".

Breton in his manifesto ("The following have performed acts of ABSOLUTE SURREALISM: Messrs. Aragon, Baron, Boiffard, Breton [...]"). This reinforces his view of Maghrebians as surrealists *avant la lettre*, as it includes all Maghrebians, or more precisely the Maghrebians in exile in Paris in the 1920s (when surrealism came into being there).

The following passage from Habib Tengour's essay offers a further parallel with Breton's manifesto:

> The passing Maghrebian is surrealist in Djeha.[74]
> Nafzawi[75] is surrealist in sexual revelation.
> Ibn Khaldûn[76] is surrealist in intrigue.
> Sidi Ahmed ben Yussef[77] is surrealist in cursing.
> Mejdûb[78] is surrealist in anguish.
> Feraûn[79] is surrealist in Si Mohand.
> Kateb[80] is surrealist in the tradition.
> Dib[81] is surrealist in the drift.
> Mrabet[82] is surrealist in his joints.
> Sénac[83] is surrealist in the streets.
> Khaïr-Eddine[84] is surrealist in his alcoholic delirium.
> I am surrealist when I am not there.
> Tibouchi[85] is surrealist in certain verses.
> Baya[86] is not surrealist despite Breton's sympathy.
> Etcetera.[87]

André Breton's manifesto reads:

> Swift is Surrealist in malice,
> Sade is Surrealist in sadism.
> Chateaubriand is Surrealist in exoticism.
> Constant is Surrealist in politics.
> Hugo is Surrealist when he isn't stupid.

---

74 Nasr Eddin Hodja is a legendary figure widespread in Muslim culture. He is a philosopher of Turkish origin and lived in the thirteenth century. In the Maghreb he is known, among other names, as Djeha.

75 Muhammad ibn Muhammad al-Nafzawi (fifteenth century) is the author of *The Perfumed Garden of Sensual Delight*, a sex manual and erotic work.

76 A leading historian, born in Tunisia in the fourteenth century.

77 An eighteenth-century theologian born in Algeria.

78 A sixteenth-century poet, Sufi and mystic born in Morocco.

79 Mouloud Feraoun translated the poems of Si Mohand, who was born in Algeria. Si Mohand was nicknamed the "Kabylie Verlaine" by French scholars.

80 Kateb Yacine (1929–1989), an Algerian writer.

81 Mohammed Dib (1920–2003), an Algerian writer.

82 Mohammed Mrabet (b. 1936), a Moroccan writer and artist.

83 Jean Sénac (1926–1973), an Algerian poet and writer.

84 Mohammed Khaïr-Eddine (1941–1995), a Moroccan writer.

85 Hamid Tibouchi (b. 1951), an Algerian painter and poet.

86 Baya Mahieddine (Fatima Haddad; 1931–1998), an Algerian artist.

87 Tengour, "Maghrebian Surrealism".

> Desbordes-Valmore is Surrealist in love.
> Bertrand is Surrealist in the past.
> Rabbe is Surrealist in death.
> Poe is Surrealist in adventure.
> Baudelaire is Surrealist in morality.
> Rimbaud is Surrealist in the way he lived, and elsewhere.
> Mallarmé is Surrealist when he is confiding.
> Jarry is Surrealist in absinthe.
> Nouveau is Surrealist in the kiss.
> Saint-Pol-Roux is Surrealist in his use of symbols.
> Fargue is Surrealist in the atmosphere.
> Vaché is Surrealist in me.
> Reverdy is Surrealist at home.
> Saint-Jean-Perse is Surrealist at a distance.
> Roussel is Surrealist as a storyteller.
> Etc.[88]

Habib Tengour's manifesto reads like a dialogue with Breton's manifesto, out of which he pulls certain key words and passages and applies them to the Maghreb. Hédi Abdel-Jaouad refers to it as a manifesto of "equivalences".[89] The names in the passage cited above are those of Algerian, Moroccan and Tunisian writers, poets, mystics, artists, theologians and historians from different centuries. The author relativizes and undermines Breton's quasi-doctrinaire surrealism by conceiving of surrealism as an integral element in Maghrebian culture. In so doing, he simultaneously exercises a subtle criticism of certain Maghrebian artists and writers who believe they have to prove something to the world:

> The Maghrebian artists, however, are often obsessed by their image, they want to prove something: that they have "*talent.*" A left bank Parisian publisher confided confidentially that he did not like to do business with Maghrebian writers because they all think they are Rimbaud. So what! It is certain that he, Rimbaud, didn't give a damn about being a Maghrebian in the Harrar and that the publisher in question is a cad despite his undeniable qualities.[90]

Breton also refers to the notion of talent in the appendix to his manifesto, titled "Secrets of the magical Surrealist art: Written Surrealist composition or first and last draft": "Forget about your genius, your talents, and the talents of everyone else. Keep reminding yourself that literature is one of the saddest roads that leads to everything. [...]"[91] Here, Habib Tengour intimates that the Maghrebians are constantly comparing themselves with their French role models ("they all think they are Rimbaud"[92]),

---

88 Breton, "Manifesto of Surrealism".
89 Hédi Abdel-Jaouad, "Tendances surréalistes dans la littérature maghrébine d'expression française", PhD thesis, Temple University, Philadelphia 1983, http://www.limag.com/new/index.php?inc=dspliv&liv=00000141. See Megan C. MacDonald's contribution to the present volume.
90 Tengour, "Maghrebian Surrealism".
91 Breton, "Manifesto of Surrealism".
92 Tengour, "Maghrebian Surrealism".

while Rimbaud (1854–1891) in no way considered it desirable to be "a Maghrebian in the Harrar" (here Tengour creates an analogy to the Maghrebians in Paris trying to be Rimbaud). As a matter of fact, Rimbaud spent several years of his life as a coffee trader in Harrar in Ethiopia after having abandoned poetry.

Tengour's manifesto is the "act of an individual" and as such is completely independent of any group with specific artistic or political goals. It is not a manifesto in the sense that it calls for the adoption of a particular political or artistic stance. It is an artwork; and it is, as suggested by the title of the English translation, an "essay"[93] that engages with Breton's manifesto from a specifically Maghrebian point of view. In the manner of surrealist repurposing (*détournement*), pieces of scenery are cut out and slotted into a new context, that is to say the Maghreb. In a certain sense, Breton is beaten at his own game by Tengour. This reminds us of Art et Liberté: with their manifesto of solidarity, they declare themselves as avant-garde and Europe as lagging behind. Breton is knocked off his pedestal as the self-pronounced inventor of surrealism by Tengour's examples of a Maghrebian "surrealism" *avant la lettre*. At the same time, the author is also critical vis-à-vis Maghrebian artists' obsession with their image and the fact that they are torn between here and elsewhere. This leads him to the question: "Who is this Maghrebian? How to define him?"[94]

Furthermore, like the Syrian poet Adonis (Ali Ahmad Said),[95] Tengour sees a connection between Sufism and surrealism: "It is finally into Maghrebian Sufism that surrealist subversion inserts itself: '*Psychic automatism in its pure state*,' '*amour fou*,' revolt, chance meetings, etcetera."[96] A direct link to local traditions is found.

Tengour's manifesto intentionally mimics Breton's manifesto pointing both in the direction of the Maghrebians and Breton's surrealism. He ends his essay/manifesto by quoting Breton again: "The Surrealist Revolution is total and '*in matters of revolt none of us can have need of ancestors*'."[97] Everything must be recreated from scratch, the old must vanish and the connection to the past must be cut. Paradoxically, Tengour invokes the rich Maghrebian history only to conclude with the necessity of cutting ties with the past. This could be interpreted as the need to provide a specifically Maghrebian narration and contribution to the history of surrealism, thereby relativizing the monopoly of French surrealism, before the revolution can begin. On the other hand, it ironically points to the fact that all avant-garde movements, including the surrealists, were obsessed with the past.[98]

---

93 Maghrebian Surrealism [Essay & Manifesto]; in French: "Manifeste du surréalisme maghrébin »

94 Tengour, "Maghrebian Surrealism".

95 Adūnīs, *al-Ṣufiyyah wa-l-sūriyāliyyah*, London: Dār al-Sāqī 1992. English translation: Adūnīs, *Sufism and Surrealism*, trans. Judith Cumberbatch, London: Saqi Books 2005.

96 Tengour, "Maghrebian Surrealism".

97 Tengour, "Maghrebian Surrealism". Italics in original.

98 Cf. Pierre Bourdieu, *Die Regeln der Kunst: Genese und Struktur des literarischen Feldes*, 7th ed., Frankfurt am Main: Suhrkamp 2016.

Conclusion

The examples of manifestos presented in this chapter show that surrealism was an idea that circulated widely but never had the same programme in the many places of its adoption. It depended largely on the specific time, the place, the context, the individual perspectives and the political and artistic intentions connected to it. It is clear that surrealism was as much a global phenomenon as modernism was. Globalism is inevitably centric; in the case of the Parisian surrealist movement, it is Eurocentric. To participate, one must float with the current. The problem is the nature of surrealism itself, which is inherently subversive and centrifugal. The examples discussed here solve this problem through a certain degree of eccentricity, which induced the drafting of a manifesto.

Surrealists need to position themselves. In the cited examples, this happens through certain key figures. André Breton is present in all three examples, although to a much lesser degree in El Janabi's group, where Georges Henein takes over the role of the key figure of surrealism. Relating to an approved authority provides authenticity and visibility and therefore is an important tool for self-legitimization. Regardless of that, a certain cult of personality cannot be denied. This is especially the case with El Janabi in his relation to Henein, whose meeting with the forefather of surrealism in the Arab world represents a kind of revelation and is the ground on which El Janabi situates his own group. Genealogy plays a central role. Both El Janabi and Tengour build their surrealist initiatives on myths: Henein is for El Janabi what Ibn Arabi is for Tengour. Eccentricity requires a centre of reference. In this sense, all cited forefathers are centres of eccentricity.

The manifesto "Vive l'art dégénéré" (Long Live Degenerate Art) generates a new pattern following which the West plunges into the Middle Ages and needs to be salvaged. The manifesto of the Arab Surrealist Movement in Exile turns around its own surreality, which is moulded into a new form, namely as a melting pot for diverse movements. In an act of surrealist *détournement*, the group "reconquers" Paris as the centre of surrealism (Arabie-sur-Seine), only to refer to it from an eccentric perspective, namely from a specifically Arab point of view. The manifesto here is highly performative and as such a work of art, just like Habib Tengour's manifesto. The latter's surrealism is an affirmation of relativity, he rejects any claims for the absolute. It is eccentric because it distances itself from Breton – while at the same time paying tribute to him – and puts the notion of surrealism in a transhistorical context, thereby linking it to Ibn Arabi and mysticism.

Finally, one can state that surrealism outside the temporal centre – that is, between the two world wars – gradually loses its surrealist core qualities, it becomes eccentric even in the former centre, Paris. The role of the manifesto mutates and becomes a game with power rather than claiming power itself.

Chapter 2

The Paris–Istanbul axis and the paradox of Turkish surrealist painting

Eyüp Özveren

> "We must go to the north all the same," said Hebdomeros to his companions, who approved of this idea. "In fact, my friends," he went on, "the north is a little bit like the west. On the other hand, the south is a little like the east. I advise you to be careful of the south and the east because these are destructive and corrosive countries. Towards the north lie life and happiness, beauty and light; joy in the work and rest without remorse; if you have something to say or to show, say it and show it to the north and the west, you will have more chance than anywhere else of being understood and rewarded for your pains. Yet this does not mean, my friends, that you should never go towards the south or the east; a day will come when not only will we go there but we will stay there."
>
> Giorgio de Chirico, *Hebdomeros*[1]

The advent of surrealism in Turkey in general, and surrealist Turkish painting during the interwar period in particular, have not yet been explored either in Turkey or abroad with a focus on surrealist networks and exchanges.[2] At first sight, we can interpret this lacuna as consistent with the remark of a Turkish art critic, who noted the outright disinterest in and unawareness of surrealism among the Turkish painters in Paris in the 1920s and 1930s,[3] which we take as a point of departure.[4] The

1 Giorgio de Chirico, *Hebdomeros* [1929], New York: PAJ Publications 1988, 75–76.

2 This paper has benefitted greatly from the comments and criticisms of the editors and two anonymous referees. I would also like to thank Ergin Ertem, Rahmi Eyüboğlu, Mine Haydaroğlu, Gül İrepoğlu, Ayşegül İzer, Burcu Pelvanoğlu, Kerem Topuz, and Filiz Yenişehirlioğlu for their assistance in various stages of research, writing, and publication. However, the usual caveat applies.

3 Ferit Edgü, "Aşkın Resimleri", in: *"Sevmek Güzel Meslek Reis": B. Rahmi*, exhibition catalogue, İzmir: Folkart Gallery Publishing 2017, 151.

4 The disinterest of Turkish artists abroad for the then controversial "hot" art movements is by no means limited to surrealism but is more general. Adnan Turani (1925–2016), a renowned Turkish painter of the post-war generation, who was in Germany in the 1950s and who had the opportunity to tour the north-west Mediterranean coastline and meet Pablo Picasso (in the French Riviera) and Juan Miró (in his village near Barcelona), and who has also written extensively about the history and theory of art, once noted with disdain the lack of concern among the interwar generation for abstract art that was then "hot" on the Parisian art scene, which he believed they knew, but, to his regret, did not pursue. See Sema

judgement becomes all the more pointed when we remind ourselves that surrealist influence penetrated deep into Turkish painting much later in the 1970s, in the works of artists such as Erol Akyavaş (1932–1999) and Cihat Burak (1915–1994).[5] In fact, the late arrival of surrealism in the 1970s had a few early signals in the 1960s which only a few have noticed.[6] However, that remains beyond the scope of this work, which is confined to the interwar period and to the specification and explanation of the paradox. The very existence of the "late surrealism" phase indicates that by then the paradox had been resolved.[7]

I assume there is no such thing as "real surrealism" that serves as a compulsive model. The specification of my research agenda as a fundamentally across-space inquiry – where time is taken as constant, fixed in the interwar period – simplifies my task immensely. This is because surrealist painting was from the moment of its birth already a loose configuration of certain stylistic and thematic attributes only some of which converged in certain artists and not others. It was a nebula, where boundaries were difficult to draw. Variety was not only tolerated but welcome. Hence one could not be denied admission just because one's work did not contain a specific feature, as long as it contained at least one of the several common characteristics, and, more importantly, the artist professed to be a surrealist. Under the same rubric both Salvador Dalí and Joan Miró could coexist peacefully, and this fostered experimentation and creativity. There was enormous room for give and take; the fluidity of the domain gave it vitality. In the course of time, the early phase of dissemination across space from the centre to the periphery would be succeeded by a new mature phase where a hundred flowers could bloom, each entitled to being qualified as an equally legitimate local variant of surrealism. This was not a betrayal of the original doctrinal principles, but was part of the essence of surrealism. This is also what classifies certain specific artworks as surrealist even if the artist in question is not known as a surrealist, or did not profess to be one. To put it differently, there are more surrealist paintings than there are paintings from surrealist painters per se. This fuzzy and flexible conception of surrealism underlies the rest of my discussion.

Öztoprak, *Adnan Turani: Yaşam Serüveni, Sanat Üzerine Düşünceleri ve Resimsel Birikimi*, Istanbul: Türkiye İş Bankası Yayınları 2005, 47–58.

5 Özkan Eroğlu, *Türkiye'de Resim Sanatı*, Istanbul: Tekhne 2015, 149. Cihat Burak's relationship to surrealism was nuanced because he used surrealist elements in his primitivism that excluded a persistent specific use of depth of field. See Necmi Sönmez, *Paris Tecrübeleri; École de Paris – Çağdaş Türk Sanatı: 1945-1965*. Istanbul: Yapı Kredi Yayınları, 118-19.

6 Ambra D'Antone's contribution to this volume, focusing on the unusual art of Yüksel Arslan, covers one such important precursor at length.

7 Among those who note the phenomenon of late surrealism in Turkey without being aware of its predecessors during the interwar period, but fully conscious of the presence of surreal elements in Ottoman-Turkish traditional arts inspired by mythology, legends and folklore since time immemorial, see Hrant Melih Suci, *Türk Resim Sanatında Gerçeküstücü Ressamlar*, Ankara: Pegem Akademi 2017. 75-105. Suci identifies Yüksel Arslan (1933-2017) and Nuri Abaç (1926-2008) as the two artists who started Turkish surrealist painting in 1955 (p. 79).

In comparison with the rival avant-garde art movements of its time, surrealist painting benefitted from its "indifference", if not outright conservatism, towards the "subject" or "story" and the figure. Rather than either destroying or totally deforming objects so as to render them undistinguishable, as would befit non-figurative painting, it vaguely played with their proportions and concentrated its energy not so much in confronting figure head on, but in associating figures with one another in unexpected ways. Most of the time, it works with concrete but strange objects.[8] This being the case, the potential viewer as a novice finds surrealist paintings easier to penetrate via the help of story or figure than, say, cubist or futurist works where both the story and the figure become hardly recognizable except with special training or effort. In the case of Turkish painters of the interwar period, the story and the figure may have provided them with convenient points of entry into surrealist painting. If they nevertheless resisted the temptation, there must have been stronger forces at work to do with politically driven convictions responsive to a particular institutional incentive structure, of which more will be disclosed later.

Turkey in historical perspective

Turkey was a world apart from the rest of the Balkans, the Middle East and North Africa during the interwar period. It was a small nation state that had won its independence the hard way, successor to a previous tricontinental multi-ethnic and multireligious empire that disintegrated after the First World War, the gravedigger of such empires. Istanbul, the capital of the Ottoman Empire, yielded to Ankara, but more importantly, found itself at a loss. Istanbul had been deeply enmeshed in centuries-long European connections with Paris serving as their cultural mediating crossroads. It was largely cosmopolitan in outlook. Istanbul had become estranged from the country into which it was now being subsumed. During the heyday of surrealism, when it exerted an attraction and spread outwards from its centre, it found Istanbul difficult to penetrate. This was unprecedented, as Istanbul had been historically welcoming to influences from Paris since the nineteenth century.

After the dismemberment of the Ottoman Empire, Turkey hosted a reinvigorated state that adopted a radical cultural enlightenment project and pursued it vehemently. It was determined to sever links with the past as a repository of tradition and embark upon developing ties with Europe in order to get the best of what was available there and diffuse it to the much neglected and therefore deprived countryside. The new state inherited and pursued with much greater rigour and determination the former Ottoman policy of turning to Europe as a model for modernization and sent students abroad in order to pursue its social and economic

---

8 Yvonne Duplessis, *Le Surréalisme*, Vendôme: Presses universitaires de France 1961.

development as well as cultural policy.[9] Artists and intellectuals were to play the vanguard role in this expected thorough transformation that was to be substantially different from other, limited, window-dressing efforts in the neighbourhood. The offer the state extended to these cadres, but especially to the painters, was indeed attractive. They would be respected and gain increased recognition in return for which they would render a valuable service to the state cultural policy. At a time when, in an impoverished country, no art market existed, the state would "value" their works and exhibit them, and give the artists employment as professors in the Academy of Fine Arts in Istanbul or as teachers in schools, thereby permitting them to make a living in a way that allowed them to pursue their artistic endeavours freely.

Institution-building within the domain of the arts

One can question how freedom could exist in such a reciprocally binding arrangement, on one side of which was a relatively strong state and on the other a nascent intelligentsia. The answer is to be found in the fact that the state's preference was for "modernity", without taking sides among its various subdivisions, at the expense of "tradition". Traditional arts and their aesthetics were thus excluded. This was supported by large-scale institution-building by innovative borrowings from Europe. Nowhere was this more visible than in the contemporaneous reformation of the Academy of Fine Arts. Far from being a bastion of tradition, this was designed as the flagship of this project of modernist art. Hence, artists committed to modern approaches, regardless of which one they preferred, were more than welcome in its ranks. This conception of the "academy" is fundamentally different to what comes to mind from the centuries-long European experience. This was an artificial substitute for what was missing in Istanbul, a microclimate within which artists could pursue their ends by civil means and by recourse to an art market and its related institutional supports, such as galleries, art criticism and specialized publications. Henri Léopold-Lévy (1882-1966) was recruited to head the Academy as of 1936. He did not belong to any particular school, in fact, he was sceptical of all schools. He did not indoctrinate his students to become his disciples in any particular direction, on the contrary, he encouraged them to develop and differentiate themselves individually. No better open-minded director could have been found

9 For further details of Ottoman Turkish history, see Bernard Lewis, *The Emergence of Modern Turkey*, New York: Oxford University Press 2002; Carter V. Findley, *Turkey, Islam, Nationalism, and Modernity: A History, 1789–2007*, New Haven: Yale University Press 2010; and Erik J. Zürcher, *Turkey: A Modern History*, London: I.B. Tauris 2004. For an interpretation of historical tendencies in conformity with the specific interpretation adopted here, see Eyüp Özveren, "In Defiance of History: Liberal and National Attributes of the Ottoman-Turkish Path to Modernity", in: *Liberty and the Search for Identity: Liberal Nationalisms and the Legacy of Empires*, Iván Zoltán Dénes, ed., Budapest: Central European University Press 2006.

for the specific purpose. He was recommended by André Lhote for the job. He knew all schools but maintained a critical distance to any one of them particularly during his time in Istanbul. He is reported by one of his students to have said that in his view, compared with the daring artistic experimentations of surrealists, Pablo Picasso represented a graceful and heroic, but far from revolutionary reaction on behalf of pure aestheticism.[10]

The academy in Istanbul was in fact more like the Académie Lhote[11] in Paris than its more conventional namesake. The atelier of André Lhote (1885–1962) played the most important role in the education of the new generation of Turkish painters, and was unrivalled in its influence in this respect.[12] The relatively relaxed and friendly atmosphere, the international clientele and the pervasive cosmopolitanism, along with the tolerance for experimentation and discussion, were very hospitable and conducive to the development of Turkish artists. Last but not least, the formal training was quite conventional in the case of model painting and adhered to the classical norms as would befit an academy proper. Turkish artists were already accustomed to the master–apprentice relation via their prior experiences in Istanbul. It is no coincidence that both painters who are the focus of the present paper, Nurullah Berk (1906–1982) and Bedri Rahmi Eyüboğlu (1911–1975), were affiliated with Lhote's academy and later joined the Academy of Fine Arts in Istanbul. As such, they are among the very best representatives of a more general trend. We will also focus on a third painter, Hale Asaf (1905–1938) – once again connected with Lhote's academy, but who ultimately chose to remain in Paris – in order to see if her work became more receptive to surrealist experimentation, thereby giving us an indirect measure of the contextual effect in Turkey from which she was immune.

Turkish painters also learned the importance of professional organization from the Parisian art scene. Upon returning to Turkey, they took part in two such organizations that worked hard to improve artists' conditions and promote their common interests and that organized exhibitions in Istanbul. Berk, Eyüboğlu and

---

10 Necmi Sönmez, *Paris Tecrübeleri*, 93-94.

11 For the relationship between the Académie Lhote, the Atelier Léger and the École des Beaux-Arts in Paris, see Claire Maingon, "L'Académie Lhote – L'Atelier Léger: Enseignements comparés", in: *L'Éducation artistique en France du modèle académique et scolaire aux pratiques actuelles, XVIIIe–XIXe siècles*, Rennes: Presses universitaires de Rennes 2010. Even if the first two institutions had more in common with each other than with the École – as they provided a more cosmopolitan, accommodating and flexible environment where fluency in French was not required as a prerequisite and women felt more at ease – they were also known for giving their students a strong formal training modelled after the classic method of academy instruction.

12 Even Sabri Berkel (1907–1993), a painter who fell more strongly under the influence of Fernand Léger, had actually acquired an important part of his training at the Académie Lhote, despite the Atelier Léger being founded in 1933, the year he went to Paris. Similarly, Nurullah Berk, a friend of Berkel, studied with both Léger and Lhote but received much of his formative training with the latter, even if his painting bears a stronger mark of Léger's influence. The formative effect on Turkish painters of the Académie Lhote has more to do with its greater institutional continuity over time.

Asaf took part in the first of these organizations, but only Berk and Eyüboğlu took part in the second, because by that time, after a brief sojourn, Asaf had returned to Paris for good. The first organization, the Independent Painters and Sculptor's Association (1929) was a more strictly professional association, which brought together modern artists irrespective of their individual preferences; whereas the second, d Group[13] (1933), was more representative of a coherent art movement with an agenda of shared aesthetic and stylistic principles.[14] Hence the Turkish art scene of the interwar period was not only caught in the throes of country-wide all-encompassing change, but was also highly organized as a partner to the development of art-specific institutions. Whatever its dynamism and merits, this context was significantly different from its regional counterparts, and the place, if any, surrealism could find in it was indeed severely constrained.

In 1960, Breton, who worked as an ambassador of good will on behalf of surrealism as long as he could, was approached by a few Turkish intellectuals to write an introduction to a special issue of a journal (that later was transformed into a book).[15] By then the cultural policy summarized above had fulfilled its mission and a new generation of Turkish intellectuals had come into being as its enlightened beneficiaries. Three of them sent a letter to Breton requesting his participation. These young and aspiring intellectuals were Selahattin Hilâv (1928–2005), Onat Kutlar (1936–1995) and Ergin Ertem (b. 1935).

Hilâv graduated from the Department of Philosophy of the University of Istanbul and then moved to the Sorbonne in 1954, where he spent four years before returning to Istanbul. He published many essays and articles in numerous journals, in addition to books that began to appear from 1970.

Kutlar studied law for while in Istanbul and then headed for Paris to study philosophy. He returned after a two-year stay. He was gifted in literature, as he would soon demonstrate with poems he published in literary journals, as well as leading the Turkish Cinémathèque and writing about cinema throughout his life.[16] Just as

---

13 The d Group (*d Grubu*) artists were mocked, because of their choice of an initial "d", as the "mad men" (*deliler*) of modern Turkish art; see Kağan Güner, *Modern Türk Sanatının Doğuşu: Konstrüktivist Türkiye Cumhuriyeti'nde Kültür ve İdeoloji*, Istanbul: Kaynak Yayınları 2014, 219. However, the original idea was suggested by Fikret Adil, the art critic, on the basis that as they were the fourth art group to be founded in Istanbul, they should be named after the fourth letter of the alphabet, and deliberately as a small letter, quite unusual for their time. The name proved successful as it attracted much attention and stirred a controversy. See Gül İrepoğlu, *Zeki Faik İzer*, Istanbul: YKY 2005, 51–52.

14 The greater coherence among these modern artists cultivated a misunderstanding that they were cubists, and this was much resented by a frustrated participant and critic, Bedri Rahmi, who reported on the Ankara exhibition in February 1936. Eyüboğlu insisted that the group brought to public attention quality modern art that belonged to the recent past, the present and the future, and not to any specific "ism". Bedri Rahmi Eyüboğlu, *Gece Yarısı*, Istanbul: İş Bankası Kültür Yayınları 2002, 225–227.

15 Selahattin Hilâv, Ergin Ertem and Onat Kutlar, eds., *Gerçeküstücülük*, Ankara: de 1962.

16 Onat Kutlar, *Sinema Bir Şenliktir*, Istanbul: Can 1991.

the earlier surrealists in Paris had been great fans of cinema, thanks to this small but highly influential institution, a generation of Turkish intellectuals and artists fell under the spell of this modern art. Kutlar's book of short stories, *İshak* (1959), situated in the provincial city where he grew up, has become a classic with its distinct character and Kafkaesque atmosphere, which also contains an oblique connection with surrealist prose.[17] Shortly before he was killed in a café by a PKK-engineered terrorist explosion in 1995, he had also published books of poetry and essays that were well received by literary critics and the public.

Of the three, Ertem remains the least known to this day because he did not pursue a literary or artistic career. He was a distinguished and specialized translator with a particular interest in surrealism. It is no coincidence that he also translated Guillaume Apollinaire's *Le Bestiaire, ou Cortège d'Orphée*.[18]

The three authors jointly became the editors of the first major book on surrealism in post-war Turkey, long after the interwar high point of surrealist avant-garde. This book was a first because it covered surrealism widely as it manifested itself in different domains of literature and art. We learn that the roots of this publication project go back to 1953–1955, and hence the idea matured under the auspices of the same group along with a number of publications and translations in journals.[19]

Without any delay, Breton responded to the prospective editors in a handwritten letter "with brotherly feelings" in the name of their "surrealist friends" in Paris, and offered them an original unpublished piece entitled "Language, Woman, and Nature in Surrealism" instead of the proposed introduction (fig. 1).

That this article had to do with an egalitarian conception of women must have had additional resonances in Turkey, where women's emancipation remained a hotly contested issue except for a brief interval during the interwar period when the state intervened to tilt the balance in favour of women. Moreover, Breton ended his discussion of the theme by referring to the initial hermaphrodite cult figure and creature from which man and woman had emerged according to the ancient Abrahamic religious tradition (to a part of which Turkey had been the homeland).[20] What more could the editors have expected from Breton than an original piece on a theme of historical as well as contemporaneous relevance to the Turkish reading public?

Not long before, in 1952, Zeki Faik İzer (1905–1988), a Turkish painter who had studied with André Lhote in the 1930s, went back to Paris. Soon after, he participated as an observer in a UNESCO-organized art congress in Venice. Benefitting from the occasion, he registered his impressions of this city in his memory. He attempted to give a new interpretation to the Sienese School and produced a

[17] Onat Kutlar, *İshak*, Istanbul: A Dergisi Yayınları 1959.

[18] Guillaume Apollinaire, *Le Bestiaire, ou Cortège d'Orphée*, Paris: Deplanche 1911.

[19] İlhan Berk, *Gerçeküstücülük: Antoloji*, Istanbul: Varlık 2004, 6.

[20] André Breton, "Gerçeküstücülükte Dil, Kadın, Doğa" (trans. Selahattin Hilâv), in: *Gerçeküstücülük*, Selahattin Hilâv, Ergin Ertem and Onat Kutlar, eds., Ankara: de 1962, 13–17.

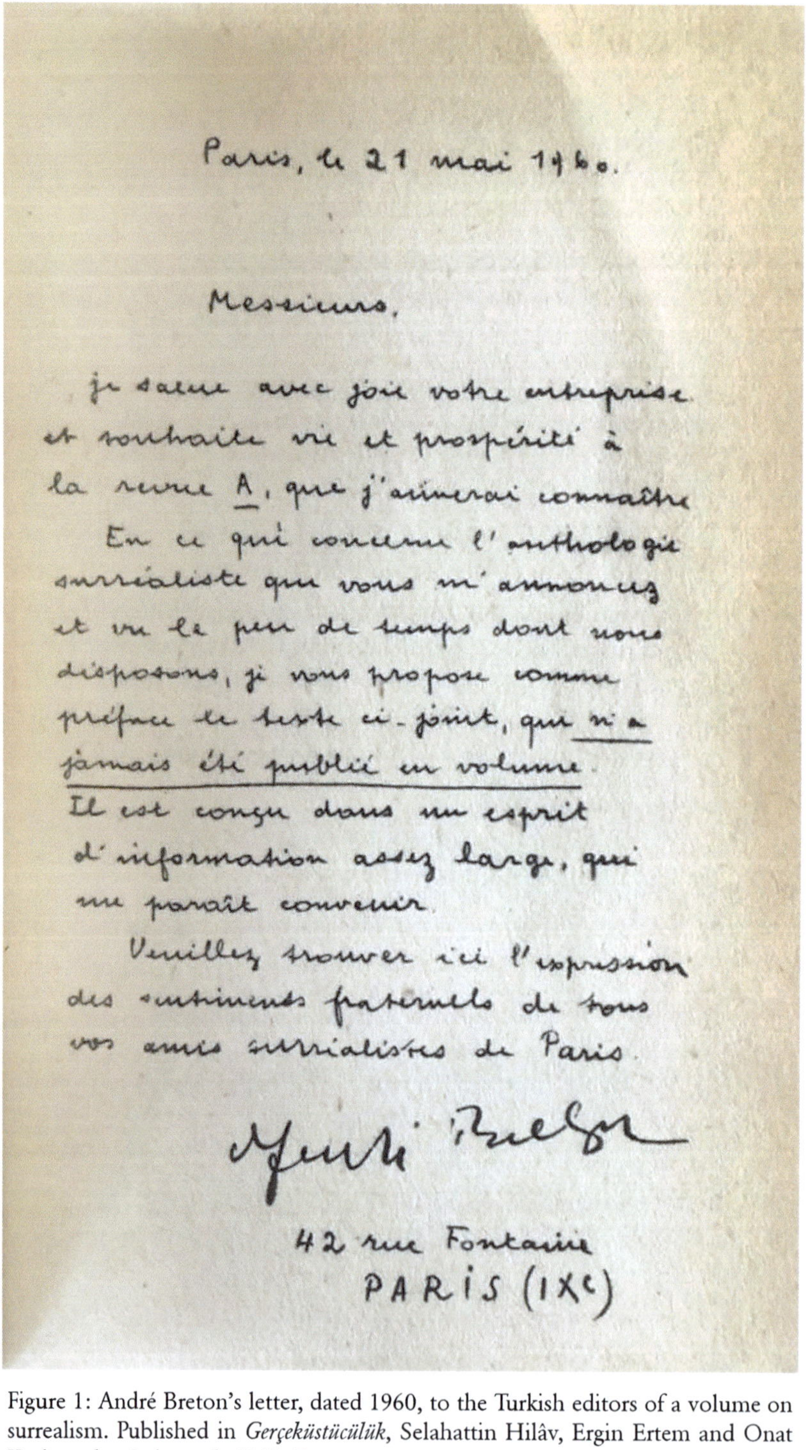

Paris, le 21 mai 1960.

Messieurs,

je salue avec joie votre entreprise et souhaite vie et prospérité à la revue A, que j'aimerai connaître.

En ce qui concerne l'anthologie surréaliste que vous m'annoncez et vu le peu de temps dont nous disposons, je vous propose comme préface le texte ci-joint, qui n'a jamais été publié en volume. Il est conçu dans un esprit d'information assez large, qui me paraît convenir.

Veuillez trouver ici l'expression des sentiments fraternels de tous vos amis surréalistes de Paris.

André Breton

42 rue Fontaine
PARIS (IXe)

Figure 1: André Breton's letter, dated 1960, to the Turkish editors of a volume on surrealism. Published in *Gerçeküstücülük*, Selahattin Hilâv, Ergin Ertem and Onat Kutlar, eds., Ankara: de 1962, 7.

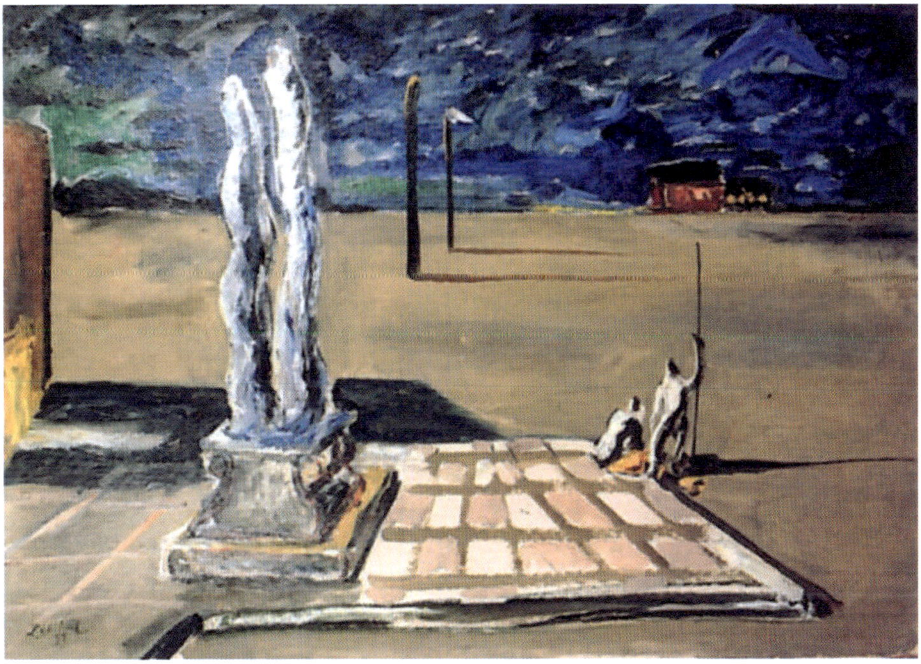

Figure 2: Zeki Faik İzer, *Composition*, 1959. Istanbul, private collection, courtesy of Ayşegül İzer.

painting titled *Masal* (Fable), with which he won the Great Prize in the State Exhibition of Painting and Sculpture in Turkey in 1955. In 1958, he represented Turkey, with his painting *Music*, in an international exhibition in Brussels to commemorate *50 Years of Modern Art*, where de Chirico was also included among many others, such as Jean Arp, Dalí, René Magritte, Miró and Yves Tanguy. He then indulged in an exercise imitating de Chirico as if he was trying to fill a persistent disturbing void in the Turkish art history of the interwar period. He painted the piece shown in figure 2 in 1959.[21] Not only with this painting of his impressions of Venice, but also with the few other works belonging to this transitional period in his career, İzer momentarily saluted the surrealism of a bygone age, before passing on to the abstract art for which he is best known.[22]

21 This is also the year of Yüksel Arslan's exhibition of his shocking Phallisme series in Istanbul. Arslan noted: "André Breton, the Pope of Surrealists, and an art dealer (Raymond Cordier) invite me to Paris." Yüksel Arslan, "Anılar", in: *Yüksel Arslan (Bir Dönem: 1951–61)*, Mazhar Şevket İpşiroğlu, Selahattin Hilâv, Orhan Duru and Ferit Edgü, eds., Istanbul: Ada 1977, 32. For more about Arslan's art, see Ambra D'Antone's chapter in this volume.

22 This paragraph is based on information in İrepoğlu, *Zeki Faik İzer*, 97–100. İzer was only one of several Turkish artists who expressed an affinity with surrealism in the 1950s. Tiraje Dikmen (1915-2014) who arrived in France in 1949 was introduced to a welcoming cohort of surrealists by Léopold-Lévy and spent her summers after 1955 in the South with Max Ernst, Jacques Hérold, Georges Hugnet, Georges Malkine, Patrick Waldberg and Yves Bonnefoy. Her works

The heavy "traffic" of Istanbul at a cultural crossroads

Istanbul bridges East and West, as has been so often repeated as to render it meaningless. A shrinking and ultimately dismembered Ottoman Empire, together with the transition to the Republic of Turkey in 1923 with Ankara serving as the capital, implied a different role for the city as a cultural capital, for which it had nevertheless long been prepared. The transition from the multicultural empire to the nation-state republic led to a significant number of cosmopolitan and "ethnic" residents, such as the Greeks and Armenians, having to migrating elsewhere – in general, nineteenth-century Istanbul was far more cosmopolitan and open to foreign influences than twentieth-century Istanbul. On the other hand, the earlier elite denizens of the city had been fewer and less equipped to benefit from foreign exposure than their equivalents in the twentieth century. It is no coincidence that many of those who went on to have a diasporic experience benefitted not only from their particular background, but also from the suitable climate that they found at the end of their migratory adventure.

Gisèle Prassinos (1920–2015) is a telling example. She was born in Istanbul and emigrated in 1922 with her family to settle in France when she was two. She was discovered by Breton in 1931 when she was fourteen, as a literary talent, in fact, as the "new Alice".[23] Her first book, *La Sauterelle arthritique* (The Arthritic Grasshopper[24]) came out the next year with a preface by Paul Éluard and photography by Man Ray of the surrealist cohort. She was thus embraced by the surrealists who saw in her work a veritable illustration of automatic language and writing as constitutive of poetry in the way they advocated. Her "Levantine Oriental" background, thanks to her early assimilation into French language and culture, manifested in neither her work nor manners, and was not noted. None of this would have been possible if she had been brought up and remained in Istanbul. Given the favourable environment in France, however, her family's Constantinopolitan background provided her with a most useful toolbox.

After the Second World War, Gisèle Prassinos moved away from poetry; she produced prints and embroidered patchwork that were reproduced in book form as *La Bible surréaliste de Gisèle Prassinos*.[25] Her work owed much to Greek Orthodox religious motifs and the legends of the inhabitants of Istanbul, as well as to the culture of iconography and folkloric illustration that had penetrated into her unconscious from early childhood. These undercurrents, once repressed and hence overlooked by surrealists, gradually resurfaced in her later work. No less important is the fact that the surrealist attributes of her painterly work were inextricably

---

representative of her first phase loaded with imagery reflect this surrealist effect that was nevertheless also a passing phase in her career. See Sönmez, *Paris Tecrübeleri*, 93-94.

23 Maurice Nadeau, *Histoire du surréalisme*, Paris: Seuil 1964, 163.

24 Gisèle Prassinos, *The Arthritic Grasshopper*, Adelaide: Wakefield Press 2017.

25 Anne Richard, *La Bible surréaliste de Gisèle Prassinos*, Wavre: Éditions Mols 2016.

linked with the ethnographic and the folkloric, the evidence for which we can still see in the reconstructed office of Breton at the Centre Pompidou (fig. 5).

What the Prassinos family left behind as a lingering backdrop included a Turkey that had been home to a strong French cultural influence. The Ottoman state, committed to modernization, had sent students to Paris to build up its future cadres. Ottoman intelligentsia looked to Paris for inspiration in general, and as one Turkish writer put it, Paris belonged more to the Young Turks who escaped from Hamidian despotism (1876–1908) than to the French during the belle époque.[26] The formation in 1923 of the republic under even more ambitiously modernist Mustafa Kemal Atatürk rekindled the role of cultural connections. In a world where everything changed fast, the fascination of Istanbul's elite with French culture survived the test of time.[27]

The advent of Ottoman and Turkish painting was part and parcel of this bigger picture. It had hesitant beginnings during the last decades of the Ottoman Empire. There had been a prolonged educative phase of imitation and improvisation with impressionism as exemplified by Şeker Ahmet Pasha who was an important precursor educated in Paris and who bore the influence of the Barbizon School (1830–1870).[28] Academic Orientalism – as championed by the founder of the Archaeological Museum in Istanbul, Osman Hamdi Bey (1842–1910), a student of Jean-Léon Gérôme (1824–1904) – was no less important.[29] Orientalism was so pervasive and taken for granted by leading Ottoman-Turkish intellectuals that its sudden disappearance after the transition to a republic, long before its wholesale criticism by Edward Said,[30] begs for an explanation. In part, this must be connected to the establishment of an association between the Ottoman Empire and Orientalism, and then the severing of this connection with the sudden drastic scaling down to a heartland republic. The modernist avalanche that came associated with the new regime and its cultural policy, embraced by a new generation of artists, was another determinant in the loss of interest in Orientalism at home. Finally,

---

26 Salâh Birsel, *İstanbul-Paris*, Istanbul: Türkiye İş Bankası Kültür Yayınları 1983, 45.

27 So much so, that until the 1980s, one could still observe the overwhelming attraction Paris held over the hearts and minds of the crème de la crème of the literary and artistic vanguard. Poles – as well as a generation – apart in Turkish literature, Attila İlhan and Enis Batur attest to this truth by placing great value on their experiences in Paris. They have deliberately nourished their literary work as well as their cultural biographies by exploiting the benefits of their affiliation with and visits to Paris. See Attila İlhan, *Hangi Batı? (Anılar ve Acılar)*, Ankara: Bilgi Yayınevi 1972; and Enis Batur, *PARIS, Ecekent*, Istanbul: Remzi Kitabevi 2012. Batur "read" and reread Paris in relation also with the surrealist literature on the city; see Batur, *PARIS, Ecekent*, 11 and 181.

28 Şeker Ahmet Pasha's painting *The Forest* intrigued John Berger by its conscious defiance of the principle of conventional perspective by introducing a "reverse perspective" instead. Durmuş Akbulut, *Türk Resminin Öncüleri*, Istanbul: Deffter 2009, 96 and 107–110.

29 Orientalism was not only acquired in Europe by Ottoman painters but also brought by resident or visiting foreign painters such as Fausto Zonaro. See *The Centennial Tale of Turkish Painting*, exhibition catalogue, Istanbul: Rezan Has Müzesi 2007, 36–45.

30 Edward W. Said, *Orientalism*, New York: Pantheon Books 1978.

Turkey's new modernist image abroad displaced the international market for Orientalist painting in favour of other geographies.

Be that as it may, the original dualism persisted in Turkish painting in various guises and under different rubrics. On the one side, there were the romantic roots of Turkish painting originally intertwined with, but increasingly liberated from, Orientalism. This current connected to the so-called generation of 1914, and found its most articulate expression in the works of Avni Lifij (1886–1927), a painter with a deep interest in art criticism at a time when this field did not yet exist in Turkey. On the other side, realist–cubist–constructivist roots evolved and took their mature form. This latter genealogy is best represented in the works of the "academic" and meticulous Sabri Berkel (1907–1993). This second current gained strength and consolidated itself as the dominant trend well into the 1950s, when a further proliferation occurred.[31]

Among the people who introduced modern painting into the Ottoman Empire were elites such as military officers including pashas, instructors like Hoca Ali Rıza (1858–1930), and Abdülmecid Efendi (1868–1944),[32] the patron of the Society of Ottoman Painters (1908). This latter was a descendent of the dynasty and the last caliph, and also a recognized writer and poet of his time; of all people, he was perhaps the least likely to defy the supposed Islamic prohibition on figurative human painting. Despite his daring endorsement, modern painting was quite naïve at that point, and, worse still, it was also cut off from traditional Ottoman painting.[33] Last but not least, it remained trapped within a claustrophobically narrow circle of artists and consumers. There was as yet no debate between traditionalists and modernists or between the followers of the two rival modern approaches. They lived in separate worlds, and neither party had specialized critics-as-advocates either – all that was to make its debut from the 1930s.

From 1924 on, the republic adopted and pursued even more vehemently the Ottoman policy of sending students abroad – some 120 students per year on average for the period 1928–1945 – to replenish its civil service and educational staff.[34] The first students to study art were sent in 1925 and returned in 1928. Among this first group were painters like Mahmut Cuda (1904–1987, who went to the atelier of Lucien Simon in the École des Beaux-Arts in Paris),[35] Refik Epikman

---

31 Eroğlu, *Türkiye'de Resim Sanatı*, 91–112.

32 Eylem Yağbasan, "Ressam Halife Abdülmecid Efendi (1868–1944)", in: *Hanedandan Bir Ressam: Abdülmecid Efendi*, Ömer Faruk Şerifoğlu, ed., Istanbul: YKY 2004, 16.

33 Traditional Ottoman painting was a largely self-contained entity; see Serpil Bağcı, Filiz Çağman, Günsel Renda and Zeren Tanındı, *Osmanlı Resim Sanatı*, Ankara: T.C. Kültür ve Turizm Bakanlığı Yayınları 2006. Hence, it had little potential for a revolutionary transformation from within into modern painting.

34 Kansu Şarman, *Türk Promethe'ler: Cumhuriyet'in Öğrencileri Avrupa'da (1925–1945)*, Istanbul: T. İş Bankası Kültür Yayınları 2015, xv.

35 In the same academy was Nurullah Berk, who was not on a scholarship. They became good friends and followed artistic activities in Paris. Upon their return, they pursued very different

(1902–1974), at the Atelier Paul Albert Laurens in the Académie Julian in Paris), Şeref Akdik and Cevat Dereli, as well as Hale Asaf and İsmail Hakkı Oygar, her first husband.[36]

These painters, along with a smaller number of others who went abroad on their own, helped transfer the approaches they observed in Paris to their homeland. A few took up residence in France, such as Fikret Muallâ (1903–1967) and Abidin Dino (1913–1993) and the unfortunate Hale Asaf, the female phantom of Turkish painting[37], of whom more will be said later. Those artists gained importance insofar as they became a part of the art scene in France and served as a bridge between Paris and Istanbul, especially after the Second World War. With respect to those who returned, it has been noted that 1925 was a major turning point: before that date, the transfer of approaches and techniques was much less frequent and therefore more observable and appreciated in itself, whereas afterwards, the role of intermediaries commanded respect only when it became part of a broader sophistication and formatting of artworks that deserved recognition in Istanbul's art scene in its own right.[38]

The artists mentioned above formed the crème de la crème of twentieth-century Turkish painters. Having studied in Paris thus became a distinction and a desirable qualification, it was a ticket to success; to be successful on the national scene without having studied abroad was extremely rare. It is beyond doubt that during their sojourn in Europe, these Turkish painters must have become acquainted with surrealism early on. Unfortunately, no direct evidence of this exists. However, very different artists have written in their letters or recounted years later how they visited without discrimination virtually all the exhibitions that were on in Paris, and given the time period, this could not be true unless they visited surrealist exhibitions. If we cannot find evidence for this in their letters, this is presumably because they wrote mostly to their families and relatives, who had hardly anything to do with art directly, and would not understand what it would mean to be a surrealist as distinct from a late cubist – in short, they did not report on the influential atelier of Lhote or cubism either. This is, at least, the situation for the many students in the arts, rather than the few in literature: even those painters who went to mainstream fine art academies have time and again recounted how they visited all kinds of exhibitions and galleries, including "fringe" events, during their stay in, as well as their periodic visits to, Paris.[39]

Given this overall assessment, the paradoxical resilience of Turkish painting to surrealist influence may well have to do with the fact that, after their historic

---

individual paths artistically, yet they collaborated to improve artists' rights by setting up a professional organization. Şarman, *Türk Promethe'ler,* 103.

36 Şarman, *Türk Promethe'ler,* 20, 24–25, 29, 37 and 102.

37 Bedri Rahmi Eyüboğlu, *Dost Dost,* Istanbul: İş Bankası Kültür Yayınları 2004,

38 Eroğlu, *Türkiye'de Resim Sanatı,* 112.

39 Eyüboğlu, *Dost Dost,* 136; and Şarman, *Türk Promethe'ler,* 178 and 332.

encounters with the art scene in Paris, Turkish painters were excited to take part in a wholesale nationalist modernization project that privileged the social and political deployment of art as an enlightening weapon *pace* the role constructivism played in revolutionary Soviet Russia.[40] No matter what they did abroad, once painters returned home, they were attracted to the glorification of work and machinery in a virgin landscape. They could combine this with their preference for strictly plastic concerns (of a cubist or constructivist kind) rather than storytelling of an agrarian revolution they witnessed in a straightforward realistic style. This overwhelming predominance of this artistic choice on the part of returning artists implied that subaltern metaphysical yearnings prone to cultivate surrealist art was left in the penumbra for several decades to come. It should also be noted that there was as yet no market for artwork in Turkey, as this only emerged in the late 1950s and especially in the 1960s. These people became painters because of the status and prestige associated with the profession: in order to make their living, they taught at the Academy of Fine Arts – and occasionally at public schools – as state employees, although it is important to note that while these European-educated artists depended on the state for their employment, their endorsement of official cultural policy in this period of revolutionary transformation was genuine. What was available as an alternative to the art market was the opportunity to exhibit in state-organized annual exhibitions, which brought them hardly any money (except when prizes were involved), but was immensely valued as it fostered public recognition. The prospects for surrealist artwork would be improved once a private art market ultimately emerged.

He who wrote about surrealism yet did not paint it: Nurullah Berk

Nurullah Berk went to Paris on his own means. He studied for four years with Ernest Laurent until 1928; he would later resent the rigid academism of his teacher. He then worked with Lhote, whom he found confusing, in 1932. Finally, he shifted to Atelier Léger, where he was more satisfied with the peaceful and more organized environment. Berk published a book, *Modern San'at* (Modern Art, 1932).[41] This was a modest book of slightly less than a hundred pages, including twenty-seven reproductions and illustrations, all in black and white, published within the technical and financial limitations of a printing house that stepped in as a second best under circumstances where publishing houses proper did not yet exist in Istanbul. It was intended to fill a vacuum and was welcomed by critics as

40 A recent study brings to light the presence of a Soviet-inspired constructivist undercurrent in modern Turkish art, which is otherwise more associated with cubism in general, as of the 1930s; see Güner, *Modern Türk Sanatının Doğuşu*, 202. In the Turkish context, cubism was reinterpreted broadly as a revolutionary movement in the arts at large.

41 Muhteşem Giray, *Müstakil Ressamlar ve Heykeltraşlar Birliği*, Istanbul: Akbank 1997, 196–201.

well as experts. Berk's style of description was at least as concise as the book itself. He handled important questions in a straightforward language more typical of the precision of scientists: it was obvious that he knew a great deal about his topic, but he put it in sparing language. Berk taught at the Academy of Fine Arts in Istanbul and took part in important Turkish art organizations and movements that assumed an avant-garde function, such as the d Group, founded as a response to the belief that Turkish art was falling desperately behind that of Europe. Berk was deservedly characterized in 1937 as the theorist of the d Group by the insider art critic Fikret Adil,[42] who frequented such circles and wrote about them. Throughout his important artistic career, Berk also continued to write as well as lecture extensively about art history, aesthetics and criticism.[43]

Berk is most closely associated with cubism in general, and in particular with Fernand Léger's cohort of Turkish students that included Berk's colleague Sabri Berkel. Even so, Berk's cubism has in retrospect been rightly qualified as a "constructivist cubism".[44] Berk's book covered impressionism, neo-impressionism, cubism, purism, futurism and surrealism, in that order. He conceived art history as a succession of movements with their distinct problems and styles. At first sight, one may be tempted to see progress in this succession. However, Berk was more interested in art movements as particular ways of "problem-solving". Hence, he was much less interested in progress per se. By implication, different movements meant solving different problems, and would-be artists were left free to choose in accordance with what appealed to them the most. The book has a very brief bibliography at the end that includes André Lhote on cubism and André Breton with his "Surrealist Manifesto" of 1924. As such, the book summarizes what he had encountered in Paris and thereby seeks to introduce the Turkish audience to these developments.

However, the motive behind this brief book was more ambitious, given that he was a professor as well as being active in organizing artists' societies and movements. Berk intended to give a sound direction to the new generation of Turkish artists. The book was expected to serve as a statement of purpose and a guidebook, if not an outright manifesto. At a time when there were hardly any specialized art critics, let alone the functioning of art criticism as an institution, this book was intended to raise the standards of artistic judgement. The book offered a description of techniques and aesthetic preferences along with an art history of successive movements. It did not express a preference in favour of, or a bias against, any one movement. The author did not advocate his own preferences. He stood for raising awareness and standards among artists as well as their future clients.

It is no coincidence that surrealism comes at the very end of the list of subjects of this concise book. It seems that the main reason for this was not chronological.

42 Güner, *Modern Türk Sanatının Doğuşu*, 209–211.
43 Giray, *Müstakil Ressamlar ve Heykeltraşlar Birliği*, 157.
44 Giray, *Müstakil Ressamlar ve Heykeltraşlar Birliği*, 202.

It was probably the least known of the movements among Turkish readers, and moreover it was perhaps the circumstantially least relevant when the country was on a path of modernization via economic development in the wake of the Great Depression. Last but not least, it was different from the others in one important sense, as Berk put it while introducing the relevant chapter. Whereas cubism and impressionism,[45] otherwise widely disparate, were movements that were basically conceived within the domain of, and therefore restricted to, the "plastic" arts concerned with form and colour, surrealism, going even further than futurism, developed from a philosophical principle – as articulated by Breton in collaboration with his friend Philippe Soupault upon an original inspiration from Sigmund Freud – and was therefore applicable to a wide range of media extending from literature to plastic arts. What Berk wrote here was a faithful representation of the then state-of-the-art understanding, and demonstrated that he knew more than he wrote, although he did not go into details. Berk included one painting from de Chirico (*Metaphysical Interior (with Small Factory)*, 1917) and one from Yves Tanguy (*West Tower*, 1931). Berk quoted Maurice Raynal, the French art critic – an ardent advocate of cubism known for his opposition to surrealism – on surrealism and then went on to emphasize that surrealism represented things as they were, in other words, did not experiment with the decomposition and montage of objects depicted. Instead, it built its artistic stratagem on bringing into unusual contact disparate objects on stages where the artists fiddled with distance and perspective so as to render the visual experiences in unusual and dream-like ways to the viewer. To put it differently, surrealists composed their paintings with familiar objects in unfamiliar settings with which they did not necessarily correspond in our usual experiences. There was thus the old (representation of the object) and the new (metaphysical setting with time and space distinctions blurred) in a novel presentation. This was hailed by Berk as a forceful style of expression bound to affect the viewer deeply. The fact that Berk parted ways with Raynal in approaching surrealism attests to the fact that Berk was not at all hostile to surrealism per se. Moreover, he wished to give his readers a fair representation rather than a critique of surrealism.

In the final chapter of his book, entitled "Yesterday, Today and Tomorrow", Berk noted that most schools of art had had their say and that even artists like Picasso, Matisse, Derain and Léger could no longer create something entirely different from the works to which they owed their reputations.[46] The novelties they had introduced had already made their effect on modern art. He separated surrealism

---

45 It is interesting that one of the best books with a sympathetic assessment of French impressionism – which came out rather late, long after it was discredited in Turkey as out of vogue – was by Salâh Birsel, a poet and essayist with certain surrealistic credentials. See Salâh Birsel, *Fransız Resminde İzlenimcilik*, Ankara: Dost Yayınları 1967, 16–17.

46 In fact, both Picasso and Matisse changed their painting significantly over time, surprising their followers again and again. Berk would have responded that they nevertheless remained loyal to their basic artistic and aesthetic preferences by indulging themselves in repetition with a difference.

from other art movements as belonging to what was at the time the more recent past and the present. According to him, it was yet to have its final say and secure itself the place it deserved in art history. Even so, according to Berk, the plastic arts in Europe were at a major crossroads where schools and movements had lost their meaning and formative power. As such, European art was left devoid of a discernible character.[47] Rethinking this final statement, we might well infer that surrealism was, in his view, likely to be normalized into becoming a chapter in art history much as this was against its original intent. In any case, if the boat of European art was lost on the open sea with a certain probability of sinking like the *Titanic*, the further prospects of a surrealist art could hardly matter.

Bedri Rahmi Eyüboğlu's indirect and oblique convergence with surrealism

Bedri Rahmi Eyüboğlu is quite different from Nurullah Berk in that he wrote much, but also painted a great deal. Whereas Berk was highly self-contained and developed his painting within the rigid artistic and aesthetic parameters he professed, Eyüboğlu was a passionate artist who relentlessly experimented with form and content. He had an enormous capacity to remain wide open to being influenced by, as well as inspired from, all kinds of stimuli, be they from different art movements or life experiences. If any of the Turkish painters from the 1930s Parisian cohort were to indulge in experimentation with something resembling surrealism, it would most likely be Eyüboğlu.

He was already a student at the Academy of Fine Arts in Istanbul when he went to Paris, the "Mecca of Art",[48] in 1930 to join his brother Sabahattin, who was already in France on a government scholarship to study literature. After visiting museums and exhibitions with his brother, Bedri Rahmi settled to study painting in the atelier of André Lhote, where he also met Ernestine, his Romanian-born future wife, later to be known as Eren Eyüboğlu.[49] He became directly acquainted with the major trends in modern art. We know that among the many exhibitions he visited with his friends was a Pierre Bonnard exhibition in Paris in 1932, of which he wrote some twelve years later.[50] Unfortunately, though he mentions that he did not miss a single opportunity to visit an exhibition, he does not usually give specific names, despite his vast correspondence with friends and relatives. This is probably because those to whom he would have written about such details were already with him in Paris, and to others back in Turkey it would have made no sense. In his 1932 correspondence from Lyon with his future wife Eren in Paris,

47 Nurullah Berk, *Modern San'at*, Istanbul: Semih Lütfi Bitik ve Basım Evi 1935, 101–102.

48 Eyüboğlu, *Dost Dost*, 94.

49 Hıfzı Topuz, "Bedri Rahmi in Paris", in: *"Sevmek Güzel Meslek Reis": B. Rahmi*, exhibition catalogue, İzmir: Folkart Gallery Publishing 2017, 29.

50 Eyüboğlu, *Dost Dost*, 225.

we do catch a glimpse of the art scene and their interest in visiting galleries, precisely because this was something they shared in addition to their then developing love.[51] As he continued his studies, he painted scenes of Paris, such as the Jardin du Luxembourg (1931) and Montparnasse (1932) – this latter was a favourite hangout of artists, including some surrealists who had "betrayed" Montmartre, which they had frequented almost as a holy site in the earlier phase of the avant-garde movement. Unfortunately, we do not know if Eyüboğlu met any of the surrealist celebrities. He had one foot in the bohemian circles, mixing with the common folk, and the other in academia with the intellectuals. His affinity to ordinary people was later reflected in his painterly preferences that turned him to folk art for inspiration.

As mentioned, throughout his career Eyüboğlu was quite open-minded when it came to influences and experimentation, and this is manifest even in his earlier paintings. His *Nude with Eiffel Tower* from 1935 (fig. 3) is suggestive of this playful ambiguity and openness to the viewer's interpretation. It is an interior scene, yet there is a painting of the Eiffel Tower in the background that emulates a window scene. Equally, though, there is an eye above the nude's shoulder, suggesting that this interior may well not be real. This Magritte-like interplay with alternating planes combined with what would appear to be an evil (male) eye along with obscure shadows, all with Freudian connotations, may lead the viewer into the world of surrealists.

In the academic year of 1936–1937, some time after he returned to Istanbul, Eyüboğlu joined the Academy of Fine Arts to work with Léopold-Lévy, and took part in Turkish avant-garde movements. It was only after the Second World War was well over that he would have an opportunity to return to Paris, to meet his artist friends as well as to frequent museums and exhibitions – his first chance was in 1950.[52]

Eyüboğlu wrote about art just as he wrote poetry, in a way reminiscent of Apollinaire – the godfather of surrealists, who also indulged in both though to different degrees. And like Apollinaire, Eyüboğlu experimented with visual poetry in the spirit of the avant-garde movement.[53] He did not care where poetry ended and art started. His correspondence as well as his sketchbooks from various trips are full of examples of such coexistence.

51 Huguette Eyüboğlu, *Biz Mektup Yazardık! Bedri Rahmi Eyüboğlu ve Çağdaşlarından Mektuplar*, Istanbul: Türkiye İş Bankası Kültür Yayınları 2015, 25–26.

52 Topuz, "Bedri Rahmi in Paris", 30–34.

53 For an example of Eyüboğlu's combination of poetry, calligraphy and design as part of a letter he addressed to Abidin Dino in the 1930s, see Hughette Eyüboğlu, ed., *Bedri Rahmi Eyüboğlu ve Çağdaşlarından Mektuplar: Biz Mektup Yazardık!*, Istanbul: Türkiye İş Bankası Kültür Yayınları 2015, 118. See also Guillaume Apollinaire, *Calligrammes*, Paris: Gallimard 1925. See Stephen C. Foster, ed., "The Avant-Garde and the Text", special issue, *Visible Language* 21, nos. 3–4 (1987).

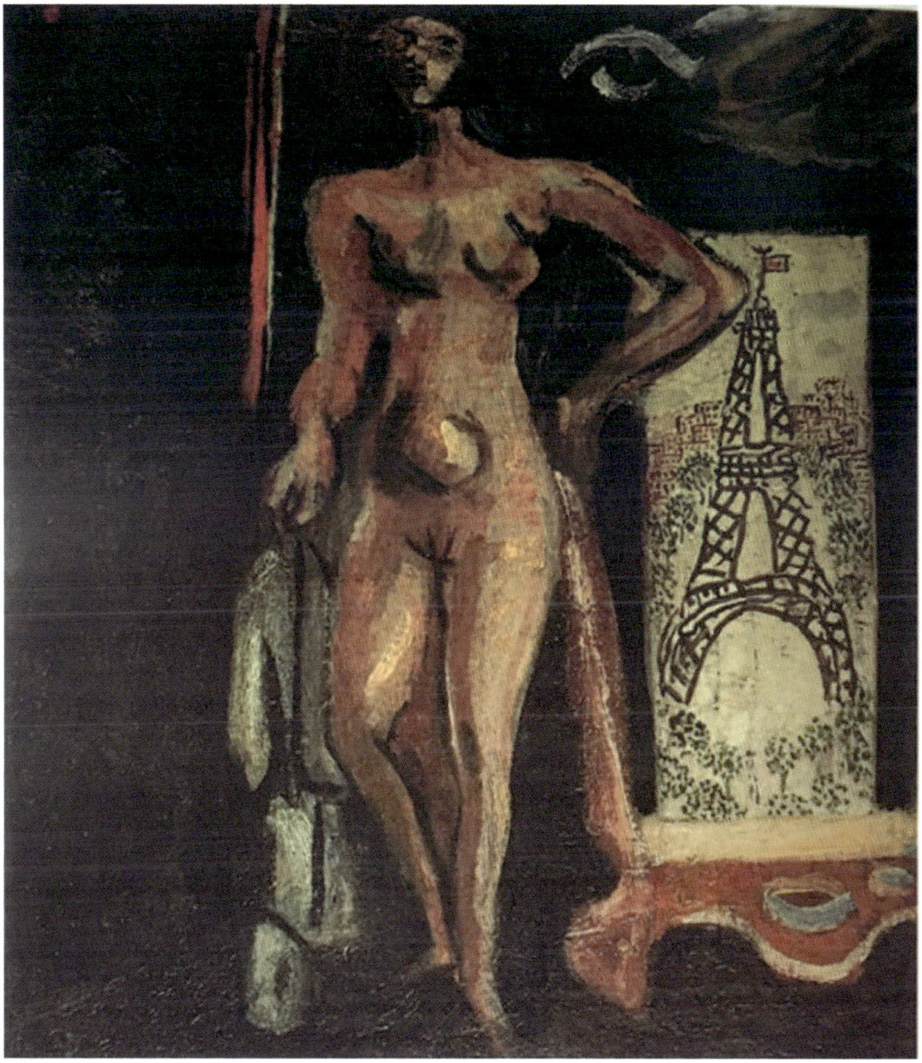

Figure 3: Bedri Rahmi Eyüboğlu, *Nude with Eiffel Tower*, 1935. Istanbul, private collection, courtesy of Rahmi Eyüboğlu.

Eyüboğlu once noted that in Anatolia he was better recognized as an art critic and poet than as a painter because paintings were not yet in wide circulation via reproductions and exhibitions hardly took place outside of Istanbul and Ankara. Hence, it was only in Istanbul and to a lesser degree in Ankara that people were familiar with his artwork through periodic exhibitions.[54] His art criticism was received positively; otherwise, he would not have found space in the Turkish press, which cared

[54] Topuz, "Bedri Rahmi in Paris", 35.

less about quality and more about how much one was followed.[55] In its eleventh exhibition of painting and sculpture in Istanbul in 1944, the d Group, in which he took part with Berk, introduced the work of Pierre Bonnard, an artist who had inspired many, to a Turkish audience;[56] and in a piece published in that same year, he considered why the d Group – many of the members of which had studied in the atelier of Lhote in Paris – nevertheless chose to give precedence to Bonnard, who had perhaps taught no one directly in his lifetime, yet who could make an ordinary ashtray the subject of his painting in a way André Derain had never done.[57] The same year, he wrote another article introducing members of the d Group to his readers, including Berk as well as his own wife Eren, and mocking himself as the unnamed fourteenth member of the group, who had a paintbrush in one hand and a fountain pen in the other because he wrote at night and painted during the day. In that same piece, he said: "If you ask the painters about him, they would say his painting was mediocre but he wrote good poetry, and if you approach the writers with the same question, they would respond that he was an average writer but a really good painter."[58]

Eyüboğlu became one of the best known and most productive painters of his generation. Years later, he regretted that no matter how much they took their original Parisian and post-war Western experience as a model for the exhibitions they organized, something remained missing. He noted that unlike the post-war large-scale exhibitions of the works of Max Ernst and Marc Chagall in Paris, London and New York, which set up a chain reaction among artists, their efforts did not have the much-needed snowball effect on Turkish art.[59]

A milestone in Eyüboğlu's career was his experience of being sent to the provinces by the government in order to paint. The Turkish government started a programme of "country excursions", sending painters to the countryside with a mission to paint every summer for a period of one to three months.[60] The primary motive of the ministry was to introduce studio-based artists from Istanbul, educated in Europe, to the rich folkloric traditions and the realities of country life in

---

55 As early as 1943, he was sufficiently versed in European painting as to notice, question and criticize that there were no cars crossing the very Parisian streets in Maurice Utrillo's urban scenes; and he looked to the earliest Turkish primitive painters and their relationship to Parisian art equally critically. Eyüboğlu, *Dost Dost*, 174 and 211–212.

56 Eyüboğlu, *Dost Dost*, 225.

57 Eyüboğlu, *Dost Dost*, 265–266.

58 Eyüboğlu, *Dost Dost*, 264.

59 Güner, *Modern Türk Sanatının Doğuşu*, 77. In retrospect, Eyüboğlu noted that his generation had mistakenly taken France as synonymous with modern art and had been blinded for about twenty-five years, with Turkish painting bearing a 90% influence from French painting, completely overlooking African art as well as Turkish traditional and folk art. Topuz, "Bedri Rahmi in Paris", 36. He had only become conscious of this once he travelled extensively in Europe as well as the United States, from the 1950s to the early 1970s, before his death in 1975.

60 Güner, *Modern Türk Sanatının Doğuşu*, 161.

Anatolia.[61] This large-scale programme was similar to the New Deal "public work" projects in photography and documentation in the USA[62] as well as to some projects to promote official "socialist realist" art in the USSR. Even Eyüboğlu, who had strong family roots in provincial culture and had made his earliest paintings on the Black Sea coast, benefitted greatly from his periodic excursions under this programme. In 1938 he went to Edirne in Thrace to paint with a group of painters, and in 1945 he recounted with great excitement his experience in İskilip, a little known but historical town in the inland Anatolian province of Çorum. By that point, it had been six years since artists had first been commissioned to paint on excursions, and a collection of some five hundred paintings had already been accumulated.[63]

Perhaps as a result, Eyüboğlu's painting and ceramic work, as well as his occasional sculptures, were enriched with colour and stylized folkloric content.[64] His work in figure 4, a folkloric fetish, obviously belongs to the same family of art objects that populated the atelier of Breton (fig. 5). Hence, it is possible to identify the subtle continuity from his Paris experiences to his explorations of Anatolian folklore.

Just like his peers, however, though he knew very well what surrealism was, Eyüboğlu did not pursue surrealist painting as a genre. His interests lay elsewhere, just as his inspiration originated from a variety of sources, among which Mediterranean themes and objects[65] occupied an important place. The connection of his work to surrealism is sometimes obscured, but will not escape the initiated viewer faced with the fetish in figure 4. Moreover, this is representative of a more general trend of oblique, if not outright hidden, and nuanced surrealist affiliations in Turkish painting. Nonetheless, the effect of surrealism was deeply and selectively pervasive, even in places where it was least expected. But then, this should come as no surprise if we remind ourselves that surrealism was best known, from its origins in its heartland, for its capacity to shock. Istanbul, secretly communicating with Paris, was no formidable exception in this respect.

Last but not least, Eyüboğlu was an artist who distilled art from his love for various women at different times, and continally illustrated his love letters. The

61 A somewhat less intended consequence was to familiarize provincials with contemporary art, or integrating "academic" art with the people; see Güner, *Modern Türk Sanatının Doğuşu*, 161.

62 See William Stott, *Documentary Expression in Thirties America*, Chicago: University of Chicago Press 1986.

63 Eyüboğlu, *Dost Dost*, 171, 267 and 299–305.

64 His broadly defined "cubist" style was engendered by local art in a fashion equal to what the Hungarian composer Béla Bartók – who was also a one-time collector of Anatolian folk music – and also Ahmed Adnan Saygun had achieved in music. Güner, *Modern Türk Sanatının Doğuşu*, 256.

65 Bedri Rahmi Eyüboğlu, *Mavi Yolculuk Defterleri*, Istanbul: Türkiye İş Bankası Kültür Yayınları 2008.

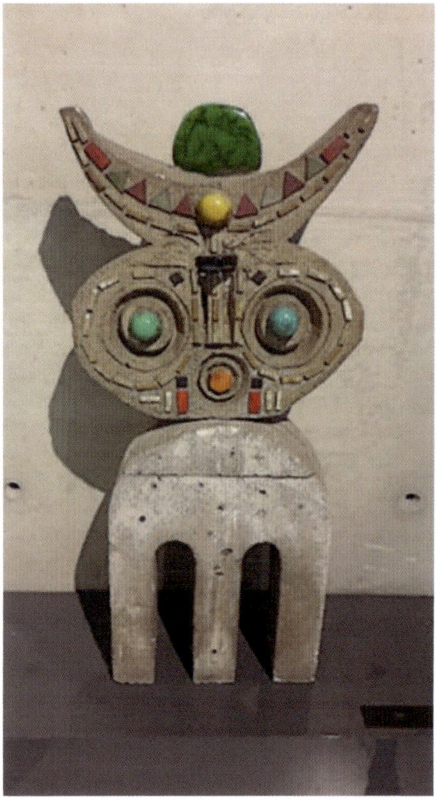

Figure 4: Unnamed and undated Anatolian folkloric fetish-like ceramic work by Bedri Rahmi Eyüboğlu. Istanbul, private collection, courtesy of Rahmi Eyüboğlu.

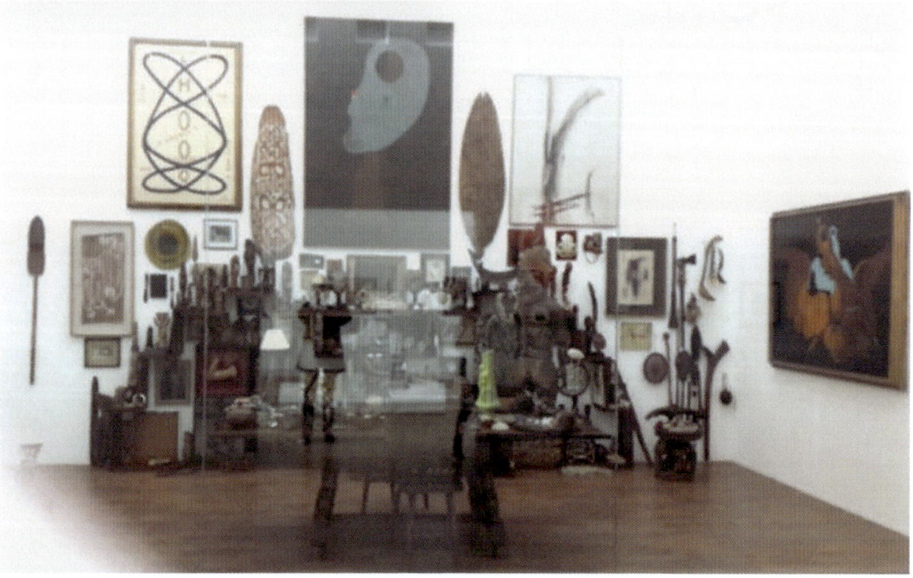

Figure 5: A reconstruction of André Breton's atelier, Centre Georges Pompidou. Photograph by Eyüp Özveren.

spontaneity, almost automatism, of his self-expression is astounding for any viewer. These numerous outbursts connect his conscious with his subconscious in a way much sought after by surrealists of the early twentieth century. Eyüboğlu thus combined painting, drawing and writing in his highly creative and self-expressive correspondence. As one art collector and critic noted, Eyüboğlu offers us a unique case among Turkish painters of an emotionally overcharged artist-as-lover who made art the medium of expression of his feelings.[66] The convergence of this art-as-life form with its once-surrealist forerunners in Paris is a pointer to the ambiguous connections lost to standard textbook art histories.

Bedri Rahmi Eyüboğlu once wrote in a short piece dated 1942 about two painters of his generation talking of a recent article about cubism as well as the persistent strength of the French cultural influence in Istanbul, while they walked slowly uphill from the Academy of Fine Arts to the historic cosmopolitan district of Pera, ironically at a time when Paris itself had fallen to the Nazis. They stopped with excitement as they saw posted on the wooden blinds of a dried nut and fruit store a shocking "surrealist composition gone wild by one of those American artists, cut out of an American magazine".[67] This was neither the first nor the last time Istanbul blinked its eyes and played a seemingly surreal trick on artists who had resisted the temptation to throw themselves wholeheartedly into the arms of the surrealist movement at its prime. This observation may also be interpreted as an early sign of what was yet to come after the Second World War, as the winds of change were already in the air, at least to the discerning eye of the privileged artist.

Conclusion as fragments of a partially recovered portrait: Hale Asaf

Istanbul, a city situated on a crossroads of civilizations, has had strong historical ties with Paris, the roots of which extend as far back as early modern history. Surrealism, which attracted international attention and spread rapidly during the interwar period, found Istanbul difficult to penetrate via local intellectuals and artists – and with Istanbul, all of Turkey surrounding it was an impregnable terrain. Surrealism remained conspicuously absent in Turkish painting before the Second World War, a fact all the more striking as many Turkish painters had been sent to Paris to study in the 1920s and 1930s. Looking at the few existing accounts, records and memoirs of Turkish painters who had been in Paris, we have seen that, far from shunning new art movements, they kept their eyes wide open, whatever they were actually taught in the various academies or ateliers where they were registered. Therefore, we can dismiss the hypothesis that they did not know of surrealism.

In this essay, we have concentrated most closely on two major painters who left behind much written evidence both of what they knew and of what they did after

66 Edgü, "Aşkın Resimleri", 151 and 157.
67 Eyüboğlu, *Dost Dost*, 152.

they returned to Istanbul's art scene from Paris. Focusing first on Nurullah Berk, we observed that he covered surrealism summarily yet without any bias in his brief but influential book about modern art movements. We concluded that he knew surrealism quite well and was cognizant of its importance, even if he chose to concentrate his own work strictly within the parameters of a late cubist aesthetics. We then shifted our attention to Bedri Rahmi Eyüboğlu, who also wrote a great deal about his own experience and aesthetic preferences, and was as familiar with surrealism as with other approaches. He was an energetic and creative artist who experimented widely and sought to express himself in his work, and synthesized his academic training with themes from folklore. In one of his works inspired by folk art, we observed an oblique convergence of his sources of influence with those of the surrealists. This was as close as this generation of plastic artists in Istanbul got to surrealism, and even then it was via folk art and in a naïve expression.[68] Ultimately, the cases of both Berk and Eyüboğlu confirm that the attention and energies of painters returning from Paris – despite knowing surrealism quite well – were attracted elsewhere by stronger forces at work.

In the 1930s, there was a concerted effort on the part of the Turkish government to engage artists with the people and their folklore, which involved introducing artists to the countryside, as well as introducing the "hidden treasures" of the country to the Istanbul-based artists. This was part and parcel of a nation-building project, an ambitious modernization-cum-industrialization programme that came in combination with a belated enlightenment project. This was truly attractive to those artists who returned from Paris, as it promised them a role in the vanguard, after they had personally observed the wide gap between Europe and Turkey, a gap that they believed needed to be narrowed quickly. There was a further "perfect fit" as well, since the toolbox of the late cubist constructivist art repertoire that they had acquired in their education abroad – particularly in the atelier of André Lhote – was highly advantageous for the glorification of work and machinery that symbolized development and progress. To put it differently, extra-artistic forces (congruent with the proclivities of their formal artistic training) encouraged the artists to take a step in this direction, and this cut them off further from potentially surrealist individualistic improvisations. The politics of the original interwar surrealism promised so much less to such people in comparison.

---

[68] It should be remembered that the boundaries of surrealism in its heyday covered a wide grey "no man's land". While Pablo Picasso is never listed among the surrealist artists per se, he nevertheless had a "surrealist period" (1925–1933), to which a room is dedicated at the Musée Picasso in Paris. Work of his that was appropriate was published in surrealist journals, and "Breton's own writings on Picasso are in a tone of complete adulation" (Simon Wilson, *Surrealist Painting*, Oxford: Phaidon 1982, 16). Breton admired him most because by changing the placement of objects and liberating them from their taken-for-granted meanings, Picasso bequeathed art a terrain beyond the conventional domain. See Duplessis, *Le Surréalisme.*

If we could come up with a Turkish painter, preferably one who studied with Lhote in Paris just like Berk and Eyüboğlu but who decided to settle in Paris rather than returning home, we would have at hand a way of testing our conclusions. If that person pursued a career leading to a gradual shift away from late cubism and in favour of surrealistic improvisation, we could then interpret her/his liberty to follow such a trajectory as further evidence of what made this option unavailable for her/his counterparts in Turkey: the prevailing contextual circumstances which we characterized as extra-artistic.

Of the three Turkish painters who went to Paris and stayed, Abidin Dino (1913–1993) had in fact already had previous experience outside Turkey, first in Geneva and Paris, where he spent his childhood with his family, and later in Moscow, where he worked with Sergei Yutkevich for Lenfilm Studios (1934–1937). Between those two experiences, he had been in Istanbul, taking part in 1933 in the formation of the d Group, which he characterized as the first avant-garde movement in Turkey. By the time he returned to Paris in 1937, where he stayed only another year, he had already shaped his aesthetic preferences, and in any case Dino was not associated with the Académie Lhote. He returned to Paris in 1951, and remained there until his death in 1993. Dino commanded respect in Turkey for his personal style that survived the test of time, and he served as a bridge between Turkish artists and the Parisian scene.

Equally unassociated with Lhote was Fikret Muallâ (1903/1904–1967). He had been in Berlin from 1920 to 1926, where his exposure to expressionism left a mark on his further formation.[69] He started his career as a prodigy with a psychologically vulnerable personality after he lost his mother at an early age from Spanish influenza (1918-20), for which he blamed himself for infecting her, and he was prone to schizophrenia, which he tried to deal with by drinking more and more alcohol; he suffered from periodic mental breakdowns throughout his career. He was impatient in general and lost his temper quickly. He had first been to Paris for a few months in 1929 and confirmed that Paris was the capital of world art.[70] He left Istanbul for Paris in 1938 and remained in France until his death in 1967, in a state of permanent self-exile because of his fear of persecution. He came to know many schools of painting before his peers[71] but also parted ways with belonging to any

[69] One art scholar notes that he discovered Dadaist art production and scandal-mongering in Berlin and was the first to introduce it among the Turkish artists. Because of his Dadaist behaviour, he deliberately sided with the few revolutionary leftists of the artistic and intellectual avant garde. See Sönmez, *Paris Tecrübeleri*, 50. He was not understood and his shocking behaviour was interpreted as evidence of his madness. Eyüboğlu was exceptionally aware of the Dadaistic character of Muallâ and associated him with Asaf Hâlet Çelebi, the poet. See Eyüboğlu, *Dost Dost*, 34.

[70] Hıfzı Topuz, *Paris'te bir Türk Ressam: Fikret Muallâ'nın Yaşamı*, Istanbul: Remzi Kitavbevi, 2014, 32-4.

[71] See Topuz, *Paris'te bir Türk Ressam*, 24-5, 35-6, 65, 105-6, and 118. For the illustrations, see Semiha Berksoy and Fikret Muallâ, *İki Aykırının Mektupları*, Istanbul, Kırmızı Kedi 2017, 34, 37 and 104.

because he believed he should pursue his own way. He knew German expressionism to which he was exposed early in his career when he was in Munich and Berlin in early 1920s where he also met and admired Hale Asaf. However he also referred to his works in Istanbul in the 1930s as essentially 'futurist'. Most interestingly for our purpose, he made some illustrations that remained unfortunately unpublished until 2005[72] that he characterized explicitly as 'surrealist' in the first half of the 1930s for a short story named *Mezardan Gelen Mektup* (Letter from a Grave) by Semiha Berksoy, presumably his lifelong Platonic love, a famous actress and the first Turkish opera artist, as well as a painter who went to to Paris in 1972 to exhibit her works after Fikret Muallâ had died (fig. 6). He also sketched some stage designs and costumes for her performances in 1935. These illustrations and sketches show a consistency in style and an affinity with the paintings of De Chrico who predated but influenced many surrealists.

Fikret Muallâ was truly talented and believed in his own genius. During the Parisian phase of his painting career he remained an autodidact and lived a bohemian lifestyle that he pursued against all odds. He also had to make his living from his painting. He had to accommodate himself accordingly. He rushed to finish many guash paintings of modest size to be able to sell them sometimes within the same day. He agreed to have occasional patrons who would support him. He also started to spell his last name as "Moualla", thereby making it more legible to Francophones. Picasso took his work seriously and bought one of his paintings. When they met, Picasso gave him an autographed painting of his own that he had to sell soon because he needed the money to survive.[73] Alberto Giacometti told other Turkish artists he met in Paris to paint like Fikret Muallâ. Fikret Muallâ provides partial support for our hypothesis insofar as he developed a distinct style that reminds one of a strongly expressionistic taste for human depiction expressed in typically French urban contexts and that uses colours which in combination stand out as substantially different on the Parisian art scene. His style burst out of the conventional expressionist confines to develop a penchant for poetic realism and occasionally a mythos-inspiring realism with forays into abstraction.[74] In 1952, he placed a distance between himself and all the "isms" and opted for a personal line. His mental crises created caesura in his artistic career, during which he fiddled with an automatic painting-cum-writing which reminds one of the original surrealist project. This was in part self-therapy to rid

---

72 The journal, *Yedigün Dergisi*, rejected the illustrations Fikret Muallâ named as *Ruhlar* (spirits) with the excuse that they had an exclusive contract with another painter, Ercüment Kalmık (1909-1971), and therefore had to work with him. Yet we infer that this might not be the whole story as they introduced the short story as representative of surrealism, a strongly controversial movement. Berksoy and Muallâ, *İki Aykırının Mektupları*, 15 and 36.

73 Orhan Koloğlu, 'Hayatı,' in Nurullah Berk and Orhan Koloğlu, *Fikret Muallâ: Hayatı, Sanatı, Eserleri*. Istanbul: Milliyet Yayınları, 1971, 33-4.

74 Abidin Dino, *Gören Göz İçin Fikret Muallâ*, Istanbul: Kırmızı Kedi 2017, 98–99.

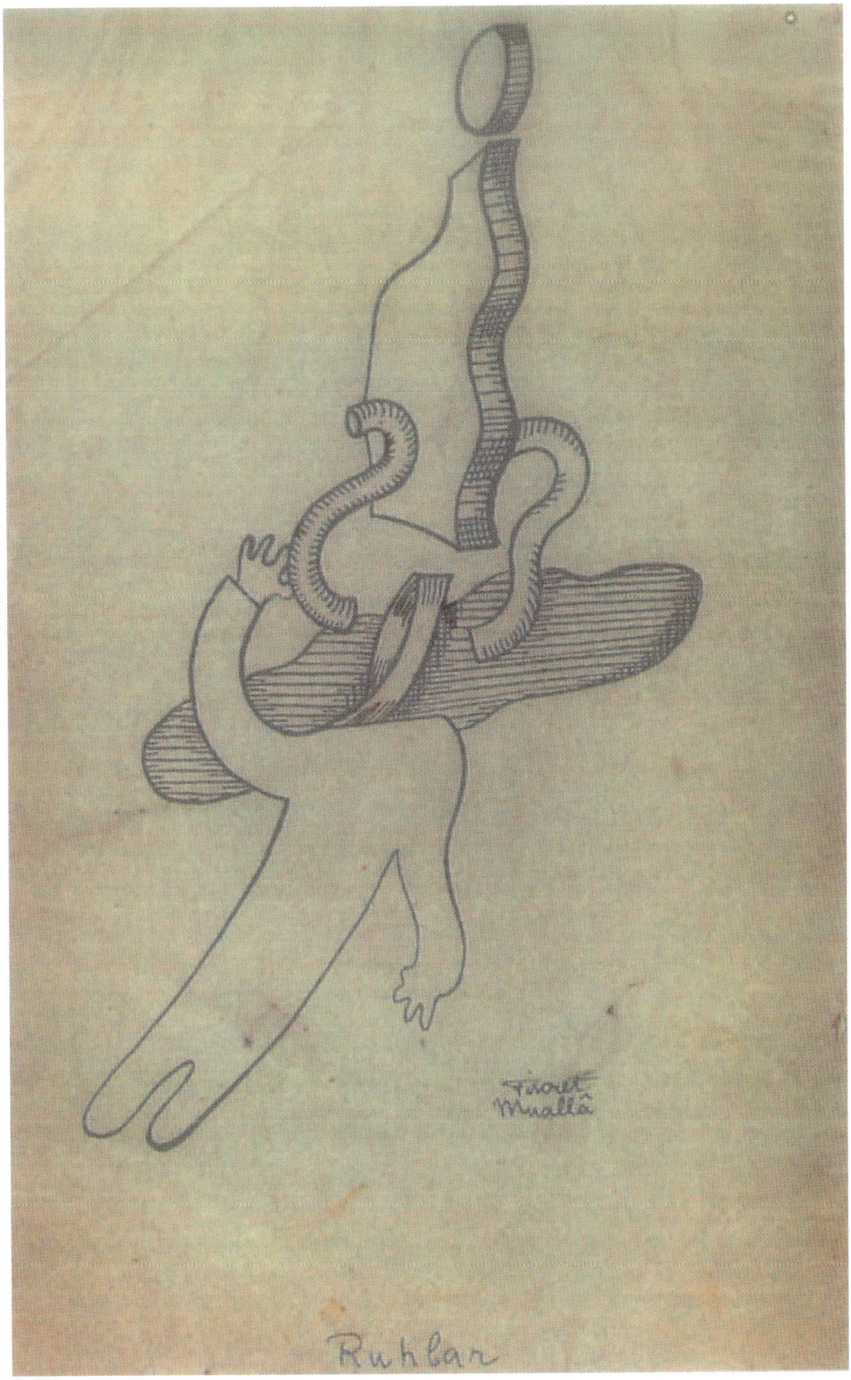

Figure 6: Fikret Muallâ, ink drawing, from the series *Ruhlar* (Ghosts), 1935. Istanbul, courtesy of the Semiha Berksoy Opera Foundation.

his mind of fears and imaginary conspiracy scenarios,[75] and is one exceptional moment where his art converged once again with surrealism, albeit in a different way. Fikret Muallâ's planar use of colours in his paintings evoking a sense of a touchable yet abstract surface was distinct, and also allowed him to undo the very sense of perspectival depth of field; attributes such as these separated him from the expressionists of the time. From being the exemplary painter of Istanbul, he developed into a painter of the Parisian scene. Abidin Dino was a good friend of Fikret Muallâ and wrote a book, first published in 1980, defending the specificity and originality of his art.[76]

Finally, there was Hale Asaf (1905–1938), to whom we referred earlier as the Turkish phantom of the Parisian art scene. Fikret Muallâ had first met Hale Asaf in Berlin in 1919, when he was seventeen. This we know through Abidin Dino, who also sang her praises for having had the courage to follow her own path in Paris. She had been a model for Fikret Muallâ.[77] She was the first of the Turkish artists to work with Lhote, with whom she maintained a connection, so much so, that he would leave his studio to her for a few summer months so that she could work.

Asaf is a plausible test-case for assessing the overall course and performance of Turkish painters of her cohort free from the direct influence of the situation in Turkey, by examining her relationship with surrealism. However, the picture is obviously complicated, as the "extra-artistic" variables in her case include her gender and the deadly illness from which she was soon to suffer. These factors alone could have sufficed to lead her work either in the direction of or away from surrealistic resonances. Thus we mean here a test-case not in any rigid scientific sense, but more as a metaphor.

In a world of men, Asaf was the only female Turkish painter, and in many ways actually led her generation of Turkish painters. Her work attracted much attention and praise in exhibitions in Turkey as well as in Paris. She had been determined

75 Fikret Muallâ, *"Çakallar"*, Istanbul: Ada 1977.

76 Dino, *Gören Göz İçin Fikret Muallâ*. This publication was probably intended as a reaction to Nurullah Berk. Berk wrote the specific part on the works of Fikret Muallâ entitled 'Eserleri' in Berk and Koloğlu, *Fikret Muallâ*, 57-87. He attempted to categorize and classify the art of Fikret Muallâ and thereby scale down the praise he had received among Turkish critics and art collectors shortly after his death. He related Fikret Muallâ to the group of 'Les Peintres Maudits' including Maurice Utrillo, Amedeo Modigliani, Chaim Soutine and Jules Pascin but also Henri de Toulouse-Lautrec. The connection is self-evident. This would have been taken naturally if only Berk himself had not been an 'academic' painter who inadvertently looked down on autodidacts and their intuition-ridden works produced with a few quick strokes which lacked patient contemplation and cold-blooded craftsmanship of the kind he professed. To his credit, Berk recognized the 'lyrical' dimension of Fikret Muallâ's expressionism in his analysis. See Berk and Koloğlu, *Fikret Muallâ*, 66. Fikret Muallâ was also well aware of his spiritual affinity with Modigliani, Utrillo, Jules Pascin as well as Wladimir Petroff, the White Russian émigré, to whom he referred collectively as "the Living Dead of Montmartre". Berksoy and Muallâ, *İki Aykırının Mektupları*, 21-25.

77 Dino, *Gören Göz İçin Fikret Muallâ*, 58 and 75.

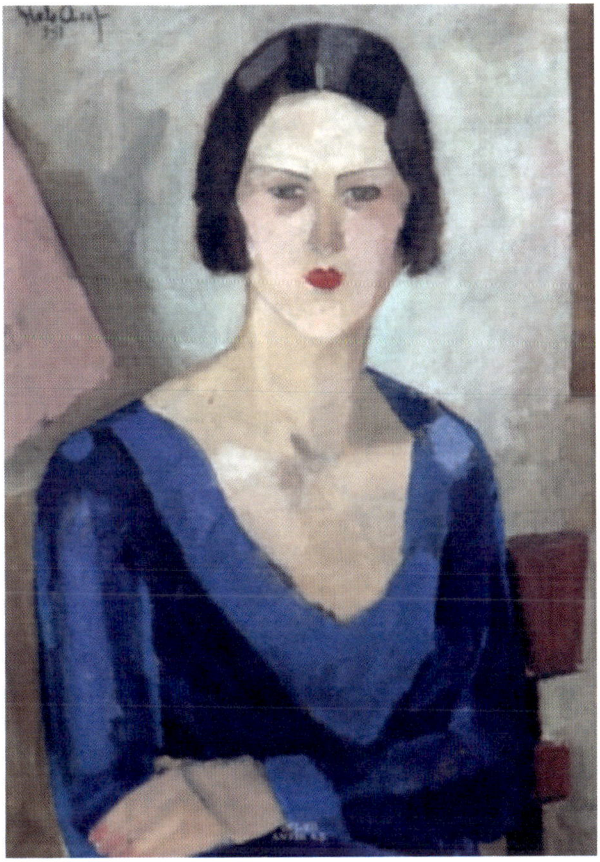

Figure 7: Hale Asaf, *The Woman in Blue*, 1931. Istanbul, private collection, courtesy of Ömer M. Koç.

to prove herself as a painter from her teenager years, and it is no surprise that she chose to settle in Paris in the end. Unlike others in the same group, she belonged to a good Ottoman family, her aunt was herself a recognized painter, and Asaf was quite international in her outlook and experiences. She studied painting in Italy, Germany and France, as well as in Turkey. However from childhood onwards, she suffered from poor health and ultimately died of cancer at a very young age, and in this respect, her determination to gain recognition as a painter was a battle against the odds, not least of which was her health. She stretched late cubist conventions to accommodate her distinct and feminine emotionalism. She came to know many artists on the Parisian scene of very different persuasions and expanded her artistic repertoire constantly in a dialogue with them. She entered the orbit of the Parisian School and yet remained an independent. As her 1931 painting *The Woman in Blue*[78] (fig. 7) – most probably a self-portrait – attests, she developed a neat lyrical aesthetics from within the parameters of Lhote-type late cubism

78 Burcu Pelvanoğlu, *Hale Asaf: Türk Resim Sanatında Bir Dönüm Noktası*, Istanbul: YKY 2007, 123.

that reminds one also of Amadeo Modigliani's portraits but with a feminine touch. It was not only her poor health and bohemian life but also a certain artistic evolution that qualified her also as an outlier.[79]

Asaf shared the last part of her life with a well-known Italian writer, Antonio Aniante (1900–1983), who had sought refuge in Paris from Benito Mussolini's fascist regime. Once her Turkish friends returned home, he remained almost[80] the only source of information on the last and most mature phase of her artistic career, as she continued a Sisyphean struggle against pending death,[81] and we are fortunate that he did write about that period. Unfortunately, he had to leave her remaining paintings with a friend before he made a narrow escape from a Paris under assault by the Germans.

It is only recently that Asaf has been rediscovered and some of her long lost or widely dispersed work is slowly emerging. A meticulous recent study has cast new light on how important she actually was as a leader and innovator among her generation.[82] Aniante's account mentions her paintings and drawings of women, flowers and children, and her reminiscences of her childhood and youth in Istanbul. I believe we have good reason to suspect that she may have indulged in some surrealistic experimentations under the effect of drugs she used that gave her hallucinations, shortly before her tragic death. If some of her final paintings are ever recovered, we will know if this was the case, and if so, how far she went in this direction. Bearing in mind that surrealist painting was always highly diverse, even in its heyday, it would not be farfetched to expect that she might develop a naïve peripheral surrealism of the Marc Chagall type by simply incorporating dreamlike memories of her childhood and youth into a few of her final works. Unlike Chagall, of course, she was from a metropolis and not from the countryside. Even so, during her sojourn in Turkey between the two phases of her Parisian experience, her appointment as a teacher in the provincial city of Bursa (1928–1929) introduced her to life in the countryside. Some of the images engraved in her memory

---

79 One author characterizes her works of the 1930s as a peculiar mix of cubism, abstraction, and new figurative art then observed on the Parisian art scene. See Sönmez, *Paris Tecrübeleri*, 50. â

80 There were occasional visitors to Paris who met with her or had news of Asaf as late as 1933. Among them is Fikret Adil, the art critic much involved in, and who wrote of, Asmalımescit in Pera/Beyoğlu, the bohemian equivalent in Istanbul of Montparnasse. He had a high opinion of her and her art. He reported of her under a false name (Sade) in his book, which also contains a few of her sketches of Parisian life. Fikret Adil, *Asmalımescit 74: Bohem Hayatı*, Istanbul: Sel 2015, 108–109 and 126.

81 Bedri Rahmi Eyüboğlu wrote an obituary when he heard of Asaf's death in 1938, several months after it happened. He had first met her in Montparnasse, and for the last time in 1933, when she looked badly undernourished and caught in the vicious circle of the bohemian neighbourhood. He qualified her as one of the most gifted and promising among her Turkish peers – naturally including himself in the reference group. See Bedri Rahmi Eyüboğlu, *Gece Yarısı*, Istanbul: Türkiye İş Bankası Kültür Yayınları 2002, 28-29.

82 See Pelvanoğlu, *Hale Asaf.*

of Bursa, and of a childhood spent on the shores of the Bosphorus and the Prince Islands on the outskirts of Istanbul, could well have made a comeback in this last phase of her art. Depending on the exact nature of the naïveté involved and the kind of expression it found in her work, she may also qualify in some ways as a forerunner of the surrealistic folkloric works that Gisèle Prassinos produced in her last phase. After all, Asaf, just like Prassinos, had deep roots in the cultural soil of *fin de siècle* Istanbul and developed her personal art in the favourable Parisian scene to which she was attracted.

Until we know if surrealism truly made an appearance in her final paintings, which one hopes might yet be retrieved, we will be able to conclude this narrative only provisionally. In an interview towards the end of his life, Aniante characterized de Chirico in their Parisian circle as "an unpleasant but interesting man".[83] Ironically, if further evidence links Asaf with surrealism – that is, if Asaf outperforms her Turkish peers in terms of her connection to the interwar surrealist avant-garde, one of the several movements that found a place in her eclectic artistic style that had gradually liberated itself from the confines of Lhote-instructed post-cubism – then the epigraph from de Chirico with which this paper began will indicate that this backward-looking metaphysical surrealist artist and writer was prophetically correct at least once. We can only wait and see.

Afterword

We did not have to wait long to see if the above anticipation was valid. A new expanded edition of Burcu Pelvanoğlu's book *Hale Asaf* (2018) came out shortly after this piece was submitted for evaluation and publication. The major difference between the two editions is that the latter introduced 37 paintings belonging to Asaf's last period and were hitherto unavailable. This was a major and unanticipated breakthrough in the scholarship, made possible by a few dedicated individuals who connected a collector in Paris with a scholar in Istanbul.

I include here only one painting (fig. 8) that can be interpreted as evidence for my above prediction that, during her final years, Asaf might have made dream-like paintings, which fused her childhood and youth memories with her desires (for an impossible motherhood) in a surrealistic manner. I was also correct in expecting a Chagall-like style with all its naivité and smooth lines and an inclination towards incorporating less used soft colours. A careful look at this work reveals two additional types of resemblances with other surrealist artists. Firstly, there exists an unexpected convergence with the deeply perceptive works of René Magritte that occasionally goes as far as generating a set of successive *trompes l'oeil*. Magritte's paintings of this sort are thought-provoking beyond being simple aesthetic illusions. At first sight, we see in Asaf's work, a figure sleeping, his bed

83 Pelvanoğlu, *Hale Asaf*, 100.

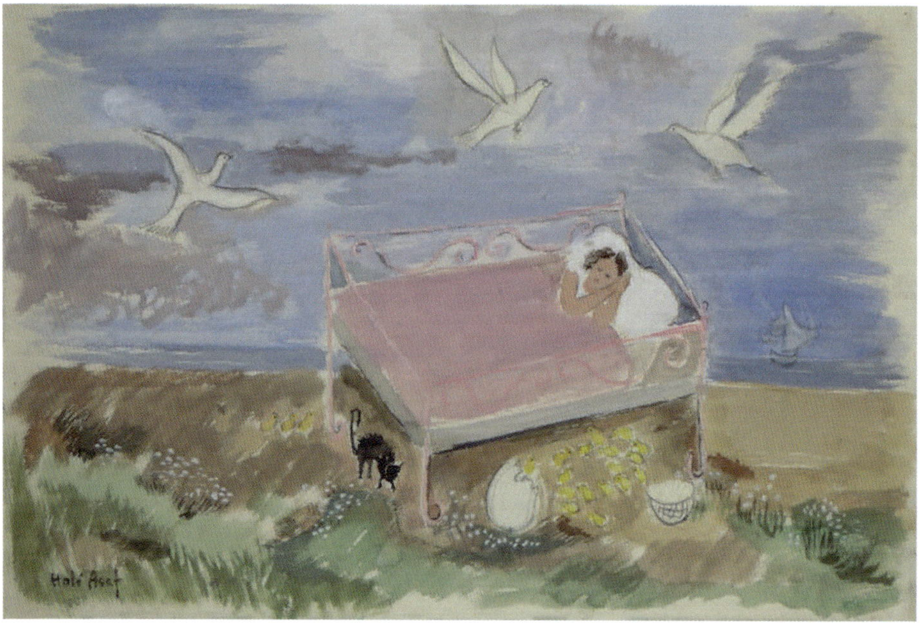

Figure 8: Hale Asaf, *The Dreaming Child*, undated. Paris, private collection, courtesy of Jean-Pierre Strauss and Kerem Topuz Archive.

and various bedroom accessories placed in the outdoors. However, the bed constitutes such a focal point, that upon second thought one has the impression that it is an indoor event that is unfolding in front of our eyes. A place where dreams and memories that have to do with the exterior are projected as illusions and efface the very walls on which they materialize. Here, the interior and the exterior are inextricably fused into a single imaginary space.[84] This fusion owes its success to the magical elimination of the house within the garden, though the bed with its roof-like (trapezoid) shape acts as a substitute for the house. Secondly, there exists an unexaggerated decorative process at work in Asaf's work that connects her with other otherwise distant kindreds. The obliqueness with which this decorative aspect is introduced makes it at first elusive. Yet upon further reflection, one can discern an affiliation with certain 'calligraphic' and seemingly simple abstract works of Joan Miró, and even the overdecorated interiors of Henri Matisse, which, in careful compositions, fuse with the outer space.[85]

84 The harmonizing unity of space and the lyrical simplicity of objects and figures assembled in it play down the shocking factor that would have been all important in Salvador Dalí's metaphysical landscapes.

85 Pelvanoğlu, while acknowledging the presence of certain surreal elements in these paintings, opts to classify them on the whole as essentially art deco. See Pelvanoğlu, *Hale Asaf*, Yapı Kredi Yayınları 2018, 9-10.

The works belonging to this final period constitute a pinnacle: Turkish painting came in the 1930s to terms most directly with surrealism of the 1930s. Another pinnacle, taking place more or less simultaneously, was Fikret Muallâ's self-conscious surrealist dossier of illustrations we referred to above. These two moments thus confirm the well-known fact that there is not one, but several surrealisms, although they share common fount and matrix.

We can thus recapitulate our conclusions in light of this important finding: That the two peaks that are identified with the two Turkish diasporic artists, both strongly connected to Paris, reinforces the underlying hypothesis relating to the paradox of Turkish surrealist painting during the interwar period. We also observe how important the links between Paris and Istanbul were for the fortunes of Turkish painters, no matter where they were based. Last but not least, the first direct conscious application of surrealism in Turkish painting in Turkey really did take place thanks to Fikret Muallâ, who benefitted from his previous experiences in Germany and France. This also supports the point made in de Chirico's *Hebdomeros,* quoted in the epigraph, about that the way to the South by southerners, to come with an ultimate tour de force better proceed via the North.

Chapter 3
Looking past: Turkish surrealism in translation

Ambra D'Antone

The study of surrealism is at a crucial stage. The underlying methods and conventions that have thus far characterized it are now being progressively exposed, challenged and negotiated. This phenomenon is concurrent with the "global turn" – an expanding discourse that has prompted a systematic questioning of normalized narratives in the way we think and write about art history, to fit the world after a postcolonial remapping.[1] Similarly, surrealism scholars have cast a wider net of inquiry over the globe, seeking to identify the geo-temporal dimensions and modus operandi of surrealism's international reach. The desire to unfurl the networks connecting the Parisian surrealist group, whose birth is generally associated with the 1924 "Manifesto of Surrealism" by French poet André Breton (1896–1966), with non-Parisian (and non-French) surrealist iterations has quickly taken over recent research endeavours.[2]

The exhilaration resulting from the development of surrealism's international spread as an overarching narrative is nevertheless matched by a considerable anxiety. Opening up surrealism to the plurality promised by the global necessarily involves allowing divergence and friction to play a part in its history, which threaten to compromise surrealism's essence as an indivisible entity.[3] As a defence mechanism, scholars are operating inquiries into the internal ontological (or "orthodox") characteristics of the Parisian surrealist group that can appear ideological and uncompromising when considered in the context of a global circulation of culture.[4] The promise of the erosion of geographical boundaries, stemming from a desire for inclusivity, has often implied an eschewal of the substantive differences of non-Parisian surrealist iterations, raising more impenetrable ideological barriers that put the authenticity and legitimation of these cultural productions in jeopardy.

1 Aruna D'Souza, "Introduction", in: *Art History in the Wake of the Global Turn*, Jill H. Casid and Aruna D'Souza, eds., Williamston, MA: Yale University Press 2014, vii–viii.

2 Michael Richardson, "'Other' Surrealisms: Centre and Periphery in International Perspective", in: *A Companion to Dada and Surrealism*, David Hopkins, ed., Chichester: Wiley Blackwell 2016.

3 Richardson, "'Other' Surrealisms", 131.

4 Wendy M.K. Shaw, *Ottoman Painting: Reflections of Western Art from the Ottoman Empire to the Turkish Republic*, London: I.B Tauris 2011, 1. The term "orthodox surrealism", used to differentiate the Parisian group from its dissidents, is still used, though its normative application is problematic.

This paper focuses on Turkish surrealism, an area that has been absent from the trajectories of global surrealism, as the chapter by Eyüp Özveren in this volume also remarks. Following the routes of intellectual trade that connected Turkey with Europe, this paper reflects on translation as an art historical methodology, beyond its primary signification as a literary tool: translation reflects a model of cultural diffusion based on a multidirectional movement of culture that functions by virtue of plurality, rather than in spite of it, revealing that surrealism itself was a movement in translation whose authority relied on motion, exchange and importation.[5] Moreover, this chapter challenges influence as a pervasive descriptor of artistic exchanges which relies on causality and imbalance and hoping to capture the plurality at the core of surrealism's international reach, testing the notion of "differential" surrealisms, after a definition by Louis Althusser employed by Ottomanist scholar Wendy Shaw.[6]

Two events serve as case studies here: the publication in 1941 of *Garip*, a poetry collection with contributions from the Turkish poets Orhan Veli Kanık (1914–1950), Oktay Rifat (1914–1988) and Melih Cevdet Anday (1915–2002); and the 1958–1959 *Phallisme* solo exhibition of Yüksel Arslan (1933–2017) at the Turkish-German Cultural Centre in Istanbul. These events provide a measure of the literary and artistic dimensions of Turkish surrealism by exposing the network of individuals involved in creating a literary and visual vocabulary for it; moreover, although they are almost two decades apart, these events reflect parallel approaches to the translation of surrealist ideas and practices. Firstly, they index a non-binary commitment to both collective and individualistic notions of artistic production, which appear fully serviceable for artists and literates and which were determined by specific historical conditions. Secondly, they reveal an added temporal dimension to translation: the creation of surrealist-informed work, in both *Garip* and Arslan's *Phallisme*, reacted to the present condition of Turkish art and poetry by actively engaging the inherited artistic forms and consciousness of Turkey's past, testing notions of conservatism and modernity.[7]

Recuperating Turkish surrealism

The understanding of Turkish surrealism in this paper warrants further clarification, since the term encapsulates two distinct, albeit deeply imbricated, meanings.

---

5 Esra Akcan, "Channels and Items of Translation", in: *Art History in the Wake of the Global Turn*, Jill H. Casid and Aruna D'Souza, eds., Williamston, MA: Yale University Press 2014, 145–146; Robyn Creswell, *City of Beginnings: Poetic Modernism in Beirut*, Princeton: Princeton University Press 2019, 85–86.

6 Michael Baxandall, "Excursus Against Influence", in: *Patterns of Intention: On the Historical Explanation of Pictures*, New Haven: Yale University Press 1985; Shaw, *Ottoman Painting*, 1-3.

7 This line of argument is inspired by Nergis Ertürk, "Surrealism and Turkish Script Arts", *Modernism/Modernity* 17 (2010).

On the one hand, it captures the reception of French surrealism amongst Turkish artists and intellectuals, with first translations and mentions appearing in the early 1930s.[8] On the other hand, Turkish surrealism also involved the creative development of surrealist strategies, appearing both in art and literature. Though often in disagreement about its ontology, Turkish art historians and literary critics acknowledged that surrealism became a significant artistic catalyst in Turkey.[9] Yet, despite André Breton's declaration of surrealism's boundaries as "non-national" in 1937 and Constantinople notably featuring in the *Surrealist Map of the World*, published in the Brussels review *Variétés* in 1929 (fig. 1), Turkey has sadly fallen off the map, revealing an asymmetry in the field and in the established methods of art history.[10]

Turkish surrealism has become a debatable denomination: scholars who have discussed it, in fact, have stipulated that there *could not* be surrealism in Turkey. Ayfer Bakkalcioğlu, in his 1974 essay "Of Surrealism in Turkey", claimed that a surrealist movement in Turkey never existed because of Turkey's sociopolitical and historical specificities.[11] Because of the social and political commitments of French surrealism, which exceeded the strictly literary and artistic, Bakkalcioğlu argued that the movement was inextricably bound to a type of society Turkey did not possess, making it impossible to conform to its perceived French standard. As he put it, "the mere fact that its birthplace is France at a given moment in history hides certain *données* which are accepted merely as facts of life in Paris but may not be so at other parts of the world".[12]

In his essay, Bakkalcioğlu exposed the ideological nature of understanding the transnational movement of culture through a model of unidirectional mimetic application, which perpetuates asymmetrical relations of power in the process of knowledge production.[13] Rather than due to a "lack" in Turkish artistic production, Bakkalcioğlu's dismissal of Turkish surrealism reflected his reservations towards harnessing a narrative which minimized the different aspects of Turkey's history and society, promoting Europe as the culmination of modernity to which Turkey could only be subsidiary.[14] Eyüp Özveren has presented the case of the Turkish author Ferit Edgü, a figure discussed more later, who also rejected the

8 Some of the earliest instances: Nurullah Berk, *Modern San'at*, Istanbul: Semih Lütfi Bitik ve Basımevi 1935; Mehmet Behçet Yazar, *Genç Şairlerimiz ve Eserleri*, Istanbul: Kanaat Kitabevi 1936, 36–42; Tahir Olgun, *Edebiyati Lügati,* Istanbul: Âsâr-i lmiye Kütüphanesi Neşriyati 1936, 120.

9 Cemal Süreya, *Şapkam Dolu Çiçekle: Toplu Yazılar I*, Istanbul: Yapı Kredi Yayınları 2006; Selahattin Hilâv, *Edebiyat Yazıları,* Istanbul: Yapı Kredi Yayınları 2008; Sezer Tansuğ, *Türk Resminde Yeni Dönem*, Istanbul: Remzi Kitabevi 1995.

10 André Breton, "Nonnational Boundaries of Surrealism" in: *Free Rein = La Clé des Champs*, trans. Michel Parmentier and Jacqueline d'Amboise, Lincoln: University of Nebraska Press 1995, 7–18.

11 Ayfer Bakkalcioğlu, "Of Surrealism in Turkey", *Boğaziçi Üniversitesi Dergisi* 2 (1974), 1.

12 Bakkalcioğlu, "Surrealism in Turkey", 2–3.

13 Shaw, *Ottoman Painting*, 1–3.

14 For a similar argument, see Ertürk, "Surrealism and Turkish Script Arts".

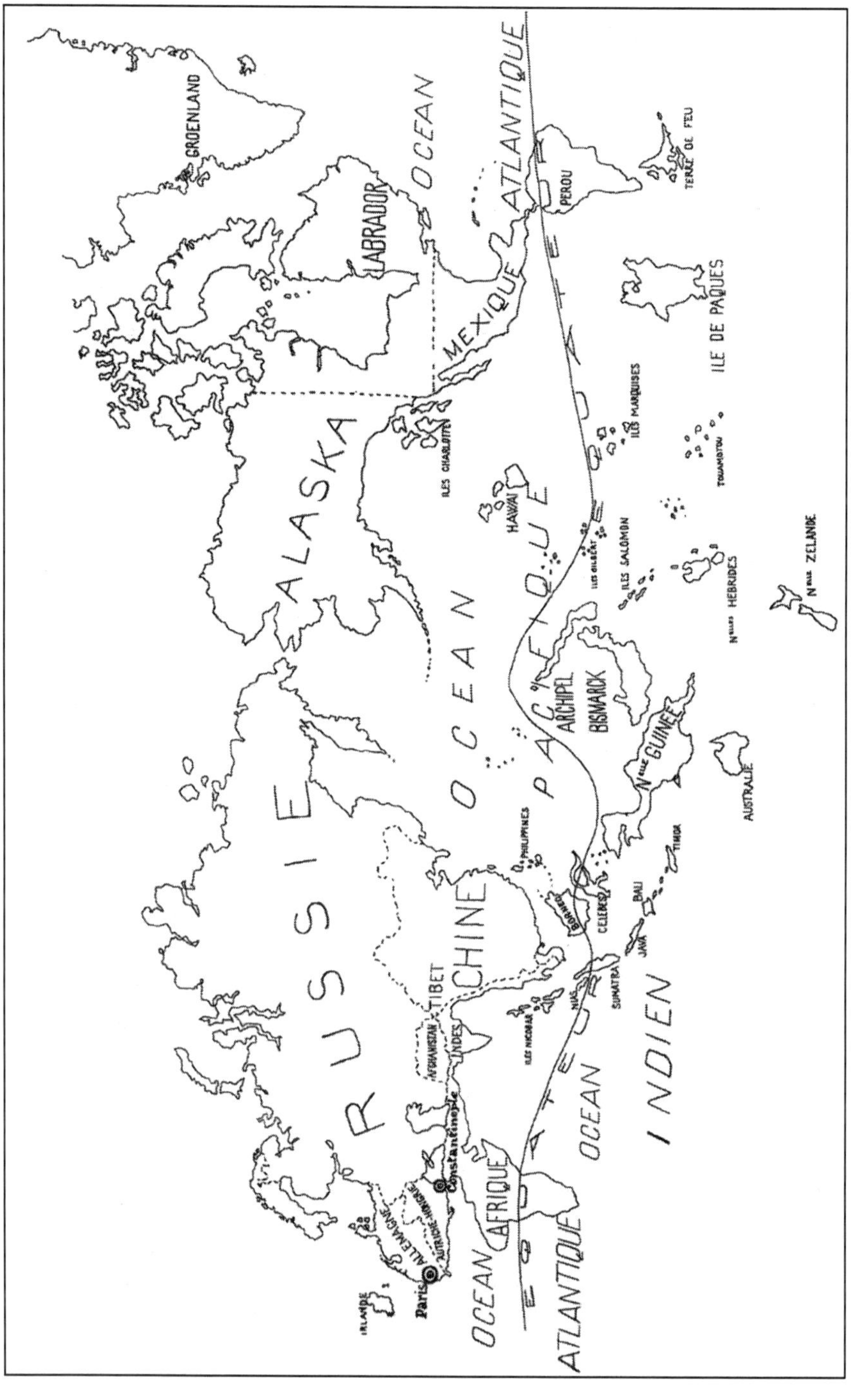

Figure 1: Anonymous, *Surrealist Map of the World*, printed in *Variétés* (Brussels), 1929.

notion of Turkish surrealism.[15] In a text which served as the introduction to the Turkish translation of André Breton's *Nadja*, Edgü reiterated that although certain Turkish productions had been described as "surrealist", an organized movement in Turkey could not come to fruition because of surrealism's philosophical stakes as an epistemological world-view, which he found untranslatable into the Turkish milieu.[16]

In a similar vein, Timour Muhidine recently denied the existence of a Turkish surrealism, because of the country's failure to meet criteria for the "importation" of surrealism, listing among these a post-war bourgeois society, the support of a rich linguistic and poetic tradition and an organized non-Muslim cultural activity.[17] Yet, this paper is of an altogether different character from Bakkalcioğlu's – the Turkish cultural milieu is here cast as epigonic, belated and lacking.[18] Bakkalcioğlu's, Edgü's and Muhidine's arguments rely on different ideological commitments, yet all point to one reason behind the delay of academic interest in Turkish surrealism: the crystallization of a perceived ontology of surrealism as an "ideal type", a totalizing and coherent set of concepts which, nonetheless, is tied to a fixed set of historical and cultural conditions.[19] The issue of organized collectivism, particularly, is at the heart of the authors' targeted criticisms: criteria have not been met to ensure the birth of an organized movement, an element which many feel to be at the very core of surrealism's essence, determined by a hermetic development and ontological cohesiveness.[20]

The need for admission criteria denounces a Eurocentric bias at the core of the surrealist discourse, facilitated by a set of essentializing historiographical tropes that have critically (mis)informed what it means to talk about modernity in Turkey.[21] The modern in Turkish history has become synonymous with the declaration of the Turkish Republic in the early 1920s and with a series of so-called "Westernizing" reforms, meant to provide a radical break from the country's Ottoman

15 See Eyüp Özveren's chapter in this volume.
16 Ferit Edgü, "Breton ve Nadja Üzerine Birkaç Söz", in: André Breton, *Nadja*, trans. Ismail Yerguz, Istanbul: Mitos Yayınları 1992, 5–6.
17 Timour Muhidine, "'Ce ciel postiche qui nous appartient à tous': Le Surréalisme en Turquie", in: *La Multiplication des images en pays d'Islam*, Bernard Heyberger and Silvia Naef, eds., Würzburg: Orient-Institut Istanbul 2016, 174.
18 A similar argument can be observed in Martine Antle, "Surrealism and the Orient", *Yale French Studies* 109 (2006).
19 In discussing the "ideal type", I am inspired here by Albert Hourani, *The Emergence of the Modern Middle East*, Los Angeles: University of California Press 1981, xvii.
20 Ferdinand Alquiè, *Philosophie du surréalisme,* Paris: Flammarion 1955, 206–207; Michael Richardson and Krzysztof Fijałkowski, "Introduction: Surrealism as a Collective Adventure", in: *Surrealism Against the Current: Tracts and Declarations*, Michael Richardson and Krzysztof Fijałkowski, eds., London: Pluto Press 2001.
21 Duygu Köksal, "The Role of Art in Early Republican Modernization in Turkey", in: *La Multiplication des images en pays d'Islam*, Bernard Heyberger and Silvia Naef, eds., Würzburg: Orient-Institut Istanbul 2016, 154.

past.[22] As a result, scholars have understood the literary and artistic productions of the Republican period as inextricably linked to a government-sponsored reformist agenda, with no possibility of an independent edge, as belated imitations of European originals.[23] Turkish modernity, in these accounts, is the culmination of a teleological development, moving unidirectionally from a centre point in the Euro-American region towards marginal peripheries.[24] This narrative eschews the authenticity of creative productions in Turkey, and more generally in the Middle Eastern region, which is often the victim of a "time lag" trope and remains ideologically anchored to the category "Islamic" as a totalizing narrative irreconcilable with modernity.[25]

Adherence to these lines of arguments has generated frustrating binaries like "centre and periphery" or "orthodox surrealism" and "other surrealisms" which, even when exposed through postcolonial gambits, are hard to eliminate.[26] Until the understanding of surrealism as a transnational entity switches from being a capillary sub-narrative of French surrealism to a self-standing discourse determined by a substantive pluralism, these infectious discourses will prevail.[27] An alternative approach is in order: we can, instead, account for the existence of Turkish surrealism as "differential". Pioneered by the Marxist philosopher Louis Althusser, the notion of "differentiality" not only promises to account for ontological diversity, but contains a temporal dimension, purporting to understand different societies as possessing their own peculiar times which might not always be in accord.[28]

Differentiality, therefore, unfurls in a "plurality of instances" and the proliferation of uneven contradictions, challenging a diachronic, Eurocentric understanding of history.[29] Applied to surrealism, differentiality entails the acceptance that

---

22 Sibel Bozdoğan, "Art and Architecture in Modern Turkey: The Republican Period", in: *The Cambridge History of Turkey*, vol. 4, Reşat Kasaba, ed., Cambridge: Cambridge University Press 2008, 452.

23 Köksal, "The Role of Art", 154.

24 Preminda Jacob, "Between Modernism and Modernization: Locating Modernity in South Asian Art", *Art Journal* 58 (1999), 48–50.

25 Anneka Lenssen, "The Shape of the Support: Painting and Politics in Syria's Twentieth Century", PhD thesis, Massachusetts Institute of Technology 2014, 11; Sussan Babaie, "Voices of Authority: Locating the 'Modern' in 'Islamic' Arts", *Getty Research Journal* 3 (2011); Finbarr Barry Flood, "From the Prophet to Postmodernism? New World Orders at the End of Islamic Art", in: *Making Art History: A Changing Discipline and Its Institutions*, Elizabeth Mansfield, ed., London: Routledge 2007.

26 Partha Mitter, "Decentering Modernism: Art History and Avant-Garde from the Periphery", *Art Bulletin* 90 (2008); Avinoam Shalem, "Exceeding Realism: Utopian Modern Art on the Nile and Abdel Hedi al-Gazzar's Surrealistic Drawings", *South Atlantic Quarterly* 109 (2010), 578.

27 This line of argument is inspired by the rhizomatic method developed in Gilles Deleuze and Felix Guattari, *A Thousand Plateaus: Capitalism and Schizophrenia*, trans. Brian Massumi, Minneapolis: University of Minnesota Press 1987, 6–20.

28 Louis Althusser and Étienne Balibar, *Reading Capital*, trans. Ben Brewster, London: Verso 1979, 99–100; Robert J.C. Young, *White Mythologies*, London: Routledge 2004, 18–20.

29 Althusser and Balibar, *Reading Capital*, 100.

some of its constitutive characteristics in its global iterations might diverge from those of the French group, echoing the cultural and historical specificities of their locale. As illustrated through the following case studies, this chapter contends that the presence of an organized surrealist movement was not a necessary parameter for the development of surrealist artistic and literary strategies in Turkey, being replaced by a non-binary commitment to collectivism and individualism in artistic productions and identity which exposes notions of avant-gardism and conservatism as artificial and fraught.

The fabrication of the Garip *movement*

In 1941, the three Turkish poets Oktay Rifat, Melih Cevdet Anday and Orhan Veli Kanık published a collection of poems under the single title *Garip* (Bizarre), with the subtitle *Thoughts on Poetry and Selected Poems by Oktay Rifat, Melih Cevdet Anday and Orhan Veli*. The three poets had been linked by friendship since their youth and frequented the literary circles of Ankara.[30] The publication, which promised a total poetic renovation, was so impactful that the poets became subsequently known under the collective denomination *Garipçiler*, the *Garip* poets, or *Garip Hareketi*, the *Garip* movement.[31] Nonetheless, unpacking both the ontological and the historical elements of *Garip* and its reception reveals elements that point to the organized collective nature of the poets' operations as a historical fabrication, rather than as a reflection of their actual aesthetic intentions.

In the years following the establishment of the Republic of Turkey, Ankara saw a proliferation of new printed periodicals devoted to the discussion of artistic and literary production, facilitating new cultural debates.[32] These platforms allowed for individual contributions to the pressing collective concerns of the time, moulding the discourse around the function of the arts and the role of the intellectual.[33] The public exposure of the *Garip* poets as possessing a shared agenda was initially ensured in the late 1930s by the periodical *Varlık* (Existence), founded in Ankara in 1933.[34] The journal, which aimed to provide an outlet for young and innovative debates on literature and the arts, enjoyed the support of the Republican People's Party as one of its organs, while maintaining an independent critical edge.[35] *Varlık* spoke to a Turkish audience, engaging with both international and local concerns.

30 Talat Sait Halman, *Türk Edebiyatı Tarihi*, Ankara: Kültür ve Turizm Bakanlığı 2006, 4:42.

31 Hakan Sazyek, *Cumhuriyet Dönemi Türk Şiirinde: Garip Hareketi*, Ankara: Akçağ Yayınları 2016.

32 Erik J. Zürcher, *Turkey: A Modern History*, London: I.B. Tauris 2004, 152. This was not a republican prerogative: periodicals had been supporting intellectual discourses since the early nineteenth century.

33 Vedat Günyol, *Sanat ve Edebiyat Dergileri*, Istanbul: Alan Yayincilik 1986.

34 Duygu Köksal, "Art and Power in Turkey: Culture, Aesthetics and Nationalism during the Single Party Era", *New Perspectives on Turkey* 31 (2004), 111–112.

35 "Varlık Ne İçin Çıkıyor?", *Varlık* 1 (1933).

Orhan Veli, Oktay Rifat and Melih Cevdet Anday published new poetry individually from 1936, garnering coverage in other newspapers as well.[36] Yet, Orhan Veli's poems, which appeared first in issue 82 in 1936, were accompanied by a note, which positioned the poets in a shared narrative of total poetic innovation:

> Orhan Veli, whose four poems you can read below, possesses a mature style though he has not published his poetry until now. Our future issues will benefit from the new atmosphere that Orhan Veli, together with his friends Oktay Rifat, Melih Cevdet and Mehmet Ali Sel, bring to our poetry.[37]

The cementing of the Garip collective in the journal took further shape in 1937, with the publication of "Sürrealist Oyunlarda Diyalog" (Dialogue in Surrealist Games), a playful poetic dialogue between Orhan Veli and Oktay Rifat based on random word associations, which experimented with the French surrealist technique of automatic writing:

> O.R.: What is religion?
> O.V.: An omelette made with rotten egg.
> O.R.: What is symbolism?
> O.V.: The mummy of Ramses II.
> O.R.: What is the sea?
> O.V.: It is the first light in my lover's window.[38]

In his 1961 text *Vingt ans de surréalisme*, French poet Jean-Louis Bédouin mentioned the existence of a Turkish surrealist group which, he claimed, edited the journal *Varlık*; Bédouin also made mention of Orhan Veli, Rifat and Cevdet as translators of surrealist texts into Turkish. We can speculate that the 1937 poetic dialogue perhaps enabled an awareness, albeit cursory, in France of surrealist activities in Turkey, signalling the international reputation of Garip in the 1960s as an organized group.[39]

The newspaper edited by the *Garip* poets was not *Varlık*, as Bédouin thought, but *Yaprak* (Leaf), which they had founded in 1948.[40] Printing contributions by prominent intellectuals, poets and visual artists, *Yaprak* ran with two issues per month for twenty-eight issues, from 1949 until 1950, the year of Orhan Veli's untimely death.[41]

---

36 The column "Yeni Eserler" (New Works) in the newspaper *Cumhuriyet* (Republic) made multiple mentions throughout 1937 of new poetry by Rifat, Orhan Veli and Anday in *Varlık*. See *Cumhuriyet*, 5 January 1937, 8; 27 March 1937, 8; 19 May 1937, 4; 20 August 1937, 4; and 23 December 1937, 8.

37 Quoted in Cemal Süreya, "Oktay Rifat'ın İlk Şiirleri" in Süreya, *Şapkam Dolu Çiçekle*, 338. Mehmet Ali Sel was Orhan Veli's nom de plume. All translations are the author's unless otherwise specified.

38 Süreya, "Oktay Rifat'ın İlk Şiirleri", 339.

39 Jean-Louis Bédouin, *Vingt ans de surréalisme 1939–1959*, Paris: Denoël 1961, 115; Talat Sait Halman, "I Am Listening to Istanbul: Orhan Veli Kanık", in: *Rapture and Revolution: Essays on Turkish Literature*, Jayne L. Warner, ed., Syracuse: Syracuse University Press 2007, 346.

40 Sazyek, *Garip Hareketi*, 68.

41 Günyol, *Sanat*, 52.

Yaprak provided a platform for discussions on international and Turkish art, literature and contemporary politics, as well as for translations of foreign texts and poetry, contributing to salient local and international intellectual debates. The newspaper engaged with surrealism quite directly: the 1 May 1949 issue contained Orhan Veli's translation of the poem "Georgia" by the French surrealist poet Philippe Soupault (1897–1990), as well as an interview between Orhan Veli and Soupault, who had visited Ankara in April 1949 on behalf of UNESCO and met with the *Yaprak* team.[42] The two poets discussed the merits and pitfalls of translation as a method of cultural diffusion, based not on passive and total semantic transposition, but on an imperfect process of reformulation.[43] Print, therefore, was instrumental in perpetuating the reputation of Garip as a poetry collective on a national and international scale, a trajectory that the 1941 publication of *Garip* had precipitated.

The Garip *manifesto*

The text of the 1941 *Garip* manifesto reveals elements that help to complicate the positionality of the *Garip* group, vis-à-vis its contemporary poetic commitments; the manifesto also places the *Garip* group within the larger discourse around the emergence of avant-garde, of art historiography and of an artistic canon in Turkey. The book encapsulated the maturation of poetic intentions that Orhan Veli, Oktay Rifat and Melih Cevdet had begun to express in the pages of *Varlık*. The poems were preceded by a foreword, an impassioned document penned by Orhan Veli. In it, Veli called for a rejection of the lofty and formulaic rhetoric of poetry, privileging a more essential and colloquial approach to poetic language. In 1945, Orhan Veli curated and published a second edition of *Garip*, where he added previously unpublished poems of his own and removed the contributions by Oktay Rifat and Melih Cevdet, turning the text and, arguably, Garip itself into a personal endeavour.[44] Nevertheless, Turkish and international scholars alike have discussed the introduction to the first edition in terms of a de facto manifesto, which stated the poetic intentions of *Garip* as a substantive collective.[45] Such an interpretation prompted the later denomination of the *Garip* poets as "Birinci Yeniciler" (the First Innovators), positioning them within a narrative of avant-gardist renovation and of temporal primacy in the perceived linear trajectory of Turkish poetic progress.[46]

---

42 *Yaprak* 9 (1 May 1949), 1. For a preview of the interview, see "Olan Biten", *Yaprak* 8 (15 April 1949), 1.

43 *Yaprak* 9, 1.

44 Orhan Veli Kanık, *Garip*, Istanbul: Ölmez Eserler, 1945.

45 Cemal Süreya, "Gerçeküstücülük ve Türk Edebiyatı", in Süreya, *Şapkam Dolu Çiçekle*, 111; Talat Sait Halman, "Introduction", in: *I Am Listening to Istanbul: Selected Poems of Orhan Veli Kanık*, trans. Talat Sait Halman, New York: Corinth Books 1971, xiv–xv.

46 Halman, "I Am Listening to Istanbul", 346.

In his analysis of twentieth-century artistic and political manifestos, Martin Puchner described the manifesto as a literary genre containing within itself the promise of modernity, "doing away with the past and ushering in the future", inherently connected to the ontology of the avant-gardes.[47] As he put it, the genre of the manifesto functions through an ideological eschewal of the text's rhetorical merit and choice of vocabulary, in order to foreground its contents as revolutionary precepts – however, it is by virtue of their formulation that those precepts gain power.[48] The *Garip* foreword presents formal qualities that prove instrumental in sustaining its historical interpretation as a manifesto. Predominantly, the text relies on a rhetoric of negation, which takes multiple forms throughout the text. Firstly, the establishment of *Garip* as a source of innovation within poetry is achieved *via negativa* by means of a repudiation of established conventions, through a hyperbolic anti-language stance:

> Squeezing certain theories into familiar old moulds cannot be a new artistic thrust forward. We must alter the whole structure from the foundation up. […] We must dump overboard everything that those literatures have taught us. We wish it were possible to dump even language itself […].[49]

Within the foreword, the suggestion of a total destruction of language plays a generative role: it functions as a statement of Orhan Veli's commitment to achieve poetic harmony by stripping poetry of rhyme, metre, figures of speech and any other artifice which could prevent an untainted experience of poetry.[50]

Orhan Veli was not the first to propose a connection between poetic language and its epistemological effects: the Turkish poet Nazım Hikmet (1902–1963) had been a pioneer of free verse in the 1920s. Nevertheless, Hikmet had not fully repudiated the use of metric strategies, and therefore Orhan Veli's mission achieved a certain sense of historical primacy.[51] As he put it, this novel approach to language was the vehicle for reaching the realm of collective human unconscious (*tahteşşuur*): only in the unconscious, the repository of the human spirit stripped raw, could one reach nature and reality in their purest manifestation, untainted by the intervention of rationality.[52] Yet, Veli posited, only the poets possessed the tools to represent it.[53] The language of this new poetry had to be as close as possible to colloquial Turkish, following its rhythms and idioms to achieve natural harmony through what he defined as "purity of expression". Childhood memories

47 Martin Puchner, *Poetry of the Revolution: Marx, Manifestos, and the Avant-Gardes*, Princeton: Princeton University Press 2006, 2–3.

48 Puchner, *Poetry of the Revolution*, 2.

49 Translation by Talat Sait Halman, quoted in "Introduction", xv.

50 Orhan Veli Kanık, "Önsözü", in: Orhan Veli Kanık, Melih Cevdet Anday and Oktay Rifat, *Garip: Şiir Hakkında Düşünceler ve Melih Cevdet, Oktay Rıfat, Orhan Veli'den Seçilmiş Şiirler*, Istanbul: Yapı Kredi Yayınları 2014, 11.

51 Halman, *Türk Edebiyatı*, 45.

52 Orhan Veli, "Önsözü", 19.

53 Orhan Veli, "Önsözü", 22.

and puerile fantasy became particularly invested with ideological power within Orhan Veli's programmatic text, turning it into a space of privileged access to poetry "untainted by rhetorical conceits", of which the 1937 "Surrealist Games" article had offered a perhaps immature example.[54] In his 1924 "Manifesto of Surrealism", André Breton had also explored childhood as a realm of authentic experience and appreciation of reality – albeit understood as the uncontradictory synthesis of dream and wakeful states.[55]

The foreword to *Garip* contained even more explicit references to French surrealism. Orhan Veli praised the technique of automatic writing, which the surrealists employed to allow the unconscious to surface in art and writing, translating it both semantically, as *ruhî otomatizm* (spiritual automatism), and conceptually: automatism became central to the Garip poetic programme, as a strategy for representing the unconscious in poetry through plainness and purity. As Veli put it,

> Breton, who knows Doctor Freud very well and is a poet with great artistic ideas, said many years ago that a consciousness gained through chance gives man the power to dig the well that we call the unconscious.[56]

In the last issue of *Yaprak*, published in 1951 as a eulogy to Orhan Veli after his untimely death, Oktay Rifat recalled sitting on a balcony in Turkey with Orhan Veli in 1937, while his sister in law read the "Manifesto of Surrealism" to them, translating directly into Turkish.[57] As Rifat recalled, they "soared with every sentence" and Orhan Veli was deeply marked by the text, although he never sought formal affiliation with the French surrealists.[58] The introduction to *Garip* itself, in fact, is markedly anti-school in its collective commitments: Orhan Veli acknowledged that the tastes and poetic aims of the *Garip* group were akin to those of the Parisian surrealist group, and that some of their readers had called them "surrealists", yet he stressed that the *Garip* poets had no direct affiliation to it, nor to any other literary school.[59] The notion of schools, for Veli, represented a static position in the historical trajectory, as opposed to the dynamism of a "movement", which was felt to contain a promise of paradigm change.[60]

---

54 Orhan Veli, "Önsözü", 12.

55 André Breton, "Manifesto of Surrealism", in: *Manifestoes of Surrealism*, trans. Richard Seaver and Helen R. Lane, Ann Arbor: University of Michigan Press 1969, 16–40.

56 Orhan Veli, "Önsözü", 19–20.

57 Cahit Sidki Taranci, "Şair Orhan Veli", *Son Yaprak* (1 February 1951), 2; Halman, "Introduction", xiv.

58 Taranci, "Şair Orhan Veli", 2.

59 Orhan Veli, "Önsözü", 19.

60 Although anachronistic, it is interesting to remark that in 1960 the French Surrealist group issued a leaflet, jointly signed with the movement Phases, expressing similar thoughts. See "Tir de Barrage", in: *Tracts surréalistes et déclarations collectives*, vol. 2, *1940–1969*, José Pierre, ed., Paris: Terrain vague 1982, 197–204.

The Syrian poet and intellectual Ūrkhān Muyassar (1911–1965),[61] whose preface to the 1947 poetry collection *Suryāl* (Surreal) also functioned as a de facto manifesto of Syrian surrealism, articulated a similar position in 1953: in an article for the Syrian-nationalist newspaper *al-Binā*ʾ (The Structure), Muyassar stressed the ahistorical nature of literary and artistic schools.[62] As he put it, the division of art into trends and movements, albeit relying on an artificial and ideological notion of artistic origins, stemmed from the necessity of modern art to break away from the constrictions of the past; in reality, he argued, artists converged and diverged with multiple trends, and art movements constituted an "organic convergence of interests and needs, [...] produced unconsciously within a longer history of progression".[63] The proliferation of anti-school sentiments in and out of Turkey reveals the discomfort felt by artists and poets, who functioned as critical agents of modern cultural productions in the region, when confronted by Eurocentric and teleological understandings of modernity in the process of fashioning an individual, as well as a collective, artistic identity. It is therefore necessary to situate *Garip* within its wider sociopolitical circumstances, to allow some nuance in its analysis as harbinger of modernity in Turkish poetry, outside the totalizing narrative which terms like "avant-garde" and "modernity" have imposed on it.[64]

Reconnecting with traditions: Bread and stars

Much of the scholarly reception of *Garip* has capitalized on its perceived hostility towards the past, felt to be incompatible with the imagination and formal needs of the modern poet, in order to feed into the narrative of *Garip* as the first Turkish poetic avant-garde.[65] In reality, the manifesto's inflammatory nature in the literary circles of the time stemmed from its critique of poetry in the present, which Orhan Veli found to be relying on outdated conventions. In particular, Orhan Veli deployed the titular notion of "garip", a sense of discomfort produced by the unfamiliar reminiscent of Sigmund Freud's *unheimlich*, to stand for a generative process

61 For Muyassar's pioneering role in translating surrealism into Arabic, refer to Arturo Monaco's chapter in the present volume.

62 Ūrkhān Muyassar, "Taqsīm al-fann ilā madāris... Gharīb ʿan al-fann!", *al-Binā*ʾ, 9 December 1953.

63 Muyassar, "Taqsīm al-fann", translated in Lenssen, "Shape of the Support", 206. A similar case is that of the Tehran-based Anjoman-e Honari-ye Khorus Jangi (Fighting Cock Art Society), which translated ideas of French surrealism, amongst others, without donning the surrealist label. See Fereshteh Daftari, "Redefining Modernism: Pluralist Art before the 1979 Revolution", in: *Iran Modern*, Fereshteh Daftari and Layla S. Diba, eds., exhibition catalogue, New York: Asia Society 2013, 29.

64 Ertürk, "Surrealism and Turkish Script Arts", 52–53.

65 Halman, "I Am Listening to Istanbul", 344.

that indexed a recognizable historical pattern.[66] As he put it, rather than impeding progress, the strangeness of the unknown had, at various points in the history of Ottoman poetry, elicited paradigm changes and innovation: the metric conventions themselves must have originally been "garip", allowing for experimentations in the poetry of the past before being normalized.[67] Nevertheless, they had outlived their relevance in present poetry, producing a progressive artificialization of language and promoting an increasing chasm between the language of poetry and the vernacular.[68] This positioned *Garip* within a lineage of revolutionary interventions, spearheading a new wave of poetic tradition.[69]

To satisfy their claim of a poetic revolution, the Garipists sought a dialectic engagement with Turkey's past, which they identified as a fertile reservoir of innovative and transgressive formal tools. The consequences of this process were aesthetic as well as political: acutely aware of the exclusion of the larger stratum of Turkish society from an active consumption of culture, the poets committed to an anti-elite poetic production, simultaneously descriptive and prescriptive of society. *Garip* aimed to function as a model of poetic language able to speak *of* and *for* the lower classes; the figure of Süleyman Efendi, an Everyman that Orhan Veli celebrated in his poem "Epitaph I" (1938), became the symbol of the collective consciousness of the labouring class.[70] Writing in a language as close as possible to vernacular Turkish was therefore instrumental in bridging class divisions and in effectively democratizing access to poetry.

In this, the poets were engaging with an urgent contemporary discourse around the role of language in the process of identity-building. In 1928, the Atatürk administration replaced the Ottoman script, based on Arabic and Persian letters, with the characters of the Latin alphabet.[71] The alphabet reform was not an overnight phenomenon, rather it was the result of a sustained discussion which had begun within the quarters of the Ottoman central administration in the 1860s, due to the difficulties in communication posed by the script: attempts to reduce the linguistic gap between the cultivated yet unpractical Ottoman alphabet, used by the upper strata of society, and the vernacular had been made as early as the nineteenth century, with the rise of new communication media and of mass print technologies.[72] This discourse gained force in the decades leading to the founding of the republic, despite

66 See Sigmund Freud, "The Uncanny" (trans. Alix Strachey), in: *The Standard Edition of the Complete Psychological Works of Sigmund Freud*, vol. 17, *1917–1919: An Infantile Neurosis and Other Works*, ed. James Strachey, London: Hogarth Press and Institute of Psychoanalysis 1955, 217–252.
67 Orhan Veli, "Önsözü", 12.
68 Orhan Veli, "Önsözü", 12.
69 Orhan Veli, "Önsözü", 12.
70 Orhan Veli, "Önsözü", 23.
71 Zürcher, *Turkey*, 188.
72 Ertürk, "Surrealism and Turkish Script Arts", 49–50.

opposition from conservative and religious circles.[73] Yet, while the reform aimed to reduce linguistic barriers between classes, it favoured an epistemological and ontological distancing of Turkey's present from its recent Ottoman past.[74]

The republican élan towards progress was also reflected in the poets' urban fabric: the city of Ankara, where they operated, had undergone considerable changes from the turn of the century. In 1892, during a period of technological innovations overseen by Sultan Abdülhamit II, a newly built railway connected Ankara to Istanbul.[75] The city served as political headquarters for Mustafa Kemal Atatürk (1881–1938) before and during the Turkish War of Independence (1921–1922), and Atatürk later appointed it the capital city of the Republic of Turkey in 1923.[76] In a short span of time, therefore, the city had gone from provincial outpost to governmental hub, with significant consequences on its architectural layout that matched its new ideologically loaded status as the seat of Turkey's new government and, consequently, its new collective identity.[77] Moreover, and not less importantly, Ankara replaced Istanbul, the historical seat of Ottoman government and the primary artistic and cultural hub, as the political and cultural centre of the new Turkish nation, under the auspices of Atatürk.[78] The nascent republican government was met unfavourably in the old capital by the political opposition, and Istanbul became ideologically distanced in Atatürk's first years of government as a symbol of the past.[79]

The *Garip* poets' historical and political engagement, testing the function of culture and of the individual poets as *socii* of a collective identity, influenced their choice of subject matter that would rightly express their poetic and social concerns.[80] Yet, although the poets wished to give a voice to the underrepresented labouring class, the poems in the 1941 *Garip* largely disengage from a configuration of modernity as a fast and industrial apparatus, the concrete reality for large numbers of Turkish workers at the time, or from representing the sociopolitical tensions brought about by World War II.[81] Instead, they celebrate the mundane aspects of the modern, determined by a quality of quiet introspection:

> Bread in my lap,
> Stars are far, far away.
> I eat bread looking at the stars.

---

73 Zürcher, *Turkey*, 188.
74 Erdağ Görknar, "The Novel in Turkish", in: *The Cambridge History of Turkey*, vol. 4, Reşat Kasaba, ed., Cambridge: Cambridge University Press 2008, 488.
75 Zürcher, *Turkey*, 77 and 150–152.
76 Zürcher, *Turkey*, 150–152.
77 Bozdoğan, "Art and Architecture", 430–435.
78 Akcan, "Channels", 147.
79 Zürcher, *Turkey*, 172.
80 David Kushner, "Self-Perception and Identity in Contemporary Turkey", *Journal of Contemporary History* 32 (1997), 219–220.
81 Zürcher, *Turkey*, 203–204.

I am so absorbed, don't even ask –
At times I get mixed up and instead of bread
I eat stars.[82]

In this poem, Oktay Rifat deploys the timeless, bucolic imagery of eating bread while stargazing as a moment of physical and metaphysical consumption by a subject whose individual identity is purposefully erased, heightening the sense of a feeling that is collectively shared. The language condensation, the representation of mundane subject matter and the absence of any geographical or temporal markers achieve a radical democratization of the poetic experience as a modern phenomenon – albeit one that seems to take place beyond the tangibility of the present moment.

When present, geographic specifications suggest even more directly a process of translation of the past into the fabric of the present. In a number of poems that have since become iconic in Turkish history, Orhan Veli immortalized the city of Istanbul as a privileged urban setting for the expression of *Garip*'s new poetry:

I am listening to Istanbul, intent, my eyes closed.
The Grand Bazaar's serene and cool,
An uproar at the hub of the Market,
Mosque yards are full of pigeons.
While hammers bang and clang at the docks
Spring winds bear the smell of sweat;
I am listening to Istanbul, intent, my eyes closed.[83]

Within the poem, Istanbul precipitates the reader into a synesthetic contemplation of mundane, marginalized realities which abandon the realm of rationality and enter the sphere of the poet's unconscious, as he experiences the city with his eyes closed. The urban markers in this passage are ancient referents of the city's Ottoman, Muslim identity, allowing a sense of visual permanence and of temporal continuity.[84]

The *Garip* poets were not alone in dialectically harnessing Turkey's past as a source of creativity which contained the promise of a modern, indigenous Turkish expression: the Turkish author and academic İsmail Hakkı Baltacıoğlu (1886–1978), with whom the *Garip* poets often sparred in the pages of *Yaprak*, had been involved since the 1920s in a project of memorialization and reinstatement of Turkish calligraphy, an ancient art form which employed the Ottoman script.[85]

---

82 Oktay Rifat, "Ekmek ve Yildizlar", in Orhan Veli, Anday and Rifat, *Garip*, 40.

83 Fragment from Orhan Veli, "I Am Listening to Istanbul", quoted in Halman, *I Am Listening to Istanbul*, 25. Translation by Talat Sait Halman.

84 The Turkish poet and critic Cemal Süreya (1931–1990), on the contrary, wrote poems in which the city intervenes as a fast and industrial centre where people live, work and are consumed by physical desires. See Talat Sait Halman, *A Millennium of Turkish Literature: A Concise History*, ed. Jayne L. Warner, Syracuse: Syracuse University Press 2011, 107.

85 *Yaprak* 13 (1 November 1949); "Dergiler", *Yaprak* 18 (15 January 1950); Orhan Veli Kanık, "Nasrettin Hoca ve Yeni Adam", *Yaprak* 20 (15 February 1950). See also Ertürk, "Surrealism and Turkish Script Arts", 50.

The book-long essay *Turkish Script Arts*, which he penned in 1958, combining thirty years of work on the subject, argued that the letters of the Ottoman script possessed a non-mimetic, anatomical dimension, suggestive of different expressive poses of the human body.[86] Baltacıoğlu defined the relationship between the letters and the body as one of chance encounter, setting up a genealogical argument which positioned Turkish calligraphers as ancient forerunners of modern surrealism, affording calligraphy the potential to inspire modern, indigenous productions and to imbue Turkish aesthetics with meaning beyond the merely "ornamental" and "traditional".[87] Through this project, Baltacıoğlu hoped to counter the art historical discourses which characterized all art forms from the Islamic world as abstract, determined by the eschewal of human figuration because of a religious interdiction, which was assumed to be an inherent characteristic of Islam.[88]

Much of Baltacıoğlu's reception by scholars has positioned his project in the conservative, marginal quarters of the early republic; yet, a critical confrontation alongside the ambiguities surrounding the intentions of the *Garip* poets can reposition both, as part of a wider tendency of poets and artists in Turkey to identify within an anachronistic outlook the frisson of modernity. An article aptly titled "Old and New", written by the Turkish critic and writer Sabahattin Eyüboğlu (1908–1973) who was a steady contributor in *Yaprak* and other cultural reviews in the 1940s and 1950s, reflected on the

> disagreements [that] come from an inability to easily distinguish between the old and the new [...] we are late to weed out the values that live with dead values, that can survive, and we still have those that remain behind and resist the future. There is no agreement between those of us who are openly connected to the past, and those who want to innovate.[89]

This article speaks to the desire of contemporary poets and artists, in the late 1940s, to redefine what it meant to be modern or conservative, exposing these terms as unstable and fraught and seeking, instead, a differential positionality, which challenged a teleological and unidirectional conception of chronology and notions of avant-gardism. The production of surrealist-informed poetry within the economy of *Garip*, therefore, was articulated through a seemingly paradoxical movement from modernity into tradition; surrealism was deployed and translated to reconcile the external modes of expression of the international avant-garde with an inherited history of art, with which modern Turkish artists could not fully iden-

86 İsmail Hakkı Baltacıoğlu, *Türklerde Yazı Sanatı: Türk Sanat Yazılarının Grafolojisi ve Estetiği Üzerine Sosyo-Psikolojik Deneme*, Ankara: S.A.Ş. Matbaası 1958, 25.

87 Baltacıoğlu, *Türklerde Yazı Sanatı*, 25–27. Sibel Bozdoğan, "Reading Ottoman Architecture through Modernist Lenses: Nationalist Historiography and the 'New Architecture' in the Early Republic", *Muqarnas* 24 (2007).

88 See Finbarr Barry Flood, "Picasso the Muslim: or, How the Bilderverbot Became Modern, Part I", *Res* 67/68 (2016).

89 Sabahattin Eyüboğlu, "Eski ve Yeni", *Yaprak* 8 (15 April 1949), 1.

tify.[90] This overarching strategy, operated in the 1940s, found a visual parallel in the 1950s in the production of the Turkish artist Yüksel Arslan (1933–2017), addressed in the following section.

Phallisme: *A failed collective?*

In 1959, Yüksel Arslan opened his second solo exhibition with the title *Phallisme* at the Türk-Alman Kültür Merkezi (Turkish–German Cultural Centre) in Istanbul. Despite the outwardly individualistic nature of the exhibition, as a one-man show in a private gallery, its analysis can provide some nuance to this interpretation and point to another instance of a process of historical fabrication – in this case, of the individual artist as measure of modernity. The concept of *Phallisme*, which gave the name to the exhibition, had initially been theorized by Arslan and his friend, the writer Ferit Edgü (b. 1936), in 1956, with the hope of starting an artistic movement. Edgü stated:

> I think it was 1956 when we decided to form an art movement we were to call "Phallisme". Yüksel and I believed in the virtue of rebellion, ascribing the highest value to anarchy. We were more interested in Dadaism and Surrealism than revolution in art, Expressionism, Cubism or Bauhaus. Thinkers, writers and poets that rebelled against the system attracted our attention. We saw the Marquis de Sade as the greatest destroyer of values of history [...].[91]

The rationale behind *Phallisme* encapsulated sociopolitical and moral concerns, seeking to formulate a collective strategy for transgressing the status quo that went beyond visual concerns. Dada and surrealism are listed as instrumental in the process of the collective's theoretical structure, in that they exceeded a purely aesthetic agenda. The project of the art movement as such was never actualized.[92] Nevertheless, between 1956 and 1959, Arslan produced a series of works named *Phallisme*, and even started signing himself as "Comte de Phallus", "de Phallus" or "Phallus Antique" after the Marquis de Sade, arguably turning *Phallisme* into a more individual endeavour through his self-fashioning as an artist.

The Marquis de Sade (1740–1814), whom Arslan and Edgü admired for his refusal to conform to normalized social and sexual behaviours, inspired Arslan to satisfy the *Phallisme* subversive agenda through an aesthetic of phallocentrism.[93]

90 Saleem al-Bahloly, "History Regained: A Modern Artist in Baghdad Encounters a Lost Tradition of Painting", *Muqarnas* 35 (2018), 229–230; Ertürk, "Surrealism and Turkish Script Arts", 52.

91 Ferit Edgü; see Necmi Sönmez, "Formation – Conceptualisation – Emancipation", in: *A Retrospective of Yüksel Arslan: Catalogue*, Levent Yilmaz, ed., Istanbul: Santral İstanbul 2010, 69.

92 Levent Yilmaz, "Without Following the Beaten Path", in: *A Retrospective of Yüksel Arslan: Catalogue*, Levent Yilmaz, ed., Istanbul: Santral İstanbul 2010, 19.

93 Donatien Alphonse François Marquis de Sade (1740–1814), a French aristocrat and author of several texts, had previously entered the sphere of influence of the French surrealists as an important precursor.

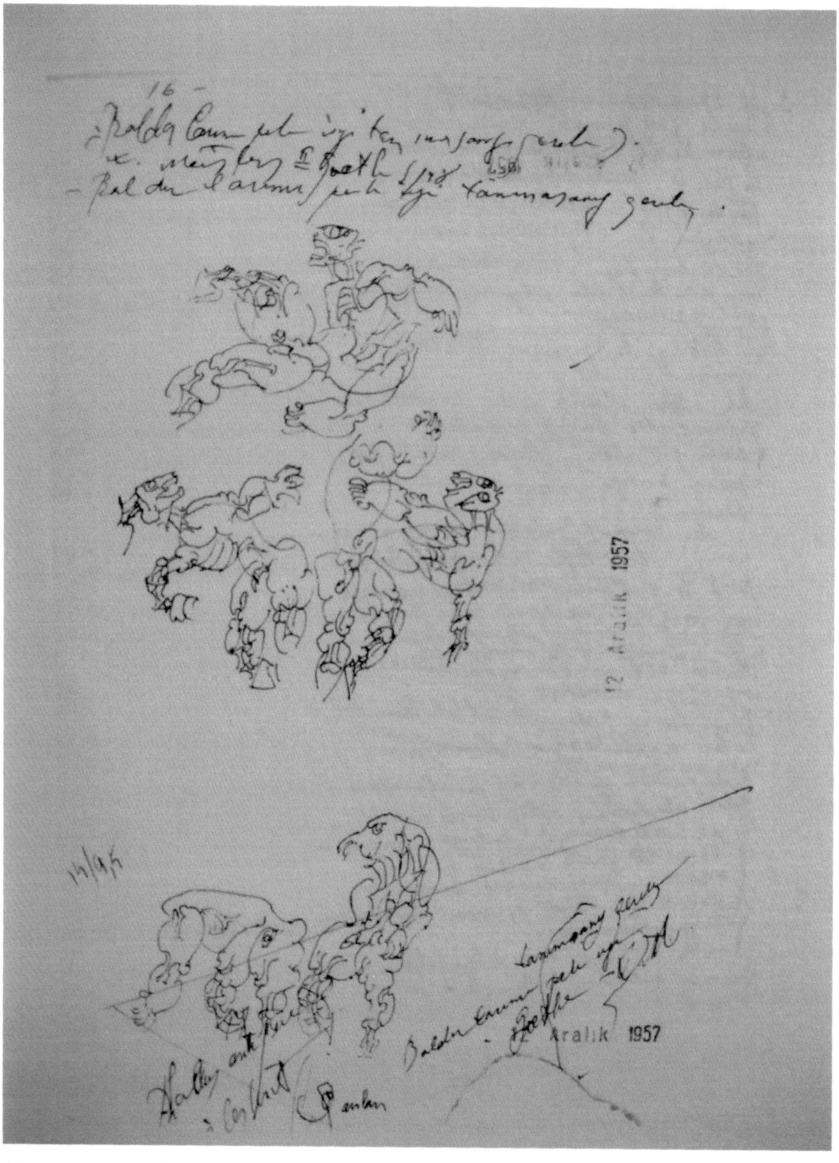

Figure 2: Letter from Yüksel Arslan to Ferit Edgü, 1957. Published in Yüksel Arslan and Ferit Edgü, *"Batı Kültürü önünde hiçbir saplantım yok", Mektuplar 1957–2008*, Istanbul: Kitap Yayınevi 2011.

The letters from Arslan to Edgü between 1956 and 1959 were often illustrated with crude sketches of gaping, barely anthropomorphic figures with scattered limbs, genderless but for recognizably human phalluses – in some instances, like the one reproduced here (fig. 2), the boundaries of sexual intercourse and violent encounter were purposefully blurred, triggering a disturbing visual experience.

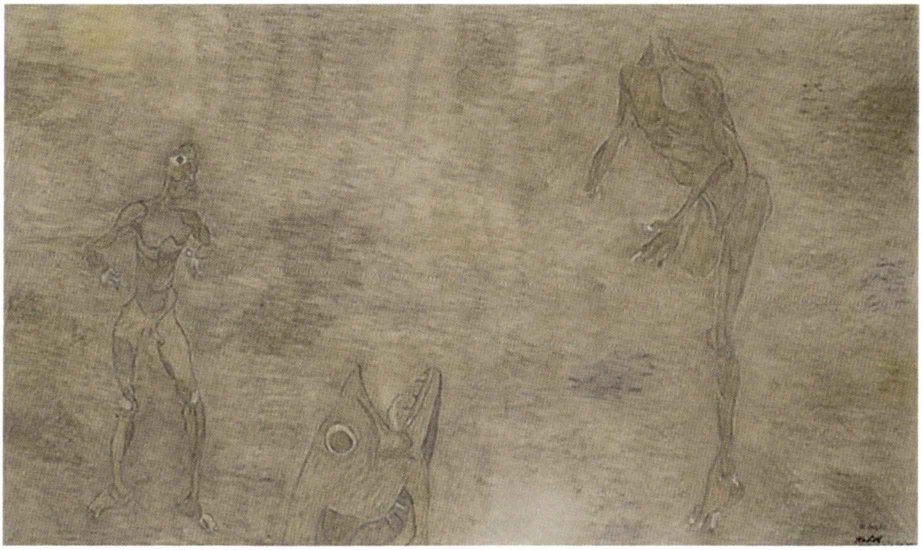

Figure 3: Yüksel Arslan, *İnsanlı Günler III*, 1955. Natural colours on paper, 44 × 76 cm. Santralistanbul Collection.

The works Arslan exhibited in 1959 witness the maturation and exacerbation of this imagery, which developed in the context of more private experimentations. For the show, Arslan selected works belonging to two different series: İnsanlı Günler (Peopled Days), which he had produced in 1955, and *Phallisme*, from the 1956–1958 period.[94] *İnsanlı Günler III* (fig. 3), executed in 1955, encapsulates some of the overarching characteristics of the works exhibited. Three figures populate the scene, detached from one another and unengaged; two are anthropomorphic, with emaciated bodies whose paper-thin skin exposes every muscle, joint and sinew. The figure on the right is headless and missing various limbs, while the one on the left appears barely whole, fragile, with one expressionless, gaping eye that mirrors the eye of the oversize fish-head that emerges, threateningly, from the bottom. The three figures communicate a sense of perpetual *non finito* as grotesque anatomical studies. There is no horizon line or vantage point to support them; the figures' floating quality is heightened by their transparency, which allow the ochre background to almost overpower them. Nevertheless, the figures are ideologically anchored in reality by their genitals, which allow us to gender them as male.

The deviancy suggested by the phallocentrism of Arslan's work proved instrumental in solidifying the artist's position in Turkish art history and historiography. Despite the near-absence of women in Arslan's works of this time, at a time in which Turkish women artists were particularly active and experimented with different strategies of self-representation, as well as the suggestion of an ahistorical, patriarchal

94 Ferit Edgü, *Arslan*, Istanbul: Ada Yayınları 1982.

rhetoric and violent sexual fantasies underlying Arslan's imagery, critics turned the phallus into a signifier of modernity and innovation.[95] Arslan was praised for producing a new style, on a par with the old masters and European avant-garde painters, which promised a paradigm change in Turkish contemporary art.[96] The *Phallisme* exhibition, which the critic Adnan Benk (1922–1998) praised as "an event of European stature", positioned Arslan at the forefront of Turkish painting and beyond, within his circle, as "the first painter of universal significance" to emerge from Turkey – a reception which blended the appreciation of artistic innovation with an agenda of collective identity-building, in dialogue with the artistic traditions of the Euro-American region.[97]

The championing of a single artist as individual harbinger of total artistic innovation on a national and international scale was partly due to Arslan's highly performative construction of his artistic persona as purposefully transgressive of established artistic, social and sexual mores, in service of which he subscribed to an individualistic rhetoric of negation, like that observed within the *Garip* foreword.[98] He professed anti-academicism by refusing to attend the Academy of Fine Arts, enrolling instead in the Art History department of Istanbul University. Additionally, Arslan rejected the category of painting and of the painter down to its material aspects, by refusing to employ artificial pigments in his practice.[99] He crafted a personal technique which involved a mixture of soil, food products, spit and even urine, which he would apply on paper before rubbing the drawing onto it with rocks and hard crayons – recalling the experimentations from this period with soil, sand and perishable elements of the Armenian-Iranian artist Marcos Grigorian (1925–2007) or the Turkish artist Bedri Rahmi Eyüboğlu (1911–1975), or indeed the French surrealist artist André Masson (1896–1987).[100] In the 1960s, having moved to Paris, Arslan coined the term *Arture*, an invented taxonomy meant to encapsulate the idiosyncrasies of his works, which allowed him a total – at least terminological – rejection of art.

---

95 Zeynep Çelik, "Speaking Back to Orientalist Discourse", in: *Orientalism's Interlocutors: Painting, Architecture, Photography*, Jill Beaulieu and Mary Roberts, eds., Durham: Duke University Press 2002, 23–25.

96 Tansuğ, *Türk Resminde*, 42–43 and 50–51.

97 Adnan Benk, "A Painter of European Stature", in: *A Retrospective of Yüksel Arslan: Catalogue*, Levent Yilmaz, ed., Istanbul: Santral İstanbul 2010, 57–58; Bozdoğan, "Reading Ottoman Architecture", 206–208.

98 Selahattin Hilâv, "Yüksel Arslan Üzerine", in: *Yüksel Arslan: İlişki, Davraniş, Sıkıntılara Övgü'den Arture'lere (1955–1970)*, Mazhar Şevket İpşiroğlu, Orhan Duru, Ferit Edgü and Selahattin Hilâv, eds., Istanbul: Yapı Kredi Yayınları 2016, 66–67.

99 Yüksel Arslan, "La Technique, ou comment on fabrique une Arture", 17 February 1981, Collection Arslan.

100 Layla S. Diba, "The Formation of Modern Iranian Art", in: *Iran Modern*, Fereshteh Daftari and Layla S. Diba, eds., exhibition catalogue, New York: Asia Society 2013, 55–56; Günsel Renda, "Modern Trends in Turkish Painting", in: *The Transformation of Turkish Culture: The Atatürk Legacy*, Günsel Renda and Max C. Kortepeter, eds., Princeton: Kingston Press 1986, 238.

Prompted by a letter from the American poet and translator Édouard Roditi (1910–1992), who recommended Arslan for his erotic subject matter and his marginal status as a "hermit" of painting, removed from all artistic movements, André Breton invited Arslan to exhibit in the 1959–1960 *EROS* surrealist exhibition (*Exposition inteRnatiOnale du Surréalisme*) at the Gallery Daniel Cordier.[101] From his letter to the exhibition secretary José Pierre, we learn that Arslan was willing yet unable to participate or send works due to governmental restrictions.[102] He then migrated to Paris in 1961 and, instead, exhibited alongside surrealist artists in 1964 at the Galerie Charpentier under direct invitation of the art critic Patrick Waldberg, who had organized the exhibition.[103] Nevertheless, throughout his career, Arslan was vocally anti-school and never agreed to be called a surrealist, claiming that his personal memories were his greatest source of influence.[104] Beyond the strictly aesthetic and artistic domain, in fact, eroticism was used by Arslan as a self-defining tool, resulting in a mythical status amongst his public which he did not refrain from fomenting.

The artist circulated personal anecdotes, claiming that they were the answer to his "obsession" with the erotic in and out of the domain of art, and these were quickly picked up by his contemporaries.[105] In his autobiographical series Autoartures, compiled in the 1980s, Arslan depicted one of these episodes, titling it *First Memory* (fig. 4). The artist recalled being mistaken for a girl at the market in his childhood because of his blond curls and exposed his penis to the crowd to re-establish his virility. In the work, the young Arslan confronts the viewer's gaze while resolutely exposing his genitals. The youthful boyishness is countered by the figure's imposing and composed presence: the boy holds his masculinity with both hands and the folds of fabric contribute to guiding our gaze towards the phallus as the centre of the composition. Resulting from this pervasive interpenetration of Arslan's personal dimensions into his artistic persona, starting from his 1959 exhibition, is a sense of failure of *Phallisme* as a collective entity of artistic transgression, and the simultaneous rise of the individual artists as a measure of modernity – an interpretation which gains some nuance from a wider historical perspective.

---

101 Édouard Roditi to André Breton, 3 September 1959, Archives of the Association Atelier André Breton. See also Yilmaz, "Without Following the Beaten Path", 24.

102 Yüksel Arslan to José Pierre, 12 November 1959, Archives of the Association Atelier André Breton. Arslan asked Breton to intercede with the French consul in Istanbul, but it is not clear why Breton did not follow through.

103 Raymond Nacentra, ed., *Le Surréalisme: Sources, histoire, affinités*, exhibition catalogue, Paris: Galerie Charpentier 1964; Esra Yıldız, "A Yüksel Arslan Biography", in: *A Retrospective of Yüksel Arslan: Catalogue*, Levent Yilmaz, ed., Istanbul: Santral İstanbul 2010, 585.

104 Yüksel Arslan, "Being a Loner is a Wonderful Thing", in: *Yüksel Arslan: Artures*, exhibition catalogue, Zurich: Hatje Cantz 2012.

105 Yüksel Arslan, "Autobiography", in: *A Retrospective of Yüksel Arslan: Catalogue*, Levent Yilmaz, ed., Istanbul: Santral İstanbul 2010, 249.

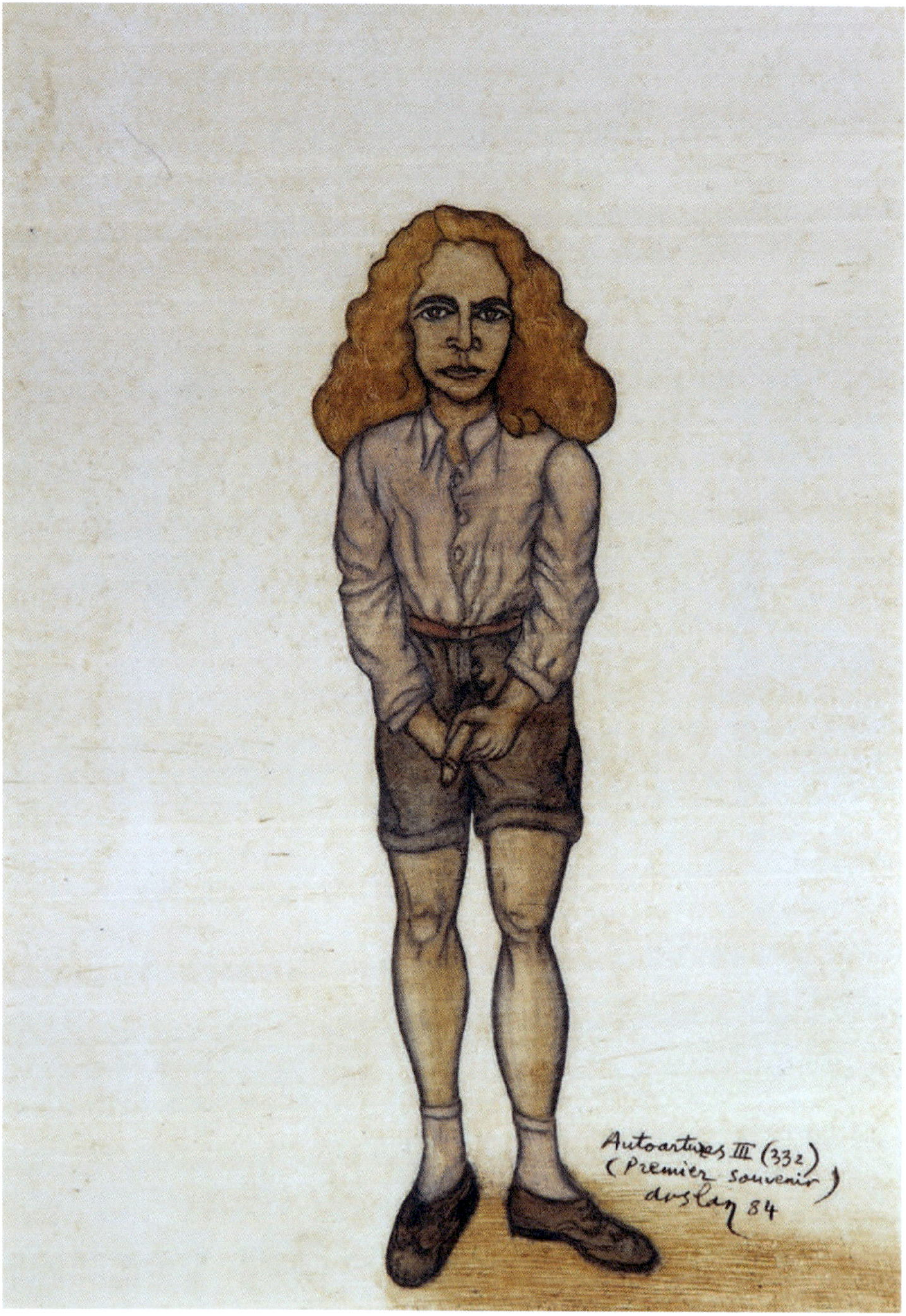

Figure 4: Yüksel Arslan, *Arture 332: Autoartures III (First Memory)*, 1984. Natural colours on paper, 24.2 × 17 cm. Private collection.

From the collective to the individual

The conflation of the individual artist with the promise of artistic innovation, in the case of Arslan, resulted in part from the artist's reaction against the past of Turkish art history. Many intellectuals and artists in the 1950s and 1960s found Turkish artistic development to have been dominated by collectives whose independence and innovative potential suffered from an excessive involvement with government-sponsored agendas.[106] The inception of this "collectivization" took place in the final decades of the Ottoman Empire – as we have seen earlier, an intense culturally metacritical moment – with the creation of the Society of Ottoman Artists around 1909, a platform for discussions around the nature and function of art.[107]

Nevertheless, the second constitutional period and the advent of the republic triggered constant reconfigurations of the discourse around art and its national role; the emergence of collectives in this period signalled the desire of artists to position themselves within these discourses. The "Impressionist School" that formed in the early 1900s, the Müstakil Ressamlar ve Heykeltraslar Birligi (Association of Independent Painters and Sculptors) of 1929 and the *d Grubu* (d Group) of 1933 are some of the collectives that most exemplify this process of ideological historical compartmentalization.[108] While these groups became accused, in retrospect, of sacrificing critical edge and artistic innovation to institutional collectivism, in fact they were all operating in continuous opposition to the previous groups – subscribing to a linear, diachronic development of history and art that recalls Orhan Veli's sequence of paradigm changes – providing a platform for artists to experiment with techniques and an array of subject matters, including eroticism.[109] The sketch from the 1930s titled *Nude* (fig. 5) by the d Group artist Zuhtu Müridoğlu (1906–1992), with its simple execution through an outline of sanguine on paper and its explicit sexual content, is but one example of an artistic precedent to Arslan's production, disrupting its primacy: the sketch depicts a close up of a reclining nude woman with spread legs, her face indiscernible and her calves and feet vanishing, offering the woman's sex and breast as the primary object of consumption for the viewer's gaze.[110]

---

[106] Nurullah Berk, *Modern Painting and Sculpture in Turkey*, [Ankara]: Turkish Press 1958, 5–6.

[107] Shaw, *Ottoman Painting*, 116–119.

[108] Berk, *Modern Painting*, 7–8; Bozdoğan, "Art and Architecture", 423–427; Zeynep Yaşa Yaman, *D Grubu 1933–1951*, Istanbul: Yapı Kredi Yayınları 2002, 12–14; Shaw, *Ottoman Painting*, 116–119.

[109] Erotica in art, in fact, had a rather long tradition in the art of the region. See Francesca Leoni and Mika Natif, eds., *Eros and Sexuality in Islamic Art*, Farnham: Ashgate 2013; and Dror Ze'evi, *Producing Desire: Changing Sexual Discourse in the Ottoman Middle East, 1500–1900*, Berkeley: University of California Press 2006.

[110] Berk, *Modern Painting*, 27.

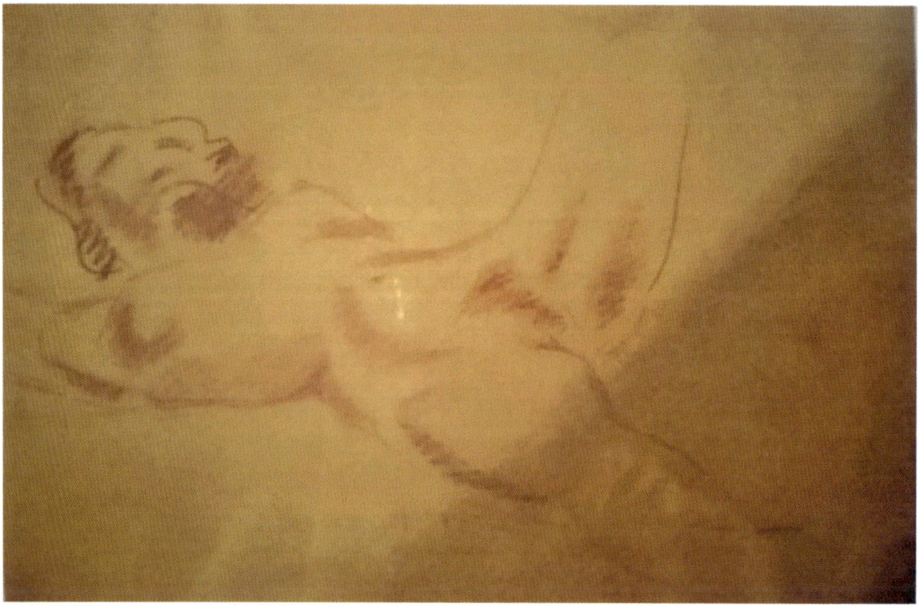

Figure 5: Zuhtu Müridoğlu, *Nude*, 1930s. Sanguine on paper, 32.5 × 50 cm. Istanbul Museum of Painting and Sculpture.

However, elements in the historical trajectory of the Turkish art world justify the greater focus on individualism in the 1950s. The general elections which took place in 1950 saw the rise to power of the Democratic Party and the defeat of the Republican People's Party, which had held the reins of government since the start of the republic.[111] The democratic government, captained by Celal Bayar (1883–1986) as president and Adnan Menderes (1899–1961) as his prime minister, implemented policies of democratization, prioritizing private enterprise and openly renouncing a centralized government hold, capitalizing on the support of the public by announcing a new era of liberalism.[112] Nevertheless, the process of liberalization or, as some would have it, Americanization, had begun after World War II, when the souring relationship with the Soviet Union pushed the government of İsmet İnönü (1884–1973) to seek support from the United States: the US political and economic support of Turkey was officialized through the Marshall Plan after 1947, creating in Turkey a pressure to conform to American policies and to loosen political restrictions.[113]

111 Zürcher, *Turkey*, 217–219.

112 Feroz Ahmad, "Politics and Political Parties in Republican Turkey", in: *The Cambridge History of Turkey*, vol. 4, Reşat Kasaba, ed., Cambridge: Cambridge University Press 2008, 226–228 and 230–235.

113 Bozdoğan, "Art and Architecture", 444.

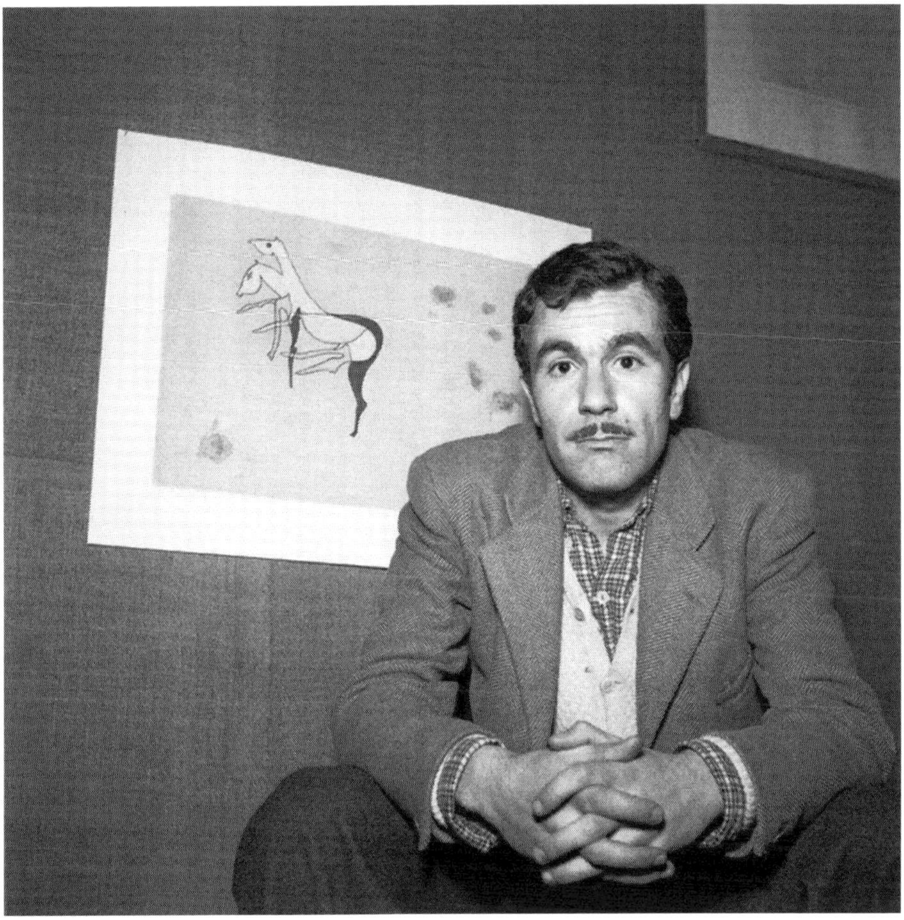

Figure 6: Yüksel Arslan at the opening of the exhibition *Homage to Relations, Gestures, Boredoms*, Maya Gallery, Istanbul. Photo: Ara Güler. Published in Levent Yilmaz, ed., *A Retrospective of Yüksel Arslan: Catalogue*, Istanbul: Santralistanbul 2010, 591.

The art market also started to gravitate towards the private sphere, shifting from state endorsement of the arts towards private sponsorship.[114] The emergence of the private gallery as an establishment had important effects on the art world of Turkey and of the Middle East for providing economic and institutional support to individual artists.[115] The popular Turkish actress and patron of the arts Adalet Cimcoz (1910–1970) opened the first private gallery in Istanbul, the Maya Gallery, in 1951 on Alyon Street in the district of Beyoğlu – Arslan held his first solo exhibition here in 1955 (fig. 6).[116]

114 Bozdoğan, "Art and Architecture", 443–445.

115 Lenssen, "Shape of the Support", 199.

116 The exhibition, named *İlişki, Davraniş, Sıkıntılara Övgü* (Homage to Relations, Behaviour, Boredom), sold out, effectively establishing Arslan's reputation. Tansuğ, *Türk Resminde*, 40.

The choice of Beyoğlu was not coincidental, as it had been an area of artistic activity and a site for exhibition spaces since the nineteenth century, providing a sense of continuity within the tissue of the city.[117] The Turkish–German Cultural Centre, where Arslan's *Phallisme* took place in 1959, was founded by the German-Swiss scholar Robert Anhegger in a privately leased space adjacent to the Maya Gallery; Anhegger's centre, which also aimed to facilitate artistic growth through privileged exchanges with German artists, quickly became a popular meeting and exhibition space.[118] Although this is by no means an exhaustive survey of these dynamics, and also does not account for the fact that many artists were active outside established institutions of the art world at this time, it allows us to see the binary distinction of collective activity and individual production as an intellectual conceit, rather than a historical reality.

Garip *and* Phallisme: *Shared experiences*

Despite the claims to individuality and independence determining the character of Arslan's *Phallisme* project, its powerful modernizing potential at the time was achieved by a systematic reliance on collective structures, both in institutional and aesthetic terms. Between 1955 and 1959, the artist effectively gathered around himself a moderate network of intellectuals who collectively aided and, somehow, curated his national and international reputation. Similarly to the *Garip* group, this process relied on print culture: Arslan benefitted from the promotion of a group of intellectuals who were involved in issuing the journal *a*, which ran for twenty-nine issues from 1956 to 1960 and supported contemporary art and poetry movements by advocating liberalism and denouncing human oppression.[119] Three contributors to the journal, the philosopher Selahattin Hilâv (1928–2005), the translator Ergin Ertem (b. 1935) and the poet Onat Kutlar (1936–1995), were also involved in the translation of French surrealist texts and published in 1962 a two-volume text titled *Gerçeküstücülük* (Surrealism): this contained translations of passages from Yvonne Duplessis's text *Le Surréalisme*, first published in Paris in 1950, as well as a letter from Breton offering his text "On Surrealism in its Living Works" (1953) in guise of a preface, with the aim of translating and reformulating surrealist concepts for the Turkish public.[120]

Arslan was also connected to the circle of scholars who gathered around the art historian Mazhar Şevket İpşiroğlu (1908–1985), professor of art history at Istanbul

---

117 Shaw, *Ottoman Painting*, 53–57.

118 Macit Gökberk, "Dr. Robert Anhegger ve İstanbul Türk-Alman Kültür Merkezi", in: *Türkische Miszellen: Robert Anhegger, Festschrift, Armağani, Mélanges*, Gudrun Schubert, ed., Istanbul: Divit Press 1987, 5.

119 Günyol, *Sanat*, 62.

120 André Breton in Selahattin Hilâv, Ergin Ertem and Onat Kutlar, eds., *Gerçeküstücülük*, Ankara: de 1962, 7. See also Eyüp Özveren's chapter in this volume.

University and Arslan's own teacher at the beginning of the 1950s; Sezer Tansuğ (1930–1998), İpşiroğlu's research assistant for a period, and Sabahattin Eyüboğlu, who contributed to the Garip journal *Yaprak* and to *a*, were both active in shaping Arslan's artistic reputation.[121] The boundaries between institutional collectivism and individuality in the theoretical formulation of *Phallisme*, therefore, appear fuzzy. Arslan's intellectual relationship with İpşiroğlu also marked the phallocentric formulation of the *Phallisme* aesthetic: as İpşiroğlu's student in the 1950s, Arslan had become familiar with the imagery of the Turkish shadow theatre, which played an instrumental role in İpşiroğlu's research as an example of collective imagery of the Turkish past.[122] Although Arslan's deployment of erotic imagery in *Phallisme* aimed to *épater les bourgeois*, so to speak, he tapped into recognizable visual codes that evoked collective, inherited artistic forms and conventions.

The shadow theatre plays, a tradition of debated origins which found its culmination within the Ottoman Empire, got their name from the translucent, two-dimensional figures held on wooden sticks which were used during the performances, held against a fabric sheet dimly lit by candle to create a shadow and light effect.[123] The plays earned their popularity from their subversive nature as weapons of political satire and brash social commentary, which did not spare the upper layers of society and provided the lower classes with chance of catharsis, a platform for a carnivalistic reversal of the status quo which enjoyed a relatively unfettered freedom from censorship, because of its nature as a temporary respite from reality.[124] The characters of Karagöz and Hacivat, the main protagonists in most plays, were crowd favourites: they embodied respectively the peasant class and the bureaucracy, creating absurd and scatological scenarios.

The plays also possessed a considerable reputation for being obscene, a quality that remained constant even when the political criticism lost its edge during the harsher censorship enforced in the 1800s: several accounts of foreign travellers reported shock and disgust at the public nature and explicit sexual content of the plays.[125] The representation of sexual encounters and the presence of phalluses on stage were formative elements for the audience, as they provided an outlet for the satisfaction of sexual repression and for education around the notion of deviant and normative sexual mores.[126] The character of Karagöz was portrayed in older

121 Tansuğ, *Türk Resminde*, 31–50. Mazhar Şevket İpşiroğlu, "Önsöz", in: *Yüksel Arslan: İlişki, Davranış, Sıkıntılara Övgü'den Arture'lere (1955–1970)*, Mazhar Şevket İpşiroğlu, Orhan Duru, Ferit Edgü and Selahattin Hilâv, eds., Istanbul: Yapı Kredi Yayınları 2016, 10.

122 A specific case is İpşiroğlu's analysis of the shadow theatre in his research on the Siyah Qalam albums; see Mazhar Şevket İpşiroğlu, *Siyah Qalem*, Graz: Akademische Druck- u. Verlagsanstalt 1976, 10–12.

123 Ze'evi, *Producing Desire*, 125.

124 Metin And, *Karagöz: Turkish Shadow Theatre*, Istanbul: Dost Yayınları 1975, 67–68.

125 And, *Karagöz*, 69. See also Andreas Tietze, *The Turkish Shadow Theatre and the Puppet Collection of the L.A. Mayer Memorial Foundation*, Berlin: Mann 1977, 19–20.

126 Ze'evi, *Producing Desire*, 127, 139 and 142.

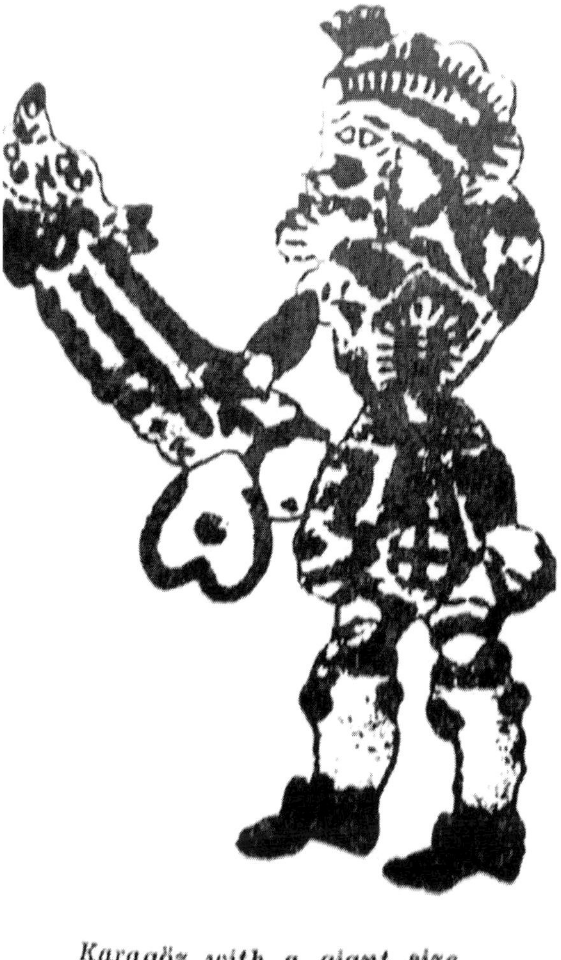
Karagöz with a giant size phallus (From the Viennese collection.)

Figure 7: Karagöz sporting a phallus. Published in Metin And, *Karagöz: Turkish Shadow Theatre*, Istanbul: Dost Yayınları 1975.

puppets sporting a giant phallus (fig. 7), replaced in more recent times by a movable arm. The plays were performed in collective spaces, speaking to and of society as a collective; every play was set in the *mahalle*, a generic local neighbourhood, which provided a familiar fabric of social interactions, and they took place during public festivals and in the coffeehouses.[127] Because of their power in moulding public discussions, the characters of Karagöz and Hacıvat were employed by

[127] Sabri Esat Siyavuşgil, *Karagöz*, Istanbul: Milli Eğitim Basımevi 1951, 8.

newspapers during the early years of the republican era in the form of satirical illustrations, co-opted as unofficial mouthpieces of the ideologies of the Republican People's Party.[128]

Arslan knew the plays intimately, both through their consumption as live or televised performances and through exhaustive reading.[129] The flat two-dimensionality and stuck-in-profile nature of the shadow theatre puppets extensively pervaded the aesthetics of the works in the 1959 *Phallisme* exhibition – as critics were quick to recognize and point out.[130]

In *Phallisme I* from 1958 (fig. 8), Arslan reproduced the puppet's perforations, which allowed them to appear colourful when hit by candlelight onto the screen: the figures on the foreground are rendered with an almost "pointillistic" method which, set against the ochre backdrop, imbues them with a similar quality of transparency. Although the bodies seem to merge in the erotic encounter, they do not overlap, instead they are stacked one on top of the other, maintaining permanent visibility in relation to the viewer. Arslan stripped these puppets of their narrative functionality and their critical edge by exacerbating their obscene, hypersexual and phallocentric qualities to fit his idiosyncratic aesthetic ambitions. Nevertheless, they are still recognizable as pertaining to the same collective imagery and, therefore, perform similar prescriptive functions and allow a similar shared visual experience, blurring the boundaries between normative and deviant and between collective and individual production.

Conclusion

In unpacking significant aspects behind the 1941 *Garip* poetry collection and Yüksel Arslan's 1959 *Phallisme* exhibition, the aim of this chapter has been to make some conceptual room for Turkish surrealist iterations in the study of surrealism as an international phenomenon. Through the methodological crutch of translation as a fairer and more realistic tool for the analysis of international and interregional movements of culture determined by a plurality of agents, this analysis has brought to the fore two elements that *Garip* and *Phallisme* shared as translations of surrealism in their divergence from fixed notions of surrealist orthodoxy, which we can perhaps understand as "differential" surrealisms. Firstly, a non-binary approach to collective and individual productions, which recalls a statement made by André Masson in 1938, defining surrealism as "the collective

[128] Yasemin Gencer, "Pushing Out Islam: Cartoons of the Reform Period in Turkey (1923–1928)", in: *Visual Culture in the Modern Middle East: Rhetoric of the Image*, Christiane Gruber and Sune Haugbolle, eds., Bloomington: Indiana University Press 2013, 189–190.

[129] Tietze, *Turkish Shadow Theatre*, 22.

[130] Hilâv, "Yüksel Arslan Üzerine", 66. This seems to have applied to foreigners as well: Levent Yilmaz, "Without Following the Beaten Path", 14, recounts that when French writer Jean Paulhan first saw Arslan's works in 1961, he said "Karagöz, I see ...".

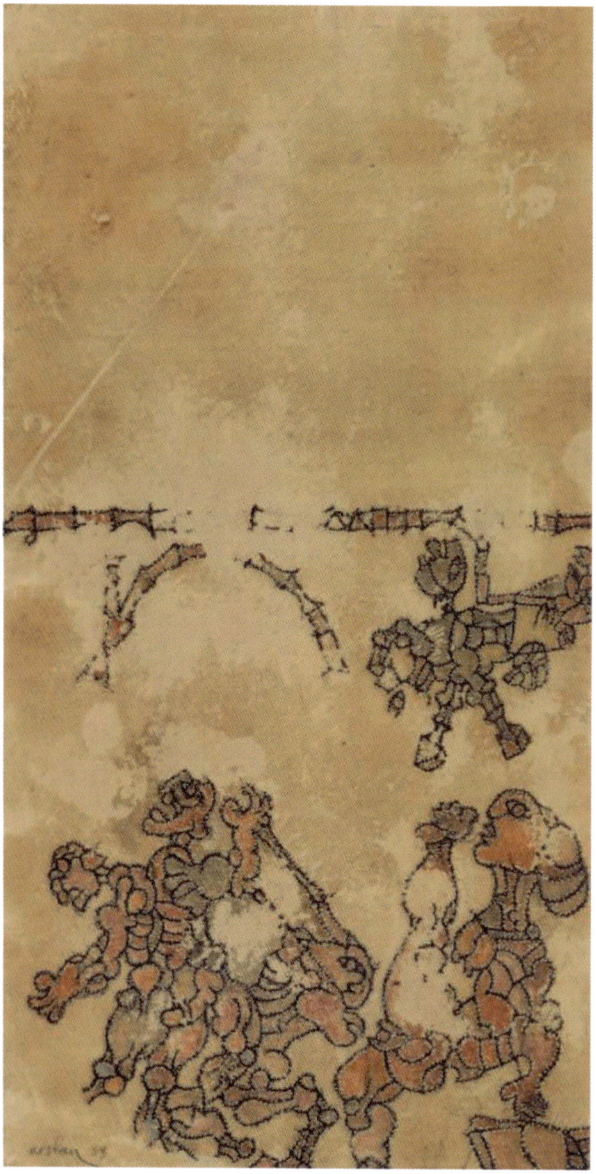

Figure 8: Yüksel Arslan, *Phallisme I*, 1958. Natural colours on paper, 31.5 × 16.5 cm. Sencer Divitçioglu Collection.

experience of individualism".[131] The imbrication of *Garip* and *Phallisme* with both individual production and collective historical and social narratives reveals just how much the distinction between the two is often due to later processes of historiographical fabrications and ideological compartmentalizations within art history. Secondly, it was suggested that *Garip* and *Phallisme* sought modernity not by

131 Robert S. Short, "The Politics of Surrealism, 1920–1936", *Journal of Contemporary History* 1 (1966), 21.

subscribing to a linear, teleological understanding of historical development, but rather by looking past and recasting inherited visual and poetic codes in the present as containing the promise of change. These two elements have constituted what was offered as a "differential" nature of Turkish surrealism as determined by a substantive diversity dictated by historical specificities.[132] This framework allows for an ontological reformulation of what it means to trace an inclusive network of international surrealist production as necessarily determined by divergence and fragmentation. This analysis is by no means an exhaustive survey of Turkish surrealism; rather, it offers an alternative approach to provide more breadth for considering these poetic and artistic productions in a manner that starts to break down some of the ideological barriers between European modernism and Turkish modernity.[133]

---

132 Shaw, *Ottoman Painting*, 1.
133 Ertürk, "Surrealism and Turkish Script Arts", 57.

Chapter 4
Ūrkhān Muyassar's pioneering role in translating surrealism into Arabic

Arturo Monaco

Surrealism was introduced into Syria in the 1940s and, surprisingly, it had no apparent link with either the Parisian centre or the contemporary surrealist experiences elsewhere in the Arab world (Egypt, Lebanon). However, the arrival of surrealism in Syria would seem unexpected only if we maintain an image of a narrow-minded country, not as open to foreign influences as other countries in the same period, such as Egypt and Lebanon.[1] In fact, a brief consideration of the context will contribute to explaining the reasons behind the appearance of surrealism in Syria, approximately a decade after Egypt.

The cultural context prior to the introduction of surrealism into Syria

First of all, we need to realize that the starting point of the Syrian surrealist adventure was the city of Aleppo, which had a remarkable and long cultural tradition, dating back to Islamic and pre-Islamic antiquity. It was a flourishing commercial pole, at least until the opening of the Suez Canal, and during the seventeenth century, the first printing press with Arabic type was brought there, leading to the development of the local press in the following centuries.[2] In addition to the cultural vitality of Aleppo, Syria had also strong links with Turkey, to which it belonged politically until the fall of the Ottoman Empire, and above all with Lebanon, which was the second main centre of the Arab cultural renaissance and the port where new ideas coming from Europe landed. Its political and cultural proximity to the land of the cedars allowed Syria to become familiar with the innovations coming from the West. However, Syria also established direct links with foreign cultures. Even before the mandate, French religious and secular missions spread the French language and culture in the country, and this process was intensified under colonial rule.[3] This led to the formation of a cultural elite able to access foreign knowledge.

1 For the situation in Egypt and Lebanon in this period, see Cléa Daridan's and Julia Drost's contributions in this volume.

2 Khalīl al-Mūsā, "Khamsat udabāʾ muʾassisūn min Ḥalab al-Shahbāʾ", *al-Maʿrifah* 508 (2006), 204–205.

3 Two examples are the Collège Saint-Vincent, in Damascus from 1787, and the Mission laïque française. See Jérôme Bocquet, "Francophonie et langue arabe dans la Syrie sous

In this context, the first, timid poetic experimentations were realized, despite the absolute dominance of the neoclassical school led by Muḥammad Kurd ʿAlī (1876–1953) throughout the first decades of the twentieth century. The Syrian surrealist adventure should be read in the frame of these experimentations, which were usually made possible thanks to the efforts of groups of intellectuals or illuminated individuals. The latter was the case of Ūrkhān Muyassar (1911?–1965), a polished, curious and eclectic intellectual from Aleppo who was unquestionably the introducer of surrealism not only into Syria but also to Arabic readers more generally.[4] Muyassar was a free thinker, and did not introduce a mere copy of French surrealism. On the contrary, he elaborated his personal version of it, even challenging André Breton's view in some respects. In order to speak about the origins of Syrian surrealism, then, specific attention must be given to this figure, and he will be the focus of this contribution. After giving a brief biographical sketch, we will engage with an analysis of his reception of Breton's surrealism, through both his critical writings and poetry.

The life of a "prince" between political and cultural engagement

When the critic Khālidah Saʿīd met Ūrkhān Muyassar for the first time, she described him in the following way:

> He looked strange to me. With time, I would find out the level of strangeness and his uniqueness. His face displayed a mix of Caucasian, Balkan and Turkish features that met with the Arabness of some of his ancestors. I saw him behaving like a prince, even if there was no princedom nor inheritance. What was left of his huge richness [...] was a few pieces of Ottoman furniture, a precious library, a polished taste, and a deep kindness towards his well-read, distinguished and elegant wife [...].[5]

As a matter of fact, Muyassar had noble and multinational origins. It is reported that among his ancestors were janissaries, the body of professional infantrymen of the Ottoman Empire. The grand vizier's daughter was an ancestor, while another was the Sultan ʿAbd al-Ḥamīd's concubine. From the seventeenth century, the family had acquired the lands of the village of al-Bāb, close to Aleppo, thanks to its commercial activities. At the end of the nineteenth century, some distinguished

---

mandat: L'Exemple de l'enseignement missionnaire à Damas", and Randi Deguilhem, "Impérialisme, colonisation intellectuelle et politique culturelle de la Mission laïque française en Syrie sous mandate", both in: *The British and French Mandates in Comparative Perspectives/Les Mandats français et anglais dans une perspective comparative*, Nadine Méouchy and Peter Sluglett, eds., Leiden: Brill 2004.

4 The majority of the output of Jūrj Ḥunayn (Georges Henein, 1914–1973) and his Egyptian surrealist comrades was in French, with very limited production in Arabic.

5 Khālidah Saʿīd, *Yūtūbiyā al-madīnah al-muthaqqafah*, Beirut: Dār al-Sāqī 2012, 249. Here and elsewhere, all translations from Arabic are mine.

members of the family took a position against Ottoman rule, which was later translated into an opposition to the French mandate.

Muyassar was born in Istanbul between 1911 and 1914,[6] and he remained there until 1918, when he moved to Aleppo with his family. After his elementary studies, he went to Lebanon and studied at *al-Jāmiʿah al-waṭaniyyah* (National University) in Aley.[7] Later, he began studying medicine at the American University of Beirut, but left it for literature and physics. After graduating, he travelled to the University of Chicago to obtain a master's degree with a thesis on the relation between the endocrine glands and human behaviour. Following his father's death, he returned to Aleppo to look after his properties and joined the nationalist movement that was building in the country, at that time both against the French presence in Syria and for the rights of the Arabs in Palestine.[8] Muyassar was politically active even after independence and drew the attention of his contemporaries to delicate issues the country was about to face in the near future. He was close to Anṭūn Saʿādah's (1904–1949) Syrian Social Nationalist Party, which led to his arrest at the beginning of the 1960s.[9]

Muyassar's engagement was not limited to politics. The critic Saʿad Ṣāʾib reports that Muyassar began writing both poetry and prose very early, while he was in Aley in 1929. His knowledge of many languages, including Arabic, English, French and Turkish, coupled with an ability to read quickly and a good memory, contributed to enriching his own cultural outlook.[10] His poetics was largely influenced by both Mahjar (Arab American) and English poets; among the latter, T.S. Eliot (1888–1965) and Rupert Brooke (1887–1915) were particularly important. As regards his philosophical and political education, his models were Arab intellectuals, such as Yaʿqūb Ṣarrūf (1852–1927), Ismāʿīl Maẓhar (1891–1962) and Fuʾād Ṣarrūf (1900?–1985), along with the German philosopher Ludwig Buchner (1824–1899), Charles Darwin (1809–1882) and Sigmund Freud (1856–1939).[11] However, Salāmah Mūsā (1887–1958) and his teacher in Aley, Mārūn ʿAbbūd (1886–1962),

6 Some discrepancies exist around Muyassar's date of birth: 1911, according to Salma Khadra Jayyusi; 1912, according to Khālidah Saʿīd and ʿAbd al-Qādir ʿAyyāsh; and 1914, according to Saʿad Ṣāʾib and Khalīl al-Mūsā. Sources agree on the place of birth, the only exception being Khālidah Saʿīd, who locates Muyassar's birthplace in Aleppo. See Salma Khadra Jayyusi, *Trends and Movements in Modern Arabic Poetry*, Leiden: Brill 1977, 513; Saʿīd, *Yūtūbiyā*, 250; ʿAbd al-Qādir ʿAyyāsh, *Muʿjam al-muʾallifīn al-sūriyyīn fī l-qarn al-ʿishrīn*, Damascus: Dār al-Fikr 1985, 507; Saʿad Ṣāʾib, "Ūrkhān Muyassar: Adīb wa nāqid", *al-Maʿrifah* 160 (June 1975), 174; al-Mūsā, "al-Shahbāʾ", 213.

7 Ṣāʾib, "Muyassar", 174.

8 Ṣāʾib, "Muyassar", 174–175.

9 Adūnīs, *al-Naṣṣ al-qurʾānī wa-āfāq al-kitābah*, Beirut: Dār al-Ādāb 2010, 172; Saʿīd, *Yūtūbiyā*, 258. The Syrian Social Nationalist Party was founded in 1932 by the Lebanese Anṭūn Saʿādah and pursued the establishment of a Greater Syria, which included Syria, Lebanon, Palestine, Transjordan, the Sinai, Iraq and Cyprus.

10 Ulfat al-Idlibī, "Ūrkhān Muyassar: Lamḥah min ḥayātihi al-khāṣṣah", *al-Maʿrifah* 160 (1975), 168.

11 Ṣāʾib, "Muyassar", 175.

turned out to be the most influential intellectuals in shaping both his critical thought and his style, which was generally fluid, ordered and concise in his essays, while enjoying complete and creative freedom in his poetry.

This rich background is reflected in the works of Muyassar that I have been able to collect: the poetry collection *Suryāl* (1947), written with his fellow poet ʿAlī al-Nāṣir (1890–1970), and a number of essays published in magazines of his time, including *al-Ḥadīth* (Conversation)[12] and *al-Maʿrifah* (Knowledge).[13] A selection of these essays was published after his death in a volume entitled *Maʿa qawāfil al-fikr* (With the Caravans of Thought, 1975).[14] We know of other works of his, and these are probably still present in libraries in Syria.[15] These works include an essay entitled "Shawqī wa ʿaṣruhu" (Shawqī and His Age), a number of translations and, interestingly, a volume devoted to surrealist art, poetry and criticism, a project he undertook together with his brother ʿAdnān (1921–1979) and ʿAlī al-Nāṣir but that apparently never came out.[16]

The present contribution will not deal with Muyassar's essays on politics, philosophy and literature in general, which still give very useful insights into his personality. In this regard, it is enough to point to the fact that these essays display a considerable interest in psychology, and Muyassar read most of the phenomena around him through that lens. This applies to the essays concerned with contemporary politics, such as those on Syrian independence or the notion of *coup d'état*, as much as to his writings dealing with philosophy, such as those revolving around existentialism and the reasons that inspired its champions. As for his literary criticism, he resorted to an analogic method, as Muyassar himself stated during an interview with Saʿad Ṣāʾib.[17] This consisted in the evaluation of local literary products in relation to high-level world literature.

However, the main focus of this contribution will be Muyassar's understanding of surrealism. How was it introduced into Syria? How did Muyassar shape his

12 Founded in January 1927 by Sāmī al-Kayyālī, Admūn Rabbāṭ and ʿUmar ʿAddās, with the first as editor-in-chief, it was a monthly magazine concerned with literature, history and society. It adopted a moderate position in the *querelle* between the supporters of tradition and modernity, drawing criticism from both sides. Many intellectuals contributed to it, including Ṭāhā Ḥusayn, Muḥammad Ḥusayn Haykal, Ibrāhīm Nājī and Tawfīq al-Ḥakīm. It was printed in Aleppo and published regularly for thirty-three years until the last issue of January 1959. See Suhayl al-Malādhī, *al-Ṭibāʿah wa-l-ṣaḥāfah fī Ḥalab*, Damascus: Dār Yaʿrab li-l-Dirāsāt 1996, 136–139.

13 Among the most important Syrian magazines, *al-Maʿrifah* was founded in 1962 with the support of Fuʾād al-ʿĀdil, the Minister of Culture and National Orientation, and is still published. Following the direction of the ministry, it aims to promote any cultural expression linked to the Arab world and Arabism, with a particular concern for literature. See Jūsif Ilyās, *Taṭawwur al-ṣaḥāfah al-sūriyyah fī miʾat ʿām (1865–1965)*, Beirut: Dār al-Niḍāl 1983, 419–422.

14 Ūrkhān Muyassar, *Maʿa qawāfil al-fikr*, Damascus: Ittiḥād al-kuttāb al-ʿarab 1974.

15 Due to the current situation in Syria, I was not able to collect them.

16 "Al-Faqīd al-adīb al-shāʿir Ūrkhān Muyassar", *al-Adīb* 9 (1965), 61.

17 Ṣāʾib, "Muyassar", 175–177.

surrealism? How did he translate theory into poetic practice? And to what degree was he an influence on his own and the following generation of poets?

The gradual introduction of surrealism: The magazines al-Ḥadīth *and* al-Qīthārah *and the poetry collection* Suryāl

The first reference to a Syrian work vaguely connected to surrealism dates back to 1933, when the symbolist poet and writer Mamdūḥ Ḥaqqī (1910–2002) published a short story in the magazine *al-Ḥadīth*. The author imagines a trip into his unconscious as it appears in a dream. He is gradually deprived of his body and lifted up to an imaginary afterlife where he meets a number of Arab and non-Arab poets. All of them enjoy the beauty and prosperity of that paradise. They are perpetually young and devoid of any imperfection and, surprisingly, even the blind poet Abū al-ʿAlāʾ al-Maʿarrī (973–1057) can see.[18] In 1936, again in *al-Ḥadīth*, the critic Sāmī al-Kayyālī reported a conversation he had with a francophone friend. What is interesting in the dialogue is the tight connection between literature, dream and unconscious. As al-Kayyālī wrote, "since the unconscious is the source of true poetry, when I weave the threads of my psyche in what are called poems, I try to go back to that first source, the unconscious, to that quiet unconsciousness, more precisely, to that new world, the world of dreams".[19]

These two examples provide evidence of some elements that will be the core of surrealism, but they still do not clearly refer to them. It is reasonable to assume that during the decade between the appearance of these two texts and the publishing in 1947 of *Suryāl* (whose introduction represents the first explanation of surrealism in Syria), these new ideas were discussed, elaborated and presented in oral or written form. However, I have not found any significant document in this respect, except for an unsigned note in the magazine *al-Qīthārah* (The Lyre),[20] where we learn of an introductory lecture on surrealism given by Ūrkhān Muyassar in

18 Mamdūḥ Ḥaqqī, "Yatakallamu min warāʾ al-qabr" (He speaks from the afterlife), *al-Ḥadīth* (July 1933), 548 and 562–567.

19 Sāmī al-Kayyālī, "Arāʾ fī l-shiʿr, al-waḥdah fī l-qaṣīdah, adab al-fikrah, al-adab wa-l-aḥlām", *al-Ḥadīth* (September 1936), 686.

20 *Al-Qīthārah* was a poetic avant-gardist magazine, very similar in its scope to the Egyptian *Majallat Abūllū* (1932–1934), by which it was clearly inspired. It was founded in Latakia in June 1946 by a group of intellectuals led by Kamāl Fawzī al-Sharābī (1923–2009) and twelve issues were published, with the last appearing in August 1947. The editorial board was made up of the members of an unidentified group called *Jamāʿat al-shiʿr al-jadīd* (Group of the New Poetry). Saʿīd ʿAql, Yūsuf al-Khāl, Badīʿ Ḥaqqī, Nizār Qabbānī, ʿUmar Abū Rīshah, ʿAlī Aḥmad Saʿīd and Mīshīl Ṭrād are just some of the outstanding poets who contributed to the magazine. For a presentation of *al-Qīthārah*, see Arturo Monaco, "The Beginning of the New Age in Syro-Lebanese Poetry: The Case of the Revue *al-Qīṯārah* (The Lyre, 1946–47)", in: *Qamariyyāt: Oltre ogni frontiera tra letteratura e traduzione; Studi in onore di Isabella Camera d'Afflitto*, Maria Avino, Ada Barbaro and Monica Ruocco, eds., Rome: Istituto per l'Oriente C.A. Nallino 2019, 391-405.

Aleppo in March 1947. As reported in the note, the lecture was widely appreciated and an American intellectual who listened to Muyassar – whose name is not reported – asked him to publish the lecture in an American magazine. The brief note was followed by two poems by Muyassar and ʿAlī al-Nāṣir, excerpted from *Suryāl*.[21] Of particular interest is that the author of the note introduces the main surrealist principles with the words "it is widely known", which suggests that the Syrian intellectual elite of that time, or at least the magazine's readership, was already familiar with surrealism. We might argue that the readership's knowledge of French and English, or the wide circulation in Syria of Egyptian magazines that had published articles on the topic (*al-Risālah* above all), meant that this Syrian intellectual elite had already been introduced to surrealism by one means or another. Nonetheless, the lack of documentation that could prove this makes any further speculation unfounded.

We do not know if the poetry collection *Suryāl* was published before or after this lecture that was given by Muyassar; what is certain is that it was in the same year. Therefore, 1947 can be considered as the official beginning of the surrealist experience in Syria.

Suryāl was elaborated in the culturally sophisticated atmosphere of Muyassar's house, which was a gathering-place for the main intellectuals of the time.[22] The first edition (1947) included an introduction, a dedication to ego, fifty-four untitled poems – thirty-four by ʿAlī al-Nāṣir and twenty by Muyassar – and an afterword.[23] The introduction and the afterword were written by Muyassar and can be read as one single essay on surrealism. After an essential history of the movement, Muyassar proposed an original interpretation of the genesis of the surrealist work of art, with some significant differences compared with the Bretonian view, as we shall see. In 1979, the *Ittiḥād al-kuttāb al-ʿarab* (Union of Arab Writers) in Damascus published a second edition of the collection. It no longer contains the poems by al-Nāṣir, but instead includes new poems by Muyassar introduced by a preface written by the poet Adūnīs (Adonis, alias of ʿAlī Aḥmad Saʿīd Isbir, b. 1930).[24]

Muyassar was able to add new reflections on surrealism in other publications, especially in the magazine *al-Ḥadīth*. In January 1948, he published an article with the title "Bīkāssū ʿabqarī l-qarn al-ʿishrīn" (Picasso, the twentieth-century genius). While describing the complexity of Picasso's art, he opened a new window on surrealism, its origins, its links with Dada, its artistic principles and its concept of

21 Ūrkhān Muyassar, "Anti… fī ruʾāī" (You… in my vision), *al-Qīthārah* 10 (1947), 22, and ʿAlī al-Nāṣir, "Shaṭra… al-ʿadam al-khāliq" (Towards… the nothing-creator), *al-Qīthārah* 10 (1947), 23.

22 Saʿīd, *Yūtūbiyā*, 251.

23 ʿAlī al-Nāṣir and Ūrkhān Muyassar, *Suryāl*, Aleppo: Maṭbaʿat al-salām 1947.

24 Ūrkhān Muyassar, *Suryāl wa-qaṣāʾid ukhrā*, Damascus: Ittiḥad al-kuttāb al-ʿarab 1979. This new edition includes both unpublished poems and a number of poems that appeared in the magazine *Mawāqif* after Muyassar's death: Ūrkhān Muyassar, "Baʿd al-mawt" (Post mortem), *Mawāqif* 32 (1978).

the world.[25] In January 1949, another article investigated the relation between surrealism and cinema, and the interaction of the latter with painting and poetry.[26] In 1950, Muyassar published what appears as the first part of an essay concerning the dream – he engaged with this topic ten years after an essay in Arabic on the same subject written by Georges Henein was published in the magazine *al-Taṭawwur* (Evolution).[27] Muyassar's essay describes the evolution of the concept of the dream, starting from the imagination of the first humans, passing through Greek and Latin philosophy, to arrive at the modern René Descartes, Arthur Schopenhauer, John Locke, Gottfried Wilhelm Leibniz, Immanuel Kant and Thomas Hobbes. Sigmund Freud appears only in the conclusion, as the one who put an end to metaphysical interpretations of the dream and provided the first scientific basis for the study of the human psyche. Unfortunately, there is no evidence in the succeeding issues of the magazine of the existence of the following parts of the study announced by the concluding statement "*li-l-baḥth baqiyyah*" (the research continues).[28]

To conclude this overview of the most significant documents related to surrealism in Syria in this period, it is worth mentioning two translations of poems by Paul Éluard that appeared between 1956 and 1958 in *al-Ḥadīth*: "al-ʿĀshiqah" (The Lover, original title "L'amoureuse"), translated by Kāmil Zuhayrī; and "al-Ḥurriyah" (Freedom, original title "Liberté"), whose translator is not mentioned.[29]

Features of Muyassar's surrealism: Para-surrealism

How did Muyassar conceive surrealism? To answer this question, I will start from his conception of the way humans behave. As he explains in the introduction to *Suryāl*, a person thinks, works and succeeds during his/her lifetime, accumulating the outcome of these activities in the huge cave of his/her unconscious. He/she keeps on in this way, convinced that he/she is pursuing his/her own goals and desires. In fact, he/she is playing his/her biological role in order to fulfil his/her ego. Everything is a "stuffed body" at its service. As soon as the person realizes this, he/she stands confused and shocked in front of this mechanism. He/she needs to say something. He/she speaks: "And there [is] art."[30]

Having explained the birth of art, Muyassar identifies four main artistic schools of modernity: realism (*al-wāqiʿiyyah*), symbolism (*al-ramziyyah*), expressionism (*al-taʿbīriyyah*) and surrealism (*mā warāʾ al-wāqiʿiyyah*). The first three schools engage

---

25 Ūrkhān Muyassar, "Bīkāssū ʿabqarī l-qarn al-ʿishrīn", *al-Ḥadīth* (January 1948).
26 Ūrkhān Muyassar, "al-Suryāliyyah taghzū Hūlīwūd", *al-Ḥadīth* (January 1949).
27 Jūrj Ḥunayn, "Min al-ḥulm ilā l-mizāḥ al-aswad", *al-Taṭawwur* 3 (1940).
28 Ūrkhān Muyassar, "al-Aḥlām wa-l-shakhṣiyyah", *al-Ḥadīth* (January 1950), 21–24, 93–94.
29 Paul Éluard, "al-ʿĀshiqah", *al-Ḥadīth* (May 1958), 342; Paul Éluard, "al-Ḥurriyah", *al-Ḥadīth* (January 1956), 8.
30 Muyassar, *Suryāl wa-qaṣāʾid ukhrā*, 14.

in different ways with logical connections in the creation of works of art. But surrealism is something different and barely fits the concept of artistic school. Muyassar recalls the origins of the movement, the first attempts to free art from rationalism, Dada's provocations, the growing need of the artist to go beyond the tangible world and disclose the unconscious. Hence, the surrealist adventure starts, aiming to discover the unexplored regions of human psyche and connect them with the outer world in a harmonic unity. Here lies Muyassar's basic concept of surrealism, which is very close to the "point de l'esprit"[31] described by Breton. In his view, surrealism is "the image painted by the unconscious through its own language, which represents its individual reality, in a mix with the yearning of the generations that live in itself [the unconscious]".[32]

To understand how this image is formed, Muyassar explains the functioning of the human psyche according to psychoanalysis. Human beings, he writes, are moved by their instincts (*al-gharāʾiz*), whose aim is self-preservation. When not satisfied, these instincts apparently disappear, only leaving a trace, to fall into the depths of our minds, the so-called unconscious (*al-ʿaql al-bāṭin*), described by Muyassar as a large reservoir. The unconscious sometimes pushes amnestic traces toward the level of consciousness so that the individual can record it. This is pure surrealism.[33]

This explanation reveals Muyassar's personal interpretation of surrealism. Certainly, it owes much to Breton's definition of surrealism as the "automatisme psychique pur par lequel on se propose d'exprimer, soit verbalement, soit par écrit, soit de tout autre manière, le fonctionnement réel de la pensée".[34] However, the very concept of this pure surrealism displays a fundamental difference in the two of them. In Breton's view, surrealism is the "pensée parlée",[35] "le nouveau mode d'expression pure";[36] it is the spoken or the written word which is expressed without the control of reason. For Muyassar, on the other hand, surrealism is not the expression, nor the product of the artist's action, whether this is conscious or not. In his opinion, surrealism is the step before the expression being the image produced "automatically" by the artist's unconscious. From their side, artists cannot but observe the images and record their traces, but never their wholeness. This interpretation implies that it is impossible to create a pure surrealist work of art. In fact, images from the unconscious do not last long. In order to record one, individuals must use the traces that are still present within them; then, they need

31 André Breton, "Second manifeste du surréalisme (1930)", in: *Manifestes du surréalisme*, Paris: Gallimard 1981, 76.

32 Muyassar, *Suryāl wa-qaṣāʾid ukhrā*, 18.

33 Muyassar, *Suryāl wa-qaṣāʾid ukhrā*, 18.

34 André Breton, "Manifeste du surréalisme (1924)", in: *Manifestes du surréalisme*, Paris: Gallimard 1981, 37.

35 Breton, "Manifeste (1924)", 34.

36 Breton, "Manifeste (1924)", 36.

to create new lines and forms in order to translate the impressions evoked by the image. The outcome is something that lies between surrealism and symbolism, since a residual activity of reason is present, though surrealism is dominant, as the image originally derives from the unconscious. This is what Muyassar defines as "para-surrealism" or "*shibh suryāliyyah*".[37]

This surrealist process forms surrealist images that are pushed to the level of consciousness of the artist, who in turn shapes para-surrealist works of art. This is the essence of surrealist artistic creation for Muyassar. Accordingly, all the experiments conducted by the different representatives of surrealism in the world are para-surrealist, and so are the poems included in the collection *Suryāl*. Muyassar goes further when he maintains that Breton's surrealist production – where the intervention of rational elements and lines is unquestionable – does not greatly differ from Homer's, Shakespeare's, Byron's or Verlaine's poetry, nor from Arabic poetry since the time of the *Jāhiliyyah*. In fact, the most remarkable difference between Breton's and Aḥmad Shawqī's (1868–1932) poetry can be reduced to the condensation of the former in opposition to the verbosity of the latter.[38]

This assertion gives rise to some doubts about the way in which it should be interpreted. Is Muyassar questioning Breton's adherence to surrealism? Or does he consider that Shawqī and the other names he quotes are surrealist poets? None of these questions are applicable, since Muyassar cites Breton's leadership of surrealism in other sources, such as the article on Picasso for instance. At the same time, there is no indication that Muyassar expands the concept of surrealism (or para-surrealism) to include different means of poetic creation not strictly connected to it. Rather, we may suppose that Muyassar conceives of one single source for poetry whose content is expressed through different processes.

Nevertheless, a polemical attitude towards a certain interpretation of surrealism, not necessarily the Bretonian one, is confirmed in the aforementioned article on Picasso. Here, Muyassar argues that some artists are mistaken in their application of surrealist principles. According to them, surrealism means recording the

37 Muyassar, *Suryāl wa-qaṣā'id ukhrā*, 19–20. Elsewhere, Muyassar translates the same phenomenon as "pseudo-surrealistic"; see Muyassar, "Bīkāssū", 36. We should remember here that Breton himself was aware of the interferences that could intervene in the surrealist mode of expression, and he does express this concern in his manifesto, even if he blames external factors for it and not the modes of expression themselves, as Muyassar does: "Je crois de plus en plus à l'infaillibilité de ma pensée par rapport à moi-même, et c'est trop juste. Toutefois, dans cette *écriture de la pensée*, où l'on est à la merci de la première distraction extérieure, il peut se produire des 'bouillons'. On serait sans excuse de chercher à les dissimuler. Par définition, la pensée est forte, et incapable de se prendre en faute. C'est sur le compte des suggestions qui lui viennent du dehors qu'il faut mettre ces faiblesses évidentes". Breton, "Manifeste (1924)", 35.

38 Muyassar, *Suryāl wa-qaṣā'id ukhrā*, 21. Most of the poets mentioned here are not quoted by Breton in his works. Here, Muyassar seems to follow Breton's same logic in tracing back surrealism in the authors of the past, but with reference to para-surrealism and including Arab poets.

psyche's reactions to external agents, borrowing the vocabulary from the unconscious. As seen before, Muyassar has a different perspective: surrealism is not the record of the image, but the image itself. The critics Salma Khadra Jayyusi and Muḥammad Jamāl Bārūt see in Muyassar's attitude an inclination in favour of extreme automatism.[39] However, Muyassar's writings seem to say the opposite. Jayyusi quotes Henri Peyre to support her opinion:

> The Surrealists did not advocate bringing to the light of clear consciousness, and dissipating eventually, the strange growths of complexes in our turbid depths. Much was made, in the early stages of Surrealism, of automatic writing, uncontrolled by reason or by critical spirit, which gave itself out as spoken and written thought seized in its spontaneous immediacy. In fact, the leading Surrealists never abused that perilous device. Their verse and their prose give evidence of elaborate composition, of skilful combination of effects, of a restrained choice made among the riches of the unconscious. But their originality lay precisely in having first proceeded to a courageous clearing of all that was worn out and effete in literature, and in having them made a fresh selection from a new and vast accumulation of materials hitherto unexplored.[40]

This quotation highlights two main aspects: the refusal of the uncontrolled use of automatism; and the intervention of rationality in the selection of the poetic subject coming from the unconscious. The use of rational elements and lines to create a work of art is required by Muyassar's para-surrealism. In addition, he repeatedly claims that not just anything coming from the unconscious embodies a potential work of art. From among all the images coming from the unconscious, the artist should select those surrealist images that obey the definition he provides, that is an image where you can see

> [...] a world whose horizons expand and whose caves deepen. A world where the philosophical outcome of reasoning descends after a hard, scientific study. A world where the kinds of human experience descend, and the abstract fusion of time, agony and pleasure too. And where everything merges with the eternal yearning that links us to the earth, and with the rebellion of the instinct, beyond any limit of age and time. The unconscious adopts this melted matter and creates bonds while refining and polishing it. Then it pushes it in a series of stories that tremble like shadows in front of the individuals in the cradle and the tomb and in front of the man in the cave, in the field, in the laboratory and in the skyscrapers.[41]

Therefore, the surrealist image is artistically valid only if it becomes a way of knowing what occurs in the individual, as well as in the collective unconscious. In Muyassar's opinion, a rational process is highly necessary to select this image. This contradicts Jayyusi's assumption about his propensity to extreme automatism.

39 Jayyusi, *Trends*, 515; Muḥammad Jamāl Bārūt, *al-Shiʿr yaktubu smahu: Dirāsah fī l-qaṣīdah al-nathriyyah fī Sūriyyah*, Damascus: Ittiḥād al-kuttāb al-ʿarab 1981, 12.

40 Henri Peyre, "The Significance of Surrealism", *Yale French Studies* 2 (1948), 42.

41 Muyassar, *Suryāl wa-qaṣāʾid ukhrā*, 20–21. Distinguishing individuals from humanity, Muyassar clearly refers to the fact that the surrealist image from the unconscious has an effect at the level of both the life of an individual (from the cradle to the tomb) and humanity (from the age of the cave to the age of skyscrapers).

Muyassar's conception of surrealism is original and innovative in some aspects, such as the concept of para-surrealism and the stress on the memory of collective experience expressed by the unconscious, together with the individual one. At the same time, it owes much to Breton in the interpretation of automatism and the concept of the unity of contradictions. Furthermore, it is undeniable that the same moral impetus animates the activity of surrealists as well as Muyassar in the relentless search for truth.

Muyassar's surrealist poetry

Muyassar's theorization of surrealism finds its best application in the collection *Suryāl*.[42] The poems in the collection provide evidence of the shift from the romantic trend that was predominant in the Syrian poetry of the first half of the twentieth century to the new surrealist techniques.[43] Moreover, the poems mark a new phase in the liberation of Arabic poetry from traditional prosody. Composed entirely in free verse (*al-shiʿr al-manthūr*) – at least in the 1947 edition – they can be included among the experiments that anticipated both the new successful versification based on the free distribution of the foot (the so-called *shiʿr al- tafʿīlah*) and the later explorers of the Arabic prose poem (*qaṣīdat al-nathr*).[44]

The matter of this poetry is the obscure world of the unconscious, imbued with ambiguities, paradoxes, hallucinations, obsessions and repressions. As the poet and critic Adonis points out, for the first time in modern Arabic poetry a poet tries to enter, explore and express what is in this world through non-prosodic versification.[45] The ego is the core of each poem and, not by chance, a dedication to it introduces the collection:

إلى	To
هذه "الأنا" النهمة التي لا ترى،	this insatiable "ego" which does not see,
والتي دأبها إبداع مسوخ تقدمها	used to invent monsters he offers
لهيكلها المليء بالمسوخ..	to its altar full of monsters...

42 As mentioned above, ʿAlī al-Nāṣir also contributed his poems to that collection, but in this paper, I will deal only with Muyassar's production, published both in the first edition of *Suryāl* (1947) and in the later one, *Suryāl wa-qaṣāʾid ukhrā* (1979). The study of this enlarged corpus gives us the chance to touch on more aspects of Muyassar's poetics, although it disregards any consideration of undoubted developments that occurred over time. For an overview of al-Nāṣir's production, see Arturo Monaco, "Ispirazione romantica e sperimentalismo surrealista in due raccolte poetiche del siriano ʿAlī al-Nāṣir (1890–1970): *al-Ẓamāʾ* (1931) e *Suryāl* (1947)", *La Rivista di Arablit* 12 (2016).

43 Al-Mūsā, "al-Shahbāʾ", 214. For an overview of the poetic movement in Syria in the first half of the twentieth century, see Jayyusi, *Trends*, 204–242.

44 Saʿīd, *Yūtūbiyā*, 253; ʿAbd Allāh al-Samṭī, "Tajārib awwaliyyah fī qaṣīdat al-nathr al-ʿarabiyyah", *Nizwā*, 1 May 2011. For further information about the role of the collection in the development of the *qaṣīdat al-nathr* in Syria, see Bārūt, *al-Shiʿr*, 7–50.

45 Adūnīs, *al-Naṣṣ*, 172–173.

لترقد بعد ذلك لحظة هنيئة	To rest thereafter for a pleasant instant
فيها استمتاع وفيها اطمئنان؛	in which there is enjoyment and in which there is reassurance;
تستجمع بينهما قواها،	between them he collects his strengths,
لتخلق مسوخا جديدة أخرى.[46]	to create new other monsters.

The goal of each poem in the collection is to give voice to those monsters from the unconscious, through automatism and, chiefly, by resorting to dreams. Automatism is extensively used in the collection, and this fragment is an example:

نفق.	Galleries.
جدران كالنهاية.	Walls as the end.
أفواه؛	Mouths;
حلقات تلتهمها حلقات،	rings swallowed by rings,
يد حلقةٍ	the collar of a ring
تتقلص وتتقلص وتتقلص.[47]	contracts and contracts and contracts.

Yet, resorting to dreams offers the most interesting examples. In Muyassar's poems, the dream embodies a series of positive characteristics, opposed to the tangible reality: dream is freedom, lines, colours, sensations, emotions and sounds. Dream is an instant to be caught before the awakening of time, as Muyassar says in the following poem:

ارقصي أيتها الشعلة،	Dance, candle,
وليعجّ فضاؤك بالأخيلة المرتعشة.	and be your space crowded with trembling spectres.
إن الزمان، اللحظة، في غفوة	The time, the instant, is sleeping
ارقصي.. ارقصي..	dance... dance...
ارقصي قبل أن تهزأ يقظة الزمان	dance before that the awakening of time makes fun
من حلمك الهزيل.[48]	of your miserable dreams.

Indeed, the dreams in the poems are crowded with spectres and monsters, but also dancers and women. The atmosphere is mysterious, illogical, occasionally repulsive and frightful. The spectre of consciousness, or the superego, hovers over it, disturbing the pleasant visions of the poet:

ولاح فوق الحفرة التي ترقد في جوفها ذاتي	And on the ditch where my ego rested
صبايا يرقصنا في حلقات لا حصر لها..	young dancers appeared in countless rings...
وكان يشق هذه الحلقات	And the rings were broken
صفوف من عجائز جلسن يصفقن في حماسة ولذة؛	by rows of old ladies who sat and applauded with enthusiasm and pleasure;
صفوف لا نهاية لها..	infinite rows...
وعملت يدايَ،	while my hands were at work,

46 Al-Nāṣir and Muyassar, *Suryāl*, n.p.
47 Al-Nāṣir and Muyassar, *Suryāl*, 54.
48 Al-Nāṣir and Muyassar, *Suryāl*, 52.

يداي المحمومتان دون كلل..	feverish, indefatigable...
كانت الحفرة ذاتها!	It was the same ditch!
إلا أنها بدت أعمقَ مما صنعته يداي قبل	Yet deeper than what I dug generations ago.
أجيال	And the breaths were the same!
وكانت الأنفاس ذاتها!	The breaths of the debris that the torrents
أنفاس الرواسب التي خلّفتها سيول	of days left behind in the primordial matter.
الأيام بين هيولى التراب.	There... at the edge of the ditch
هناك.. هناك في زاوية الحفرة،	there was:
كان:	a monster, many limbs, anchored
مسخ ذو أطراف عديدة شدت كلها إلى	at the sides of the ditch through transparent
جوانب الحفرة بشرايين شفافة	arteries
يسيب فيها سائل غريب اللون	a strange coloured liquid flowed in it
يغلي،	boiling;
تتصاعد من فوهة في رأس المسخ	Toxic gases
أبخرة مسكرة.[49]	poured out from a crater in the monster's head.

Rarely are the images from the dream mere descriptions. Rather, they hide deep reflections where bitterness mixes with optimism in portraying the complexity of reality. For instance, this is the case for a poem in which Muyassar plays with the double meaning (literal and metaphorical) of the word "puppet" and reflects on the sad position of the man-puppet in real life.[50]

This constant connection between the products of the unconscious and the outer world responds to Muyassar's definition of surrealism. Likewise, it seems to respond also to Breton's call in his second manifesto when he condemns those who "se satisfirent généralement de laisser courir la plume sur le papier sans observer le moins du monde ce qui se passait alors en eux" (were generally content to let their pens run rampant over the paper without making the least effort to observe what was going on inside themselves).[51] Muyassar aims to investigate that world, to contribute to its knowledge through an endless search for truth that looks inside and outside, to the past, the present and the future of the human existence. Consequently, we can recognize a series of issues and themes that are the primary concern of the poet's reflections: rebellion and freedom, patriotism, the woman, the solution of opposites, God, relationships with other artists.

The instinct of rebellion and freedom is diffusely present in the collection. It can arise in the "uprising" (*intifāḍah*) of the eye of an infant in the cradle, trying to open up to a new dawn, or in the rebellion of a painting against the limits of its creator, as in these lines:

49 Al-Nāṣir and Muyassar, *Suryāl*, 59–60.

50 Muyassar, *Suryāl wa-qaṣāʾid ukhrā*, 64.

51 Breton, "Second manifeste (1930)", 116; English translation: André Breton, *Manifestoes of Surrealism*, trans. Richard Seaver and Helen R. Lane, Ann Arbor: University of Michigan Press 1969, 158.

قافلة،
لا ألوان ولا حدود؛
قافلة تنتفض للمسات الخالق.
الخالق، اللوحة، ألوان
غفوة..
القافلة تجتاز اللوحة
الريشة تستيقظ
لا ألوان ولا حدود.[52]

A caravan,
not colours nor borders,
a caravan uprising at the creator's touch.
The creator, the painting, colours
rest...
The caravan crosses the painting
the brush awakes
not colours nor borders.

Inebriety is often the starting point of the rebellion. Like a lost shadow "who stumbles / in the middle of a mist of petrified dew... with frozen feet / firmly on the ground",[53] the poet sees at the bottom of his glass syncretic visions of his existence, in which inexhaustible images of the past, the present and the future merge in an endless, dreamy mix:

هنا، في قعر كأسي رؤى لا تنضب.
رؤى يحيلها فراغ الكأس، أحيانا، إلى
مآتم شفافة تولول فيها غصات من
زمن مبتور، وتعربد حولها بقايا
صلوات مجت التحنط والالتصاق
بجدران هياكل دأب لبناتها التثاؤب.
غير أن الأنفاس الشاردة التي تطوف
في فراغ كأسي تطوافاً محموماً، تذيب
أمسي الذي كنته، وغدي الذي أحياه،
ويومي الذي ما زال يتسكع في الظلمة
بقدم واحدة وبنص عين،
تذيب هذا الكل في صيغوغة من
جمال ينضح بألف لون ولون، فأصبح
كأني والقعر والأمس والغد واليوم،
رشقة سادرة لحلم لا يعرف الفجر،
وليقظة لا تفقه اليقظة![54]

Here, inexhaustible visions at the bottom of my glass.
Visions at times transformed by the emptiness of the glass into transparent funerals where the mourning of a broken time moans and the rests of prayers riot refusing embalming and being hung at the walls of temples which bricks are used to yawn.
And yet the breaths that wander in the emptiness of my glass
blend the yesterday I was, the tomorrow I will live,
and the today that still gropes in the dark one-footed and half-eyed,
blend this all in a mixture of beauty that emanates one thousand and one colours, as if the bottom of the glass, the yesterday, the tomorrow, the today and myself were a misplaced flash of a dream that doesn't know the dawn, and of a wakefulness that doesn't realize the wakefulness.

These visions can restore a life that has been petrified by the gaze of the conscience-Medusa, as we read in another poem, which is representative of Muyassar's intolerance to any constraining moral or political rule, as much as of his patriotism.[55] In this kind of poetry, the poet expresses his deep love for his

52 Al-Nāṣir and Muyassar, *Suryāl*, 64.

53 Al-Nāṣir and Muyassar, *Suryāl*, 53.

54 Muyassar, *Suryāl wa-qaṣāʾid ukhrā*, 53. This poem was published for the first time in *al-Adīb* with the title *Kaʾs* (Glass). Ūrkhān Muyassar, "Kaʾs", *al-Adīb* 12 (1959), 4.

55 Al-Nāṣir and Muyassar, *Suryāl*, 56. I attempted an interpretation of this poem during the eleventh EURAMAL conference in Madrid (2014). See Arturo Monaco, "Syria and the Reception of Surrealism: *Suryāl* 1947 vs. Radio Sūriyālī (SouriaLi) 2012", in: *New Geographies:*

country, which is taking its first steps after independence. He envisages a brilliant future, which sadly fails soon after with the fall of the democratic system. This very delusion probably inspired the following lines, which tell of the love for a country that he longs for, but that is still unborn:

بلادي يا أسطورة تجترها أسطورة	My country, oh myth which turns over a myth
يا أزرة يعانق أنفاسك النرجس	oh cedar which breaths embrace the narcissus and the
والريحان	basil
بلا لون ولا رائحة،	with no colour nor smell,
يا قمة تطأ القمم، يا قمة بلا قمة،	oh peak which towers over the peaks, oh peak without
بلادي يا روعة الوجود	peak,
يا عطرها الممزوج بشهقة دم،	my country, oh marvel of the existence
بشريحة جلد، بولولة أرملة، بزفير دن،	oh scent mixed with the fragrance of blood,
بحلم بنفسجة،	with slices of skin, with a widow's grievance, with the
برتابة العقارب في ساعة لا تفقه	exhalation of a barrel, / with the dream of violet,
الزمن،	with the monotony of clock hands that ignore time,
يا عطرها المستحم في ذوب القمح	oh scent bathing in a field of wheat
يا عارها،	oh shame,
لا عار،	not shame,
بلادي،	my country,
إنها لم تولد بعد[56].	it has not been born yet.

When delusion threatens the poet's spirit, the woman emerges as the one that can rescue him. In Muyassar's poems, the woman is in close connection with nature, she is romantically identified with it, transcending its physical elements in surreal images. In addition, the woman is also the connection with the inner world, with the dream and the unconscious. The poet finds peace in the union with her after they become one single being where their dreams and visions merge together, as in this poem that Muyassar dedicated to his wife Fikriyyah:

إلى زوجتي وهي مريضة	To my ill wife
أعانقك وكأنك ظلال لأنغام شفافة	I hug you as if you were the shadows of
تنطلق من فم الفجر لتنسكب في مسامع	diaphanous melodies
الغروب،	released by the dawn's mouth to pour in the
حيث الأحلام التي تفجر ذاتها	sunset's ears,
مع رقصة كل نغمة	where the dreams which blow up
لتنطلق سمفونياً	with the dance of each melody
ترتد إلينا رؤاها	and release a symphony
مداً وجزراً،	convey visions to us,

Texts and Contexts in Modern Arabic Literature, Roger Allen, Gonzalo Fernández Parrilla, Francisco Rodríguez Sierra and Tetz Rooke, eds., Madrid: Universidad Autónoma de Madrid 2018.

56 Muyassar, *Suryāl wa-qaṣāʾid ukhrā*, 68.

وكأنها ظلالك	ebb and flow,
وكأني كونك الذي يضم.[57]	as if they were your shadows
	and as if I were your universe who is embracing.

The union between man and woman is a key issue in most surrealist poetry, which considers love as a solution to the existing contradictions in life. The search for the Bretonian "point suprême",[58] where these contradictions could find a solution, is the ultimate goal of surrealism, and *Suryāl* also displays some attempts in this direction. The following example is quite illuminating in this respect, as much as it is representative of the ambiguity that permeates most of Muyassar's poetry in the collection:

حدباء	A hunchback:
في فقرتها العابسة	in her frowning spinal column
عين من زجاج.	there is an eye of glass.
الأم:	The mother:
مأتم صامت.	a silent funeral.
فينوس	Venus:
في برقعها النابت من جسدها الحار،	in the veil which grows from her passionate body,
عين من زجاج.	there is an eye of glass.
الأم:	The mother:
مأتم صامت.[59]	a silent funeral.

In other contexts, different time levels are the opposed poles that merge. However, the entirety of human existence is made of contradictions and only through facing and overcoming them is life possible. As Muyassar asserts in a poem, he would rather refuse life if he did not bring about the solution of these contradictions in the world.[60]

This is possible, because in Muyassar's view, humans are the creators of the world, and are therefore capable of connecting the creatures of the outer and the inner world. This leads us to some considerations about the poet's conception of God and religion. The anticlerical and antireligious stand of the French surrealists is known. As far as Arabic surrealism is concerned, this aspect was not at the core of the poets' and intellectuals' preoccupations, at least until the 1960s. In general, we observe a polemic stand against any reactionary force, and this includes religious institutions, but not against religion itself. However, Muyassar provides remarkable examples that differ from this trend. As a matter of fact, it is very common to find in his poetry the attribution of divine powers to humans,

57 Muyassar, *Suryāl wa-qaṣā'id ukhrā*, 87.

58 Michel Carrouges, *André Breton et les données fondamentales du surréalisme*, Paris: Gallimard 1950, 22.

59 Al-Nāṣir and Muyassar, *Suryāl*, 63.

60 Muyassar, *Suryāl wa-qaṣā'id ukhrā*, 108.

especially when it comes to the act of creation. The following poem displays an original way of dealing with the subject. Turning upside down the traditional image of the man-creature who rebels against the god-creator, Muyassar portraits the sense of confusion of a man-creator facing the rebellion of a god-creature who tries to overpower him:

هذا الإله الذي فغر فاه منذ أن خلقناه	This God who spread out his mouth since we
وجعلناه	created and put him
في السماء الوهمية،	in the illusory sky,
ليته ظل مطبقاً شفتيه	if only his lips had remained stitched
فاتحاً قلبه وذراعيه	opening his heart and arms
ليضم أولئك الذين خلقوه	to embrace those who created him
وجعلوا منه أسطورة أبدية	and made an eternal myth out of him
ليت ظله مكث دون أن تتخلله ألوان	if only his shadow had stopped before being
وليت خطوطه بقيت دون أن يحسها	coloured.
انسياب	If only his lines had remained before starting their
وليت لفظته استمرت دون أن تقضمها	flow
أشداق	If only his word had stayed before being nibbled at
قضمتها من قبل أشداق	by mouths already nibbled by mouths
إلا أنه تمرد على خالقه	He revolted against his creator though
وأراده أن يكون مخلوقا	and he wanted him to be the creature
وضاع الانسان ما بين خلقين	and thus the man got lost between two creations
خلقه للإله	his own creation of God
وخلق الإله له.	and God's creation of man.
إلا أن المصير واحد لكليهما،	The fate is one for both though,
للخالق والمخلوق.	for the creator and the creature.
إنهما يسيران معا	They walk together
نحو الانصهار في كيان ما زلنا نجهله.[61]	toward the fusion into a being which is still
	ignored.

It is worth observing also how Muyassar paints the image of Christ. In the period when he was working on these poems, he was one of the recurrent figures of what was called Tammuzian poetry, because, like the god Tammuz, Christ was one of the myths of suffering and resurrection to which some poets resorted to express their desire for the rebirth of their countries.[62] In one of his poems, Muyassar displays a very different attitude, which one might rather consider blasphemous. The poet compares himself to the crucified Christ, but his cross is not the symbol

61 Muyassar, *Suryāl wa-qaṣāʾid ukhrā*, 49.

62 On the Tammuzian poets, their use of the myth of Tammuz and its association with Christ, see Jayyusi, *Trends*, 724–740. The poem "al-Masīḥ baʿd al-ṣalb" (Christ after the crucifixion) by Badr Shākir al-Sayyāb is a notable example of the Tammuzian use of the figure of Christ. See Badr Shākir al-Sayyāb, *Poesie*, trans. P. Minganti, Rome: Istituto per l'Oriente 1968, 41–49.

of suffering and resurrection but of alcoholism and inebriation. Muyassar's cross leads to life, a life that flows from the juice of the grapevine, intoxicating like the dreams it generates:

كلانا مصلوبان	We both are crucified
أنا والمسيح	Christ and I
هو مصلوب على خشب	he is crucified on wood
وأنا مصلوب على الكحول	and I am crucified on alcohol
أما الفرق أنه مات بعد الصلب	the difference is that he died after the crucifixion
أما أنا فقد حييت بعد الصلب	while I lived after the crucifixion
شبعت من الكروم أنفاسي	I pleased with vineyards my breaths
فما زالت تنفث الأحلام	which keep spitting out the dreams
التي كانت تراود جذور الكرمة	that were enthralling the roots of the vineyard
منذ أن وجدت.[63]	since they existed.

In concluding this exposition of Muyassar's poetry in *Suryāl*, it is worth pointing out the fact that he dedicated a number of poems to a series of notable figures from the world of arts and music, including Max Ernst, Salvador Dalí, Louis Guglielmi and Vincent Van Gogh, as well as the Egyptian singer Umm Kulthūm.

Conclusion

In 1965, Ūrkhān Muyassar died after more than a year of fighting against lung cancer. A life spent for the sake of literature and his country was over, and very few would remember this fascinating personality. His was the first vigorous attempt at translating surrealism into Arabic – it is true that Georges Henein and his group of Egyptian surrealists tried to do the same almost ten years before him, but their results were limited to the field of art and to a couple of magazines which they edited (chiefly *al-Taṭawwur* and *al-Majallah al-jadīdah*). Muyassar not only translated surrealism into Arabic and spread it through various different means, but he also elaborated a personal version of it based on his knowledge and anchored to his environment. And even if he did not establish an official surrealist group in Syria, he gathered around him a relatively large number of intellectuals who were affected by his ideas in one way or another.

As Saʿad Ṣāʾib asserts, it was not only a person who passed away with the death of Muyassar, but also "an atmosphere of thought that we still wanted to enjoy".[64] This cultural atmosphere held sway in Muyassar's houses in Aleppo and Damascus, which were the meeting-places for anyone who desired to learn something new. Ulfat al-Idlibī reports that from 5 pm, the house was open to the public, and the meetings continued on until after midnight. Conversation

---

63 Muyassar, *Suryāl wa-qaṣāʾid ukhrā*, 89.
64 Ṣāʾib, "Muyassar", 181.

revolved around the contemporary trends in art and poetry, and freedom of speech and debate was the golden rule. Unfortunately, nothing of the content of these meetings was recorded. Otherwise, they would have testified not only to the significance of this cultural salon, but also to the thought of the majority of the Syrian educated class of that time.[65]

However, Muyassar had a significant impact on those who were fascinated by his personality. These include the closest members of his family – his wife Fikriyyah al-Ṭarābīshī and his brother ʿAdnān – but also many poets, writers and artists. ʿAlī al-Nāṣir, ʿUmar Abū Rīshah (1910–1990), Fātiḥ al-Mudarris (1922–1999), Ulfat al-Idlibī and a young Adonis with his wife Khālidah Saʿīd were all regular visitors to his houses in Aleppo and Damascus. A detailed study of these and other intellectuals and of the cultural network among them would show the true extent of the influence of Muyassar's ideas on his own as well as on the following generation.

65 Al-Idlibī, "Muyassar", 166.

Part II:
Surrealist encounters

Chapter 5
They entered art from the kitchen door – Being twenty in Beirut in the 1930s

Jad Tabet

J'entrai à mon insu chez l'art
Par la porte de la cuisine
Beaucoup rirent de ce hasard
Comme d'un chapeau envolé.

Georges Schehadé, "Anthologie"[1]

This is the story of five young men during the French mandate era in Beirut and their encounter with the literary and artistic avant-garde.[2] This forgotten story is part of the radical cultural, political and social upheavals that affected the region during the first half of the twentieth century, from the fall of the Ottoman Empire until the rise of national movements during the 1950s.

Everything started in a garden in the Ghouta plain outside Damascus, an oasis formed by the Barada river that separates the city from the dry grasslands bordering the Syrian desert. Four brave young men travelled regularly once a month from Beirut to Damascus by train to visit their friend Nehmé Eddé, whose family had settled in the Syrian capital several years before. These five young men had met in the secondary school of the Frères des écoles chrétiennes in Beirut and had become inseparable friends. They were Antoine Tabet (1907–1964), my father, who was studying engineering and dreamt of painting and architecture, Georges Schehadé (1905?–1989) and Antoine Mourani (1907–1967), who were both studying law but dreaming of poetry, Alexandre Abouchaar (1905–?), who wanted to become a painter, and Nehmé Eddé (1902–1992), the oldest of the friends, who was finishing his law studies and whose family was living in Damascus. Five young men who entered the field of art "from the kitchen door" ("par la porte de la cuisine") as Georges Schehadé wrote in one of his first poems.[3]

1 Georges Schehadé, "Anthologie", in: *L'Écolier sultan*, Paris: Gallimard 1973, 36.
2 This is not an academic paper. It is rather an introduction to a story that I have been trying to reconstruct for several years, more as a dilettante than as a serious researcher, trying to fill the gaps of the archival material through the memories of family and friends. The networks and relationships of Georges Schehadé and the surrealists in Paris are also dealt with in Julia Drost's contribution to this volume.
3 Georges Schehadé, "Anthologie", 36.

Lebanon and Syria under French mandate

Lebanon and Syria were at that time under French mandate. After the defeat of the Ottomans in 1918 and the consequent dismantling of the Ottoman Empire, the San Remo Conference followed by the Treaty of Sèvres instituted the British Mandate for Palestine and the French Mandate for Syria and the Lebanon, in accordance with the Sykes–Picot Agreement between the two European powers. In September 1920, General Henri Gouraud proclaimed the establishment of the state of Greater Lebanon with Beirut as its capital, and the new territory was granted a flag, merging the French flag with the Lebanese cedar.[4] This settlement imposed by European powers was not accepted by large segments of society. In August 1925, the Druze leader Sultan Pasha al-Atrash called upon Syria's various ethnic and religious communities to oppose the foreign domination of their land. Although it failed to liberate Syria from French mandate, the Great Syrian Revolt was one of the largest and longest-lasting popular insurgencies in the interwar Arab East and had a deep influence on the spread of nationalistic and anti-colonial ideas.[5]

Meanwhile, the establishment of the French mandate accelerated the process of modernization already engaged by the Tanzimat[6] all over the Ottoman Empire since the mid-nineteenth century. This process was mainly visible in Beirut, which became the capital of Greater Lebanon, the headquarters of the mandate's central administration and the showcase of France in the Levant. Through expropriations and demolitions, French authorities carried out a renewal of Beirut's urban core. New arteries were opened bearing the names of the winners (General Allenby Street, Marshal Foch Avenue, Marshal Weygand Street, ...) and the old city's urban fabric was cleared to make room for new layouts, designed along Beaux-Arts principles.[7]

On the cultural scene, the Phoenicianism movement and its advocacy of a Lebanese identity separate from that of the surrounding Middle Eastern countries was favoured by French officials. The writer and industrialist Charles Corm (1894–1963) is considered to be the leader of this movement.[8] He was the publisher of *La Revue phénicienne*, which catered to the Lebanese Christian intellectual elite.[9]

---

4 Carol Hakim, *The Origins of the Lebanese National Idea: 1840–1920*, Berkeley: University of California Press 2013.

5 Michael Provence, *The Great Syrian Revolt and the Rise of Arab Nationalism*, Austin: University of Texas Press 2005.

6 A mid-nineteenth-century Ottoman reform movement.

7 Jad Tabet, "La Ville imparfaite: Le Concept de centralité urbaine dans les projets d'aménagement et de reconstruction de Beyrouth", in: *Reconstruire Beyrouth: Les Paris sur les possibles*, Nabil Beyhum, ed., Lyon: Maison de l'Orient 1991, 85–120.

8 Charles Corm is the son of the painter Daoud Corm (1852–1930) and the brother of the painter Georges Daoud Corm (1896–1971).

9 Asher Kaufman, *Reviving Phoenicia: The Search for Identity in Lebanon*, London: I.B. Tauris 2004.

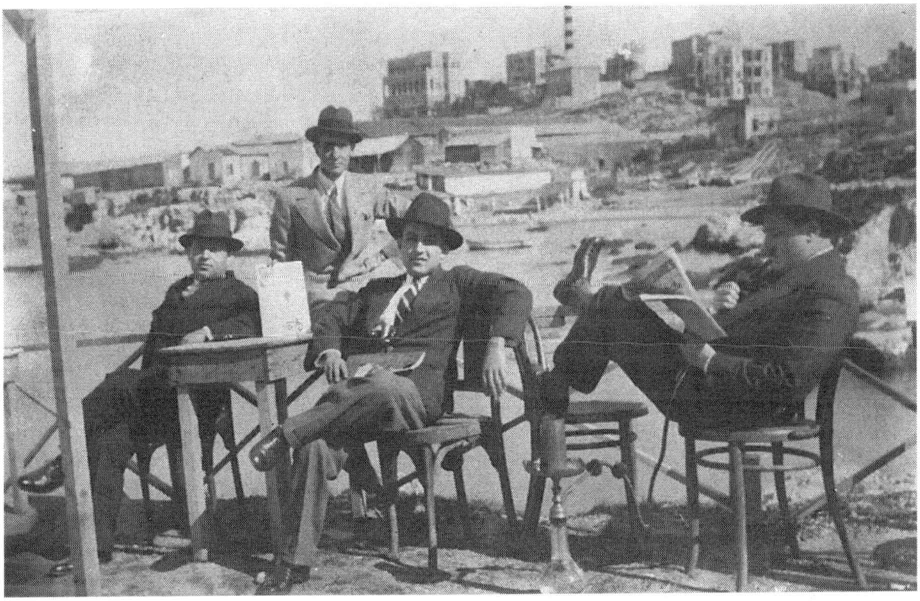

Figure 1: The *mousquetaires*, at the café du Phare, Beirut, 1929. From left to right: Porthos (Antoine Tabet), D'Artagnan (Georges Schehadé), Aramis (Antoine Mourani), and Athos (Alexandre Abouchaar). Nehmé Eddé is not in the picture. Archives Georges Schehadé / IMEC.

In the artistic field, academic painting still prevailed and painters favoured portraits and folklore images. Orientalist references and religious themes dominated the artistic scene, with a vocabulary oscillating between neoclassicism and tempered romanticism.

The five mousquetaires *and their encounter with Gabriel Bounoure*

It is in this atmosphere that our five *mousquetaires*, as they called themselves (fig. 1), were wandering between Beirut, Damascus and the neighbouring summer resorts in the Lebanese mountains, between Bhamdoun, the homeland of Antoine Tabet's family, and Bikfaya, where Georges Schehadé's family was renting a summerhouse.[10]

Our young *mousquetaires* were all French-educated, and although they spoke Arabic, French was for them the language of culture. However, they felt uncomfortable with the conservative traditional environment that characterized the society of French mandate Beirut, marked by a mélange of provincialism and pomposity.

"My dear Antoine, everything is fine in Beirut, we are bored, we are bored ...", wrote Georges Schehadé to Antoine Mourani in 1926. "I was offered a little

10 Danielle Baglione and Albert Dichy, *Georges Schehadé: Poète des deux rives, 1905–1989*, Paris: Éditions de l'IMEC and Beirut: Éditions Dār al-Nahār 1999, 34.

Browning revolver as a present two weeks ago, six or seven bullets. Here's a nice occasion to kill myself when the time comes ... I have three bullets, I will keep one for you."[11]

The salvation came from Barcelona: Gabriel Bounoure (1886–1969), the director of the French Institute in the Catalan capital, was appointed Inspector of Secondary Education in Syria and Lebanon in 1923, then French Cultural Counsellor in 1928. In addition to being a close disciple of the French poet and critic André Suarès (1868–1948), Bounoure was a poetry critic at the *Nouvelle Revue française*, where he followed in particular the surrealist movement and helped promote the works of Max Jacob, Marcel Jouhandeau, Henri Michaux, René Char, Pierre Jean Jouve and others.[12] At that time, the surrealist movement had become well established in Europe's cultural scene. The magazine *La Révolution surréaliste* started publication in 1924 and the first surrealist exhibition organized by André Breton and Robert Desnos was launched one year later at the Galerie Pierre in Paris. It is not very clear how Bounoure met our *mousquetaires*. Nevertheless, a solid relationship was quickly established and this opened new horizons for the five young men.

A turning point occurred in 1927 when Antoine Tabet travelled to Paris to "specialize" in architecture after having obtained his degree in engineering. Bounoure introduced him to André Lhote (1885–1962), the French painter who was in charge of covering painting in the *Nouvelle Revue française*, and to Auguste Perret (1874–1954), the promoter of reinforced concrete architecture in France at that time. Through these contacts, Tabet met the Parisian surrealists and discovered the artistic and political concerns shared by the surrealist movement. It was a time when surrealism was undergoing a shift in its position from a non-political stance that rejected affiliation to a specific ideology, to an alignment with Marxism and the adoption of an anti-colonial discourse that appeared clearly in the radical position they adopted vis-à-vis the Rif War.[13] Considered from the perspective of the anti-colonial struggle within France, the war in the mountainous Moroccan region of the Rif was the first attempt by the newly formed French Communist Party (PCF) to initiate a mass mobilization in France, culminating in a general strike on 12 October 1925. It also coincided with a rapprochement between the surrealists and the militants grouped around the review *Clarté*, providing them with a shared practical focus for political action.

---

11 "Mon cher Antoine, tout va bien à Beyrouth, on s'ennuie, on s'ennuie… On m'a fait cadeau il y a deux semaines d'un petit revolver Browning, six balles ou sept. Voilà une belle occasion de me tuer quand viendra l'heure… J'ai trois balles, je t'en garde une." Georges Schehadé to Antoine Mourani, 21 June 1926, Collection Paul and Anne Mourani. Also see Baglione and Dichy, *Georges Schehadé*.

12 Gérard D. Khoury, ed., *Vergers d'exil: Gabriel Bounoure*, Paris: Geuthner 2004.

13 David Drake, "The PCF, the Surrealists, *Clarté* and the Rif War", *French Cultural Studies* 17 (2006).

In 1929, after Tabet's return to Lebanon, a new opportunity was offered to the group by Georges Naccache (1887–1978), the well-known journalist who directed *L'Orient*, the most important French speaking newspaper in Beirut. On the 16th of June of that year a literary supplement – the *L'Orient littéraire* – was published, with a presentation by Georges Naccache, poems by Georges Schehadé and his sister Laurice (1908–2009), a compilation of *cadavres exquis* by Antoine Mourani and a non-conventional architectural chronicle by Antoine Tabet (fig. 2).

L'Orient littéraire was supposed to be a monthly publication. In fact, only one issue was published. As my father told me, the reason was the strong animosity between the group and a well-known painter of the time, Georges Daoud Corm (1896–1971), who used to publicly criticize Marxism, psychoanalysis, surrealism and all forms of modern art, praising the revival of the classical Renaissance.[14] The second issue of *L'Orient littéraire* was supposed to include a picture representing a foot carrying a brush and entitled "The painter Georges Corm"; the implicit meaning of this relies on a French expression and means that Corm was a failed artist ("Il peint comme un pied"). Such a provocative stance could not possibly be accepted in a bourgeois newspaper such as *L'Orient* and the publication was stopped, leaving us with a single issue of the literary supplement.

In the first years of the new decade, a series of events affected the group. Georges Schehadé was hired by Gabriel Bounoure as his assistant in the public education service created by the mandate authorities and had his first poems published in the review *Commerce*, produced by Paul Valéry, Léon-Paul Fargue and Valéry Larbaud.[15] Antoine Mourani joined the offices of the DHP (Damas, Hama et Prolongements) railway lines, while Nehmé Eddé practised as a lawyer in a big legal firm in Damascus, and Antoine Tabet opened his own architectural office in Beirut, rapidly becoming a pioneer of modern architecture in Lebanon and Syria.

By 1933, Schehadé in turn travelled to Paris, where he became close to a young poet from Alexandria, Henri El Kayem (1912–2000), and his friend Marthe Cazal (1907–1983),[16] who inspired the character of Justine in Lawrence Durell's tetralogy of novels *The Alexandria Quartet*. With his new friends, he visited André Lhote, Saint-John Perse, Jean Paulhan and Max Jacob. After his return to Beirut, the group was enlarged with the integration of two newcomers. One of these was Georges Cyr (1880–1964), a French painter who arrived in Beirut in 1934 and brought with him the influence of modernist movements in Paris. His atelier in the quarter of Ain al-Mreisseh in Beirut, where he trained young generations of artists, became the meeting-place for the group. The other newcomer who joined the group was Rose-Marie Ollier (1908–1979), a French poet who became a close assistant of Bounoure and incidentally Antoine Tabet's lover (fig. 3).

---

14 See Georges Daoud Corm, *Essai sur l'art et la civilisation de ce temps*, Beirut: Dār al-Nahār 1966.

15 Georges Schehadé, "Poèmes", *Commerce* 26 (Winter 1930), 133–143.

16 Baglione and Dichy, *Georges Schehadé*, 55–65.

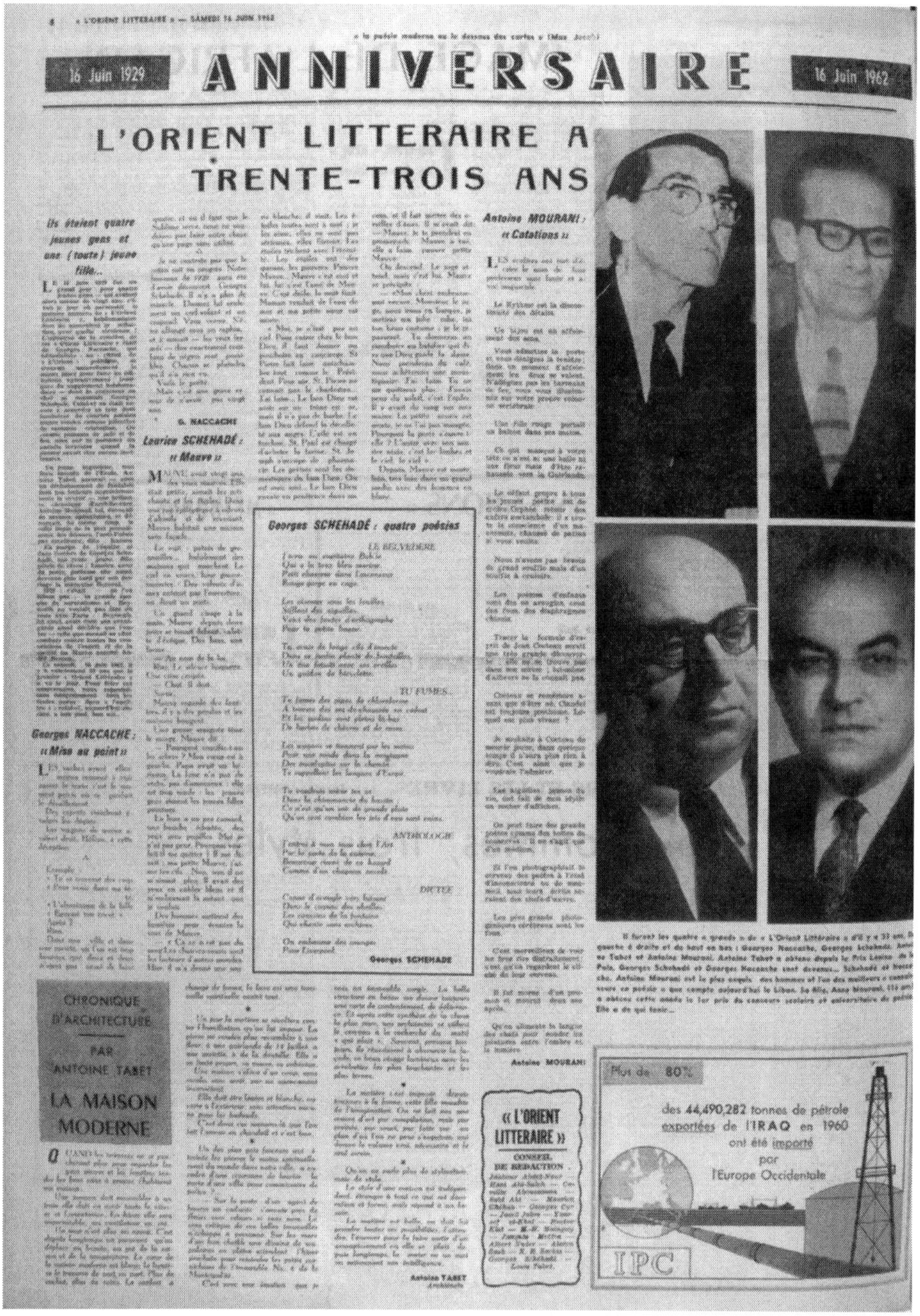

16 Juin 1929 ANNIVERSAIRE 16 Juin 1962

L'ORIENT LITTERAIRE A TRENTE-TROIS ANS

Ils étaient quatre jeunes gens et une (toute) jeune fille...

Lourice SCHEHADÉ : « Mauve »

Georges NACCACHE : « Mise au point »

Antoine MOURANI : « Catalions »

Georges SCHEHADÉ : quatre poésies

LE BELVEDERE

TU FUMES...

ANTHOLOGIE

DICTEE

CHRONIQUE D'ARCHITECTURE PAR ANTOINE TABET

LA MAISON MODERNE

« L'ORIENT LITTERAIRE »

CONSEIL DE REDACTION

Figure 2: *L'Orient-Le Jour* from 16 June 1962, a special edition celebrating the thirty-third anniversary of the first issue of *L'Orient littéraire* (16 June 1929).

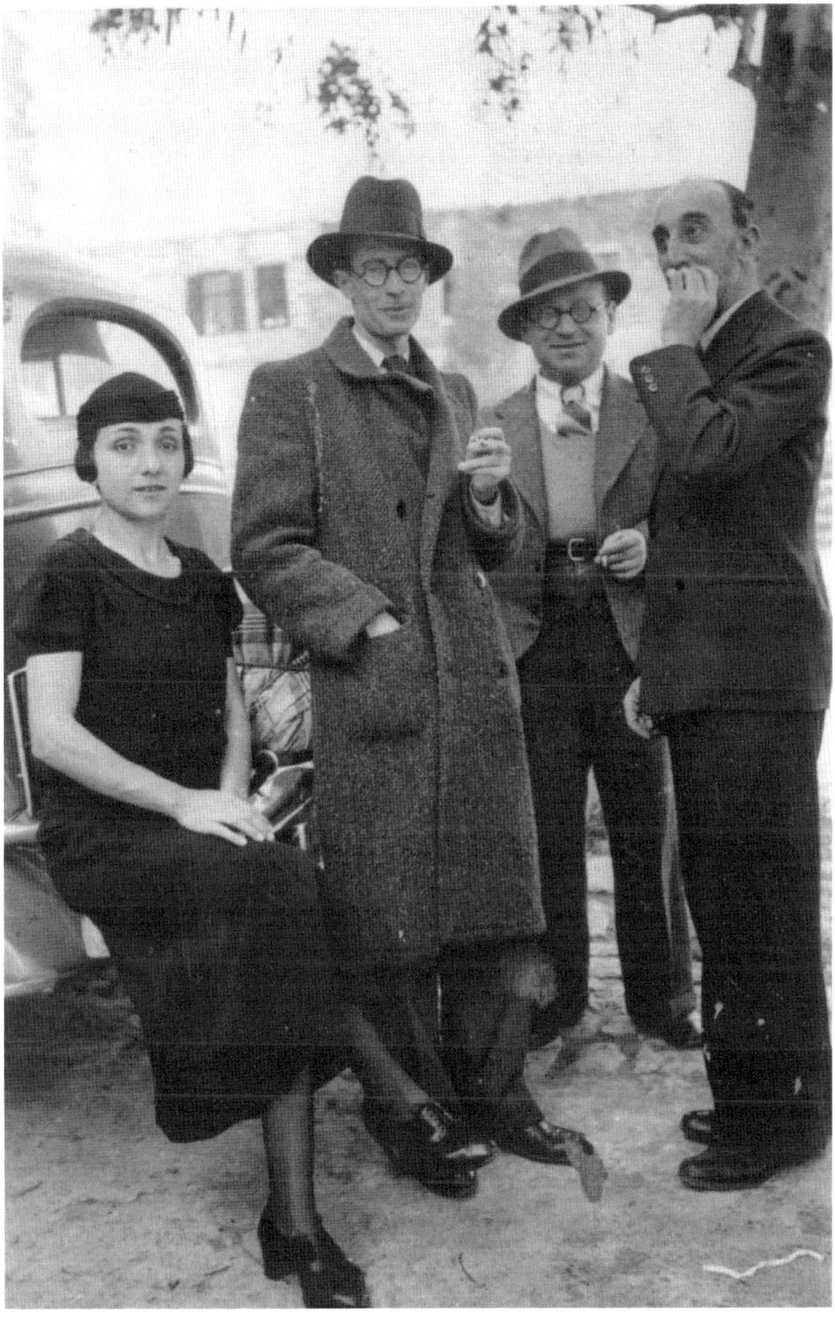

Figure 3: Beirut, *c.* 1935. From left to right: Rose-Marie Ollier, Georges Schehadé, Antoine Tabet, Georges Cyr. Archives Tabet/Mourani.

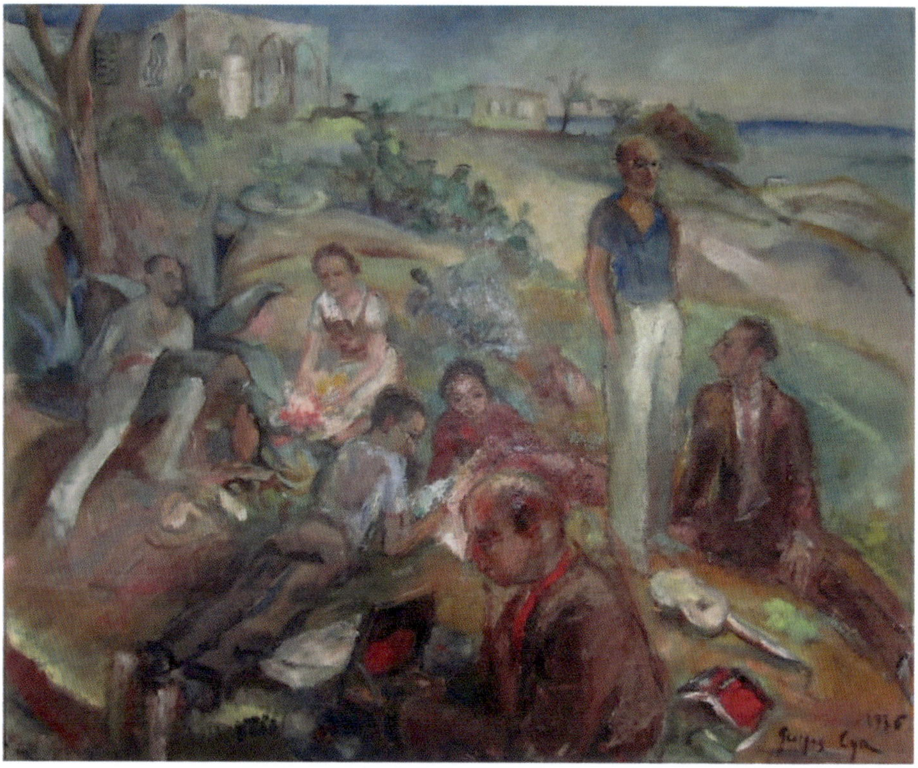

Figure 4: Georges Cyr, *Untitled*, 1936. From left to right: Georges Cyr, Suzanne Pernod, Georges Schehadé, Rose-Marie Ollier, Antoine Tabet, Gabriel Bounoure and Pierre Lafond. Archives Jad Tabet.

A painting offered by Cyr to my father who used to call it *Déjeuner sur l'herbe*, dated 1936, depicts a picnic in the meadow in the Tallet al-Khayat hills in Beirut, with the house of the Lebanese painter Omar Onsi (1901–1969) in the foreground. Symbolically, the setting of the different figures in the scenery revolves around Gabriel Bounoure, who stands alone at the centre of the composition (fig. 4).

From the same period are portraits of Georges Schehadé by Georges Cyr and Antoine Tabet; a portrait by Cyr of Tabet, carrying a big bunch of flowers wrapped in the French communist newspaper *L'Humanité*; and a poem by Schehadé entitled "Antoine Tabet architecte", written in the early thirties and first published in 1950 in Paris by Guy Lévis Mano (GLM, 1904–1980), a typographer and bibliophile French editor.[17]

[17] Georges Schehadé, "Antoine Tabet architecte", in: *L'Écolier sultan*, Paris: Gallimard 1973, 50-51.

The five mousquetaires *in the turmoil of World War II*

But the mid-thirties also witnessed major events which played a significant role in redefining the political affiliations within the group. In October 1935, Mussolini invaded Ethiopia, clearly violating Article X of the Covenant of the League of Nations. Both the United Kingdom and France gave Italy a free hand in order to secure Italian neutrality in case of conflict with Germany. The colonial character of the war and the use of chemical weapons by Italian troops brought about contrasting reactions in public opinion around the world. While a group of right-wing French intellectuals issued a manifesto praising the superiority of the West and its right "to bring civilization to backwards countries",[18] a counter-manifesto for the respect of international law was signed by many European writers and artists, with the active participation of the surrealist movement.

In Lebanon and Syria, the momentous rise of Italian Fascism and German Nazism attracted some imitators. After attending the 1936 Summer Olympics in Munich, Pierre Gemayel (1905–1984) founded the Lebanese Phalange Party, a semi-militarized right-wing Christian organization.[19] The rise of totalitarian ideologies was also evidenced by the foundation of the Syrian Social Nationalist Party by Antoun Saadeh (1904–1949), which aimed at unifying the territory of what he called "Natural Syria",[20] as well as by the creation of the Najjadeh Party, an Arab nationalist organization active among Muslim Sunni youth, founded by Muhi al-Din al-Nsuli (1896–1961) and Adnan al-Hakim (1914–1990), both keen admirers of Adolf Hitler and Benito Mussolini.[21]

In May 1936, the creation of the Anti-Fascist League in Syria and Lebanon was announced through a manifesto written by Antoine Tabet.[22] In the cultural and artistic domain, the manifesto praised a revolutionary art that would take part in the struggle against fascism. After his election to the head of the new organization, Tabet moved closer to the Communist Party and became more and more engaged in political activities. Although his friends did not follow him on this path, the links were never cut and the group continued to meet regularly. But the different political stances were exacerbated after Schehadé's sister married the Italian diplomat Giorgio Benzoni, who represented the Fascist regime in Poland and Yugoslavia. An inscription written by Schehadé in 1937 on the front page of a poetry

---

18 "Manifeste des intellectuels français pour la défense de l'Occident et la paix en Europe", signed by sixty-four French intellectuals and published in the newspaper *Le Temps,* 4 October 1935.

19 Jacques Nantet, *Pierre Gemayel,* Paris: J.C. Lattès 2001.

20 Götz Nordbruch, *Nazism in Syria and Lebanon: The Ambivalence of the German Option 1933–1945,* New York: Routledge 2008.

21 Michael C. Hudson, "Democracy and Social Mobilization in Lebanese Politics", in: *Analyzing the Third World: Essays from Comparative Politics,* Norman W. Provizer, ed., Cambridge: Schenkman 1978, 274.

22 The manifesto is no longer available.

typescript offered to Tabet seems to indicate that this period witnessed heated debates between the two friends: "A mon manager poétique Antoine [...] malgré toutes les démocraties et toutes les dictatures" ("To my poetic manager Antoine [...] despite all democracies and dictatorships").[23]

The outbreak of the Second World War created a completely new situation. After the surrender of France in June 1940, Lebanon and Syria passed into the control of the Vichy government. The Anti-Fascist League was banned and Tabet was jailed for a short while. But in May 1941, after a coup brought the pro-Axis Rashid Ali al-Gillani (1892–1965) to power in Iraq, Britain reoccupied Iraq and launched a military campaign with the support of the Free French Forces to take control over Syria and Lebanon.

The defeat of the Vichy Armée du Levant did not, however, eliminate the danger of a counter-offensive by Axis troops. In April 1942, Rommel's Afrika Korps was less than 150 miles away from Cairo, threatening the Suez Canal and the Middle Eastern and Persian oil fields. It was only in November of that year that the last-minute British victory at El Alamein turned the tide in the North African Campaign.

In Syria and Lebanon, pro-fascist propaganda was reinforced when the nationalist leaders Hajj Amin al-Husseini (1895–1974) and Rashid Ali al-Gillani fled to Berlin. Bounoure, Ollier and Cyr had joined Free France from the very beginning and were highly active in organizing the ideological counter-offensive. The Anti-Fascist League was renamed the Anti-Fascist and Anti-Nazi League and resumed its activities, while Tabet – together with renowned intellectuals such as Omar Fakhoury (1895–1946), Raif Khoury (1913–1967) and the poet and militant feminist Emilie Fares Ibrahim (1914–2011) – founded an Arabic-language cultural magazine *al-Ṭarīq* (The Road), which aimed at linking the struggle against fascism with that for liberty and national independence.

In fact, ever since the Free France forces had defeated the Vichy army, General Georges Catroux, delegate general under Charles de Gaulle, had proclaimed the independence of Lebanon in the name of his government. However, the French continued to exercise effective authority until November 1943, when popular protests and international pressure led to the independence of Lebanon.

Meanwhile, Beirut had become a meeting-place for many French intellectuals, writers and artists fleeing from Vichy's reactionary regime. The Lebanese capital also provided a relatively safe haven for anti-fascist militants and Jewish refugees. Under the direction of Henri Seyrig (1895–1973)[24] and Daniel Schlumberger (1904–1972),[25] the French Archaeological Centre, housed in the old Abdel Kader palace near the Zeitouneh quarter of Beirut, became a forum for debates and

23 Georges Schehadé, "Poésies 1930–1936", typescript, Jad Tabet Collection.
24 Frédérique Duyrat et al., *Henri Seyrig (1895–1973)*, Beirut: IFPO Press 2016.
25 Mathilde Gelin, ed., *Daniel Schlumberger: L'Occident à la rencontre de l'Orient*, Beirut: IFPO Press 2010.

heated discussions about the links between culture and politics. The first Thursday of the month, Antoine Tabet's office in Beirut's Maarad area also hosted public lectures about Marxism given by the French-Jewish Orientalist Maxime Rodinson (1915–2004).[26] The members of the group actively participated in these intellectual activities.

Incidentally, the relationships between the members of the group became even closer, with the marriages of Antoine Tabet and Antoine Mourani with Nehmé Eddé's sisters Marie and Sarah. At the same time, the political misunderstanding that had affected these relationships disappeared with the imprisonment of Schehadé's brother-in-law, the Italian diplomat Giorgio Benzoni, by the Fascist regime due to his opposition to the alliance between Mussolini and Hitler.[27]

Lebanese artists exhibiting in Cairo and Jerusalem

The cultural scene was particularly rich in the first years of Lebanese independence. In 1944, Gabriel Bounoure founded the École des Lettres, a higher educational institution for literature and human sciences, of which Schehadé became general secretary. The Lebanese Fine Arts Academy (Académie Libanaise des Beaux-Arts) had been created in the previous year, offering architecture, painting, sculpture and music courses. Over the years, modern art had won its spurs and become largely accepted by Lebanese society.

Breaking beyond national boundaries, modern artists started establishing links with their counterparts in neighbouring countries. Several artists from Lebanon were invited by the Egyptian Art et Liberté group (1938–1948) to take part in the third Exhibition of Independent Art (*Exposition de l'art indépendant*), which took place at the Continental Hotel in Cairo.[28] In addition to Georges Cyr and Antoine Tabet, the two French painters Henri Pierre Fortier (1914–1977) and Geneviève Moron (dates unknown), who were working in Lebanon, and the Lebanese painter Omar Onsi (1901–1969) participated in the exhibition. Given the strong anti-fascist stance of the participants, the exhibition which took place from 21 to 30 May 1942[29] represented a strong act of resistance, since Rommel's Afrika Korps was at Cairo's doorstep in the spring of that year.[30]

---

26 Maxime Rodinson, *Marxisme et monde musulman*, Paris: Éditions du Seuil 1972, 11.

27 Baglione and Dichy, *Georges Schehadé*, 106.

28 See Sam Bardaouil, *Surrealism in Egypt: Modernism and the Art and Liberty Group*, London: I.B. Tauris 2017, 185–186.

29 Samir Gharieb, *Surrealism in Egypt and Plastic Arts*, Cairo: Prism Publications Offices 1986, 18.

30 The Greek novelist Stratis Tsirkas masterfully recreated the atmosphere prevailing in Egypt and the Middle East during World War II in his trilogy *Drifting Cities*, first published in 1965.

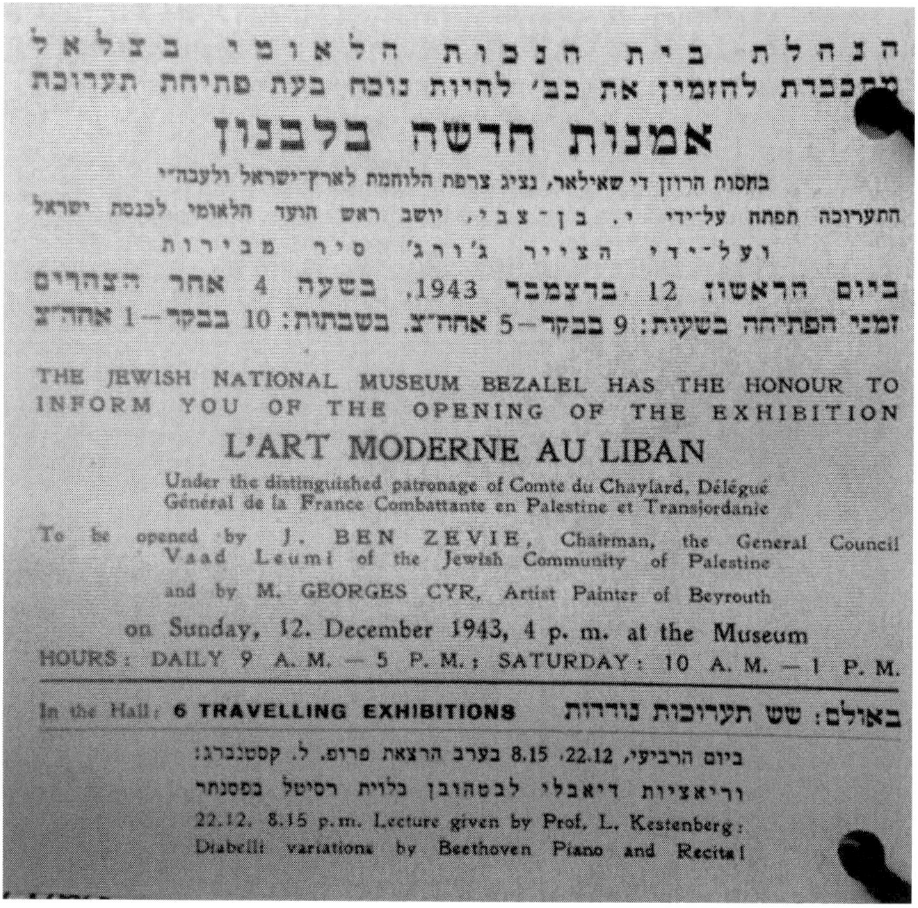
הנהלת בית הנכות הלאומי בצלאל
מתכבדת להזמין את כב׳ להיות נוכח בעת פתיחת תערוכת
אמנות חדשה בלבנון
בחסות הרוזן די שאילאר, נציג צרפת הלוחמת לארץ־ישראל ולעבה״י
התערוכה תפתח על־ידי י. בן־צבי, יושב ראש הועד הלאומי לכנסת ישראל
ועל־ידי הצייר ג׳ורג׳ סיר מביירות
ביום הראשון 12 בדצמבר 1943, בשעה 4 אחר הצהרים
זמני הפתיחה בשעות: 9 בבקר—5 אחה״צ. בשבתות: 10 בבקר—1 אחה״צ

THE JEWISH NATIONAL MUSEUM BEZALEL HAS THE HONOUR TO INFORM YOU OF THE OPENING OF THE EXHIBITION

L'ART MODERNE AU LIBAN

Under the distinguished patronage of Comte du Chaylard, Délégué Général de la France Combattante en Palestine et Transjordanie

To be opened by J. BEN ZEVIE, Chairman, the General Council Vaad Leumi of the Jewish Community of Palestine

and by M. GEORGES CYR, Artist Painter of Beyrouth

on Sunday, 12. December 1943, 4 p. m. at the Museum

HOURS: DAILY 9 A. M. — 5 P. M.; SATURDAY: 10 A. M. — 1 P. M.

In the Hall: 6 TRAVELLING EXHIBITIONS באולם: שש תערוכות נודדות

ביום הרביעי, 22.12, 8.15 בערב הרצאת פרופ. ל. קסטנברג:
וריאציות דיאבלי לבטהובן בלוית רסיטל בפסנתר

22.12. 8.15 p.m. Lecture given by Prof. L. Kestenberg: Diabelli variations by Beethoven Piano and Recital

Figure 5: Invitation to the opening of the exhibition *L'Art moderne au Liban* at the Bezalel National Museum in Jerusalem (12 December 1943–4 January 1944). Bezalel National Museum, Jerusalem.

Although Art et Liberté was essentially a surrealist movement, it is clear that the artworks sent from Lebanon had little in common with surrealism. The invitation sent to artists from Lebanon could thus be interpreted as an attempt by the Egyptian group to build regional networks beyond the links established with major international surrealist figures.

This attempt to create a regional artistic network was further extended later the same year with a large exhibition at the Bezalel National Museum in Jerusalem entitled *Modern Art in Lebanon* (fig. 5). The exhibition was organized by Gabriel Bounoure, Rose-Marie Ollier and Georges Cyr, representing the General Committee of France Combattant in Lebanon.[31] The exhibition comprised seventy-two

[31] A copy of the exhibition catalogue is preserved in the archives of the Bezalel National Museum, Jerusalem.

artworks and ran from 12 December 1943 through to 4 January 1944. Seven Lebanese and French painters, sculptors and architects representing modern artistic currents in Lebanon participated, including the artists who had taken part in the exhibition organized by Art et Liberté in Cairo. Another exhibition entitled *Modern Art in Palestine* was supposed to be organized in Beirut later in 1944, but this exhibition never took place for unknown reasons.[32]

The correspondence preserved in the archives of the Bezalel National Museum reveals the differences in the expectations of the various actors participating in this artistic event. While the Free France authorities considered the Jerusalem exhibition as a political event expressing French revival in a British-dominated territory, the artists participating in the exhibition primarily wanted to strengthen their ties with the modern Palestinian art scene, with the aim of creating cultural synergies at the regional level. On the other hand, the correspondence between Mordechai Narkiss (1898–1957), director of the Bezalel National Museum from 1925 to 1957, and the World Zionist Organization expresses the wish that the exhibition would be a first step towards the recognition in Lebanon and Syria of the Zionist movement. It is perhaps due to these conflicting expectations that the attempt to create permanent links between modern artists in Lebanon and Palestine, and more broadly at the regional level, ended in failure.

"Méfie toi des souvenirs comme d'une montre arrêtée"[33] *or the dissolution of the "circle of the friends of surrealism"*

In contrast to the euphoric atmosphere that prevailed after the victory over fascism and during the first years of independence, the political situation became much gloomier from the late 1940s onwards. The first Arab–Israeli war resulted in the Palestinian Nakba in 1948 and triggered significant changes throughout the Middle East. Palestinian refugees were settled in refugee camps throughout the Arab world while Jewish communities started leaving Arab countries and migrating to the newborn Israeli state as well as to Europe and the Americas. The Arab defeat resulted in a series of upheavals that shocked the Arab region. Syria and Egypt witnessed military coups that overturned previous equilibriums and adopted a staunchly nationalist, anti-imperialist agenda, which came to be expressed through a vehement patriotic discourse. The state of cold war that replaced post-war international cooperation introduced new polarizations as well as political and military tensions that reflected on an unstable regional situation.

---

32 Letter from the director of the Bezalel National Museum, Mordechai Narkiss, to Georges Cyr, 20 October 1943, archives of the Bezalel National Museum, Jerusalem.

33 Georges Schehadé, *Monsieur Bob'le* [1951], in Georges Schehadé, *Œuvre complète, Le Théâtre, Tome 1*, Beirut: Dar an-Nahar 1989, 35.

The new conditions that arose out of these radical transformations led to the shrinking of the capacity of local cultures to communicate with each other and to their withdrawal into narrow conformist attitudes. Modernity was perverted by the nationalist political discourse that revolved around unilateral simplistic interpretations of the notions of progress, growth, advancement and development. Hence, the attempts of Arab cultural avant-gardes to instigate a rupture with national barriers in order to partake in the project of radical modernity, as well as their commitment to the international character of culture, seemed outdated in the face of these new local realities.

The times were burdened with issues and concerns that affected the relationships among the members of the Lebanese group. Despite occasional encounters, like the collective writing of Schehadé's *La Soirée des proverbes* in 1952 or the opposition to the campaign launched by French militaristic circles when *Histoire de Vasco* played at the Odeon Theatre in 1958,[34] the group split apart into separate destinies, telling individual stories.

Rose-Marie Ollier left Lebanon in 1947 and was appointed cultural attaché at the French Embassy in Australia. There, she was caught in a murky affair of espionage.[35] Suspected of giving information to the KGB about French military plans in Indochina, she was acquitted after a long trial but subsequently suffered from paranoia. When I visited her in Paris in 1968, she received me in a small maid's room because she was convinced that her apartment in avenue de la Bourdonnais was full of microphones put there by the CIA. She died in Paris in the late 1970s.

Gabriel Bounoure left Lebanon in 1952, after a magazine published a private letter he had sent to an Egyptian friend, the philosopher Abdelrahman Badaoui (1917–2002), criticizing French policy in Algeria and Morocco. Summoned by the Quai d'Orsay to retract, he refused and resigned from the French administration.[36] He moved to Egypt, where he chaired the Department of French Literature at Ain Shams University in Cairo, then to the University of Rabat in 1959. He retired in 1965 and returned to his native village in Brittany where he died in 1968.

Towards the end of the 1940s, Georges Cyr went through an existential crisis, questioning his place in the contemporary art scene. Trapped in a difficult dialogue with post-cubism, he remained split between his strong attachment to Lebanese cultural life and his desire to be recognized in the Parisian art scene.[37] He died in Beirut in 1964. His art collection was bequeathed in his will to his housemaid and also to Georges Schehadé's wife, Brigitte Collerais.

Antoine Mourani and Nehmé Eddé tried to open an import–export business during the 1950s. Unfortunately, they were not business-minded, or rather, they

---

34 Baglione and Dichy, *Georges Schehadé*, 196–202.

35 Robert Manne, *The Petrov Affair: Politics and Espionage*, Sydney: Pergamon Press 1987.

36 Gérard D. Khoury, "Portrait de Gabriel Bounoure", in: *Dictionnaire des orientalistes*, François Pouillon, ed., Paris: Karthala 2008, 139.

37 Michel Fani, *Dictionnaire de la peinture au Liban*, Grenoble: Éditions de l'Escalier 1998.

were more interested in poetry than in management. They went bankrupt several times and Antoine Tabet regularly covered the debts of his old friends. Antoine Mourani died in 1967. Nehmé Eddé moved to Paris after the outbreak of the civil war in Lebanon. He suffered from Alzheimer's during the later years of his life and recited the early poems of Schehadé all day long.

Antoine Tabet became one of the most important representatives of the Lebanese modern architectural movement during the 1950s and was more and more involved in politics. He was a member of the World Council for Peace, an international organization close to the communist movement, participated actively in the birth and development of the non-aligned movement in Asia and Africa, and received the Lenin Peace Prize together with Fidel Castro in 1962. He died in Beirut in 1964. Several years after his death, his family found letters and pictures related to his group of friends, locked in a safe and secret drawer.

Georges Schehadé became ... Schehadé. His poems were extensively published and translated into several languages and his plays were performed in all European capitals. After the outbreak of the war in Lebanon, he moved to Paris in 1976, and died there in 1989. His visitors say that, towards the end of his life, he was always recalling the stories of the group of *mousquetaires* and evoking the memory of his old friends.

Chapter 6
Beyrouth – Paris. Georges Schehadé et le surréalisme

Julia Drost

L'exploration du surréalisme au Liban en est encore à ses débuts et doit être considérée ici dans le contexte d'un tournant dans la recherche qui, depuis quelques années, s'intéresse d'une manière plus approfondie au surréalisme en tant que phénomène « global[1] ». Le poète libanais Georges Schehadé (1905?–1989) est une figure majeure si l'on tente de comprendre l'impact de l'avantgarde surréaliste dans cette partie du monde. « Poète des deux rives », son parcours poétique et artistique se situe à la croisée de l'Orient et de l'Occident, donnant lieu à une biographie profondément marquée par les relations politiques et culturelles entre la France et le Liban au XXe siècle[2]. Depuis la capitale libanaise sous mandat français, Georges Schehadé était un fervent observateur de la vie artistique et intellectuelle parisienne, à la fois source d'inspiration, d'échanges et de transferts[3].

Dans une lettre adressée en 1958 à Benjamin Péret, Schehadé nous livre un indice particulièrement intéressant quant à l'importance de la philosophie surréaliste pour son travail. Péret, ami et allié de longue date d'André Breton, avait demandé à Schehadé de lui envoyer un poème inédit ainsi que des renseignements biographiques. Le poète fait d'abord preuve de sa retenue habituelle : « Je ne sais pas quoi dire, et, en vérité, je n'ai rien d'intéressant à communiquer. » Toutefois, il ajoute : « En tout cas, si vous voulez bien dire quelque chose à mon sujet, je vous prie de dire, avant tout, que je suis un fils du surréalisme ». À la fin de la lettre, il ajoute « Un grand bonjour à Elisa et à André Breton qui m'a beaucoup oublié[4] ». Cette lettre semble donc comporter une sorte de « concession » par rapport à la signification et à l'importance que le surréalisme a pu avoir pour son parcours et son œuvre. Le lecteur comprend également que la relation entre les deux hommes est désormais moins intense, moins profonde, Breton l'ayant « beaucoup oublié ».

---

1 Voir à ce sujet notamment l'introduction de Monique Bellan et Julia Drost ainsi que la contribution d'Ambra D'Antone dans le présent volume. Pour le surréalisme au Liban, voir aussi l'étude d'Alfred el-Khoury.

2 Tel est le titre de la première et pour l'instant unique monographie éditée par l'Institut Mémoires de l'édition contemporaine (IMEC) où sont déposées ses archives : Danielle Baglione et Albert Dichy, *Georges Schehadé, poète des deux rives, 1905–1989*, Paris : Éditions de l'IMEC ; Beyrouth : Dār al-Nahār 1999.

3 Voir aussi l'article de Jad Tabet dans le présent ouvrage.

4 Lettre de Georges Schehadé à Benjamin Péret, Beyrouth, 16 décembre 1958, Bibliothèque littéraire Jacques Doucet, Paris (Ms 34.712).

À partir de cette métaphore de la filiation surréaliste, le présent article se propose d'analyser les liens entre Schehadé et les surréalistes parisiens. Nous cherchons par ailleurs à démontrer que son œuvre poétique fut profondément marquée par l'expérience de la mobilité et de la migration. Les circonstances de sa biographie, ses rencontres et multiples allers-retours entre le Liban et la France, ont favorisé le brassage et la réception d'idées issues de différents milieux intellectuels et artistiques, comme en témoigne la production du poète. La connaissance et la réception du surréalisme, notamment, s'inscrivent dans cet horizon particulier.

« Une bande de copains, tous fous de littérature »

Lorsque que l'aventure surréaliste commence à Paris au début des années 1920, autour d'André Breton, Paul Éluard, Philippe Soupault et bien d'autres, Schehadé est encore adolescent. Sa date de naissance précise n'est pas connue, mais on suppose généralement que le poète naît en 1905 en Alexandrie, à une époque où ni la nationalité égyptienne, ni la nationalité libanaise n'existent encore[5]. Il naît sujet ottoman, dans une famille de religion chrétienne et de rite gréco-orthodoxe. La famille quitte l'Égypte vers 1921 – lorsque le Liban devient un état indépendant sous mandat français – pour s'installer dans le quartier chrétien de Beyrouth[6]. Dès son enfance, Schehadé connaît donc l'expérience du déracinement et de la migration, qui constitue en même temps un enrichissement culturel. Il est habitué depuis toujours à vivre sous le signe de la dualité, lui le poète francophone en terre arabe, dans un monde en transformation perpétuelle. Schehadé conserve sa résidence principale au Liban jusqu'en 1978. S'il s'installe après la Seconde Guerre mondiale à Paris avec sa femme Brigitte Collerais, c'est pour faire des allers-retours entre la France et le Liban, car il reste très attaché à son pays. Le décor de son appartement parisien semble d'ailleurs évoquer cette situation d'entre-deux permanent, ou plutôt un « non-décor », comme le remarque en 1985 un journaliste du *Monde* : « Un immense appartement, presque vide ; aux murs, des toiles de Dufy, Masson, Mathieu, un canapé, des valises.... Schehadé vit comme en exil à Paris...[7] » On peut en effet identifier dans la description de cet appartement quelques éléments-clés qui resurgissent régulièrement lorsqu'il s'agit de l'exil. L'impression de vide de la pièce et le manque de mobilier renvoient ainsi au statut de celui qui n'a pas de domicile véritable. Et en effet, le

---

5 Pour la biographie de Schehadé, nous renvoyons à la monographie parue en 1999, Baglione et Dichy, *Schehadé*. Schehadé lui-même donne 1910 comme année de naissance dans les notices biographiques envoyées à Péret.

6 Pour le contexte historique et politique, nous renvoyons à l'article de Jad Tabet dans ce volume.

7 Raphaël Sorin, « Georges Schehadé, le magicien », dans *Le Monde*, 8 mars 1985 ; http://abonnes.lemonde.fr/archives/article/1985/03/08/georges-schehade-le-magicien_2743197_1819218.html.

motif de la valise, symbole du voyage et de la circulation des idées et des connaissances, est aussi le symbole phare de la migration[8]. L'artiste Etel Adnan (née en 1925), ancienne étudiante et amie de Schehadé, racontera plus tard que cette situation d'entre-deux a été pour lui un véritable déchirement : « Le poète regrettait Paris lorsqu'il était à Beyrouth, parce qu'il y était mieux compris et Beyrouth, lorsqu'il était à Paris, parce qu'il s'y ennuyait[9] ».

En Égypte et au Liban, Schehadé reçoit une éducation en langue française et écrit toujours en français. Issu d'une famille libanaise bourgeoise aisée qui le destine à des études commerciales, il préfère se tourner vers le droit. Lors de ses études, il se lie à un groupe d'amis, Antoine Mourani (1907–1976), Nehmé Eddé (1902–1992), Antoine Tabet (1907–1964) et Alexandre Abouchaar (dates de vie inconnues) que la contribution de Jad Tabet dans ce volume évoque plus en détail (voir aussi ill. 1 dans son chapitre). Leur petit groupe se surnomme « les mousquetaires », plus tard « les émerveillés d'eux-mêmes[10] » : « Nous formions une bande de copains, fous de littérature, francophiles à un point que l'on n'imagine pas ...[11] ».

Sa licence obtenue, Schehadé entre dans l'administration de l'État. En 1930, il devient d'abord rédacteur au ministère de la Justice, puis assistant dans un service dirigé par l'écrivain Gabriel Bounoure (1886–1969) et ensuite encore conseiller pour l'Instruction publique au sein du Haut-commissariat en Syrie et au Liban. Arrivé au Liban en 1923, Bounoure allait jouer un rôle important dans le parcours de Schehadé. Ainsi, lorsqu'il crée l'École Supérieure des Lettres à Beyrouth en 1943 dans le Liban indépendant, Schehadé en devient le secrétaire général. Et lorsque Bounoure doit quitter le Liban en 1952 pour avoir critiqué la politique arabe de la France, Schehadé devient peu de temps après, en 1959, conseiller artistique auprès de l'ambassade de France au Liban. L'écrivain français associe ainsi Schehadé, tout au long de sa carrière, à la vie éducative et culturelle française au Liban. Bounoure devient par ailleurs son professeur en matière de littérature et de poésie. L'écrivain s'occupe d'une chronique sur la poésie à *La Nouvelle Revue française* (NRF), dirigée par Jean Paulhan. C'est par la revue qu'il essaye dès la fin des années 1920 de faire connaître en France les poètes libanais, Schehadé et ses amis. En 1929, il rédige ainsi une note de lecture sur le recueil *Étincelles* de Schehadé, saluant la naissance d'une jeune poésie libanaise[12]. Il souligne notamment l'immense source d'inspiration que représentent Paris et la littérature française pour ces poètes

8 Burcu Doğramacı, « Objekte der Migration. Zeitgenössische künstlerische Strategien und produktive Aneignungen », dans *Dinge des Exils*, Doerte Bischoff et Jochaim Schlör, dir., Munich : edition text und kritik 2013.

9 Éric Dussert, « Notice biobibliographique », dans : Georges Schehadé, *Les Poésies* [1952], Paris : Gallimard 2001, 161.

10 Sorin, « Schehadé ».

11 Baglione et Dichy, *Schehadé*, 34.

12 Georges Schehadé, *Étincelles. Poèmes*, Paris : Éditions de la pensée latine 1927. Schehadé a renié ce recueil par la suite.

alors au début de leur itinéraire[13] : « Les jeunes libanais commencent à pénétrer les secrets de Baudelaire, ce parisien du plus vieil Orient[14] ».

Si les « émerveillés d'eux-mêmes » observent avec intérêt ce qui se passe en France, notamment en matière de poésie surréaliste, Breton et ses amis vont quant à eux nourrir dans l'entre-deux-guerres une vision essentiellement mythique de l'Orient, voyant dans la culture du Levant une civilisation à l'opposé du rationalisme du monde occidental[15]. En 1924, Breton écrit ainsi : « Pour ma part il me plaît que la civilisation occidentale soit en jeu. C'est d'Orient que nous vient aujourd'hui la lumière[16] ». Edward Saïd a rappelé combien cette vision de l'Orient relève d'une « expérience européenne », une expérience de l'*autre* conçu comme contre-modèle, antithèse, caractère opposé, par rapport à la culture constituant la référence[17]. C'est dans cette même logique que la célèbre carte *Le monde au temps des surréalistes*[18], parue en 1929 dans la revue belge *Variétés*, renvoie à Constantinople, ville mythique et métonymique de toute la région, dans l'esprit d'une « géographie imaginaire ». L'Orient et ses symboles représentent une source d'inspiration, il fascine dans la perspective d'une recherche de tout ce qui se démarque de ce que l'on trouve chez soi.

L'information ne circule d'abord que dans un sens. Ce sont les émerveillés qui s'intéressent à la vie culturelle et artistique parisienne. L'anecdote veut que le premier contact de ces jeunes poètes avec la littérature française d'avant-garde ait eu lieu au milieu des années 1920 à Beyrouth grâce à une valise qu'un membre du groupe, Antoine Mourani, avait ramenée d'un voyage à Paris : « C'est cette malle de livres qui met le petit groupe au courant de la plus récente actualité littéraire et leur fera découvrir Cocteau, Max Jacob et les auteurs surréalistes[19] ». On retrouve ici l'idée de la valise comme symbole de la circulation des idées. Nous ignorons à ce jour quels livres elle contenait. Mais il n'est pas difficile de supposer qu'il pouvait s'agir des *Champs magnétiques*, publiés par André Breton et Philippe Soupault en 1920, de poèmes de Max Jacob ou encore de quelques numéros de *Littérature* ou de *La Révolution surréaliste*.

---

13 Toute sa vie, Schehadé se montre redevable vis-à-vis de son maître : « Je travaillais auprès de Gabriel Bounoure, un homme extraordinaire. [...] Entre deux travaux administratifs, je lui montrais mes brouillons. Il était la bonté même. Il me disait : "Georges lisez m'en encore". » Voir Sorin, « Schehadé ».

14 Gabriel Bounoure, « Étincelles, par Georges Schehadé (Ed. de la Pensée Latine) », dans *La Nouvelle Revue française*, 187 (avril 1929), 584.

15 Martine Antle, « Surrealism and the Orient », dans *Yale French Studies* 109 (2006), 4–5. Le mythe de l'Orient s'inscrit avant tout et est instrumentalisé dans le contexte de la guerre du Rif et du communisme. Voir Marguerite Bonnet, « L'Orient dans le surréalisme. Mythe et réel », dans *Revue de littérature comparée* 54, fasc. 4 (1980).

16 André Breton, « Réponse à l'enquête des "Cahiers du mois": Orient/Occident », dans *Œuvres complètes*, dir. Marguerite Bonnet, Paris : Gallimard/Pléiade 1988–2008, 1:898.

17 Edward W. Saïd, *Orientalismus*, Francfort/Main : Fischer 2009, 9–10.

18 Voir la reproduction de cette carte dans l'introduction de Monique Bellan et Julia Drost, 18.

19 Baglione et Dichy, *Schehadé*, 34.

« *Marcher dans les rues, fumer des cigarettes et voir du monde* »

Le premier séjour de Schehadé à Paris n'a lieu qu'en 1933. Il se lie d'amitié avec le poète égyptien Henri El Kayem[20]. « Ma vie est assez misérable à Paris déjà [...] », écrit-il à sa sœur Laurice depuis la capitale française, « et je te jure que jusqu'à présent, je n'ai pris qu'une fois le taxi et c'est Kayem qui me l'a payé. Je ne sors que très peu jusqu'à présent, je n'ai pas été à un cinéma, je me contente de marcher dans les rues, de fumer des cigarettes et de voir du monde[21] ». Même s'il cherche à faire croire à sa sœur qu'il ne sort pas beaucoup, il semble développer une activité importante. Il visite le musée du Louvre, fait la connaissance des poètes Saint-John Perse et Jules Supervielle et se fait inviter chez Max Jacob que Kayem tient pour « le chef de file des surréalistes[22] ».

Il s'avère difficile de reconstituer avec exactitude la chronologie des rencontres. On peut lire que c'est Paul Éluard qui, après avoir découvert ses poèmes dans la revue *Commerce*, l'introduit dans le cercle des surréalistes[23]. Schehadé rencontre de nombreux poètes, personnellement ou en lisant leurs poèmes. Un an plus tard, en 1934, de retour au Liban, il fait la connaissance du peintre Georges Cyr, récemment arrivé de Paris. Ce dernier réalise plusieurs portraits du poète, dont un à la manière de Cézanne. Dans son style, son exécution contraste étrangement avec le motif du portrait qui, lui, renvoie à la tradition de l'artiste bohème. Le poète y apparaît dans une pose de réflexion, en quête d'inspiration, sous la lumière d'une lampe de bureau (ill. 1).

Il fait nuit. Le poète semble mal installé sur sa chaise, vautré sur son bureau, la tête appuyée sur le bras droit, devant un livre ouvert. Une tasse de café sur le bureau, une bouteille de vin posée par terre à droite du meuble, sous la fenêtre, et un objet qui pourrait être un paquet de cigarettes sont les attributs qui accompagnent la scène faussement bohème, car on devine une certaine aisance matérielle dans le meuble de bureau ancien et le tableau encadré qui le surmonte. Plus tard, Georges Cyr reviendra sur son premier contact avec Schehadé :

> Celui-ci [Schehadé], à ma grande surprise, se met tout de suite à me parler d'André Breton, de Max Jacob, d'Éluard, personnes qui m'étaient chères. Le petit secrétaire n'était pas encore (le grand) Georges Schehadé mais il semblait à fond connaître le surréalisme et ses tenants[24].

---

[20] Baglione et Dichy, *Schehadé*, 55.

[21] Lettre de Schehadé à sa sœur Laurice, Paris, 19 février 1933, cit. dans Baglione et Dichy, *Schehadé*, 57.

[22] Lettre de Henri El Kayem à Marthe Cazal, s. l., 26 février 1933, cit. dans Baglione et Dichy, *Schehadé*, 58.

[23] Nous renvoyons à Dussert, « Notice biobibliographique », 161.

[24] Cité dans le catalogue de l'exposition *L'eau dans l'œuvre de Georges Cyr* (mai 1997), Beyrouth : Centre culturel français 1997, 9.

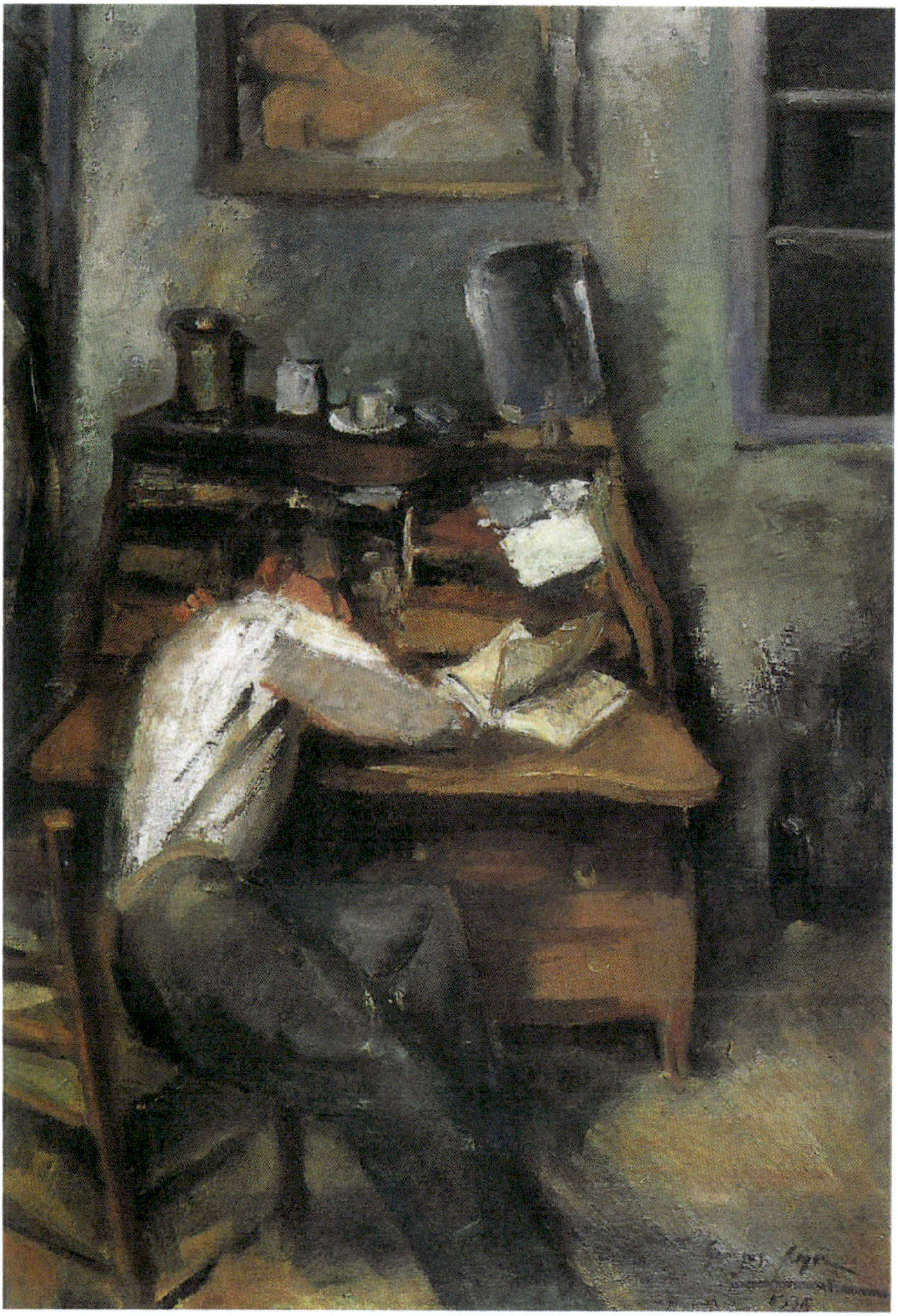

Illustration 1 : Georges Cyr, *Georges Schehadé à son bureau*, 1936. Huile sur toile. © Archives Albert Dichy.

« *Avec vous, la poésie est revenue nouvelle* »

En 1938, ses *Poésies* paraissent chez Guy Lévis Mano, typographe, poète et éditeur bibliophile, qui publie principalement les poètes surréalistes dans les années 1930[25]. C'est aussi chez lui que paraissent d'autres ouvrages de poésies de Schehadé, en 1948 et 1949, ainsi que *Rodogune Sinne* en 1947 et *Poésies zéro ou L'Écolier Sultan* en 1950. Le recueil *Poésies* est très apprécié par Paul Éluard en 1938 qui lui écrit (ill. 2) :

> Je lis et relis chaque jour vos poésies. Je vous en remercie. Avec vous, la poésie est revenue nouvelle. Depuis longtemps, je lisais peu, désespérais (d'écrire aussi). Vos poésies me rapportent une vue profonde, un chant juste que j'oubliais. Votre livre me fait un bien que vous ne pouvez évaluer[26].

Georges le remercie dans une lettre, soulignant de son côté la profonde gratitude qu'il ressent envers le poète français : « Vous ne pouvez pas croire ce que vous représentez pour moi, incomparable aîné ![27] ». Il lui dédicace un poème (ill. 3) :

> Je me déciderai dans un jardin de pommes
> Dans cette eau de la campagne
> Au pas immaculé des charbonniers
> Et pour toi amie des saules de la mort
> Les colombes qui volent sans air
> L'absence plus longue que les années[28].

Arrêtons-nous quelques instants sur cette poésie pour tenter d'en dégager certaines particularités que Paul Éluard a pu apprécier. Ce poème qui date du premier recueil de 1938 est une composition en vers libres[29]. Notons d'abord qu'aucune localisation n'est possible dans ce poème qui parle de jardin et de campagne, évoquant un paysage éminemment subjectif. Si les images-énoncés et les enchaînements peuvent nous paraître énigmatiques, ils s'inscrivent néanmoins dans un ensemble bien structuré. Leur thématique récurrente repose sur un lexique très générique, le poème désigne les éléments d'un paysage naturel et une conscience nostalgique du temps qui passe. Il est tout empreint d'une ambivalence affective: domine d'abord un sentiment de bonheur ou de quiétude qui est ensuite fragilisé

---

25 Parmi les poètes et écrivains édités par Mano, nous comptons Breton, Éluard, Péret, Tristan, Georges Bataille et aussi Schehadé. Ayant son propre atelier-librairie rue Huygens, à Montparnasse, il met beaucoup de soin à la recherche d'un équilibre entre texte, format, typographie et illustration.

26 Lettre de Paul Éluard à Georges Schehadé, Antibes, 30 mars 1938, cit. dans Baglione et Dichy, *Schehadé*, 86.

27 Lettre de Georges Schehadé à Paul Éluard, s. l., 10 avril 1938, cit. dans Baglione et Dichy, *Schehadé*, 86.

28 Poème manuscrit joint à la lettre adressée par Schehadé à Éluard, 10 avril 1938.

29 Stéphane Baquey, « Georges Schehadé, Edmond Jabès et Kateb Yacine, une époque de la littérature de langue française en Méditerranée », dans *Med-Mem*, Marseille : INA Med-Mem 2013. http://www.medmem.eu/fr/folder/47/georges-schehada-edmond-jabas-kateb-yacine.

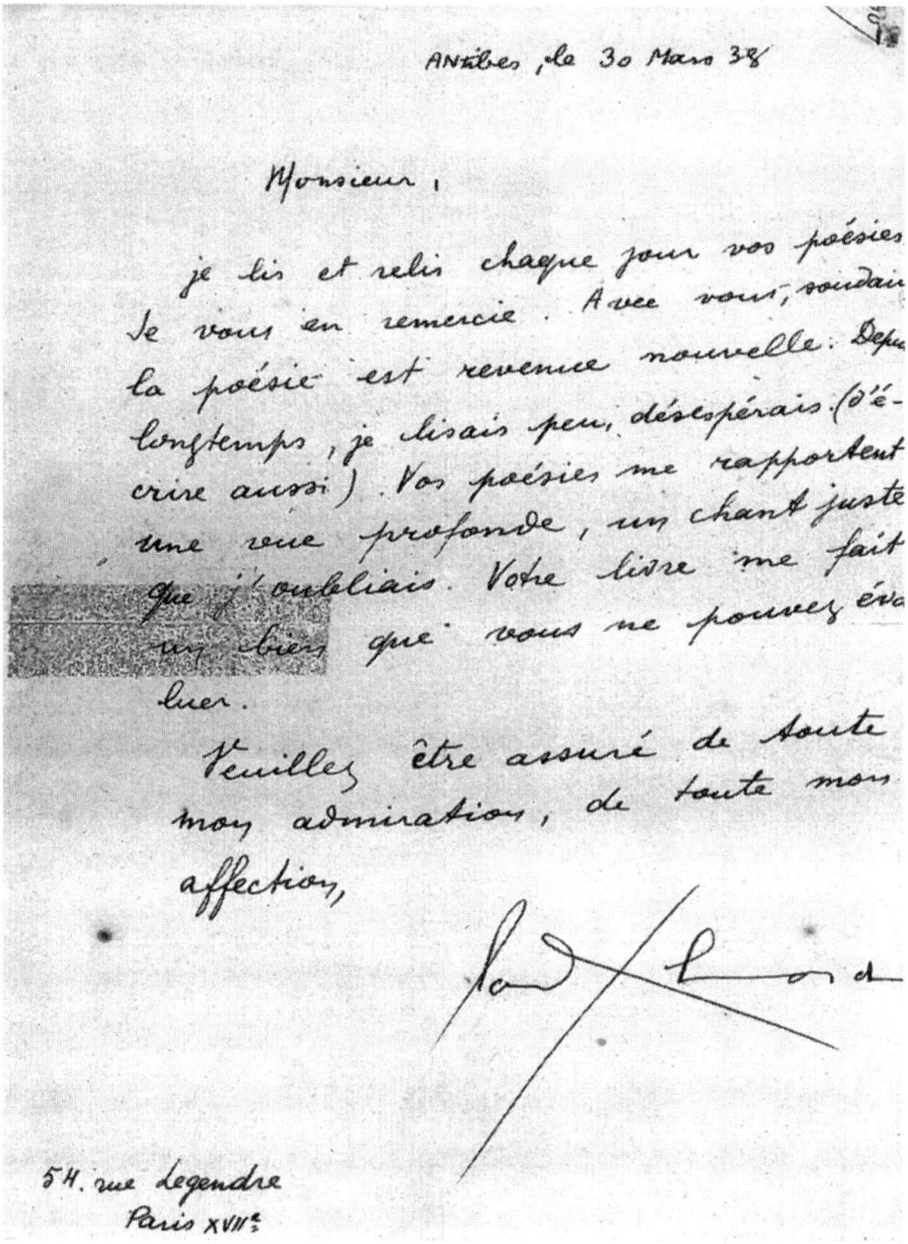

Antibes, le 30 Mars 38

Monsieur,

je lis et relis chaque jour vos poésies
Je vous en remercie. Avec vous, soudain
la poésie est revenue nouvelle. Depu
longtemps, je lisais peu, désespérais (d'é-
crire aussi). Vos poésies me rapportent
une vue profonde, un chant juste
que j'oubliais. Votre livre me fait
un bien que vous ne pouvez éva
luer.

Veuillez être assuré de toute
mon admiration, de toute mon
affection,

Paul Éluard

54. rue Legendre
Paris XVIIe

Illustration 2 : Lettre de Paul Éluard adressée à Georges Schehadé après la lecture du premier recueil des *Poésies*, 1938. © Archives Albert Dichy.

par des notions de rupture, de nostalgie et de mort. Comme le décrit Stéphane Baquey, « la perception de cette grâce fragile [du poème] se passe fort bien de la localisation dudit “jardin” en un “pays” » et de ce qu'un récit de vie pourrait

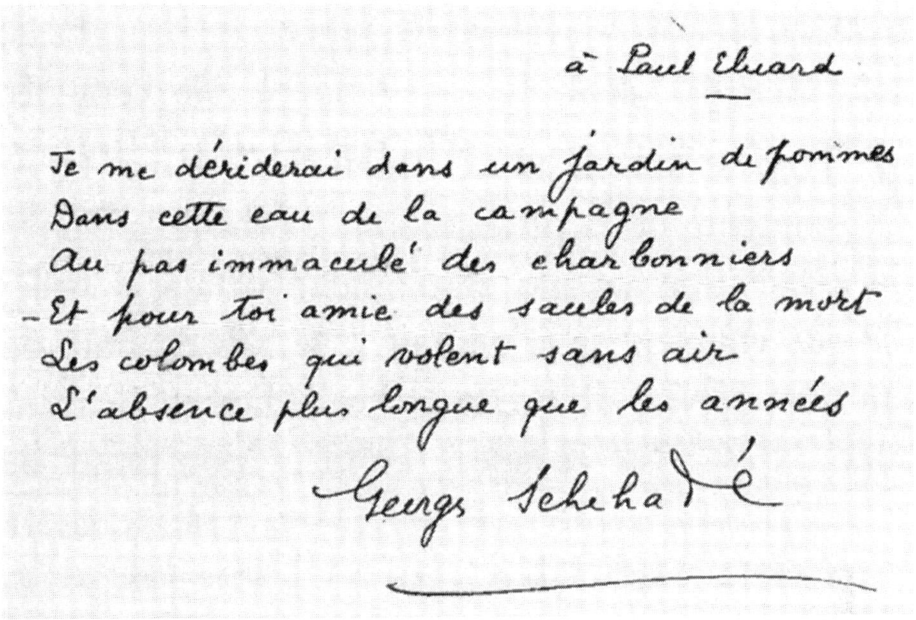
à Paul Eluard

Je me dériderai dans un jardin de pommes
Dans cette eau de la campagne
Au pas immaculé des charbonniers
– Et pour toi amie des saules de la mort
Les colombes qui volent sans air
L'absence plus longue que les années

Georges Schehadé

Illustration 3 : Poème manuscrit joint à la lettre adressée par Georges Schehadé à Paul Éluard, 10 avril 1938. © Archives Albert Dichy.

apporter sur ce qu'ont été les années que réactualise le poème[30]. C'est une poésie qui, de par la rigueur de sa composition, doit beaucoup à Max Jacob et à Paul Éluard[31]. Il convient par ailleurs de souligner que les surréalistes et Schehadé partagent une prédilection pour le romantisme allemand ainsi que pour Rimbaud[32].

Poète des deux rives, comme on l'a appelé, Schehadé se nourrit des imaginaires des deux cultures, de l'Orient et de l'Occident. Sans toutefois évoquer l'un ou l'autre pour insister sur l'altérité, comme ont pu le faire les poètes de l'époque romantique, Schehadé s'enrichit de ces deux pôles en les rapprochant dans l'imaginaire[33]. Son œuvre se nourrit des deux univers de sorte que, bien souvent, il paraît impossible de dire si c'est l'Orient ou l'Occident qui est convoqué, si ce sont les fastueux jardins du Levant ou le jardin d'Eden que le poète fait surgir. À l'instar de la vie du poète, les imaginaires se confondent, se mêlent et donnent

30 Baquey, « Georges Schehadé, Edmond Jabès et Kateb Yacine ».

31 Pour l'influence de la poésie surréaliste sur les intellectuels libanais des années 1930, voir aussi la contribution d'Alfred el-Khoury dans ce volume.

32 Nous renvoyons à Julia Drost, « "Caspar David Friedrich – peintre de l'angoisse romantique". Le surréalisme et l'héritage romantique allemand », dans *« Le Splendide XIXe Siècle » des surréalistes*, Julia Drost et Scarlett Reliquet (dir.), Dijon : Les Presses du réel 2013. Voir aussi *Trajectoires du rêve du romantisme au surréalisme*, Vincent Gille (dir.), Paris, Paris musées 2003.

33 Charis Goer et Michael Hofmann, dir., *Der Deutschen Morgenland. Bilder des Orients in der deutschen Literatur und Kultur von 1770 bis 1850*, Munich: Wilhelm Fink Verlag 2008.

naissance à un monde poétique propre, singulier. Le poète Gaëtan Picon, ami de Schehadé, préface *Les Poésies* pour une réédition chez Gallimard en 1952 et revient sur la métaphore de la valise, ici un « coffre » qui symbolise à ses yeux la valeur hors du temps et de l'espace de la poésie de Schehadé : « J'ouvre ce recueil – Les Poésies – comme un coffre que l'on peut transporter partout avec soi. » La poésie de Schehadé tiendrait son caractère « unique et incomparable » justement de l'impossibilité de la rattacher à une origine spécifique. C'est ce déracinement qui est pour lui la source d'une « senteur si complexe et si subtilement équilibrée que je ne la retrouverai nulle part et que les mots me manquent pour la décrire […]. C'est sans doute qu'elle appartient à une terre plus lointaine que celle dont je viens de parler … celle d'un "lointain intérieur": L'Orient [de Schehadé] est celui du cœur et de l'imaginaire[34] ».

« Charmant, redoutable et très enfant »

C'est seulement après la guerre que Schehadé séjourne à Paris pour la deuxième fois. Par l'intermédiaire de Max-Pol Fouchet, il rencontre – enfin – André Breton et se lie d'amitié avec de nombreux artistes et poètes : Benjamin Péret, Julien Gracq, René Char, Octavio Paz et bien d'autres. Breton vient lui-même de rentrer à Paris après cinq ans d'exil aux États-Unis. Dans un entretien, le poète et journaliste libanais Unsi al-Hajj lui demandera plus tard comment il a rencontré le chef de file des surréalistes :

> In Paris. I was walking with one of his friends. Suddenly, he took my arm violently, shook it and cried: "Georges! Georges! There is Breton!" We were on the pavement, and there was Breton, alone, walking in the middle of the street, keeping the same distance to those on his left and those on his right. Like a Red Indian chieftain. And the hair on his head like a lion's mane. He was sublime [*ʿālī*, lit. high] and noble. He said to me: "It is an honour." He said it in a certain way, stressing all the chivalry in the [word] honour. He was the greatest sorcerer [*kāhin*, which means a pagan priest and in Modern Standard Arabic would mean mostly a Christian priest] of French poetry[35].

Entre le pape du surréalisme et Schehadé naît une amitié spontanée qui durera quelques années. Le poète se souvient :

> The French mind, which insisted on loading poetry with ideas, embarrassed him. The Cartesian French mind, which surrealism has blown up by looking to the Orient. He probably found in my poetry an encounter with the spontaneity that surrealism tried to revive through the unconscious, and through dreams, automatic writing, and the blowing up of language[36].

---

34 Gaëtan Picon, « Préface », dans Georges Schehadé, *Les Poésies* [1952], Paris : Gallimard 2001, 7.

35 « Jūrj! Jūrj! Innahu Brūtūn! » dans Unsī al-Ḥājj, *Kalimāt, Kalimāt, Kalimāt*, Beyrouth: Dār al-Nahār li-l-Nashr 1987, 2:611–614. Je remercie Alfred el-Khoury de m'avoir fait connaître cette édition et d'avoir traduit ce passage en anglais.

36 Unsī al-Ḥājj, « Jūrj! Jūrj! Innahu Brūtūn! », 611–614.

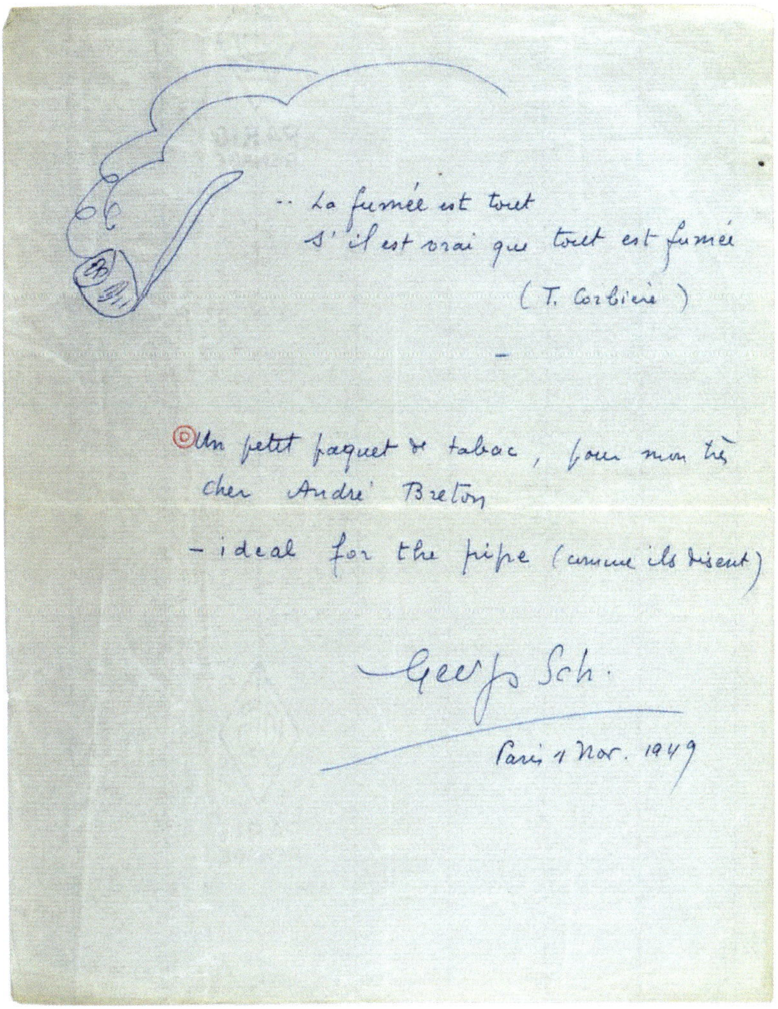

– La fumée est tout
s'il est vrai que tout est fumée
(T. Corbière)

–

Un petit paquet de tabac, pour mon très
cher André Breton
– ideal for the pipe (comme ils disent)

Georges Sch.
Paris 1 Nov. 1949

Illustration 4 : Lettre de Georges Schehadé adressée à André Breton, 1er novembre 1949. © Bibliothèque littéraire Jacques Doucet, Paris.

En 1949, Schehadé écrit à sa sœur : « Je vois souvent Breton avec qui je suis lié. Il est charmant, redoutable et très enfant[37] ». De nombreuses lettres, des dédicaces dans des livres, des petits mots et attentions envoyés par Schehadé à Breton témoignent de la profonde affection qu'il lui portait[38]. Schehadé se révèle aussi fin connaisseur de l'œuvre littéraire de Breton et lui envoie du tabac accompagné du dessin d'une petite pipe (ill. 4), allusion probable aux « Notes sur la poésie », parues

[37] Lettre de Georges Schehadé à Laurice Schehadé-Benzoni, s. l., 20 octobre 1949, cit. dans Baglione et Dichy, *Schéhadé*, 122.

[38] Ces documents datant du début des années 1950 sont conservées dans le fonds Breton à la Bibliothèque littéraire Jacques Doucet.

en décembre 1929 dans *La Révolution surréaliste*, dans lesquelles Breton avait écrit « La poésie est une pipe[39] » évoquant à son tour la célèbre peinture de René Magritte[40].

Le foisonnement de la capitale internationale des arts inspire et stimule Schehadé qui, pour la première fois, dit avoir l'impression de travailler dans des conditions favorables et accueillantes. Il décide donc de rester et de s'installer à Paris où vit de plus sa future femme, Brigitte Collerais, une Française rencontrée lors d'une traversée de la Méditerranée. À sa sœur Laurice, il écrit le 13 avril 1949 : « [...] on t'a dit que je comptais m'installer à Paris [...] Mon dernier voyage à Paris a été très fructueux [...] j'ai eu des contacts très intéressants. [...] GLM me dit que les jeunes poètes achètent mes livres, qu'ils trouvaient ce que j'écrivais magnifique et qu'il n'avait jamais vu auparavant : des poètes aimer un poète[41] ».

Après quelques difficultés, Schehadé trouve un travail à l'UNESCO, et comme s'il lui devait des excuses, il écrit à sa sœur : « Si je suis nommé à l'Unesco, je toucherai un traitement princier de l'ordre de 200 000 à 300 000 francs par mois ce qui me permettrait largement de vivre à Paris et d'envoyer de l'argent à papa et maman. À Beyrouth, je touche 1000 livres, soit 120 000 francs...[42] ». C'est alors que Schehadé entre dans le sérail des surréalistes, fréquentant même leurs réunions au café de la place Blanche. Dans un entretien pour *Le Monde*, il en dira plus tard avec humour et distance :

> Je suis allé aux fameuses réunions de la place Blanche. On aurait dit la Cène. Jean-le-Bien-Aimé (Benjamin Péret) prenait place à la droite du Maître. Les autres disciples l'écoutaient religieusement. Breton était comme un violoncelle. Il suffisait de glisser une pièce dans la fente pour qu'il résonne à l'infini... Je l'aimais[43].

---

39 André Breton, « Notes sur la poésie », *La Révolution surréaliste* 12 (15 décembre 1929), 53.

40 Cette affection est tangible également dans une lettre qu'il adresse à André Malraux en 1953 : « Je viens d'apprendre par Barrault [...] que vous vous proposez d'organiser une souscription pour aider André Breton à payer l'amende que vient de lui infliger le tribunal à la suite de la stupide histoire que l'on sait » (Lettre de Georges Schehadé à André Malraux, s.l., 15 décembre 1953, Bibliothèque littéraire Jacques Doucet, Paris, MLX, C. 734). « La stupide histoire que l'on sait » est un procès : Breton doit comparaître en 1953 au tribunal correctionnel de Cahors pour dégradation d'une peinture rupestre représentant la trompe d'un mammouth à la grotte de Pech-Merle. Il est condamné à une amende de 25 002 francs et doit payer 1 franc à la commune, 1 franc à l'État, 5000 francs d'amende et 20 000 francs de dommages et intérêts. Voir aussi Jean Record, « Un procès surréaliste : Abel Bessac contre André Breton », dans *La Dépêche*, 30 août 2017, https://www.ladepeche.fr/article/2017/08/30/2635946-un-proces-surrealiste-abel-bessac-contre-andre-breton.html. « Je serai heureux que vous songiez à moi... », écrit Schehadé à Malraux, « J'aimerais beaucoup aider, dans la mesure de mes moyens, mon ami Breton », Schehadé à Malraux, 15 décembre 1953.

41 Lettre de Schehadé à sa sœur Laurice, s.l., 13 avril 1949, cit. dans Baglione et Dichy, *Schehadé*, 120.

42 Lettre de Schehadé à Laurice, s. l., 13 avril 1949, cit. dans Baglione et Dichy, *Schehadé*, 120.

43 Sorin, « Schehadé ».

« *L'*Almanach *est une chose qui donne chaud au cœur* »

Dès lors, Schehadé ne semble plus seulement fortement inspiré par la modernité de la poésie surréaliste mais participe affectivement et activement au mouvement, même s'il ne devient jamais membre officiel du surréalisme et ne signe ni pétitions ni tracts. Ses poèmes sont publiés pour la première fois dans le cadre de l'*Almanach surréaliste du demi-siècle* dirigé par André Breton. À son retour d'exil, Breton avait trouvé la capitale française et la vie artistique profondément changées. Pour le chef de file du mouvement, l'enjeu est donc de lui donner un nouveau visage, de façonner le surréalisme de l'après-guerre. Son livre *Arcane 17*, paru en 1945, en est la première démonstration, signe d'espoir et de résurrection, tout comme l'Exposition internationale du surréalisme à Paris qui a lieu en 1947 à la galerie Maeght. Y participent un grand nombre de nouveaux artistes surréalistes qui ont rejoint le groupe pendant la guerre, toutefois ce n'est pas encore le cas de Schehadé qui a rencontré Breton trop tard. À travers l'*Almanach*, il s'agit non seulement de célébrer les trente ans du surréalisme, mais aussi de montrer qu'il est toujours bien vivant, contrairement à ce que peuvent dire de nombreuses voix malveillantes depuis la fin de la guerre. Publié en mars 1950 sous la forme d'un numéro spécial de la revue *La Nef*, avec un frontispice de Max Ernst, l'*Almanach* s'ouvre sur un calendrier recensant un certain nombre d'évènements mémorables de l'histoire de l'humanité envisagés au prisme du surréalisme[44]. Dans ce « Calendrier tour du monde des inventions tolérables » figurent les objets les plus ordinaires, tels une échelle ou une fourchette à escargots : les auteurs Breton et Péret rendent ainsi hommage à l'objet surréaliste et à la rêverie poétique que peut déclencher tout objet, aussi désuet soit-il. À ce calendrier répond en fin de volume un « Panorama du demi-siècle », restituant année par année les évènements retenus comme significatifs pour le surréalisme. Entre les deux, un certain nombre de textes et contributions rythment la structure de l'*Almanach*. Parmi les auteurs se trouvent notamment les nouvelles recrues du surréalisme, comme Schehadé. L'*Almanach* sert par ailleurs à inscrire le surréalisme dans la filiation des écrivains et philosophes dont il se réclame : c'est ainsi qu'on y trouve les noms de Sade, Lautréamont, Rimbaud et d'autres[45]. Schehadé contribue à cet *Almanach* par trois poèmes qui sont illustrés par l'artiste tchèque Toyen (1902–1980), comme le souhaitait Breton[46]. Bounoure et Schehadé, depuis Beyrouth, accusent réception de l'ouvrage dans une lettre

---

44 Gérard Durozoi, *Histoire du mouvement surréaliste*, Paris : Hazan 2004, 509–510 ; Jean-Pierre Cauvin, « Petites histoires d'almanach : tour du monde des inventions tolérables », dans *Pleine marge* 12 (1990).

45 Durozoi, *Histoire*, 512.

46 « J'ai reçu une lettre adorable de Breton, très affectueuse, où il insiste beaucoup pour mon retour à Paris – il dit que l'*Almanach* paraîtra dans quinze jours et qu'il me l'enverra, mes poèmes sont illustrés par Toyen […]. Il me demande ma collaboration pour une revue qu'il va diriger en octobre etc. etc. », Lettre de Georges Schehadé à Brigitte Collerais, s.l., 10 mars 1950, cit. dans Baglione et Dichy, *Schehadé*, 124.

commune datée du 26 avril 1950. Ils donnent leur impression en écrivant chacun une phrase à tour de rôle, un peu selon le principe d'un cadavre exquis.

> Mon cher Breton,
>
> Voici une lettre qui commence à 2 voix :
> G. Schehadé – l'Almanach est magnifique, nous avons surtout admiré et aimé
> G. Bounoure – Ce poème en prose de ce Dauphin et la Dauphine
> entre les plumes des ribauds et des ribaudes
> G. Schehadé – oui particulièrement ça…, et puis les mites qui recouvraient certains visages comme les moisissures de la conscience… (il s'agit d'un bouquet de visages comme une collection d'escargots)
> G. Bounoure – mais libres & pures, certaines effigies
> aimées comme les seins refermés des îles
> G. Schehadé – nous avons, Bounoure et moi, partagé
> Les deux exemplaires par vous adressés
> Un pour lui, un pour moi, comme les deux battants d'une porte aux merveilles…
> Merci pour leur envoi…[47] »

La lettre nous apprend par ailleurs que la collaboration entre Schehadé et Breton était harmonieuse. Le poète attire l'attention de Breton sur une erreur de temps dans un poème. Il aurait voulu dire « couvre de mirabelles » et non « couvrira » de mirabelles, mais n'en tient point rigueur : « Ce futur n'est pas très joli, tant pis ! Mais l'ensemble de l'*Almanach* est une chose qui donne chaud au cœur, vive la tribu ! […] Et n'oubliez pas de remercier Toyen pour les illustrations de mes poèmes – j'ai beaucoup aimé ces dessins (soleil et monde sont inclus)… très cher Breton, cette lettre écrite autour d'une cigarette, avec la plume paresseuse du matin ».

« L'ensemble de l'*Almanach* est une chose qui donne chaud au cœur. Vive la tribu. » Cette phrase cible avec humour une ou peut-être *la* raison d'être de cet almanach, à savoir l'existence même et la cohésion du surréalisme qui préoccupe tellement Breton, plus que toute autre chose. Il s'agit pour lui dans cet ouvrage de rassembler les artistes et les poètes, de développer de nouveaux apports théoriques, notamment sur l'automatisme et son avenir possible, en vue aussi d'inclure de nouveaux artistes dans la lignée du surréalisme, tels que Ramsès Younane (1913–1966) qui fut parmi les artistes majeurs du mouvement Art et Liberté au Caire ou, Jaroslav Serpan (1922–1976) et Simon Hantaï (1922–2008).

À l'instar de la fin des années 1930, lorsque l'arrivée d'artistes comme Roberto Matta (1911–2002), Kurt Seligman (1900–1962) ou Wifredo Lam (1902–1982) avait marqué un nouvel élan et le début d'une deuxième génération de surréalistes, l'après-guerre connaît une exceptionnelle ouverture, une nouvelle configuration nourrie de nouveaux noms et de nouveaux apports, comme Breton le précise dans ses entretiens radiophoniques en 1952 :

---

47 Lettre de Georges Schehadé à André Breton, Beyrouth, 26 avril 1950, Bibliothèque littéraire Jacques Doucet, Paris.

> […] Il ne manque pas aujourd'hui de se produire d'œuvres qui, sans être surréalistes à la lettre, le sont plus ou moins profondément par l'esprit. Il n'y a pas, à mes yeux, de différence intrinsèque entre ce qui peut animer le lyrisme de Jean-Pierre Duprey et celui de Malcolm de Chazal. Au théâtre, deux œuvres récentes de très haut timbre comme Le Roi pêcheur de Julien Gracq et Monsieur Bob'le de Georges Schehadé doivent, au même titre, être tenues pour intégralement surréalistes[48].

Pour Breton, cela ne fait pas de doute, Schehadé est un poète et écrivain surréaliste. Dans la même optique, il inscrit Schehadé dans une chronologie du surréalisme à laquelle il travaille en 1953. Ce dossier intitulé « Flair » se veut une chronologie commentée, année après année, de l'activité littéraire et artistique qui a eu lieu autour du surréalisme et de ses prémices. Pour Breton, il ne fait aucun doute que Schehadé y ait sa place. Il y figure en 1938, année de parution des *Poésies* chez GLM, et en 1951, avec *Monsieur Bob'le* (ill. 5 et 6).

Qu'y-a-t-il de surréaliste dans cette pièce de théâtre en trois actes, mise en scène en 1951 par Georges Vitaly au théâtre de la Huchette, avec des décors et costumes de Dora Maar et une musique de Maurice Ohana ? Les trois actes tournent autour de la figure de Monsieur Bob'le, admiré de tous : il part en voyage dans le premier acte, est absent dans le deuxième, et on attend son retour dans le troisième. Un critique écrit dans *Combat* : « La pièce coule comme une source d'eau transparente et secrète, et l'auteur y a mis des moments de drôleries et d'émotion tout à fait en dehors des chemins battus. Un auteur dramatique ? Je ne sais. Un poète ? Sans aucun doute[49] ». Si l'on excepte cette critique favorable, la presse parisienne se déchaîne. La pièce fait scandale, elle rompt complètement avec les habitudes théâtrales, car elle se passe d'action et de tout enchaînement dramatique. Par la suite, on rapprochera le théâtre de Schehadé du Nouveau Théâtre de Samuel Beckett et d'Eugène Ionesco. Seul Breton défend l'« exceptionnelle beauté[50] » de la pièce, alors que les réactions de la critique rappellent l'onde de choc des premiers temps du surréalisme. Ainsi, Robert Kemp se moque dans *Le Monde* : « Que c'est beau ! Que c'est beau cette patience du public à chercher pendant deux heures le sens d'une pièce ! Il essaie de l'attraper, par la moustache ou par la queue, comme un rat. Mais le sens est malin et s'esquive par tous les trous du texte […] il n'entend qu'un mélange rance d'images fatiguées ; une parodie du surréalisme à ses débuts… Des phrases d'enfants arriérés, de vieillards à l'asile […] C'est le triomphe du faux, du piège, de l'attrape-nigaud[51] ». Art de fous, art enfantin, jeu du piège et du non-sens, *Monsieur Bob'le* réunit tous les ingrédients pour plaire au chef de file

---

48 « Entretiens radiophoniques » dans André Breton, *Œuvres complètes*, dir. Marguerite Bonnet, Paris : Gallimard/Pléiade 1988–2008, 3:563.

49 Critique de Thierry Maulnier dans le journal *Combat*, du 9 février 1951, cit. dans Baglione et Dichy, *Schehadé*, 133.

50 André Breton, « [Pour Monsieur Bob'le de Monsieur Schehadé] », dans *Œuvres complètes*, dir. Marguerite Bonnet, Paris : Gallimard/Pléiade 1988–2008, 3:1034.

51 Robert Kemp, « Monsieur Bob'le », dans *Le Monde*, 3 février 1951, http://abonnes.lemonde.fr/archives/article/1951/02/03/monsieur-bob-le_2066305_1819218.html.

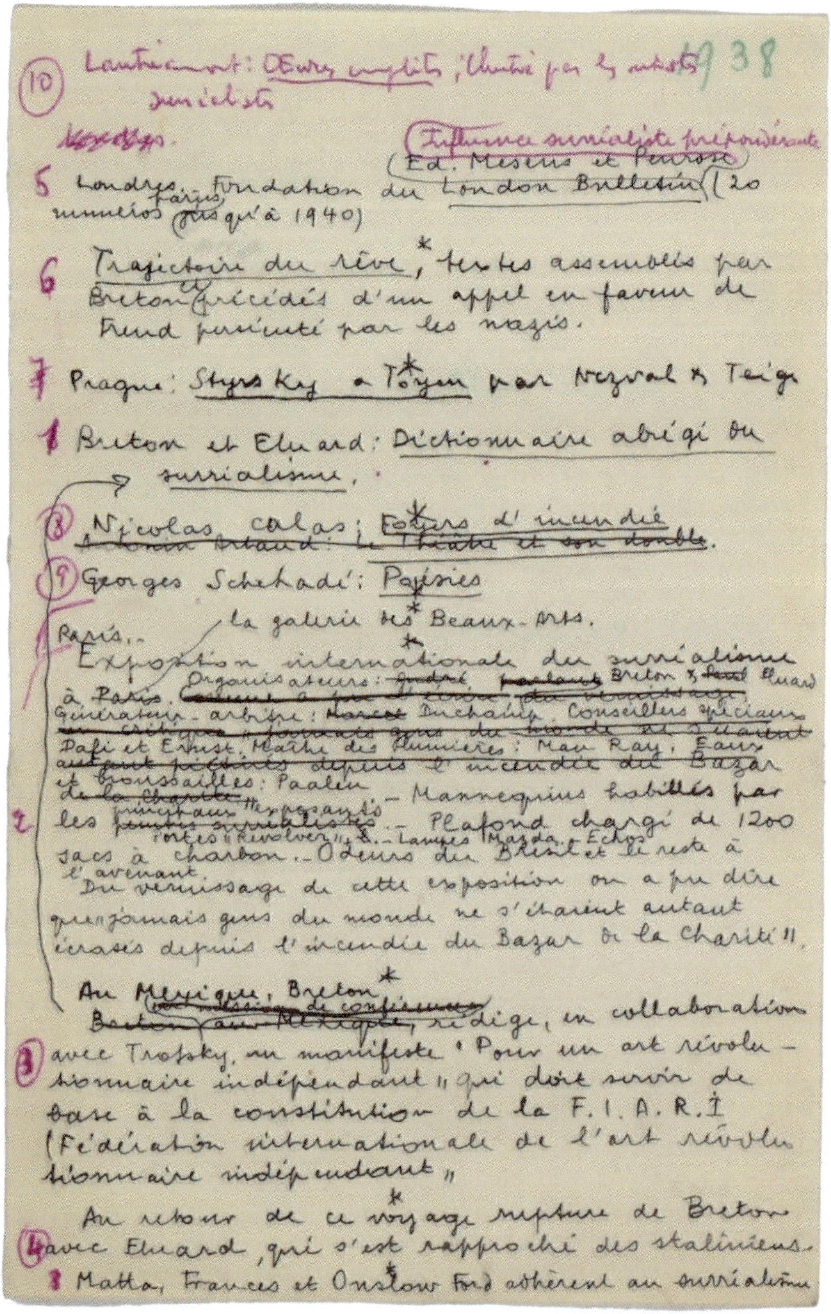

1938

(10) Lautréamont : Œuvres complètes, illustrées par les artistes surréalistes

(Influence surréaliste prépondérante)
(Ed. Mesens et Penrose)

5 Londres, Paris : Fondation du London Bulletin (20 numéros jusqu'à 1940)

6 Trajectoire du rêve, textes assemblés par Breton et précédés d'un appel en faveur de Freud persécuté par les nazis.

7 Prague : Styrsky et Toyen par Nezval et Teige

1 Breton et Eluard : Dictionnaire abrégé du surréalisme.

(8) Nicolas Calas : Foyers d'incendie
~~Antonin Artaud : Le Théâtre et son double~~.

(9) Georges Schehadé : Poésies

2 Paris. – Exposition internationale du surréalisme à la galerie des Beaux-Arts. Organisateurs : Breton & Eluard. Générateur-arbitre : Duchamp. Conseillers spéciaux Dali et Ernst. Maître des lumières : Man Ray. Eaux et broussailles : Paalen – Mannequins habillés par les principaux exposants. – Plafond chargé de 1200 sacs à charbon. – Portes « Revolver », Lampes Mazda, Echos, Odeurs du Brésil et le reste à l'avenant.
Du vernissage de cette exposition on a pu dire que « jamais gens du monde ne s'étaient autant écrasés depuis l'incendie du Bazar de la Charité ».

(3) Au Mexique, Breton rédige, en collaboration avec Trotsky, un manifeste « Pour un art révolutionnaire indépendant » qui doit servir de base à la constitution de la F.I.A.R.I. (Fédération internationale de l'art révolutionnaire indépendant »

(4) Au retour de ce voyage rupture de Breton avec Eluard, qui s'est rapproché des staliniens.

8 Matta, Frances et Onslow Ford adhèrent au surréalisme

Illustrations 5 et 6 : Manuscrit d'André Breton pour « Flair », une chronologie commentée de l'activité littéraire et artistique autour du surréalisme. © Bibliothèque littéraire Jacques Doucet, Paris.

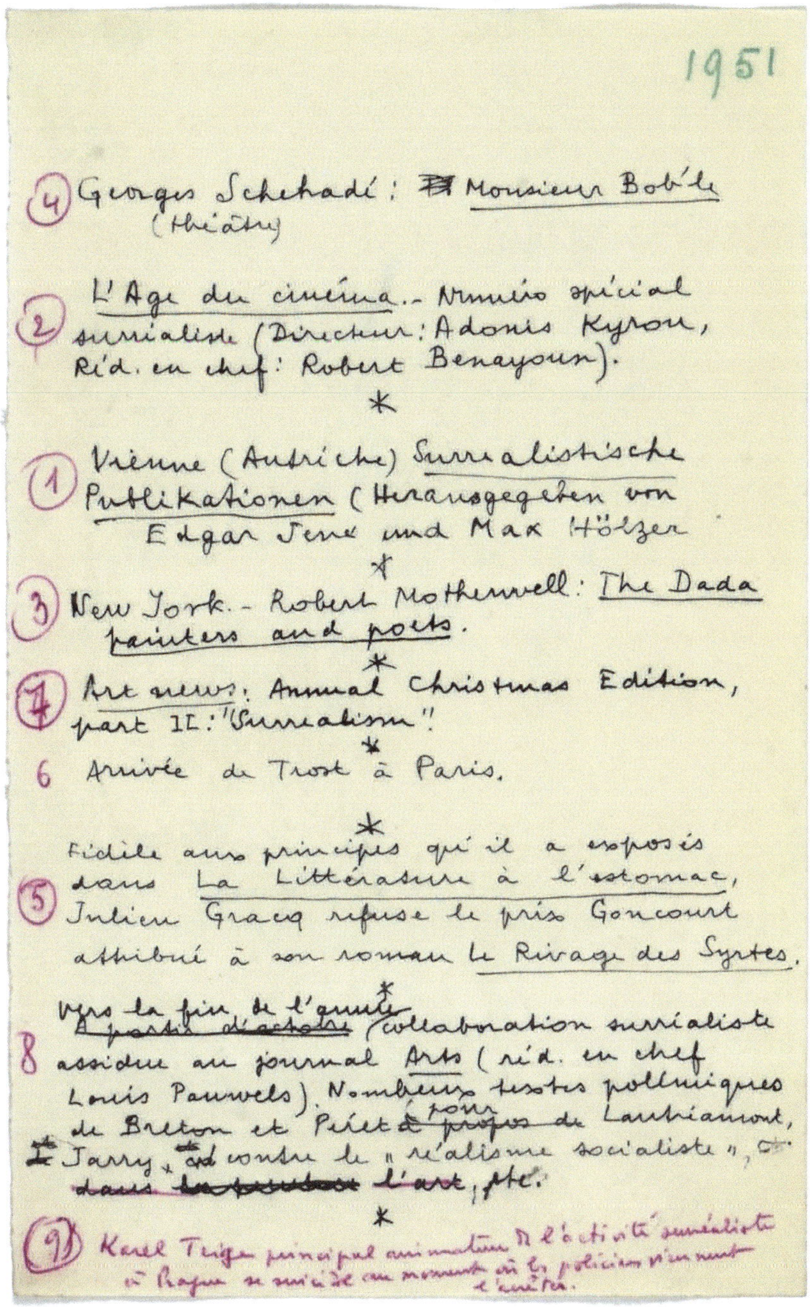

1951

(4) Georges Schehadé : ~~M~~ Monsieur Bob'le
(théâtre)

(2) L'Age du cinéma. – Numéro spécial surréaliste (Directeur : Adonis Kyrou, Réd. en chef : Robert Benayoun).

*

(1) Vienne (Autriche) Surrealistische Publikationen (Herausgegeben von Edgar Jené und Max Hölzer

*

(3) New York. – Robert Motherwell : The Dada painters and poets.

*

(7) Art news : Annual Christmas Edition, part II : "Surrealism".

*

6 Arrivée de Trost à Paris.

*

(5) Fidèle aux principes qu'il a exposés dans La Littérature à l'estomac, Julien Gracq refuse le prix Goncourt attribué à son roman Le Rivage des Syrtes.

*

8 Vers la fin de l'année ~~A partir d'octobre~~ collaboration surréaliste assidue au journal Arts (réd. en chef Louis Pauwels). Nombreux textes polémiques de Breton et Péret ~~à propos de~~ pour Lautréamont, Jarry, et contre le « réalisme socialiste », ~~dans les problèmes~~ ~~l'art~~, etc.

*

(9) Karel Teige principal animateur de l'activité surréaliste à Prague se suicide au moment où les policiers viennent l'arrêter.

des surréalistes, même si la relation de Schehadé avec le surréalisme semble rester ambivalente.

Schehadé n'appartient pas à un surréalisme vécu ou affiché dans une dimension collective. Le poète libanais a laissé une œuvre singulière qui se nourrit d'un certain nombre « d'outils » poétiques surréalistes ainsi que des réseaux du mouvement, et qui sera accueillie en France comme une œuvre francophone majeure, en premier lieu par les surréalistes. Sa réussite a dépendu très largement, comme nous l'avons vu, du soutien que Schehadé a trouvé en France, son pays d'accueil où il a su fusionner ses origines et son parcours marqué par la migration.

Le philosophe et théoricien de la communication Vilém Flusser a proposé de voir cette situation entre deux rives ou cultures comme une problématique de deux ordres de réalités qui se rencontrent. Dans ses essais « We Need a Philosophy of Emigration » et « Exile and Creativity », Flusser développe une conception large de l'émigration qui peut s'appliquer à l'analyse de la vie entre les deux rives de Schehadé[52]. Ayant fait lui-même l'expérience de l'émigration et de l'exil, Flusser non seulement rend compte de sa vie personnelle, mais tente aussi de saisir l'état d'émigration de manière dialectique : à savoir comme un état dans lequel l'ancien et le nouveau se rencontrent ; dans lequel le passé et le présent se pénètrent et se conditionnent mutuellement :

> The immigrant [...] is partially opened to the new contingence, precisely at those points where the old contingence has been ironically rejected. At these points he is able to assimilate the new contingence and assimilate himself to it. And at those points where he chooses to retain pieces of his old contingence, he is able to act on the new one as well[53].

L'émigration est interprétée comme une sorte de condition conflictuelle, résultant de la tension permanente entre le nouveau et l'ancien, entre deux cultures. En fin de compte, c'est précisément grâce à cette tension que peut se libérer l'énergie créative. L'exil devient ainsi une source de créativité, comme l'illustre l'exemple du poète libanais. C'est en France que Schehadé crée sa plus grande œuvre, nourrie et inspirée par la poésie française et notamment par le surréalisme. C'est ici d'ailleurs que Schehadé a reçu le Grand prix de la francophonie en 1986. Il en ressort que la réception officielle de son œuvre est largement passée par l'Europe : par la France, mais également par l'Allemagne par exemple, où son théâtre a connu un grand succès[54].

52 Vilém Flusser, « We Need a Philosophy of Emigration » et « Exile and Creativity », dans *The Freedom of the Migrant. Objections to Nationalism*, dir. Anke K. Finger, Champaign : University of Illinois Press 2003, 21–24 et 81–87.

53 Flusser, *Freedom of the Migrant*, 23.

54 Voir « Durch die Blume », dans *Der Spiegel* 41 (1960), 81–82. La recherche sur Schehadé en est à ses débuts. Ainsi, une étude sur son théâtre fait toujours défaut.

« Je l'ai échappé belle »

Qu'en est-il de sa réception au Liban ? Son œuvre y est également connue, mais en différé. Car si Schehadé a été en France officiellement reconnu par les autorités de la francophonie, c'est surtout auprès de jeunes lettrés que ses écrits ont trouvé un écho au Liban en passant par l'Europe où la censure, le conservatisme et le conformisme régnant dans les pays arabes obligent les poètes à s'installer, notamment en France. C'est le cas du Libanais Ghazi Younès (né en 1950) qui semble être particulièrement marqué par l'œuvre de Schehadé[55]. Son travail encore mal connu mériterait d'être étudié plus en détail. Selon Narjess D'Outreligne, « ce dessinateur, poète et acteur de théâtre de la nouvelle génération […], a participé activement à la continuité de la production artistique surréaliste au Moyen Orient[56]. » Il est ainsi « intervenu dans les traductions de Tzara et Soupault » en arabe[57]. Aux côtes de l'Irakien Abdul Kader El Janabi (né en 1944), Younès fonde en 1973 la revue *Le Désir libertaire* qui « appelle à tout détruire, à se révolter contre les valeurs du nationalisme islamique et à rejeter toutes les valeurs et traditions arabo-musulmanes[58]. » La revue sous-titrée *Revue du surréalisme interdit dans les pays arabes sous l'irresponsabilité d'Abdel Kader al-Janabi* est bilingue, se revendique d'une orientation révolutionnaire démocratique, étrille le règne du capital et se réclame à la fois du surréalisme et du marxisme[59].

Schehadé n'a jamais participé à un numéro du *Désir libertaire*, qui publie par ailleurs des contributions d'auteurs comme Georges Henein, Benjamin Péret, Paul Celan, Unsi al-Hajj, Theodor Adorno et bien d'autres. Il n'a jamais voulu adhérer à un collectif, et a fortiori à un collectif politique engagé. On pense dans ce contexte notamment au groupe Art et Liberté[60]. Il paraît surprenant qu'on ne trouve dans les archives du poète, à notre connaissance, aucune mention de ce collectif qui s'est pourtant formé dans le pays où il est né. Dans l'exposition présentée au Musée national d'art moderne à Paris en 2016, sur le schéma mural figurant les

55 Narjess D'Outreligne, « Le surréalisme en Orient », dans *Arabica* 50, fasc. 2 (avril 2003), 249.

56 D'Outreligne, « Le surréalisme en Orient », 249.

57 Voir Marc Kober, « Introduction », dans *Le Désir libertaire. Le Surréalisme arabe à Paris, 1973–1975*, Abdul Kader El Janabi, dir., Toulouse : L'Asymétrie 2018, 15. Voir également la contribution de Monique Bellan dans le présent ouvrage.

58 Cinq numéros paraîtront entre 1973 et 1975 (n° 1 : 5 décembre 1973 ; n° 2–3 : 15 avril 1974 ; n° 4 : 26 juillet 1974 ; n° 5 : 1 novembre 1974), puis trois autres en 1980 et 1981 (n° 1 : « L'Amnésie administrée », [1980] ; n° 2 : « L'Islam brûle », 25 décembre 1980 ; n° 3 : « SU-BobJECTIVITÉS », [1981]). Voir D'Outreligne, « Le surréalisme en Orient », 249. Dans son article, l'auteure compte par ailleurs les Irakiens Haifa Zangana (1950) et Salah Failk (1945) ainsi que l'Algérien Farid Lariby (1937–1990) parmi les membres fondateurs de la revue. Ces informations ne sont toutefois pas confirmées par Marc Kober qui ne nomme qu'al-Janabi et Younès comme fondateurs du *Désir libertaire*. Voir Kober, « Introduction », 13.

59 « Avis aux lecteurs », dans *Le Désir libertaire* (25 décembre 1980), 6.

60 Sam Bardaouil et Till Fellrath, dir., *Art et Liberté. Rupture, guerre et surréalisme en Égypte, 1938–1948*, cat. exp., Paris : Skira/Centre Georges Pompidou 2016.

réseaux surréalistes dans le monde, la flèche reliant Le Caire à Beyrouth renvoyait à Gabriel Bounoure qui était présent à Beyrouth et non à Schehadé à Paris. Et ce fut Unsi al-Hajj qui fit connaître le surréalisme au Liban[61]. Alfred el-Khoury montre dans le présent volume que Unsi al-Hajj a non seulement joué un rôle important de médiateur par le biais des traductions qui rendaient des textes de Jacques Prévert (1900–1977), Antonin Artaud (1896–1948) et André Breton accessibles au public libanais et arabophone. Sa fine connaissance des auteurs surréalistes ainsi que de ceux dont se réclamaient ces derniers, comme Rimbaud, Sade, Lautréamont et d'autres, l'a par ailleurs conduit à inventer une poésie moderne « appealing to the Arab literati, who might have found in its exaltation of love and lyric tonalities a discourse that they could admire and identify with[62] ».

En résumé, le mérite d'avoir fait connaître le surréalisme au Liban, ne revient donc pas d'abord à Schehadé mais à son homologue cadet, Unsi al-Hajj, alors que Schehadé développe ses activités à Paris où il devient une figure importante du renouveau du mouvement après la Seconde Guerre mondiale.

Les surréalistes parisiens ont aidé Schehadé à trouver sa voie. C'est grâce aux rencontres avec Éluard, Breton, Péret et d'autres que le Libanais parvient à développer une poésie et un théâtre poétique singuliers. La signification de ces échanges est à elle seule soulignée par la métaphore à travers laquelle Schehadé se décrit comme un fils du surréalisme. Cependant, il lui aura fallu s'en défaire pour aller plus loin, se sentir libre de toute contrainte et trouver sa propre voix : « Je l'ai échappé belle (au surréalisme) » dira-t-il en 1985, se félicitant de n'avoir rencontré le chef de file du mouvement que sur le tard, sinon « Breton m'aurait aspiré dans ses réacteurs[63] ».

61 Nous renvoyons au texte d'Alfred el-Khoury dans ce volume.
62 Voir la contribution d'Alfred el-Khoury dans le présent volume, 195.
63 Sorin, « Schehadé ».

Chapter 7
Unsī al-Ḥājj's surrealist encounters

Alfred el-Khoury[1]

In the history of surrealism, there are very few notions that have proved as instrumental and significant as the notion of "encounter". Even in the pre- and early history of the surrealist venture, this notion plays a formative role, as the first tremors of surrealism

> [...] occurred in the form of a series of encounters between individual writers and painters during the First World War: André Breton and Jacques Vaché in a mental hospital in Nantes; Marcel Duchamp and Francis Picabia in New York; Tristan Tzara and Richard Huelsenbeck and Hans Arp in Zürich.[2]

It is, likewise, by means of encounters that the artistic conceptions and literary lineages of the early surrealists were shaped: their encounter with Giorgio de Chirico's *Mystère et mélancolie d'une rue* (1914), with Pierre Reverdy's reflections on the poetical image, and with Lautréamont's *Les Chants de Maldoror* (1868–1869), to mention only a few examples.[3] It is not surprising, moreover, that what mostly struck the surrealists in Lautréamont's work was an image of a strange encounter taken for the epitome of the beautiful: "beau [...] comme la rencontre fortuite sur une table de dissection d'une machine à coudre et d'un parapluie!" (beautiful... like the chance encounter on a dissecting table of a sewing machine and an umbrella!).[4]

One facet of the encounter notion are those instances when, at different stages and historical junctures, the surrealists' paths came to cross those of revolutionaries, artists and writers from all over the world. On the one hand, these encounters had the merit of bringing refreshing light into surrealism in times of crisis and

---

1 An earlier version of this chapter was presented as a public lecture at the Orient-Institut Beirut on 26 May 2016. The present version has benefited from the comments and remarks I received during the lecture, especially those from Prof. Lucy McNeece and Prof. Stefan Leder. I would also like to thank Fatras/Succession Editions for giving me permission to publish the manuscripts of Jacques Prévert (figs. 2–5) in this chapter, and to the staff at the archives of the American University of Beirut Libraries for providing me with scanned copies of this material.

2 Roger Shattuck, "Love and Laughter: Surrealism Reappraised", in: Maurice Nadeau, *The History of Surrealism* [1945], trans. Richard Howard, Harmondsworth: Penguin Books 1978, 13.

3 See, for example, the "Chronology of Surrealist Engagement with Ideas" in Krzysztof Fijałkowski and Michael Richardson, eds., *Surrealism: Key Concepts*, London: Routledge 2016, 255–266, which is, for a large part of it, nothing but a chronology of surrealist encounters.

4 See translation in Keith Aspley, *Historical Dictionary of Surrealism*, Lanham: The Scarecrow Press 2010, 7.

schisms, while on the other hand they represented to the surrealists the confirmation of the veracity and universality of their practices, positions and beliefs. Although the extent of the surrealists' openness to the "Other" remains a contested matter,[5] surrealism would emerge different after each of these encounters, the chronicles of which have not yet been written or thought out as they deserve.

The present chapter deals with an obverse instance of this last facet of encounter: the encounters of the Lebanese poet and journalist Unsī al-Ḥājj (1937–2014) with three pivotal figures of French surrealism: Jacques Prévert (1900–1977), Antonin Artaud (1896–1948) and André Breton (1896–1966). Through discussing al-Ḥājj's translation of these three surrealists, the chapter aims at shedding light on his surrealist mission, its reception among the Arab literati and the resonances it left in Arabic literature. While presenting al-Ḥājj's surrealist engagements against the backdrop of modernist attempts in Arabic poetry since the 1930s, I try to show, equally, that these were not disconnected from his own poetical itinerary. On the contrary, the latter's developments, stages and detours could appear under an illuminating light when read in relation to al-Ḥājj's surrealist encounters.

The literary context: The reception of surrealism among Lebanese intellectuals since the 1930s

In his *Rawābiṭ al-fikr wa-l-rūḥ bayn al-ʿarab wa-l-faranjah* (The Intellectual and Spiritual Ties Between the Arabs and the French, 1943), Ilyās Abū Shabakah (1903–1947) – a romantic Lebanese poet who came to fame in the late 1930s – evokes the school of Rimbaud and Verlaine, which, as he asserts, has corrupted (*afsadat*) the young generation of Lebanese writers. For these writers have abandoned "the spiritual, Sufi poetry and turned to the symbolist poetry as they understood it, or, more precisely, to the insane side of this literature [*al-jānib al-mariḍ min hādhā l-adab*]".[6] In the same vein, the *tammūzī*[7] poet Khalīl Ḥāwī (1919–1982) speaks of Rimbaud, who "exceeded all bounds in drinking and drug [use]", observing that "some adepts of surrealism have found delight in inventing imaginary worlds

5 Cf. Martine Antle, "Surrealism and the Orient", *Yale French Studies* 109 (2006).

6 Ilyās Abū Shabakah, *Rawābiṭ al-fikr wa-l-rūḥ bayn al-ʿarab wa-l-faranjah*, 2nd ed., Beirut: Dār al-Makshūf 1945, 162–163. All translations in this chapter, unless noted otherwise, are my own.

7 The term *tammūzī* (from Tammuz, the lover of the goddess Ishtar in the religious literature of Babylonia) was first coined by Jabrā Ibrāhīm Jabrā to designate the Arab poets of the late 1950s who were inspired by the Mesopotamian myths of resurrection and fertility. Per Jabrā, the *tammūzī* poets included Adonis, Yūsuf al-Khāl, Badr Shākir al-Sayyāb and Khalīl Ḥāwī. The term was later applied to other poets and has gained considerable prominence since its first usage. See Jabrā Ibrāhīm Jabrā, "Yūsuf al-Khāl: al-Mafāzah wa-l-biʾr wa-l-lāh", *Shiʿr* 7–8 (1958), 57–67, esp. 60. The article was republished in: Jabrā Ibrāhīm Jabrā, *al-Nār wa-l-jawhar: Dirāsāt fī l-shiʿr*, Beirut: Dār al-Quds 1975, 37–47, see esp. 40n1.

which have no meaning, devoid, fragile, endlessly threatened by nothingness and their foundations permeated by the absurd".[8]

These two stances, separated by some two decades, provide us with a glance into the unsympathetic, and at times hostile, positions stirred by surrealism among Lebanese poets and intellectuals since the 1930s.[9] At the root of these positions there lie, I would suggest, a partial conception and a confusion. The latter is the total assimilation of surrealism to Dadaism and to extreme cases of symbolism (Rimbaud and Verlaine, for instance),[10] while the former, i.e. the partial conception, is that surrealism was conceived of and represented only through its most extreme and turbulent aspects, which constitute but one side of the complete picture: its iconoclasm, its blasphemous activities, and its "adolescent provocations", to borrow Henri Peyre's words.[11] Those Lebanese intellectuals, although they were under the spell of French literature and culture[12] and open to an assorted variety of Western influences, saw in surrealism a threat, a strange and dangerous practice that has nothing to do with "true" literature and thus went to denigrate it.[13] The "positive"[14] achievements of surrealism, namely, its "mythical and magical ambitions", its endeavours to prepare the way for "[t]he release of Desire and the triumph of Love",[15] are hardly reflected in these early definitions and conceptions.

With this in mind, one grasps the full implications of a Lebanese poet writing in Arabic and adopting the views and agenda of surrealism at the time. Unsī al-Ḥājj was not unaware of these implications and the challenges awaiting him as he

---

8 Khalīl Ḥāwī, *Khalīl Ḥāwī: Falsafat al-shiʿr wa-l-ḥaḍārah*, ed. Ritā ʿAwaḍ, Beirut: Dār al-Nahār 2002, 105–106.

9 The attack on surrealism and its "adepts" in Arabic literature was later taken over by the review *al-Ādāb* (Beirut, 1953–2012; published electronically as of 2015) in its *querelle* with the review *Shiʿr*, which broke out in the early 1960s. Although not always mentioned by name, al-Ḥājj was the main target for many of *al-Ādāb*'s attacks. He was represented as a foolish adolescent, a mercenary for the West and an enemy of Arab nationalism. See, for instance, "Ūlāʾika al-muzayyafūn…", *al-Ādāb* 9, no. 3 (1961); and "Falsafat 'al-irtizāq'", *al-Ādāb* 9, no. 4 (1961). See also Suhayl Idrīs's editorial, "al-Wujūh al-mustaʿārah", *al-Ādāb* 9, no. 7 (1961).

10 Abū Shabakah contrasts these extreme cases with what he calls "orthodox symbolism" (*al-ramziyyah al-mustaqīmah*), of which he is considered a pioneer in Arabic poetry. See Abū Shabakah, *Rawābiṭ al-fikr*, 66.

11 Henri Peyre, "The Significance of Surrealism", *Yale French Studies* 2 (1948), 38.

12 "Perhaps we will not be mistaken", writes Abū Shabakah, "if we affirm that France is the breast of the world, and that all the social, political and literary movements were nurtured from this breast". Abū Shabakah, *Rawābiṭ al-fikr*, 7.

13 As ʿIṣām Maḥfūẓ has noted, "the surrealist adventure seemed, at the time, the utmost revolutionary extremism, [held] against the utmost reactionary extremism, the roots of which go back more than a thousand years in our tradition [*ʿindanā*]". ʿIṣām Maḥfūẓ, *al-Sūryāliyyah wa-tafāʿulātuhā l-ʿarabiyyah*, Beirut: al-Muʾassasah al-ʿArabiyyah li-l-Dirāsāt wa-l-Nashr 1987, 83–84.

14 I employ the term "positive" here merely as a contrast to the "negative" reception of surrealism discussed above.

15 Peyre, "Significance", 34.

engaged in his poetical journey in the late 1950s. His surrealist mission seems, from this standpoint, remarkably cognizant and self-reflexive, especially in its beginnings.[16] Early on, he was careful to differentiate himself not only from the literati of the *nahḍah* (the Arab Renaissance) and the neoclassical poets, but also from the *tammūzī* poets, his peers and colleagues at the review *Shiʿr* (Beirut, 1957–1964 and 1967–1970). These poets, in the footsteps of T.S. Eliot's *The Waste Land* that they held in great admiration, became so fascinated by the Mesopotamian myths of fertility and the cycles of death and rebirth as to employ them to excess:

> [...] as the [Tammuz] myth originally belonged to our part of the world it seemed natural that Arab poets would incorporate it into their work. Thus the dominant theme in the Arabic poetry of the fifties was that of the parched land waiting for rain; of fertility restored through the blood of Tammuz, murdered by the wild boar; of death and resurrection.[17]

Al-Ḥājj, on the other hand, seemed to be evolving in another orbit. His sources – so to speak – were to be sought elsewhere. Eliot's magnum opus had not spoken to him and the myths of death and rebirth did not appease his fears and doubts. He was, as Khālidah Saʿīd has noted, driven by a "desperate, nihilistic rejection".[18] Thus we find him declaring in one of his early poems, in a mixture of sarcasm and bitterness:

> *aḥtariq lā ubʿath, lā arjiʿ li-usfak*[19]
>
> (I burn [but] am not resurrected, I do not come back to be sacrificed)

The extra-literary dimension: Khālidah Saʿīd's narrative

This is not to say, however, that al-Ḥājj's surrealist mission was solely driven by, or confined to, literary claims and agendas. These were just one side of the coin, the other side being his extra-literary occupations: the issues of love, the woman,

---

16 Besides his adoption of surrealism as both a literary affiliation and *état d'âme*, al-Ḥājj's radicalism and provocations were amplified by his choice of the *poème en prose* as the exclusive and quintessential medium for modernist poetry, unleashing thus an attack upon the hegemony of traditional forms of Arabic metrics and dressing himself as the spokesperson of this new form in Arabic literature – see his celebrated introduction/manifesto to his first poetry collection, *Lan* (Beirut: Dār Majallat Shiʿr 1960, 5–15). On the reception of al-Ḥājj and the Arabic *poème en prose*, see Muhammad A. Deeb, "The Critical Reception of al-Ḥājj and the *Poème en prose*", *Canadian Review of Comparative Literature* 12, no. 3 (1985). On the other hand, many critics have noted the complementary role played by the *poème en prose* as an avant-gardist literary medium and linked its advent into Arabic literature to that of surrealism: see, for instance, Vénus Khoury-Ghata, "La Poésie arabe au Moyen-Orient", *Europe* 609 (1980), 75; and ʿIṣām Maḥfūẓ, *al-Sūryāliyyah wa-tafāʿulātuhā*, 84.

17 Jabra I. Jabra, "Modern Arabic Literature and the West", *Journal of Arabic Literature* 2 (1971), 83–84.

18 Khālidah Saʿīd, "Bawādir al-rafḍ fī l-shiʿr al-ʿarabī l-ḥadīth", *Shiʿr* 19 (1961), 95.

19 Al-Ḥājj, *Lan*, 82.

the body, the wonderful, death, freedom, madness and the like. His orientation toward surrealism was thus motivated by a "genuine", personal experience. An articulation of this formative experience was first attempted by the literary critic Khālidah Saʿīd. In a lengthy review of al-Ḥājj's first poetry collection, *Lan* (Never, 1960), she writes:

> In 1945, at seven years old, his mother died. His bark was removed. The warm protective curtain was torn and he was left naked. In 1945, at seven years old, the war came to an end, one camp triumphed over another, after the world had been filled with death, and the first atomic bomb exploded in Hiroshima. Those who survived death lived in decaying and disintegrating bodies, and many atomic explosions followed. He probably heard of all of this, due to his father's work in journalism. The elderly people discussed the causes and effects; they philosophized the events, either with remorse or wonder. He was a child with a naked soul, deprived of tenderness, and thus he was wounded.[20]

This narrative, which is interestingly reminiscent of that of the genesis of surrealism itself – from Maurice Nadeau's *locus classicus*, *History of Surrealism* (1945), to Hal Foster[21] and other later historians of surrealism – has left a trace in almost all the studies that were subsequently written on al-Ḥājj, especially on his early phase. Almost all later attempts at deciphering al-Ḥājj's hermetic imagery, or at piercing his tightly concealed world of symbols and riddles, were informed, whether directly or indirectly, by Khālidah Saʿīd's remarks. The death of the mother, due to cancer, was to become the golden key to pierce al-Ḥājj's poetics.[22] Another important aspect was first pointed out by Saʿīd: that of al-Ḥājj's relation to surrealism, and particularly to Antonin Artaud: "[...] al-Ḥājj resembles the early Dadaists and surrealists: he writes poetry by chance", she affirmed.[23]

There could be little doubt as to the originality and intensity of al-Ḥājj's engagement with the Artaudian experience of insanity and the body, as will be pointed below. Moreover, it would be injudicious to overlook the impact of the mother's death at such an early stage of the poet's life, or to ignore the relevance of such an event in the surrealist context. And yet, to take these as immutable guidelines with which to read the entirety of al-Ḥājj's experience is to condemn a rather multifaceted, unremittingly evolving itinerary to a single, pre-oriented reading. For, as I will try to show, al-Ḥājj soon *fled* the Artaudian cluster of the body and turned to other surrealist figures, conceptions and horizons. Indeed, his subsequent surrealist encounters and poetical engagements attest to the richness and

---

20 Khālidah Saʿīd, "Lan, li-Unsī al-Ḥājj", *Shiʿr* 18 (1961), 153.

21 Hal Foster, *Compulsive Beauty*, Cambridge, MA: MIT Press 1993.

22 See, for instance, ʿAbd al-Karīm Ḥasan, *Qaṣīdat al-nathr wa-intāj al-dalālah: Unsī al-Ḥājj unmūdhaj^an^*, Beirut: Dār al-Sāqī 2008; Otared Haidar, *The Prose Poem and the Journal Shiʿr: A Comparative Study of Literature, Literary Theory and Journalism*, Reading: Ithaca Press 2008, 136–150; Nabil Ayyūb, "Unsī al-Ḥājj al-mukhtalif fī qirāʾah tafkīkiyyah nafsiyyah: al-Aṣl wa-l-muhammash; Aṭyāf al-Masīḥ/ashbāḥ Frūyd", in: *Naṣṣ al-qāriʾ al-mukhtalif (2) wa-sīmyāʾiyyat al-khiṭāb al-naqdī*, Beirut: Librairie du Liban 2011, 173–186.

23 Saʿīd, "Lan, li-Unsī al-Ḥājj", 149.

vivacity of his itinerary. More importantly, they tell us that, although he remained faithful to the concerns and credos of surrealism, al-Ḥājj never became an adept or a militant in the ideological sense of the word. For him, this was by no means a trivial threat. When the journalist ʿAbduh Wāzin asked him about the nature of his relation to surrealism, he explained:

> I often wonder: If I had the chance to be in Paris in the twenties, and, consequently, to meet Breton, Aragon, Soupault, Artaud, Éluard and Char, would I be attracted to surrealism to the extent of joining it? And if we suppose that I joined it, would I remain committed for a long time? I do not think so. I have several contradictions in my character that make me uncomfortable and uncomforting inside any movement.[24]

Before turning to examine al-Ḥājj's surrealist encounters, another central aspect of his mission should be taken into consideration, namely, his double role as poet and journalist. At first, he joined *Shiʿr* as a literary critic, contributing mainly book reviews for newly published poetry collections, before starting, as of the review's second year, to publish his own poems on its pages. And in 1964, he founded *al-Mulḥaq* (Beirut, 1964–1974 and 1992–2015), the literary and cultural weekly supplement of the newspaper *al-Nahār*, which was quickly upgraded into a full-fledged media enterprise and a manifold battleground.[25] Al-Ḥājj's vehement, and at times scandalous, tone, which brings to the fore the tone of surrealism's *période héroïque*,[26] turned his weekly articles into small vanguard manifestos.[27] In the pages of *al-Mulḥaq* he would rage over all kinds of traditionalism, conformism and oppression, while paying homage to surrealist writers and surrealist themes, praising the virtues of madness and the capabilities of psychic automatism, discussing issues of delirium and glossolalia,[28] and indulging in an assorted variety of provocations: one of his early articles in *al-Mulḥaq* was titled "[More] insults are needed".[29]

---

24 Unsī al-Ḥājj, "Ayna al-mutahawwirūn ḥāriqū l-ḥayāt: Ajmal al-ḥarīq wa-dhurwat al-jiddiyyah fī muntahā l-ḥubb wa-l-ʿabath", interview with ʿAbduh Wāzin, *al-Nahār*, 23 January 1983, 9.

25 On al-Ḥājj's experience at *al-Mulḥaq*, see Khālidah Saʿīd, "Unsī al-Ḥājj: Ḍawʾ fī khalīj al-ʿawāṣif", in: *Yūtūbiyā l-madīnah al-muthaqqafah*, Beirut: Dār al-Sāqī 2012, 224–237. And for a brief comparison between al-Ḥājj's articles in *al-Mulḥaq* and Georges Henein's journalistic writings, see ʿAbd al-Qādir al-Janābī, "ʿIndamā qāl al-shiʿr li-l-jamīʿ: Lan", in: *Unsī al-Ḥājj: Min qaṣīdat al-nathr ilā shaqāʾiq al-nathr, mukhtārāt min ashʿārihi wa-khawātimihi*, Beirut: Jadāwil li-l-Nashr wa-l-Tarjamah wa-l-Tawzīʿ 2015, 24–25.

26 See Maurice Nadeau, *Histoire du surréalisme* [1945], Paris: Éditions du Seuil 1964, 41–90.

27 Al-Ḥājj's articles in *al-Mulḥaq* were published in 1987 in a three-volume book under the title *Kalimāt kalimāt kalimāt* (Words, Words, Words) – which is the title of the rubric under which these articles appeared. See Unsī al-Ḥājj, *Kalimāt kalimāt kalimāt*, 3 vol., Beirut: Dār al-Nahār li-l-Nashr 1987–1988.

28 See, for instance, Unsī al-Ḥājj, "Jūrj! Jūrj! Innahu Brūtūn!" in: *Kalimāt kalimāt kalimāt*, 2:611–614; "Ayyuhumā yukhifuk akthar?" in: *Kalimāt kalimāt kalimāt*, 3:1136–1139; along with the articles mentioned in footnote 44 below.

29 Unsī al-Ḥājj, "Maṭlūb^{un} shatāʾim", *al-Mulḥaq*, 4 October 1964, 19. On the history of *al-Mulḥaq* and its role as an avant-gardist platform, see Alfred el-Khoury [Alfrād al-Khūrī], "'Mulḥaq' al-khamsīn ʿām^{an} wa-ʿām", *al-Mulḥaq*, special issue, 20 June 2015, 19.

Through these two media platforms – *Shiʿr* and *al-Mulḥaq* – al-Ḥājj was assuming his role as the spokesperson of a generation, the Lebanese 1960s, but, with no less ingenuity, he was dealing with his own "personal pains" (*al-awjāʿ al-shakhṣiyyah*), which count on their own terms and deserve to be set as "a rule for respect" (*qāʿidah li-l-iḥtirām*), as we read in "al-ʿĀṣifah" (The Tempest), the poem that opens his third poetry collection.[30] It is this twofold aspect of al-Ḥājj, I would suggest, that makes up his originality among his peers and draws him nearer to the surrealists, especially to André Breton. It enabled him to embrace and reconcile the exterior and the interior, the literary and the extra-literary, the prosaic and the poetic, the role of the social agitator and the persona of the *poète maudit.*

Al-Ḥājj's translation projects

Al-Ḥājj's first translation project was published in 1954 in *al-Adīb* (Beirut, 1942–1983), a Beirut-based literary review with a French inclination that constituted a predecessor for *Shiʿr* and a bridge between the innovative attempts of the interbellum period and the poetic revolution that crystallized in the early 1960s.[31] The then 17-year-old poet chose to turn into Arabic a long symbolist poem: "Le Cœur de Hialmar" by Leconte de Lisle (1818–1894),[32] a French poet who was popular among the Lebanese literary circles of the 1940s. This was but the prelude, for al-Ḥājj's subsequent translation projects would appear on the pages of *Shiʿr* and would rather draw from and revolve around a new inspiration, that is, surrealism. Three of these projects/encounters will be considered here.

Winter 1959: Al-Ḥājj translates Jacques Prévert

In the winter 1959 issue of *Shiʿr*, an Arabic translation of sixteen poems by Jacques Prévert appeared. The first seven poems were translated by Unsī al-Ḥājj, and the remaining ones by Fawwāz Ṭrābulsī.[33] Al-Ḥājj wrote also a short study on Prévert,

---

30 See Unsī al-Ḥājj, "al-ʿĀṣifah", in: *Māḍī l-ayyām al-ātiyah*, Sidon: al-Maktabah al-ʿAṣriyyah 1965, 14–15.

31 It is worth noting here that a poem by Albert Adīb (1908–1985), *al-Adīb*'s founder and editor-in-chief, was published in the first issue of *Shiʿr*. See Albert [Albīr] Adīb, "Ṣabr", *Shiʿr* 1 (1957). As far as I am aware, there is no extensive published study dealing with this periodical. Such study is a desideratum.

32 Leconte de Lisle, "Qalb Hyālmār li-l-shāʿir al-faransī Lū Kūnt Dī Līl", trans. Unsī Luwīs al-Ḥājj, *al-Adīb* 12 (1954).

33 Jacques Prévert [Jāk Brīfīr], "Mukhtārāt shiʿriyyah", trans. Unsī al-Ḥājj and Fawwāz Ṭrābulsī, *Shiʿr* 9 (1959). The translated poems cover thirteen pages of the review and include: "Déjeuner du matin", "Le Cancre", "La Rivière", "Maintenant j'ai grandi", "Le Temps perdu", "L'Éclipse", "Chanson du mois de mai", "Pour toi mon amour", "Chanson", "Dimanche", "Le Jardin", "Le Miroir brisé", "L'Automne", "Paris at Night", "Le Bouquet", and "Chanson pour vous".

which was appended to the translated poems, and from which the reader can remark al-Ḥājj's acute understanding of surrealism and his awareness of its controversies and complex concerns.

He begins the study by describing Prévert as "the greatest singer of the proletariat in Paris today", and then proceeds to distinguish him from the "oriented poets" (*al-muwajjahūn*), such as Louis Aragon, "the communist poet", as he intently labels him:

> Prévert's specificity in comparison with the oriented ones, is that he is not oriented, and a poet like Aragon cannot be described as a poet of the people [*shāᶜir al-jamāhīr*], except from the point of view of the political doctrine to which he adheres, and this suffices not.[34]

Prévert, however, although "he witnessed the inception of the surrealist adventure", did not succeed inside the "church" (*kanīsah*) of André Breton; "the successful ones at the time were Louis Aragon, Pierre Naville, Benjamin Péret, Éluard, René Crevel, Antonin Artaud and their likes".[35] The sarcastic overtones of this statement could certainly not be mistaken, and the metaphor of the surrealist group as "Breton's church" is emblematic.

The study turns next to examining a number of issues related to Prévert's poetry, elaborating on his stylistic techniques and quoting the critic Gaëtan Picon numerous times. But what mainly concerns us here is the criticism that al-Ḥājj levies against the "official" surrealists, to which we pointed above. This criticism will attain its paroxysm and turn into a fervent attack in al-Ḥājj's translation of Antonin Artaud, duly examined below.

As for al-Ḥājj's encounter with Prévert, this did not come to an end with the 1959 translation project. In 1967, al-Ḥājj met Prévert in person in Paris. The nocturnal encounter, which began in the celebrated Le Dôme restaurant and resumed the following day in Prévert's Parisian house, has been related by al-Ḥājj in a *compte rendu* that appeared in the summer 1967 issue of *Shiᶜr*.[36] The text, titled "In the Room of Jacques Prévert", was headed by a portrait of Prévert (fig. 1) and accompanied by new, unpublished poetical texts. These were produced on the review's pages in Prévert's own handwriting without being translated into Arabic (figs. 2–5).[37]

---

34 Prévert, "Mukhtārāt shiᶜriyyah", 80.

35 Prévert, "Mukhtārāt shiᶜriyyah", 80.

36 Unsī al-Ḥājj, "Fī ghurfat Jāk Brīfir", *Shiᶜr* 35 (1967). The text was republished in 1997 as the foreword to a translation by ᶜAbduh Wāzin of a selection of Prévert's poetry. See Unsī al-Ḥājj, "Fī ghurfat Jāk Prīvīr", in: Jacques Prévert [Jāk Prīvīr], *Khamsūn qaṣīdah*, trans. ᶜAbduh Wāzin, Beirut: Dār al-Nahār 1997.

37 These texts consist of two poems (figs. 4 and 5, respectively): "Le Bon jeune temps" (published in 1972 in *Choses et autres*, Prévert's last published work during his lifetime) and "Sancta Senilità" (first published in the 1980 posthumous collection *Soleil de nuit*); an aphorism (fig. 2, from a suite of aphorisms titled "Graffiti", published in *Choses et autres*); and a text (fig. 3) that I was not able to locate in Prévert's complete works published by Gallimard

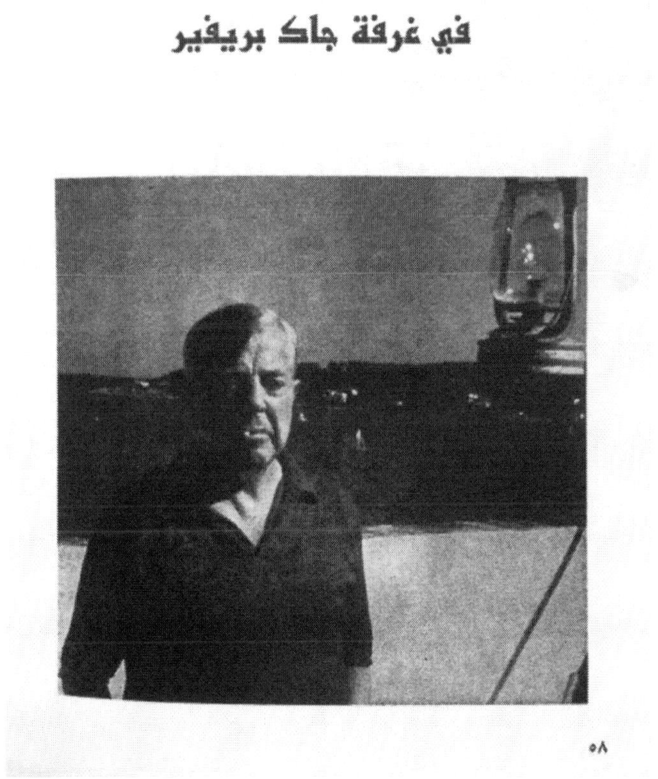

Figure 1: Portrait of Jacques Prévert. Published in *Shiʿr* 35 (1967), 58.
© *Shiʿr.*

After describing the circumstances of the fortuitous meeting, al-Ḥājj's text turns into a monologue of Prévert: the visitor asking him about a wide array of themes, about abstract art, poetry, Breton, Lebanon, modern theatre, freedom and the cinema, and Prévert replying at length. The first few lines of the text encapsulate the fascination of al-Ḥājj toward his French host and thereby deserve to be quoted here in full:

> I encountered him in the restaurant Le Dôme, Montparnasse, after midnight, he was sitting with a woman who was fifty years old, maybe less, maybe more. He was eating, she was eating. But she was [doing] more than that, she was contemplating him as he ate.
> A man with a weird haircut passed by and greeted him.
> I said to the waiter: "Could you please tell the madam that I would like to introduce myself to the monsieur."
> The monsieur was the first [poet] I read after leaving school, after getting rid of school.

(Jacques Prévert, *Œuvres complètes*, ed. Danièle Gasiglia-Laster and Arnaud Laster, 2 vol., Paris: Gallimard/Pléiade 1992–1996).

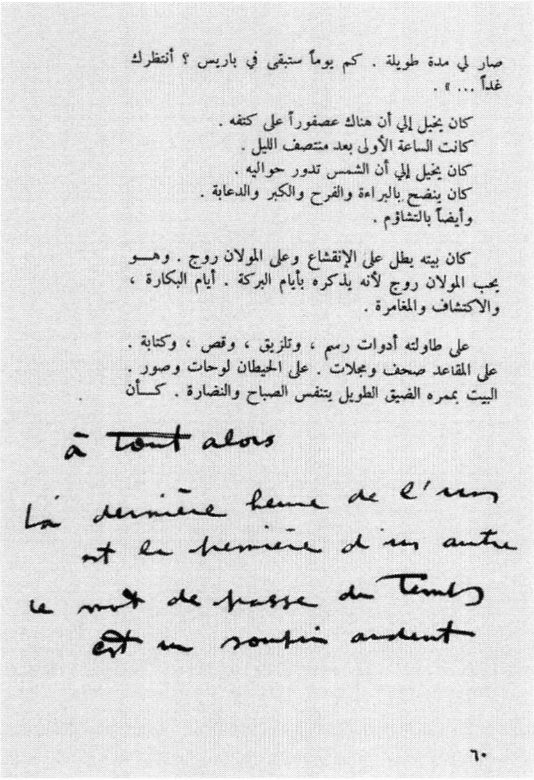

صار لي مدة طويلة . كم يوماً ستبقى في باريس ؟ أنتظرك غداً ... » .

كان يخيل إلي أن هناك عصفوراً على كتفه .
كانت الساعة الأولى بعد منتصف الليل .
كان يخيل إلي أن الشمس تدور حواليه .
كان ينضح بالبراءة والفرح والكبر والدعابة .
وأيضاً بالتشاؤم .

كان بيته يطل على الإنقشاع وعلى المولان روج . وهو يحب المولان روج لأنه يذكره بأيام البركة . أيام البكارة ، والاكتشاف والمغامرة .

على طاولته أدوات رسم ، وتلزيق ، وقص ، وكتابة . على المقاعد صحف ومجلات . على الحيطان لوحات وصور . البيت بممره الضيق الطويل يتنفس الصباح والنضارة . كـأن

à ~~Tout~~ alors
La dernière heure de l'un
est la première d'un autre
le mot de passe du Temps
est un sourire ardent

٦٠

Figure 2: Aphorism from a suite titled "Graffiti". *Shiʿr* 35 (1967), 60. In Jacques Prévert, *Œuvres complètes*, 2:277. © *Shiʿr* and Fatras / Succession Jacques Prévert / Gallimard.

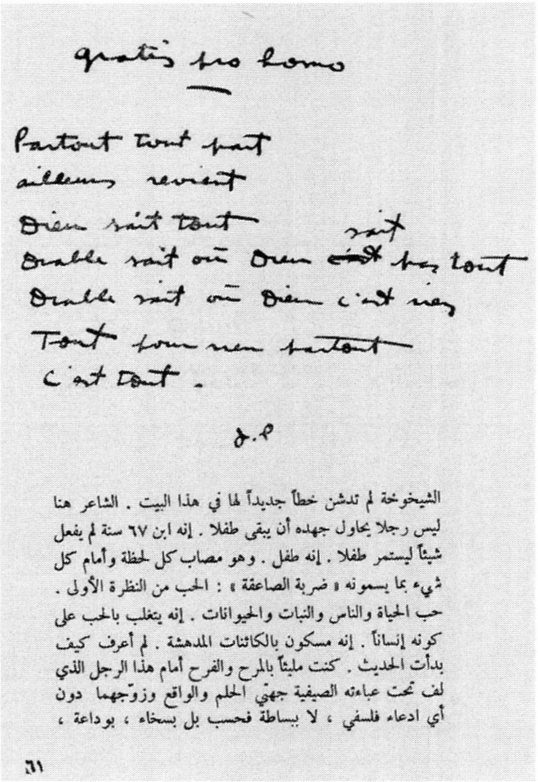

gratis pro homo

Partout tout part
ailleurs revient
Dieu sait tout
Diable sait où Dieu ~~c'est~~ sait pas tout
Diable sait où Dieu c'est rien
Tout pour rien partout
c'est tout.

J.P

الشيخوخة لم تدشن خطاً جديداً لها في هذا البيت . الشاعر هنا ليس رجلا يحاول جهده أن يبقى طفلا . إنه ابن ٦٧ سنة لم يفعل شيئاً ليستمر طفلا . إنه طفل . وهو مصاب كل لحظة وأمام كل شيء بما يسمونه « ضربة الصاعقة » : الحب من النظرة الأولى . حب الحياة والناس والنبات والحيوانات . إنه يتغلب بالحب على كونه إنساناً . إنه مسكون بالكائنات المدهشة . لم أعرف كيف بدأت الحديث . كنت ملبثاً بالمرح والفرح أمام هذا الرجل الذي لف تحت عباءته الصيفية جهتي الحلم والواقع وزوّجهما دون أي ادعاء فلسفي ، لا ببساطة فحسب بل بسخاء ، بوداعة ،

٦١

Figure 3: A text by Jacques Prévert that I could not locate in his *Œuvres complètes*. *Shiʿr* 35 (1967), 61. © *Shiʿr* and Fatras / Succession Jacques Prévert / Gallimard.

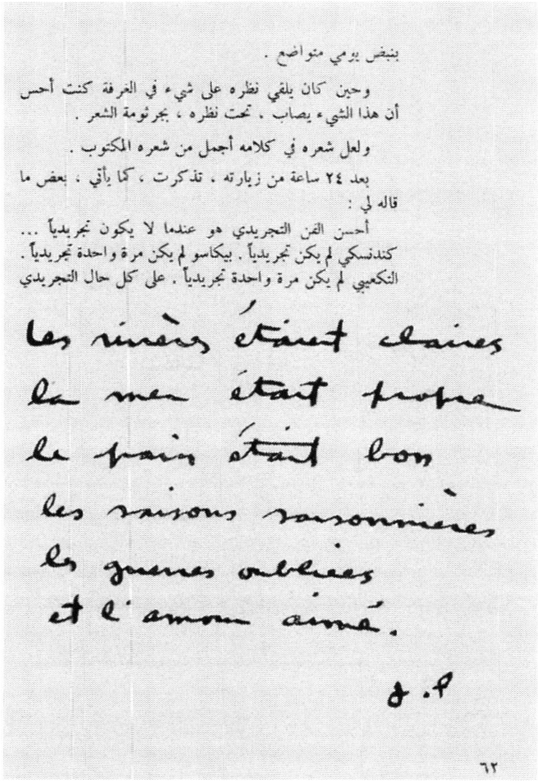

بنبض يومي متواضع .

وحين كان يلقي نظره على شيء في الغرفة كنت أحس أن هذا الشيء يصاب ، تحت نظره ، بجرثومة الشعر .

ولعل شعره في كلامه أجمل من شعره المكتوب .

بعد ٢٤ ساعة من زيارته ، تذكرت ، كما يأتي ، بعض ما قاله لي :

أحسن الفن التجريدي هو عندما لا يكون تجريدياً ... كندنسكي لم يكن تجريدياً . بيكاسو لم يكن مرة واحدة تجريدياً . التكعيبي لم يكن مرة واحدة تجريدياً . على كل حال التجريدي

les rivières étaient claires
la mer était propre
le pain était bon
les saisons saisonnières
les guerres oubliées
et l'amour aimé.

J.P

٦٢

Figure 4: Jacques Prévert, "Le Bon jeune temps". *Shiʿr* 35 (1967), 62. In Jacques Prévert, *Œuvres complètes*, 2:293–294. © *Shiʿr* and Fatras / Succession Jacques Prévert / Gallimard.

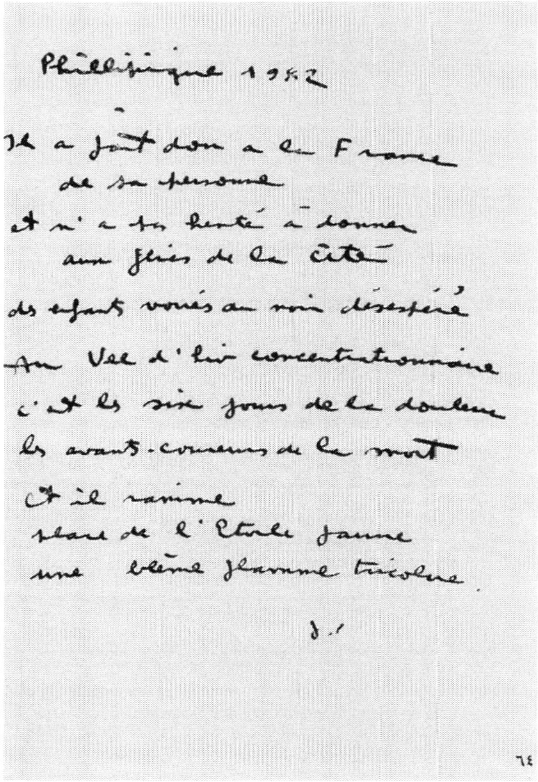

Philippique 1962

Il a fait don à la France
de sa personne
et n'a pas tenté à donner
aux fleurs de la Cité
des enfants voués au noir désespéré
au Vel d'Hiv concentrationnaire
c'est les six jours de la douleur
les avant-coureurs de la mort
Et il ranime
place de l'Étoile jaune
une blême flamme tricolore.

J.P

٦٤

Figure 5: Jacques Prévert, "Sancta Senilità". *Shiʿr* 35 (1967), 64. In Jacques Prévert, *Œuvres complètes*, 2:811. © *Shiʿr* and Fatras / Succession Jacques Prévert / Gallimard.

> I had written about him and translated some of his poems in the review *Shiʿr* more than eight years ago.
> The madam, of a short and thin stature, turned to me and smiled. So, I went to sit with them, filled with a muted laugh, the laugh of the enchanting coincidence. I was confused, and I noticed that Jacques Prévert, the man facing me with his rounded blue eyes, had become, after the first few words, as confused as I was. This, however, did not last long and he began to talk.[38]

Fall 1960: The encounter with Antonin Artaud

In the fall 1960 issue of *Shiʿr*, nearly two years after his translation of Prévert, al-Ḥājj published his third translation project, which would mark his second surrealist encounter: a translation of eleven poems by Antonin Artaud, followed by a study on him.[39]

After using a celebrated passage from Rimbaud's "Letter to Paul Demeny" (1871) as an epigraph and applying it to Artaud's case, al-Ḥājj opens his study with the following notice: "I am incapable of giving a coherent study about him [i.e. Artaud]; he haunts me and I am incapable".[40] This notice gives the text its warm and intimate tone from the very beginning while revealing the intensity of al-Ḥājj's engagement with Artaud. Indeed, it was not difficult to infer that, at this stage, the 23-year-old poet was haunted by the persona of Artaud, his experimentations with language and the body and his experience of insanity and cancer. This was conspicuously reflected in al-Ḥājj's first poetry collection, *Lan*, which belongs to the same phase (fall 1960) and in which the themes of cancer, heresy, articulation and the body are central.[41]

In his study on Artaud, al-Ḥājj identifies himself radically with the Artaudian persona and thus unleashes an inflammatory attack upon the official surrealists, charging them with cowardice and pretentiousness: "the surrealists were – their heads at least – lovers of life, whereas Artaud was sick and torn apart"; "the surrealists promoted the unconscious, automatic writing and psychic automatism [*al-āliyyah al-nafsiyyah*]; however, they did not cease in any instance to rely on the

---

38 Al-Ḥājj, "Fī ghurfat Jāk Brīfir", 59.

39 Antonin Artaud [Anṭūnān Ārtū], "Iḥdā ʿashratah qaṣīdah", trans. Unsī al-Ḥājj, *Shiʿr* 16 (1960). The translated poems cover twenty-four pages of the review and include: "L'Enclume des forces", "Poème" (published in 1948 under the title "J'étais vivant" in the magazine *84*), "Lettre à Pierre Loëb", "Cri", "Poète noir", "Musicien" (the title given by al-Ḥājj is "Musique"), "L'Arbre", "Nuit", "L'Amour sans trêve", "Prière", and "Sur Van Gogh" (an excerpt from "Van Gogh le suicidé de la société").

40 Artaud, "Iḥdā ʿashratah qaṣīdah", 94.

41 Robyn Creswell has delivered an illuminating discussion of al-Ḥājj's translation of Artaud, situating it in the context of modernist projects in Arabic poetry. His "Artaudian" reading of some of *Lan*'s poems sheds light on the nexus of cancer, articulation and the body between Artaud and al-Ḥājj; this, in turn, is related to al-Ḥājj's own conception and origin story of the Arabic *poème en prose*. See Robyn Creswell, *City of Beginnings: Poetic Modernism in Beirut*, Princeton: Princeton University Press 2019, 127–146.

rational mind, the mind that sees clearly and enables [one] to properly pursue a given task".[42] Artaud, on the other hand, is more authentic and daring, for he went in his delirium to the limit: "Artaud's delirium was that of a dead person, and his deadly convulsion was the only sign that he was 'living' and breathing".[43]

The practice of automatism is another crucial concern for al-Ḥājj at this stage. This is attested through the many texts he dedicated in *al-Mulḥaq* to discussing its capabilities and the difficulties inherent in it.[44] And in his study on Artaud, the notion of automatism constitutes the undercurrent for his criticism of the surrealists. This idea will bring al-Ḥājj to discuss the poetical image, "the barrier that the surrealists did not cross", as he affirms, in order to uncover the internal world of the human being: "the surrealists did not open up the image to look over the peril [*al-muhlik*] that lies behind it".[45]

Other key issues discussed in the study are the issues of suffocation (*al-ikhtināq*) – understood both physically and figuratively – claustrophobia, the shattered body, cancer and the (un)literariness of literature, and these happen to be the central themes of al-Ḥājj's early poetry. Georges Charbonnier's monograph, *Essai sur Antonin Artaud*, published a year prior to al-Ḥājj's study (that is, in 1959),[46] constitutes a main reference for al-Ḥājj.[47] Some passages are verbatim renderings from Charbonnier and some phrases repeated throughout the latter's book are encountered in al-Ḥājj's study as well. This, however, does not lessen the originality of the study, marked by a remarkable intensity, an emotional tone and an uncompromising admiration for Artaud's persona and undertakings.

Aspects of Contemporary French Poetry

Al-Ḥājj's translation of Artaud, and probably also his translation of Prévert, were conceived as part of a larger translation project. In the section "Akhbār wa-qaḍāyā" (News and Issues) of the summer 1960 issue of *Shiʿr*, we come across an announcement of a forthcoming publication by al-Ḥājj: a book on contemporary French poetry. The following is an English translation of the announcement:

> The forthcoming issue of *Shiʿr* will feature Unsī al-Ḥājj's study on Antonin Artaud, together with a translation of some of the latter's poems. This study is from his [i.e. al-Ḥājj's] book, *Aspects of Contemporary French Poetry* [*Malāmiḥ min al-shiʿr al-faransī al-muʿāṣir*], the first section of which traces, through historical sketches and interpretation,

---

42 Artaud, "Iḥdā ʿashratah qaṣīdah", 95.

43 Artaud, "Iḥdā ʿashratah qaṣīdah", 96.

44 See, among other articles, Unsī al-Ḥājj, "al-Junūn saṭḥī", in: *Kalimāt kalimāt kalimāt*, 1:8–9; "Waḥsh ʿalā l-ṭarīq", in: *Kalimāt kalimāt kalimāt*, 1:31–32; and "al-Alfāẓ hiya al-afkār", in: *Kalimāt kalimāt kalimāt*, 1:46–47.

45 Artaud, "Iḥdā ʿashratah qaṣīdah", 95.

46 Georges Charbonnier, *Essai sur Antonin Artaud: Bibliographie, dessins, portraits et fac-similés*, Paris: Seghers 1959.

47 This was noticed by Creswell in *City of Beginnings*, 131 and 230n47.

> the evolution of modern trends in French poetry from the twentieth century onwards, focusing specifically on the surrealist movement, and studying it in the light of its own conceptions of art and life, and of what it has nowadays become and what it represents in these times that seem to have surpassed it.
> As for the book's second section, it consists of studies of five poets, together with translations from their poetry, and those poets are: Paul Éluard, René Char, Antonin Artaud, Jacques Prévert and Henri Michaux, who represent, each on his own, a unique trend in poetry.[48]

This announcement has several things to tell us. Suffice it to point out for now that, interestingly enough, none of the aforementioned poets – with the exception of Éluard – was "surrealist" in the typical sense of the word: Michaux was never an official member of the group; Artaud and Prévert joined early, left early, and were soon found among Breton's fiercest "attackers";[49] and Char did not join the surrealist group until 1930, when it had entered its *période raisonnante*.[50] We do not encounter such inevitable surrealist names as Aragon, Péret or even Soupault. And the main absent is certainly André Breton.

Fall 1962: Rediscovering Breton, the dawn of a lifelong admiration

Al-Ḥājj's *exclusion* of Breton is by no means accidental, and it certainly cannot be attributed to an unawareness of his central position within surrealism: in 1958, as al-Ḥājj would later recall, he was on the point of sending him a letter – which "[he thanks God that he] did not send".[51] The exclusion of Breton ought to be rather seen in the light of al-Ḥājj's rejection of orthodox surrealism. It thus takes on an interesting dimension in this respect: how can a book on French poetry in the twentieth century, with a focus on surrealism, not include Breton?

Al-Ḥājj's awaited book, in fact, did not see the light of day.[52] Instead, the fall 1962 issue of *Shiʿr* brought out al-Ḥājj's fourth – and longest – translation project. It consisted of thirteen poems by André Breton, among them the celebrated "L'Union libre" (The Free Union, 1931) but also the "Ode à Charles Fourier" (Ode

48 "Akhbār wa-qaḍāyā fi thalāthat ashhur", *Shiʿr* 15 (1960), 143–144.

49 Having been, from the outset, a heretic among the heretics, Artaud was expelled from the surrealist group in 1926 for "incompatibility of goals". As for Prévert, he was officially expelled in 1928, and was one of the contributors to "Un Cadavre" (A Corpse), the notorious pamphlet against Breton published in 1930. On the crisis within the surrealist group, see Nadeau, *Histoire du surréalisme*, 100–101 and 118–131; and Aspley, *Historical Dictionary of Surrealism*, under "Artaud, Antonin" and "Prévert, Jacques".

50 See Nadeau, *Histoire du surréalisme*, 91–137.

51 Unsī al-Ḥājj, "Unẓur ilyah bi-ʿayn al-raḍīʿ", *al-Akhbār*, 25 September 2010, 32.

52 The editorial of the following issue of *Shiʿr* made mention of al-Ḥājj's translation of Artaud, "which deserves to be praised", and noted that "al-Ḥājj is still working on his book *Aspects of Contemporary French Poetry*, which will be published by *Shiʿr* publications probably in the coming spring". See "Ilā l-qāriʾ", *Shiʿr* 16 (1960), 8.

to Charles Fourier, 1947).[53] And as was the case with the two previous translation projects, this one was accompanied by an insightful study on the "pope of surrealism". The study, more detached and focused than the one on Artaud, opens by presenting Breton as – first and foremost – a poet, refuting thereby "the prevailing tendency to emphasize his role as the leader of surrealism and not as a poet".[54] Al-Ḥājj considers this a sort of injustice (*ijḥāf*), for inasmuch as he is a theorizer, Breton is "equally a great poet, and as his poetry constitutes a continuation of his theories, so do his prose [works] and manifestos: they are poetry".[55]

Interestingly, al-Ḥājj harks back to the same questions he discussed in his study on Artaud. The positions he holds are, however, antagonistically different. He stresses the extra-literary dimension of the surrealist adventure, praises Breton's lyricism and vindicates his progression from symbolism to Dadaism to surrealism, passing through communism, observing that "the key to understanding this rich personality is to proceed by approaching it as an unbreakable unity".[56] Then, he dwells on Breton's conception and "practice" of the poetical image at some length and illustrates his postulations through passages carefully extracted from the first (1924) and second (1930) manifestos of surrealism, as well as from *Nadja* (1928) and *L'Amour fou* (1937).

This study would thus herald the returning of al-Ḥājj to the Bretonian fortress. From then on, his admiration for the leader of surrealism never waned and remained radiant until the end of his life. On the death of Breton, in 1966, al-Ḥājj published a now celebrated[57] text in *al-Mulḥaq*, with the title "The King of Djinns Passed Away in Paris" – an overtly, yet sincerely, eulogistic obituary, which opens with the following lines:

> They used to compare him to a lion. His head, his voice, his stature. He was greater than a lion. He was a man who lived in the twentieth century for three [things]: Love, Poetry and Freedom.[58]

Simultaneously, there appeared in the pages of *Shiʿr* another obituary for Breton, with the title "An Eternal King" (*Malik abadī*; fig. 6). Although this was not signed, al-Ḥājj's metaphors and eulogies for Breton – which make one recall the surrealists' own celebration of their ancestors – could not be mistaken: "He [Breton] was a

53 André Breton [Andrīh Brūtūn], "Thalātha ʿashratah qaṣīdah", *Shiʿr* 24 (1962). The translated poems – ordered chronologically – cover thirty pages of the review and include: "Coqs de bruyère", "Usine", "L'Union libre", "Un homme et une femme absolument blancs", "Vigilance", "L'Air de l'eau I", "L'Air de l'eau II", "Au lavoir noir", "À Pierre Mabille", "Plus que suspect", "Uli", "Ode à Charles Fourier" (excerpts), and "Rano Raraku".

54 Breton, "Thalātha ʿashratah qaṣīdah", 101–102.

55 Breton, "Thalātha ʿashratah qaṣīdah", 102.

56 Breton, "Thalātha ʿashratah qaṣīdah", 102.

57 See Narjess D'Outreligne, "Le Surréalisme en Orient", *Arabica* 50, no. 2 (2003), 249.

58 Unsī al-Ḥājj, "Māt malik mulūk al-jān fī bārīs", in: *Kalimāt kalimāt kalimāt*, 1:295. A literal translation of the title would read as follows: "The King of Kings [*malik mulūk*] of Djinns Passed Away in Paris".

ملك ابدي

عاش اندريه بريتون في أحلامنا أكثر مما عاش في فرنسا .

كان قدوة لنا أكثر من شعرائنا . كان شرقاً وغرباً أبعد من الكلمتين. وعندما ختم حياته بالقول انه لم يعد يؤمن الا بالحب كان يؤكد، مرة أخرى، انه كبير شرفاء ذلك الجزء من العالم الذي زور كل شيء ، حتى الحب .

هذا العصر ، الواضح الانحطاط ، مدين لبريتون بالسوريالية: مدين له بانهاض الحرية والشعر والخيال من الموت . نحن أيضاً مدينون لبريتون : أعطانا المثل الحي على التمرد ، والرفض ، وشق الجدران . وسلمنا في الشعر مفاتيح أعاد نبشها من الغمر والظلم وسوء الفهم .

كان منارة ، رأسه كرأس أسد وصوته سيف . كان صوته حضناً للنار والذهب .

ونحن نعتقد أن الفرنسيين الميالين الى اعتبـــاره منطق السريالية أكثر من اعتبـــاره شاعراً ، هم مخطئون . وعلى عكس الرأي السائد ، نحن نعتقـــد ان بيانات بريتون وإظهاراتـــه النثرية هي امتداد حيوي وشعري لشعره . وليس شعره ، كما يظن كثيرون من الغربيين، برهاناً على أفكاره الفلسفية . هذا تحقير لبريتون ولا يشفع به كونه غالباً ما ينبع من انحراف روحي وثقافي مركب الاسباب .

جر" بريتـــون وراءه مقلدين ومشعوذين ومزيفين وأقزاماً ، وألب حوله معارك بعضها تافه . وكان له في سلوكه تصرفات ثانوية . لكنه ، في النهاية ، ربح الجولة وظل ملكاً .

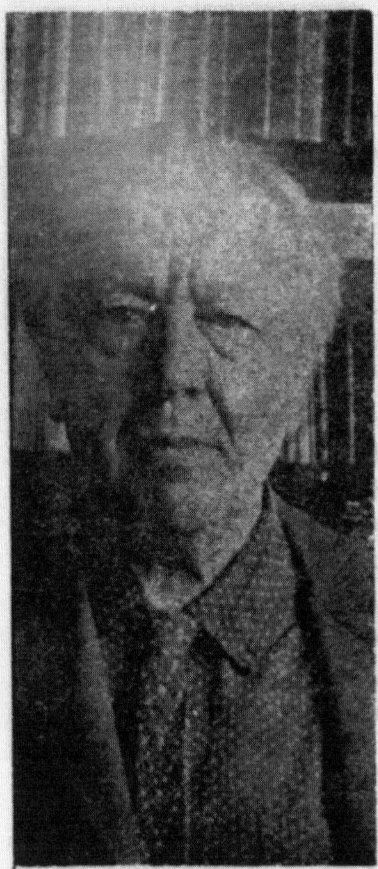

اندره بريتون (١٨٩٦ – ١٩٦٦)

ملك من ملوك الروح والشعر والحب في عصر الدمامة والهلاك والحقارة .

ملك عاش في أحلامنا أكثر مما عاش في فرنسا ، وسيعيش كالنور في المستقبل إذا كان المستقبل سيظل يحتمل الحقيقة .

١٩١

Figure 6: *Shiʿr*'s Obituary for Breton, "An Eternal King" (*Malik abadi*). Published in *Shiʿr* 33–34 (1967), 191.

guiding light. His head like the head of a lion and his voice a sword. His voice was a bosom for fire and gold."[59]

And forty years later, on the anniversary of Breton's death, al-Ḥājj published in the newspaper *al-Akhbār* – where he had just begun to contribute a weekly text under the rubric "Khawātim III" – a text with the title "West Is This East", which opens with the following lines:

> Yesterday, forty years have passed since the death of André Breton, in whom the spirit of the triumphed revolt [*al-tamarrud al-muntaṣir*] was wholly incarnated, the revolt of the passionate shadows against the barren lights, [the revolt] of the lively margin against the dead body, [the revolt] of France's white night against its dark day, and of the gardens of the imagination against the deserts of the intellect.[60]

In this same text al-Ḥājj describes Breton as

> [t]he one who rescued Atlantis from the depths of despair, and who dressed the rejection on its feet, the rejection that safeguards the honour of the humans, and who directed modern cultural sensibility and modern poetry and modern art to the purest springs, vigorous since the dawn of history, fresh and modern and surreal since the dawn of history.[61]

Hence, Breton became for al-Ḥajj a refuge, both poetically and – I am tempted to say – existentially, whereas Artaud became, I would argue, a haunting spectre of a remote past, a spectre to be fled and evaded, as he incarnated al-Ḥājj's fears, anxieties and phobias. Breton's idealization of Love and the Woman, in whom he placed all the energy and meaning of his resurrectional project, his conception of the Poet as both a visionary and a revolutionary, became central credos in al-Ḥājj's poetics.

Al-Ḥājj's surrealist itinerary

In fact, al-Ḥājj's progression from Artaud's system of cruelty to Breton's passionate "philosophy" of "mad love" is, in surrealist terms, quite relevant.[62] For one should not forget that the schisms inside the surrealist group – which resulted in a wave of exclusions and departures – were not only related to the political involvements of the surrealists and the upheavals of the time. The disagreement extended to other conflicting issues of a more lasting character. Central to these issues was the conception of love.[63] On this question, Breton and Artaud represented two

59 "Malik abadī", *Shi'r* 33–34 (1967), 191.

60 Unsī al-Ḥājj, "al-Gharb huwa hādhā l-sharq", *al-Akhbār*, 11 November 2006, 24.

61 Al-Ḥājj, "al-Gharb huwa hādhā l-sharq", 24.

62 For a reading of al-Ḥājj's surrealist itinerary, covering the entirety of his poetical works, see Alfred el-Khoury [Alfrād al-Khūrī], "Unsī al-Ḥājj wa-l-suryāliyyah al-faransiyyah: Min al-jasad al-hādhī ilā l-ḥubb al-majnūn", MA thesis, American University of Beirut, Department of Arabic and Near Eastern Languages 2015.

63 Breton is peremptorily lucid on this point. In "Ajours" (1947) he affirms: "Chose frappante, j'ai pu vérifier *a posteriori* que la plupart des querelles survenues dans le surréalisme et qui

radically conflicting poles. The sixth of the twelve sessions the surrealists held between 1928 and 1932 under the title "Recherches sur la sexualité" reveals much of the fierce disagreement between the two. Whereas Breton insisted on placing "love above everything else" and refused to differentiate between love and sexuality, Artaud had a very low esteem for love, and an equally low one for the beloved. Breton affirmed that he had "the very highest opinion" of the destined woman, to which Artaud replied that "it's highly probable that [he'll] never meet her".[64] Artaud then left the session – which was the only session in which he participated – but not before declaring: "We do not agree about a single word we're saying. If we have to analyse every word, any discussion will be impossible".[65]

If we turn to al-Ḥājj, we notice that whereas his early poetry can be considered "Artaudian" in its position on the question of love, his late works are uncompromisingly "Bretonian". The idealization of the Woman attains its culmination in his fifth poetical work: *al-Rasūlah bi-shaʿrihā l-ṭawīl ḥattā l-yanābīʿ* (The Messenger with her Long Hair to the Springs, 1975, henceforth *al-Rasūlah*). In this long, incantatory poem, al-Ḥājj adopts a prophetical tone to relate to the world "the story of the other side of genesis" (*qiṣṣat al-wajh al-ākhar min al-takwīn*),[66] where love is sublimed and the woman is exalted, but is also assigned a colossal task, to deliver the human race from its curse and to restore to humans their lost paradise and their former, perfected body: the androgyne. According to al-Ḥājj's poem, it is the arrogance of the male, his greed and his desire to dominate and undermine his other feminine component that led to this loss. We are certainly not far from the programme set by Breton in *Arcane 17* (1945), the closing and densest movement in his prose quartet that began with *Les Vases communicants* (1932).[67]

Breton and "Bretonian" themes and occupations also enjoy an eminent presence in al-Ḥājj's late writings in the newspaper *al-Akhbār*. Among these is a text that carries the cryptic title "Who are you, Nadja?" (*Man anti, Nādjā?*). It begins as a review of a freshly published book on Léona Delcourt,[68] the "real" woman

---

ont pris prétexte de divergences politiques ont été surdéterminées, non, comme on l'a insinué, par des questions de personnes, mais par un désaccord irréductible sur ce point [i.e. the conception of love]". André Breton, *Œuvres complètes*, dir. Marguerite Bonnet, 4 vol., Paris: Gallimard/Pléiade 1988–2008, 3:106–107.

64 José Pierre, ed., *Investigating Sex: Surrealist Research 1928–1932*, trans. Malcolm Imrie, London: Verso 1992, 86–88.

65 Pierre, *Investigating Sex*, 86.

66 Unsī al-Ḥājj, *al-Rasūlah bi-shaʿrihā l-ṭawīl ḥattā l-yanābīʿ*, Beirut: Dār al-Nahār li-l-Nashr 1975, 11 and *passim*.

67 With *Nadja* and *L'Amour fou* as the second and third movements, respectively. On the role of the Woman in Breton's *Arcane 17*, see Maryse Laffitte, "L'Image de la femme chez Breton: Contradictions et virtualités", *Revue romane* 11, no. 2 (1976), 286–305, esp. 296–298; and Bethany Ladimer, "Madness and the Irrational in the Work of André Breton: A Feminist Perspective", *Feminist Studies* 6, no. 1 (1980).

68 Unsī al-Ḥājj, "Man anti, Nādjā?", *al-Akhbār*, 20 February 2010, 32. The reviewed book is Hester Albach, *Léona, héroïne du surréalisme*, Paris: Actes Sud 2009.

believed to be behind the persona of Nadja, but soon turns into an homage to Breton's book (i.e. *Nadja*) and to the theme of the surrealist encounter. In another text, al-Ḥājj's spirit (*shabaḥ*) encounters Jābir b. Ḥayyān, one of the most famous figures of Arabic alchemy, and communicates to him his dream of converting money into life and units of time.[69] Tracing the entirety of al-Ḥājj's "Bretonian texts" would be an interesting exercise; it is of course beyond the scope of this chapter.

Reception and later resonances

In the end, I would like to return to the reception of al-Ḥājj as a surrealist among his contemporaries and among later generations of Arab poets. For, although his blatant surrealist affiliation has made him a despicable figure for many Arab poets and critics,[70] this very aspect contributed to his originality and brought him admiration and respect among the avant-garde. In addition to Khālidah Saʿīd's seminal remarks pointed to above, it is interesting to note that Adonis (ʿAlī Aḥmad Saʿīd), in a letter sent to Yūsuf al-Khāl from Paris in 1961, acknowledges that "Unsī is, among us, the purest one" (*Unsī huwa baynanā, al-anqā*).[71] This declaration recalls to mind Suzanne Bernard's description of Artaud as "the purest revolutionary" (*le révolté le plus pur*),[72] – especially given that, at the time, Adonis was quite familiar with Bernard's study on the *poème en prose*[73] while being aware of al-Ḥājj's admiration for Artaud. More conspicuous is the declaration of Yūsuf al-Khāl in one of *Shiʿr*'s weekly gatherings that "had Unsī al-Ḥājj been an assassin instead of a poet, he would have carried a revolver and started killing people"[74] – a position that mirrors Breton's famous dictum at the outset of the second manifesto that "the purest surrealist act consists of dashing down into the street, revolver in hand, and firing blindly, as fast as you can pull the trigger, into the crowd".[75] Later, the painter and art critic Maḥmūd al-Zibāwī would describe al-Ḥājj as "a mystic in the savage

69 Unsī al-Ḥājj, "Liqāʾ maʿ Jābir", *al-Akhbār*, 26 November 2011, 32. Jābir b. Ḥayyān flourished in the early ʿAbbasid age; he is known in Latin under the name of Geber.

70 See footnote 9 above.

71 Adūnīs, "Ḥawla 'Qaṣāʾid fī l-arbaʿīn' wa-ḥamlat al-tazwīr wa-l-istighlāl", *Shiʿr* 18 (1961), 181.

72 Suzanne Bernard, *Le Poème en prose de Baudelaire jusqu'à nos jours*, Paris: Librairie Nizet 1959, 703.

73 As far as I am aware, Adonis was the first to introduce Bernard's work into Arabic, in his 1960 article on *qaṣīdat al-nathr* (the Arabic *poème en prose*) – recognized as the earliest theoretical text on this poetic form in Arabic – which was largely based on Bernard's study. See Adūnīs, "Fī qaṣīdat al-nathr", *Shiʿr* 14 (1960).

74 "Akhbār wa-qaḍāyā fī thalāthat ashhur", *Shiʿr* 28 (1963), 99.

75 André Breton, "Second manifeste du surréalisme", in: *Œuvres complètes*, 1:782–783. The translation (which has been slightly modified here) is from André Breton, *Manifestoes of Surrealism*, trans. Richard Seaver and Helen R. Lane, Ann Arbor: University of Michigan Press 1969, 125.

state", employing thus the celebrated image concocted by Paul Claudel to describe Rimbaud ("un mystique à *l'état sauvage*").[76]

This last connection is particularly relevant. For al-Ḥājj's originality and "authority" as a surrealist were not solely established on the basis of his encounters with and translations of pivotal figures of surrealism. His role as a pioneering figure of surrealism in Arabic literature was further consolidated by the fact that he went on to discover and engage with surrealism's spiritual fathers and ancestors. This is reflected in a great number of his texts, poems and interviews: Rimbaud is present everywhere in al-Ḥājj, and so are Baudelaire, Lautréamont, Apollinaire, Nerval and others. In his interview with ʿAbduh Wāzin, al-Ḥājj asserts:

> when I say "poet", I understand by it every holder of a poetical "vision". Not only that, but also every holder of a poetical "vision" toward a world governed by the [two] principles of desire and pleasure [*mabdaʾā l-shahwah wa-l-ladhdhah*]. In this sense, I have in mind, besides Baudelaire, Rimbaud, Lautréamont, de Nerval, Novalis and Jung, and besides Artaud, Breton, Char and Michaux, I have, in a radical sense, Le Marquis de Sade, Dostoevsky, Jesus Christ, Hermes Trismegistus, Nicolas Flamel, Paracelsus, Éliphas Levi, Plato, Charles Fourier and many others, whether they were minor or great, who broke through, or wanted to break through, the prison of oppressing polarities governing us, in order to reach the promised land of divinity.[77]

It is interesting to note that the names that al-Ḥājj summons up in this passage overlap with the ones recurrently mentioned in Breton's works; many of them are present in the first manifesto, where Breton lists the surrealists *avant la lettre*,[78] and in the second manifesto, where he reconsiders Rimbaud's "alchimie du verbe" (alchemy of the word),[79] and in many other places.[80]

However, with the publication of *al-Rasūlah*, al-Ḥājj was no longer considered a surrealist, or, at best, he was seen as a "repentant" one. *Al-Rasūlah*, unlike his earlier poetical works, received praise from all camps, the detractors of modernist poetry as well as its exponents and sympathizers. Its unanimous success culminated in Saʿīd ʿAql – the leading figure of Arab neoclassicism, who had never been on good terms with the modernist poetry of the late 1950s – awarding al-Ḥājj his literary prize and describing *al-Rasūlah* as "the book of love that the present generation will read as its own book". "In [this work]", continues ʿAql, "love is sung in the most beautiful fashion, together with values that spring from it and make it even more shining and architectural. And we shall remember that Unsī's pencil, which is of fire, is our most prominent craftsman [*miʿmāriyyunā l-amthal*]."[81]

---

76 *Unsī al-Ḥājj, al-mutamarrid, al-ḥālim, al-naqī: Shahādāt wa-aqwāl*, unknown editor, Beirut: Muʾassasat Jūzīf Rʿaydī li-l-Ṭibāʿah and Dār al-Nahār 1995, 20–21. Note that al-Zībāwī uses the word *mythique* instead of *mystique*, although it is probably the latter that is intended.

77 Al-Ḥājj, "Ayna al-mutahawwirūn", 9.

78 André Breton, "Manifeste du surréalisme", in: *Œuvres complètes*, 1:328–330 and *passim*.

79 Breton, "Second manifeste du surréalisme", 818–820.

80 See, for instance, André Breton, "Arcane 17", in: *Œuvres complètes*, 3:113 and *passim*.

81 *Unsī al-Ḥājj, al-mutamarrid, al-ḥālim, al-naqī*, 15.

As I tried to establish earlier, in *al-Rasūlah*, al-Ḥājj was still in the heart of surrealism.[82] By no means did he "repent", and his conception of poetry remained at odds with any kind of craftsmanship or mannerism. Only one aspect had changed about him: he was now embracing another version of surrealism from the one we encounter in his early poetical works, which we could call Bretonian in its mediums and vision. This version of al-Ḥājj's surrealism seemed more appealing to the Arab literati, who might have found in its exaltation of love and lyric tonalities a discourse that they could admire and identify with. Hence, this "positive" version of al-Ḥājj – whose role as a surrealist and publicist of surrealism we have already indicated – implies, in one sense or another, and whether consciously or not, a "positive" presence of surrealism in Arabic literature.

This last point deserves further consideration. For the resonances of al-Ḥājj should not solely be sought among later Arab surrealists, who have continually recognized him as their forerunner,[83] but also among Arab poets of later generations who had no direct affiliation with surrealism. Where the question of surrealism's *relation* to the Orient and to Orientalism has already drawn some scholarly attention, the question of the resonances left by surrealism in the Arabic artistic scenes, and more precisely in literature, has barely been touched upon. Whether intentionally or not, al-Ḥājj has contributed, through both his poetry and translations – which I have tried to present as genuine encounters and determining experiences – to making surrealism less despised and to communicating its universal values, aspirations and dreams. The names – and relative projects – of Rimbaud, Artaud and Breton, among others, have certainly been offered through him a brighter place in Arabic literature.

Although we have been able to explore al-Ḥājj's multifaceted connections to surrealism, an appreciation of his poetry remains incomplete without a consideration of its relationship to language. It is precisely this passionate enterprise of stirring the Arabic language from within, of making it tremble and stutter and howl; this challenge of proclaiming oneself the aggressor of the language one

82 Celebrating the publication of the translation into French of *al-Rasūlah* (*La Messagère aux cheveux longs jusqu'aux sources et autres poèmes*, Paris: Sindbad/Actes Sud 2015), Christophe Dauphin wrote that for the group of *Supérieur inconnu*, the surrealist review founded in 1995 by Sarane Alexandrian and the editorial board of which included among others Dauphin himself, *al-Rasūlah* was "nothing but the book of the Lebanese *Mad Love*". Christophe Dauphin, "'L'Éternité volante' de la messagère d'Ounsi el Hage", *K-Log Diffusion*, 7 October 2015, http://www.klogdiffusion.fr/leternite-volante-de-la-messagere-dounsi-el-hage/. A translation of excerpts from *al-Rasūlah* was published in the ninth issue (1998) of *Supérieur inconnu*.

83 Most prominent among these is the Iraqi poet ʿAbd al-Qādir al-Janābī (b. 1944), who throughout his career has paid several homages to al-Ḥājj. On his surrealist experience and relation to al-Ḥājj, see Sibylla Krainick, *Arabischer Surrealismus im Exil: Der irakische Dichter und Publizist ʿAbd al-Qādir al-Ǧanābī*, Wiesbaden: Reichert 2001, esp. 17, 78–79 and 91. See also al-Janābī's introduction to the French translation of selected poems of al-Ḥājj in Ounsi El Hage, *Éternité volante*, ed. and trans. Abdul Kader El Janabi, Paris: Sindbad/Actes Sud 1997, 9–12.

writes with and within; this yearning for a new rhetoric that breaks with traditions, recent and remote, that made of him the uncontested *enfant terrible* of Arabic poetry. This enterprise was by no means separate from his engagement with surrealist ideas and projects. What one has to take into consideration, nevertheless, are the transformations and adaptations these had to go through when drawn into the context of Arabic poetry. To what extent could the problems raised by al-Ḥājj, both in his poetry and critical writings, find a fertile ground in Arabic literature? How deeply could they resonate? What significance has surrealism had to the modernist project(s) in Arabic poetry since the 1950s? As a provisional closing, I shall excerpt the following lines from a lengthy text that al-Ḥājj wrote for the review *Mawāqif* (Beirut, 1968–1994) to be included in a 1979 special issue on the conceptions of modernism among Arab intellectuals:

> […] [modernism] is the clash inside me of the wonderful and the dead.
> […] It is surrealism complemented by what it rejected, that is, faith.
> […] It is the will of imagination to become reality.
> […] It is Lautréamont's saying "beautiful […] like the chance encounter on a dissecting table of a sewing machine and an umbrella!"
> […] It is my impact on André Breton and his impact on me at the same time and prior to both of us.
> […] It is Paul Éluard's vertigo of tenderness when he closes his eyes.
> […] It is [the fact] that my poetry is not Arabic […][84]

[84] Unsī al-Ḥājj, "al-ʿĀlam, munḥallan fi māʾ al-raghbah", *Mawāqif*, al-Ḥadāthah fi l-fikr wa-l-adab 1, no. 35 (1979), 104–108.

Chapter 8
Le surréalisme égyptien à la lumière de la presse francophone d'Égypte

Cléa Daridan

Implanté dès 1939 au Caire, le mouvement Art et Liberté était probablement le seul groupe de la région à être en lien avec André Breton. Portée par la pratique du français dans la région du Levant et particulièrement en Égypte, la diffusion du surréalisme s'est faite grâce à des personnes – écrivains, artistes, journalistes – ayant voyagé, travaillé ou vécu à Paris et ayant véhiculé ses idées dans leurs pays d'origine. Aussi, dans le cadre de recherches sur le surréalisme à Paris, en Afrique du nord et au Moyen-Orient depuis les années 1930, nous semble-t-il intéressant de proposer une étude approfondie de la presse francophone d'Égypte afin de mettre en lumière le surréalisme égyptien comme phénomène non seulement artistique mais politique et social, d'établir les liens structurant ce mouvement et ses échanges avec Paris, autant que les conditions de sa réception.

L'expédition d'Égypte menée par Napoléon Bonaparte entre 1798 et 1801 a contribué à l'introduction du français en Égypte, entraînant dès lors une relation de dépendance entre francophonie et pouvoir politique. La situation linguistique de l'Égypte dans la première moitié du XXe siècle peut se résumer ainsi :

> Sont pratiquées sur le sol égyptien une langue considérée comme nationale, la langue arabe […] la langue de l'occupant, l'anglais […] une langue étrangère principale, minoritaire d'un point de vue démographique mais dans une relation d'égale priorité avec la langue de culture autochtone dans la communauté qui la pratique, la langue française[1].

La francophonie atteint son apogée en Égypte dès les années 1920, et la pratique du français devient incontournable pour qui souhaite intégrer la haute société. Dans un numéro du *Phare égyptien* de 1926, Michel Paillares affirme :

> En Égypte, la connaissance du français est indispensable si l'on veut se faire une place honorable dans la société, dans les administrations et dans les affaires. Nous sommes dans un pays où l'arabe est la langue nationale et où l'Angleterre occupe, depuis 1882, une situation privilégiée, et cependant, que voyons-nous ? C'est en français qu'est rédigé le « Journal Officiel », c'est en français que les avocats, même les Anglais, plaident devant les tribunaux mixtes. C'est en français que les magistrats de ces juridictions rendent leurs jugements. C'est en français que se publient une douzaine de quotidiens et de périodiques.

1 Irène Fenoglio, « Le choix d'une langue étrangère : enjeu non modique d'un mode de fonctionnement social : la "mode" du français en Égypte », dans *Transidis* 1, décembre 1992, 86.

> C'est en français que l'on s'exprime de préférence dans les grands magasins. C'est en français que sont composées les enseignes et les affiches[2].

Le français est donc la langue pratiquée par une élite détentrice d'un important capital à la fois socio-économique et culturel.

La presse francophone d'Égypte qui a pris son essor sous le règne du Khédive Saïd Pacha (1854–1963) s'étoffe dès lors. En 1926, sur 283 périodiques, 174 sont en arabe et 50 en français - dont 15 quotidiens - sur les 109 en langue étrangère. Douze ans plus tard, en 1938, l'importance des périodiques en français relativement à ceux écrits dans d'autres langues étrangères est encore plus frappante puisque l'on en compte 67 sur un total de 101, dont des quotidiens qui impriment à un tirage moyen de 10000 exemplaires[3]. Il s'agit ainsi d'une époque des plus brillantes tant par le nombre des organes de presse concernés que par la compétence de ses journalistes. On citera *La Semaine égyptienne* qui voit le jour en 1926, hebdomadaire social, politique et littéraire qui a paru durant vingt ans, *Un effort*, organe du groupement artistique et littéraire de tendance révolutionnaire des Essayistes paru entre 1929 et 1937, ou *La Revue des conférences françaises en Orient* publiée de 1936 à 1951. On pourrait également mentionner les quotidiens *Le Progrès égyptien* (depuis 1893), *La Bourse égyptienne* (1898–1960) ou *Le Journal d'Égypte* (1936–1994), l'hebdomadaire politique *L'Égypte nouvelle* (1922–*c.*1943), les hebdomadaires sociaux *La Gazette d'Orient* (1927–1942) et *Images* (1929–1969), ou le mensuel féminin *La Femme nouvelle* (1945–1953) ainsi que les revues littéraires, mensuelle *La Revue du Caire* (1938–1962), ou trimestrielles *Messages d'Orient* (1925) et *Valeurs* (1945–1947) qui demeurent d'irremplaçables témoins des échanges intellectuels cosmopolites de l'époque. Il est en effet nécessaire de rappeler que l'Égypte d'alors était devenue la terre d'asile de milliers d'étrangers fuyant l'Europe et l'Occupation, ainsi que la plaque tournante des troupes alliées venues d'Afrique, d'Extrême-Orient ou d'Australie. Accessibles sur le site du Centre d'études alexandrines qui recense plus de 2375 exemplaires de quotidiens, journaux politiques, périodiques ou autres revues littéraires, féministes ou mondaines publiés durant plus de 200 ans en Égypte en langue française et scannés depuis 2004, ces sources, cependant non exhaustivement conservées, représentent une contribution irremplaçable à l'histoire de l'Égypte contemporaine, à la compréhension de l'évolution sociétale et culturelle, littéraire et artistique, du Proche-Orient ainsi qu'un intéressant apport à la francophonie[4]. L'examen attentif de la presse francophone d'Égypte permet ainsi de comprendre le retentissement qu'a pu connaître le surréalisme égyptien au sein d'une société où les échanges culturels internationaux passaient essentiellement par le biais de la francophonie.

---

2 Michel Paillares (dates inconnues), journaliste, historien. « La langue française en Égypte », dans *Le Phare égyptien*, 9–10 mars 1926.

3 Jean-Jacques Luthi, *La Presse égyptienne d'expression française*, Alexandrie : Éditions de l'Atelier 1978, 28.

4 La Presse francophone d'Égypte, Centre d'études alexandrines, http://www.cealex.org/pfe. (© Archives CEAlex/CNRS.)

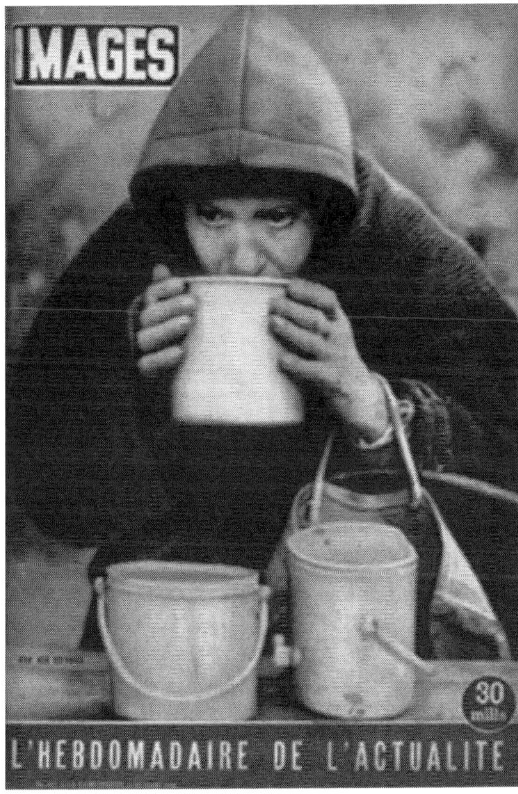

Illustration 1 : *Images*, 25 mars 1945. © Archives CEAlex/CNRS.

Quelle était donc la situation de l'avant-garde égyptienne, à la fois artistique et littéraire, à l'aube des années 1930 ? De quelle manière le surréalisme a-t-il été reçu en Égypte ? Quels ont pu être les acteurs médiatiques, institutionnels ou particuliers de sa réception et de son expansion, notamment à travers Art et Liberté ? Enfin quelles étaient les relations, relayées par la presse, entre Paris et l'Égypte ?

La scène artistique égyptienne à l'orée des années 1930 et l'émergence des Essayistes à l'avant-garde littéraire (1935–1939)

Depuis 1909, la scène artistique égyptienne était dominée par la tenue du Salon annuel du Caire. Événement mondain de premier ordre auquel assistait le monarque, le Salon était organisé par la Société des amis de l'art avec le soutien de l'État égyptien. Ces manifestations conservatrices, conçues sur le modèle des salons parisiens, contribuaient à instaurer une hiérarchisation des artistes selon leur pratique et leur nationalité. En 1945, la revue *Images* (ill. 1) énonçait ainsi dans son compte rendu :

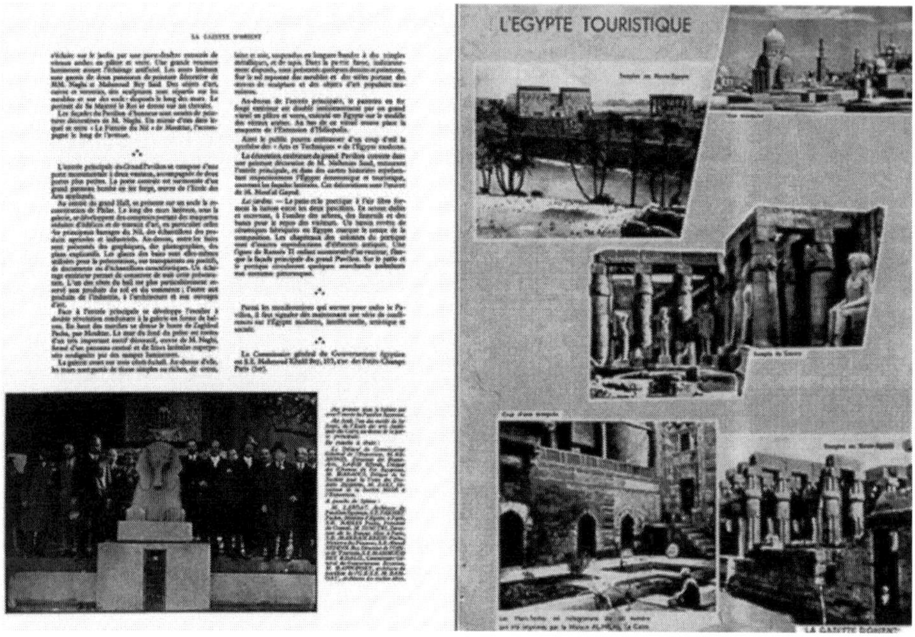

Illustration 2 : *La Gazette d'Orient*, mai 1937. © Archives CEAlex/CNRS.

> Sur les deux cent cinquante numéros du catalogue, c'est tout juste si le quart retient l'attention du visiteur averti. Il y a là de bonnes études propres à rappeler à plusieurs artistes du rez-de-chaussée qu'à la base de toute peinture personnelle, instinctive ou inspirée, il y a inéluctablement la connaissance du dessin, des valeurs de la composition. *Tempête sur la Corniche* de Mahmoud Saïd est, sans conteste, la plus belle toile du Salon qu'elle domine par son rythme tumultueusement harmonisé. Elle est composée avec discipline[5].

En 1937, *La Gazette d'Orient* (ill. 2) relatait la contribution égyptienne à l'Exposition internationale des arts et techniques de Paris en 1937 sous le commissariat de Mahmoud Bey Khalil, par ailleurs fondateur de la Société des amis de l'art. Il y était fait mention de trois artistes-contributeurs : Mahmoud Moukhtar (1891–1934), Mahmoud Saïd (1897–1964) et Mohammad Naghi (1888–1956)[6].

En 1939, *La Revue du Caire* publiait un article intitulé « Les Nouvelles Acquisitions du Musée d'art moderne du Caire » dans lequel on pouvait lire :

> Le Musée d'Art Moderne offre par la diversité de ses nouvelles acquisitions un spectacle d'un grand intérêt. Moukhtar, comme toujours, nous conquiert par la prodigalité, la verve et, par-dessus tout, par la mesure dans le trait vif. Il y a dans son ciseau un souci de perfectionnement, une technique souple et ample qui donne à ses créations un sentiment à la fois profond et délicat. Chaque attitude des figures prises dans l'existence courante est

5 « Compte rendu », dans *Images*, 25 mars 1945.
6 *La Gazette d'Orient*, mai 1937.

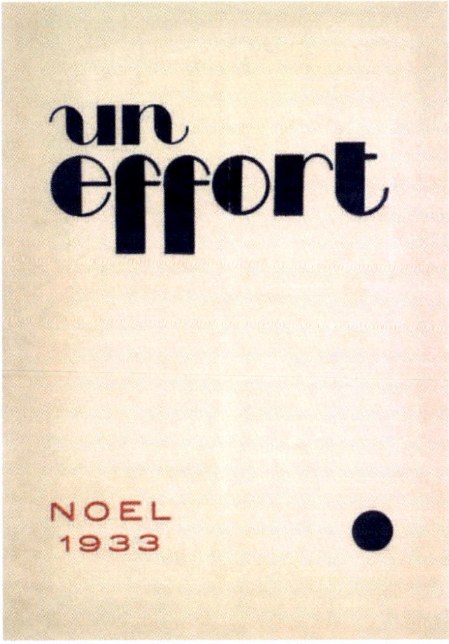

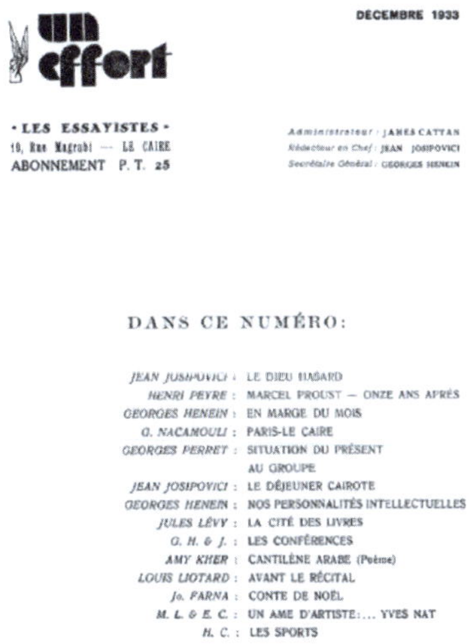
un effort

DECEMBRE 1933

• LES ESSAYISTES •
19, Rue Magrabi — LE CAIRE
ABONNEMENT P. T. 25

Administrateur : JAMES CATTAN
Rédacteur en Chef : JEAN JOSIPOVICI
Secrétaire Général : GEORGES HENEIN

DANS CE NUMÉRO:

JEAN JOSIPOVICI : LE DIEU HASARD
HENRI PEYRE : MARCEL PROUST — ONZE ANS APRÈS
GEORGES HENEIN : EN MARGE DU MOIS
G. NACAMOULI : PARIS-LE CAIRE
GEORGES PERRET : SITUATION DU PRÉSENT AU GROUPE
JEAN JOSIPOVICI : LE DÉJEUNER CAIROTE
GEORGES HENEIN : NOS PERSONNALITÉS INTELLECTUELLES
JULES LÉVY : LA CITÉ DES LIVRES
G. H. & J. : LES CONFÉRENCES
AMY KHER : CANTILÈNE ARABE (Poème)
LOUIS LIOTARD : AVANT LE RÉCITAL
Jo. FARNA : CONTE DE NOËL
M. L. & E. C. : UN AME D'ARTISTE : ... YVES NAT
H. C. : LES SPORTS

Illustrations 3–4 : *Un effort*, Noël 1933. © Archives CEAlex/CNRS.

> captée dans ce qu'elle a d'essentiel et de sculpturalement significatif : en particulier *À la porte du Village, Retour du Marché* sont animés de grâce finement sensuelle et en même temps d'indiscutable noblesse. Voilà une collection qui contribuera à étendre le rayonnement des forces artistiques de l'Égypte[7].

Une poignée d'artistes occupaient donc le devant de la scène, pour l'essentiel réduite à une activité institutionnelle détentrice du bon goût, relayée par de nombreux journaux et revues dans les rubriques expositions ou mondanités.

En 1933, alors que Georges Henein rentre en Égypte après avoir étudié en Europe, symbolisme, romantisme et orientalisme ont les faveurs du public et de la Société des amis de l'art, au contraire des avant-gardes qui suscitent des réactions hostiles. Ainsi, en 1927, *La Bourse égyptienne* dénonçait-elle les surréalistes et leur « haine de l'esprit, de la langue et du sentiment de leur pays », ainsi que leurs applaudissements aux « vers anti-français » de Rimbaud[8]. Lorsque que Henein rejoint les Essayistes en 1933, ils constituent un groupe dynamique et influent. Si *Un effort*, organe du groupement des Essayistes, ne peut être considérée comme une revue révolutionnaire à proprement parler, elle est néanmoins ouverte aux expressions contestataires et permet à Henein d'entrer en scène (ill. 3–4).

---

[7] « Les Nouvelles Acquisitions du Musée d'art moderne du Caire », dans *La Revue du Caire*, mai 1939.

[8] *La Bourse égyptienne*, 9 novembre 1927.

Il y affirme la position qu'il entend prendre comme polémiste d'avant-garde, sur les plans esthétiques et littéraires. En 1935, Henein y publie « De l'irréalisme » :

> Rien n'est inutile comme le réel. Le seul monde véritable est celui que nous créons en nous. En avant pour l'irréalisme, artifice par rapport au réel, vérité par rapport à moi, à l'extrême-moi. Écrire n'importe quoi qui vous soit advenu intérieurement et qui n'ait pas été provoqué par une cause extérieure, et qui ne puisse pas se transporter ni s'utiliser dans le monde extérieur[9].

À Paris, la même année, Henein soumet à la revue marxiste *Les Humbles* « Le Chant des violents » qui appelle les prolétaires à la révolte tandis qu'il consacre au suicide de René Crevel un article paru dans le numéro d'octobre 1935 d'*Un effort* à la lecture duquel on comprend qu'il était déjà acquis au surréalisme[10]. Pourtant Henein trouve difficilement à exprimer le radicalisme de ses positions politiques contre le capitalisme bourgeois et le fascisme dans les publications égyptiennes francophones et publie à compte d'auteur deux écrits controversés : *Suite et fin* en 1934 et *Le Rappel à l'ordure* en juin 1935. La formule employée par Ahmed Rassim pour décrire Henein au Congrès des écrivains étrangers de langue française qui se réunit à Paris en 1937, relayé par *Le Journal d'Égypte* la même année, résume clairement la manière dont le jeune auteur est alors perçu : « Georges Henein dont les articles et conférences sur le problème social et l'art d'avant-garde sont souvent écrits au vitriol[11] ».

Lorsque Filippo Tommaso Marinetti se rend en Égypte en 1938, l'opposition entre futuristes et surréalistes sur le plan politique est à son comble. L'essor du fascisme et l'adhésion du poète italien au mouvement provoque de violentes réactions chez certains intellectuels cairotes, dont Georges Henein[12]. Le scandale éclate au cours du débat organisé au cercle des Essayistes en présence de Marinetti et Henein, ce dernier opposant le futurisme nationaliste et impérialiste au surréalisme internationaliste qui se réclamait affranchi de toute idée reçue. « Par exemple, aurait dit Georges Henein, nous n'avons aucun préjugé en ce qui concerne l'inceste. » Ce à quoi Marinetti aurait répondu : « Mes félicitations et mes vœux à votre sœur ![13] » Gabriel Boctor raconte quant à lui en 1944, dans *La Bourse égyptienne*, comment Henein « prit à parti le chef de ce mouvement, lui reprochant d'être inféodé au fascisme et le barde de ses guerres d'expansions coloniales », et comment la réunion faillit « mal tourner[14] ».

---

9 Georges Henein, « De l'irréalisme », dans *Un effort*, février 1935.

10 Georges Henein, « René Crevel », dans *Un effort*, octobre 1935.

11 Ahmed Rassim (Alexandrie, 1895–Alexandrie, 1958), écrivain. *Le Journal d'Égypte*, 15 juin 1937.

12 Daniel Lançon, *Jabès l'Égyptien*, Paris : Jean Michel Place 2009, 4 : « [l'évènement] illustre la divergence de vues de quelques hommes de gauche et de la quasi-totalité du monde francophone/italophone du Caire ».

13 Nelson Morpurgo, « Marinetti in Egitto », 1938, archives Nelson Morpurgo, Beinecke Rare Book and Manuscript Library, Yale University, New Haven.

14 Gabriel Boctor (dates inconnues), fondateur de la revue *Images*, critique. *La Bourse égyptienne*, 16 décembre 1944.

La scène culturelle égyptienne du début du XXe siècle, bien que dominée sur le plan artistique par le très conservateur Salon annuel du Caire, voit naître dès 1935, à l'avant-garde littéraire, le groupement des Essayistes dont Georges Henein est un membre actif. Une transformation dans le statut de Henein sur la scène littéraire cairote se produit néanmoins au cours des années 1937–1938 car, se ralliant au surréalisme, l'introduisant au Caire et contribuant activement à sa diffusion, il en devint de fait le chef de file égyptien.

Réception et appropriation du surréalisme en Égypte

Alors en pleine expansion grâce, notamment, à de nombreux journalistes et critiques français installés en Égypte, la presse francophone n'a pas manqué de se faire le relais des innovations littéraires et esthétiques apparues en Europe avec le surréalisme. En 1926 déjà, René Crevel écrivait au sujet d'André Breton dans *Messages d'Orient,* attestant ainsi du fantasme lié à l'Orient : « Le *Manifeste du surréalisme*, rend grâce à Freud d'avoir accordé au songe toute sa valeur psychologique. Mais déjà l'Orient s'imposait aux jeunes par l'idée la plus simple sinon la plus juste qu'ils s'en faisaient : L'Orient était la terre même du surnaturel, du surréel[15] ». Une des illustrations de Mayo orne la couverture de la revue culturelle *La Semaine égyptienne*, datée du 30 novembre 1933, accompagnée d'une note de la rédaction confirmant que « Mayo qui nous vient de Paris a été en contact avec les meilleurs surréalistes ». Dans un article intitulé « L'Évolution littéraire de 1900 à 1940 » publié par *La Revue du Caire* en 1942, Edmond Jaloux admet quant à lui : « Par leur volonté implacable de créer en dehors du monde une sorte d'univers du songe ou du rêve éveillé, de la dictée inconsciente et du alogique de l'esprit, André Breton, Aragon, Paul Éluard, René Crevel, Robert Desnos, Georges Ribemont-Dessaignes, Antonin Artaud et tant d'autres, nous ont donné des œuvres dont la singularité apparaîtra d'autant plus à mesure que les années passeront[16] ». En 1942, Gabriel Bounoure publie dans *La Revue du Caire* un article de référence sur le destin et la poésie chez Mallarmé dans lequel il expose textuellement que : « La conscience voudrait triompher du hasard. Mais c'est le hasard, sans doute, qui triomphe d'elle[17] ». Dans le hors série numéro 23 de *La Semaine égyptienne*, Georges Henein souligne également le rôle essentiel joué par Mallarmé :

> La gloire de Mallarmé aura été de marquer l'aube du XXe siècle d'une orientation poétique inédite, reprise après lui par Reverdy, Apollinaire et Breton. C'est de cette orientation que nous avertit son : « *Toute pensée émet un coup de dés* » dans lequel les jeunes poètes de 1910 et de 1920, trouvèrent un encouragement décisif à risquer fortune ou faillite sur une

15 René Crevel, « Pour la liberté de l'esprit », dans *Messages d'Orient* (Alexandrie), avril 1926.

16 Edmond Jaloux (Marseille, 1878–Lutry, 1949), écrivain et critique. « L'Évolution littéraire de 1900 à 1940 », dans *La Revue du Caire*, février 1942.

17 Gabriel Bounoure (Issoire, 1886–Lesconil, 1969), écrivain. « Destin et poésie chez Mallarmé », dans *La Revue du Caire*, juin 1942.

image, sur une idée, sur un malentendu, sur un jeu de mots, nés on ne sait plus où, dans la rue, sur une vitre, au hasard de l'amour, dans une des salles étincelantes de ce Casino de l'Inspiration où les tricheurs sont priés de se suicider à la sortie[18].

Enfin plusieurs articles paraissent en 1945 au sujet de Max Jacob, précurseur de Dada et du surréalisme. Le compte rendu d'une conférence donnée aux Amitiés françaises est publié dans *La Réforme*, une critique de ses lettres à Edmond Jabès éditée par Etiemble parait à Alexandrie dans *Images*, ainsi que des fragments de correspondance dans *Valeurs*, en juillet 1945, dont voici un extrait : « Ne vous faites pas d'illusions sur Montparnasse, pays du Kant, du qu'en-dira-t-on, de la Morgue, de la morve, de la mort aux rats. Le vrai désert d'Égypte avec chameaux etc. est Montparnasse. Il n'y a pas d'Égypte. Il n'y a pas de Paris[19] ».

Si le présent survol ne peut retracer l'ensemble des critiques telles qu'elles ont pu être formulées dans la presse francophone d'Égypte durant la période qui nous occupe, il semble important de souligner leur diversité, qu'elles appartiennent au champ littéraire, esthétique ou politique, afin de comprendre quels ont pu être les acteurs intellectuels et médiatiques de sa réception ainsi que les mécanismes d'appropriation mis en place.

En 1936, Georges Henein rencontre André Breton. Dans une lettre datée du 8 avril 1936, Breton révèle déjà qu'il est conscient des efforts de Henein pour diffuser le surréalisme en Égypte : « Le démon de la perversité, tel qu'il daigne m'apparaître, semble avoir une aile ici et l'autre en Égypte[20] ». Ce à quoi Henein répond : « Oui, mais une aile qui bat bien faiblement[21] ». À partir de ce moment, Henein est le canal de diffusion principal des développements de la scène internationale vers le circuit local. Le 3 septembre 1936, il signe la déclaration de Breton intitulée « La vérité sur le procès de Moscou ».

Le 4 février 1937, Henein donne chez les Essayistes une conférence radiodiffusée intitulée « Bilan du mouvement surréaliste »[22]. Cette conférence est présentée le 1er mars 1937 à l'Atelier à Alexandrie[23]. Elle bénéficie d'une audience assez large auprès des publics francophones et marque l'introduction du surréalisme en

[18] Georges Henein, « Hommage à Mallarmé », dans *La Semaine égyptienne*, décembre 1942.

[19] Amitiés françaises (1943), groupe intellectuel destiné à promouvoir la culture française, avec deux centres autonomes implantés au Caire et à Alexandrie. *La Réforme*, 9 mai 1945. Jean Moscatelli (Le Caire, 1905–Le Caire, 1965), écrivain, critique. « Lettres de Max Jacob », dans *Images*, 9 septembre 1945. René Etiemble (Mayenne, 1909–Vigny, 2002), fondateur de la revue *Valeurs*, écrivain, critique. « Revue des livres », dans *Valeurs*, juillet 1945.

[20] Lettre d'André Breton à Georges Henein, 8 avril 1936, archives André Breton, Bibliothèque littéraire Jacques Doucet, Paris.

[21] Marc Kober, « Le Démon de la perversité : à propos d'un échange entre André Breton et Georges Henein », dans *André Breton*, Michel Murat, dir., Paris : L'Herne 1998, 377.

[22] Georges Henein, « Bilan du mouvement surréalistes », dans *La Revue des conférences françaises en Orient*, octobre 1937.

[23] L'Atelier (depuis 1934), association destinée à promouvoir les arts plastiques implantée à Alexandrie.

Égypte. La *Revue des conférences françaises en Orient* en publie le texte, tout en l'introduisant de la manière suivante :

> Georges Henein a fait et continuera, croyons-nous, de faire en Égypte, pour une certaine forme d'idée et de littérature – il vaudrait mieux préciser : d'alittérature – c'est ce que l'on saura peut-être un jour. Qu'en attendant l'on sache que Georges Henein est l'auteur de deux brochures : un essai déjà renié, *Suite et fin* ; un pamphlet qui ne l'est pas encore, *Le Rappel à l'ordure*, et qui a peu de chances de l'être. Car on ne renie honnêtement ses propres violences que pour adhérer à des violences majeures.[24]

Au cours de cette conférence, Henein détaille les origines du mouvement et la signification des renouvellements qu'il apporte, ainsi que le non-conformisme absolu qui les oppose aux institutions et aux régimes chargés d'opprimer les individus rebelles à leur pouvoir. Il explicite les attendus de l'écriture automatique, ses liens avec la théorie freudienne du subconscient, les sommeils hypnotiques et l'importance du « domaine du rêve dont le subconscient n'est que la province limitrophe ». Il évoque les tableaux d'Angelo de Riz, exposés au Caire au moment où il prononce sa conférence et dont « plusieurs ne sont que des instantanés de rêves ». Il commente abondamment Breton, Tzara, rejette les futuristes et « le caractère exhibitionniste des manifestations de Monsieur Marinetti, le dynamisme artificiel et spectaculaire qu'il préconise ». Achevant de mettre en avant les liens établis avec la mouvance française, Henein insiste : « Les surréalistes ne dédaignent pas non plus l'étude des superstitions orientales, de l'occultisme et affectionnent la plupart des troubles mentaux[25] ». Soulignons que, pour *La Bourse égyptienne* datée de 1937, le travail de Kamel El Telmisany (1915–1972), qui participait à la même exposition qu'Angelo de Riz, est plutôt « surréaliste qu'oriental[26] ». En décembre de la même année, Jean Moscatelli écrit dans *Images* à propos d'une exposition d'Angelo de Riz à la Galerie Nistri du Caire : « Le surréalisme a ses adeptes en Égypte[27] ».

L'année suivante, Henein adhère à la Fédération internationale de l'art indépendant (FIARI), fondée par Breton et Trotski qui élaborent en commun le manifeste « Pour un art révolutionnaire indépendant » revendiquant « toute licence en art » et dénonçant les régimes totalitaires qui prétendent contrôler la production artistique. La même année, Marie Cavadia, mécène du groupe et poétesse, souligne son intérêt pour le surréalisme dans *La Revue du Caire* :

> Chez le poète surréaliste l'inspiration s'emploie sur un plan très différent : doué de facultés étranges, son esprit s'évade de l'enclos habituel où s'exerce [sic] nos cinq sens pour aller inquisitionner dans d'arrière-sphères obscures, et c'est là, dans ces souterrains de la conscience, qu'il retrouve les racines des images et des pensées logiques servant de butin aux poètes plastiques[28].

---

24 *La Revue des conférences françaises en Orient*, octobre 1937.

25 Georges Henein, *Œuvres : poèmes, récits, essais, articles et pamphlets*, Paris : Denoël 2006, 372.

26 *La Bourse égyptienne*, 12 mars 1937.

27 Jean Moscatelli, *Images*, 11 décembre 1937.

28 Marie Cavadia, « Dix chansons de Marie l'Égyptienne », dans *La Revue du Caire*, avril 1938.

La prolifération de débats sur les « vertus » du fascisme au contraire de la démocratie a eu pour conséquence une montée du sentiment totalitaire qui se fit sentir dès le milieu des années 1930. La population ressentait une frustration liée aux conditions sociales et politiques, comme l'atteste une lettre adressée par El Telmisany à Henein en 1937 dans laquelle il lui écrit que « des épouses et des sœurs » sont contraintes de se prostituer[29]. À l'aube de la Seconde Guerre mondiale, les institutions culturelles du Caire traversaient donc une crise existentielle poussant certains jeunes artistes à se réunir en collectifs autonomes afin d'outrepasser les pratiques institutionnelles et les critères académiques établis par la Société des amis de l'art organisatrice du Salon du Caire. Ainsi, l'emprise autoritaire de l'*establishment* étatique sur la pratique des arts, combinée aux activités d'une section locale de futuristes liés au parti fasciste, achevèrent de manifester, quoique dans des conditions différentes, la présence, en Égypte, d'une idéologie proche de celle qui qualifiait les mouvements d'avant-garde d'*entartete Kunst* (art dégénéré) expliquant notamment l'attrait pour le surréalisme et son expansion à travers Art et Liberté.

Art et Liberté (1938–1948). Un creuset littéraire et artistique militant

Publié au Caire le 22 décembre 1938, « Vive l'art dégénéré » dénonce l'Allemagne et l'Italie fascistes où l'art qualifié de « dégénéré » doit « céder la place à la platitude et à l'ineptie de l'art national-socialiste[30] ». Le manifeste est signé par trente-sept intellectuels égyptiens (artistes, écrivains, journalistes, avocats) révoltés contre « l'hostilité » avec laquelle « la société actuelle regarde toute création littéraire et artistique menaçant plus ou moins directement les disciplines intellectuelles et les valeurs morales ». Il se clôt sur ces mots : « Intellectuels, écrivains, artistes ! Relevons ensemble le défi. Cet art dégénéré, nous en sommes absolument solidaires. En lui résident toutes les chances de l'avenir. Travaillons à sa victoire sur le nouveau Moyen-Âge qui se lève en plein cœur de l'Occident ». Le tract est, dans un premier temps au moins, mal perçu en Égypte même si quelques revues et journaux égyptiens en signalent la parution tels que *La Bourse égyptienne* et *Le Journal d'Égypte*, *La Revue des conférences françaises en Orient*, le quotidien grec *Kiryx*, la revue publiée en arabe *al-Majallah al-jadīdah* (La Nouvelle Revue) et, plus tard, *Images*[31]. Georges Henein parvient également à faire signaler le manifeste dans

29 Sam Bardaouil et Till Fellrath, dir., *Art et Liberté. Rupture, guerre et surréalisme en Égypte, 1938–1948*, cat. exp., Paris : Skira/Centre Georges Pompidou 2016, 105.

30 Art et Liberté, « Vive l'art dégénéré », manifeste, dans *Revue des conférences françaises en Orient*, janvier 1939.

31 Le numéro 1 d'*Art et Liberté*, publié en mars 1939, fait état du fait que seule *La Bourse égyptienne*, « moins bassement réactionnaire, a consenti à signaler l'apparition du manifeste » et que le 2 janvier 1939, *Le Journal d'Égypte* en « résume le contenu et énumère les signataires ». *La Revue des conférences françaises en Orient* en publie le texte intégral ainsi que l'importante revue égyptienne *al-Majallah al-jadīdah*.

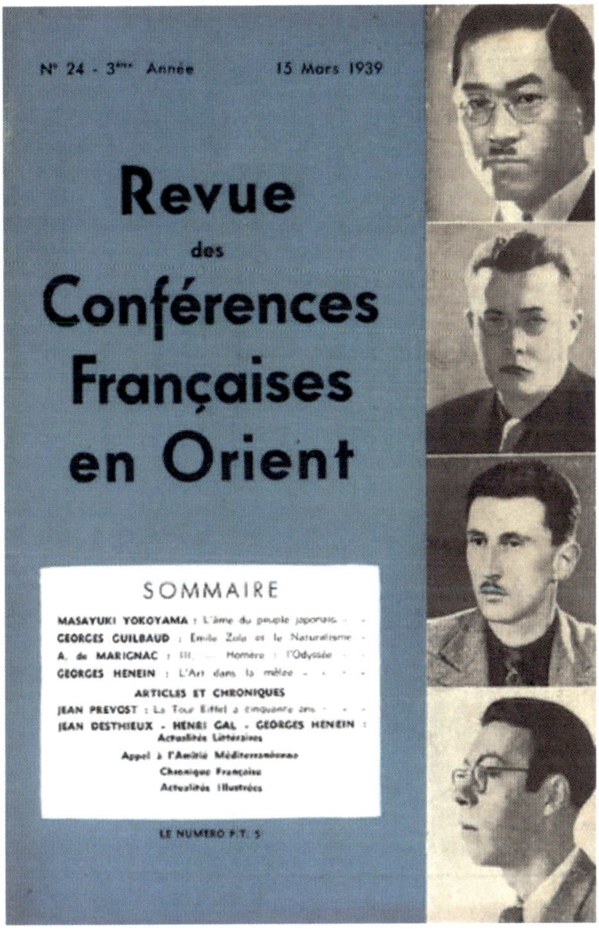

Illustration 5 : *La Revue des conférences françaises en Orient*, mars 1939. © Archives CEAlex/CNRS.

La Nouvelle Revue française par l'intermédiaire de son ami Henri Calet (1904–1956) qui rédige un bref communiqué paru dans le numéro du 1er février 1939 avec l'en tête : « L'Orient travaille pour la défense de la culture occidentale ». Les statuts de l'association sont également publiés dans le deuxième numéro de *Clé*, le bulletin de la FIARI publié en français depuis Paris en 1939[32].

Dans une conférence prononcée chez les Essayistes le 26 janvier, retranscrite dans *La Revue des conférences françaises en Orient* sous le titre « L'art dans la mêlée » (ill. 5), Georges Henein développe l'idée que :

> L'Art est descendu dans la grande mêlée humaine où nous voici tous jetés, d'une manière presque inconsciente […] Enlevez Picasso, et tout l'art moderne tombe dans la nuit.

32 *Clé*, 2 février 1939.

> Enlevez Chirico, et l'immense vague de rêve qui, avec le surréalisme triomphant, recouvre la littérature et la peinture contemporaines, perd toute origine, toute profondeur.

L'auteur poursuit :

> Je terminerai même en citant une phrase du Dr. Goebbels avec laquelle il m'est difficile de n'être pas absolument d'accord : « Au moment où la politique écrit le drame d'un peuple, où un monde est renversé, où toutes les valeurs sombrent et où d'autres s'élèvent, à ce moment l'artiste n'a pas le droit de dire que cela ne le concerne en rien ». En effet, tout cela le concerne, et l'artiste, lui-même, est le premier à en convenir. La seule formalité à régler, formalité déjà réglée pour la plupart d'entre eux, est de savoir de quel côté du monde, de quel côté du peuple, de quel côté des valeurs anciennes et nouvelles, de quel côté du drame, il appartient aux artistes de se ranger. Certainement pas du même côté que Mr Goebbels[33].

Le second bulletin du groupe, daté de mai 1939, nous apprend que l'Assemblée générale du 8 mars avait été présidée par Roland Penrose, chef du groupe surréaliste anglais alors de passage en Égypte. À cette occasion, Penrose prononça un discours sur la corrélation entre art et activisme politique contre le fascisme. Penrose fit en sorte que le texte intégral en français et en arabe de « Vive l'art dégénéré » soit republié en avril dans le *London Bulletin*, la revue des surréalistes britanniques[34].

Outre les bulletins d'*Art et Liberté*, dans un premier temps, Henein et quelques autres membres du groupe Art et Liberté collaborent, entre 1939 et 1940, à la revue francophone, politique et littéraire *Don Quichotte*, « première revue littéraire et artistique d'avant-garde, en langue arabe ». Sa consœur arabophone *al-Taṭawwor* (L'Évolution), publiée entre janvier et septembre 1940, a vocation à soutenir les réformes sociales, économiques et morales, et à lutter contre les traditions et les archaïsmes. Deux ans plus tard, des membres d'Art et Liberté prennent la direction de la revue arabe *al-Majallah al-jadīdah* (La Nouvelle Revue), fondée dans les années 1930 et qui sera interdite en 1944. En 1947, ils créent *La Part du sable* (ill. 6) – qui sera éditée jusqu'en 1953 – et Henein anime avec trois autres membres, pour une année, *Cause*, un secrétariat international du surréalisme ayant pour objectif d'établir la liaison avec les différents groupes étrangers.

Étienne Mériel, dans *Le Progrès égyptien* du 4 avril 1947 conseille la lecture du premier numéro de *La Part du sable* à tous ceux qui sont curieux de découvrir une manifestation vivante du surréalisme, et il y loue « la valeur humaine de ce document » et son état d'esprit qui révèle « une des formes les plus aiguës de l'inquiétude contemporaine[35] ».

---

33 Georges Henein, « L'Art dans la mêlée », dans *Revue des conférences françaises en Orient*, mars 1939, 272.

34 Roland Penrose était alors en relation avec Art et Liberté, notamment via Lee Miller rencontrée à Paris en 1937 et avec qui il vivra à Londres après qu'elle avait quitté Le Caire et son époux égyptien Aziz Eloui Bey en 1939.

35 Étienne Mériel (dates inconnues), critique. *Le Progrès égyptien*, 4 avril 1947.

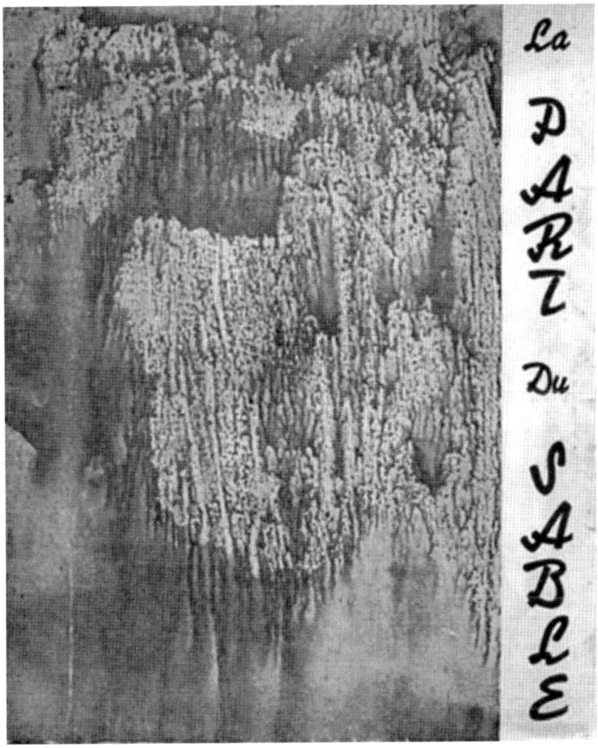

Illustration 6 : *La Part du sable*, 1947. © Archives CEAlex/CNRS.

Dès le début de la guerre, Art et Liberté redéfinit sa mission et devient un phénomène non seulement littéraire mais artistique, de portée sociale et politique. Au-delà de la lutte pour l'indépendance de l'art face aux régimes totalitaires, il s'agit de permettre la survie des avant-gardes menacées de disparition, avec l'appui de villes libres comme Londres et New York.

En effet, l'émergence d'une conscience nationale voit naître un nouveau courant de pensée, *nahḍah*[36], revendiquant un « art authentiquement égyptien » contre lequel Art et Liberté concentrera son action. Le manifeste du groupe affirmait ainsi : « Nous trouvons absurdes et ridicules le racisme, la religiosité et le nationalisme fanatiques, sur lesquels certaines personnes tentent d'aligner la destinée de l'art moderne[37] ». Pour les avant-gardes, et notamment Georges Henein, les revendications identitaires de particularismes régionaux n'ont aucun sens. La volonté

[36] *Nahḍah* (l'éveil) est un mouvement qui émerge dès la fin du XIXe siècle dans les domaines religieux, politiques, économiques et culturels et se caractérise par la volonté de concilier valeurs nationales et modernisation.

[37] Art et Liberté, « Vive l'art dégénéré ».

d'enraciner la création dans une réalité nationale ne trouve pas d'écho chez Henein qui refuse de s'identifier à un pays.

De 1940 à 1945, cinq expositions indépendantes sont organisées. En 1940, Henein affirme dans *Don Quichotte* l'autonomie de l'art face aux enjeux politiques d'identité nationale :

> Tous ceux qui ont essayé ou s'obstineront à essayer de fonder un art national conçu en fonction des caractères spécifiques d'un pays déterminé se condamneront à l'échec et au ridicule le plus complet. L'art, qui devient chaque jour davantage un moyen d'unifier le sentiment humain, ne doit pas servir à rendre compte des modes, coutumes, des idées et des visions locales – autant de fausses frontières plus absurdes et détestables que les vraies, dressées entre des esprits qui n'osent pas encore se reconnaître pour solidaires les uns des autres. L'art n'a pas de patrie, pas de terroir. Chirico n'est pas plus italien que Delvaux n'est belge, que Diego Rivera n'est mexicain, que Tanguy n'est français, que Max Ernst n'est allemand, que El-Telmisany n'est égyptien. Tous ces hommes participent d'un même élan fraternel contre quoi les raisons de clocher ou de minaret ne sauraient élever qu'une barrière dérisoire[38].

Ainsi la quête picturale était-elle bien plus ancrée intellectuellement que plastiquement ou politiquement, suivant les préceptes de la *nahḍah.*

Défini dans le catalogue de la IIe Exposition de l'art indépendant en 1941, l'objectif est ainsi :

> [d']intégrer l'activité des jeunes artistes d'Égypte au grand circuit de l'art moderne, de l'art passionnel et mouvementé, rebelle à toute consigne policière, religieuse, ou commerciale, de l'art dont nous sentons battre le pouls à New York, à Londres, à Mexico, partout où luttent les Diego Rivera, les Paalen, les Tanguy, les Henry Moore, partout où luttent des hommes qui n'ont pas encore désespéré de la libération totale de la conscience humaine[39].

On lit dans *Images* une critique signée de Marie Cavadia :

> Avant d'entrer chez les « Indépendants » vous feriez bien de déposer au vestiaire votre honnête petite logique quotidienne et je ne suis pas certaine, qu'après cette belle aventure que vous venez de traverser dans l'irréel, vous ne songiez point à l'abandonner pour toujours[40].

Au contraire, dans la veine conservatrice du Salon du Caire, Mohamed Saddik écrivait la même année :

> L'autre lundi a eu lieu le vernissage du IIe Salon des Indépendants au milieu d'une grande affluence de public cairote à une manifestation de cet ordre. Monsieur Eric de Nemès était inattendu dans la cohue des exposants. Sa peinture tue toutes les autres. Aussi convient-il de porter sur lui un jugement à part des autres. Il serait cruel de permettre la comparaison. Monsieur de Nemès n'est pas d'ici, il n'est pas un débutant, c'est un artiste connu en Europe, qui a remporté de grands succès et l'admiration des connaisseurs à

---

38 George Henein, « El Telmisany », dans *Don Quichotte*, 29 mars 1940.

39 « L'Art indépendant en Égypte », dans *Catalogue de la IIe Exposition de l'art indépendant*, Le Caire, 1941.

40 Marie Cavadia, « La 2ème Exposition de l'art indépendant », dans *Images*, 18 mars 1941.

> Paris. Monsieur Ramsès Younane est d'une inégalité étonnante, mais il est jeune et nous espérons qu'il apprenne la rigueur et cesse de s'abandonner trop vite à son goût qu'il a mauvais. [...] Monsieur Kamel El Telmisany nous change de ses compositions terriblement embrouillées par un portrait de femme intitulé Lucienne où sa peinture calmée laisse rêver un pessimisme qui ne manque ni de sympathie ni de caractère, ni d'exercer une sorte d'envoûtement. Espérons que ce soit pour Telmisany le début d'une nouvelle manière. Deux dessins agréables et une tête de nègre sculptée amusante de Monsieur Angelo de Riz. Monsieur Laurent Marcel Salinas s'est égaré dans la peinture. Monsieur Fouad Kamel est bien jeune, sa palette franchement embrouillée et sa cervelle aussi[41].

Dans *Le Journal d'Égypte* daté du 16 mars 1941, l'article s'achève de la façon suivante : « On aimerait beaucoup savoir comment sortir[42] ». Dans *L'Égypte nouvelle* du 18 mars 1941, paraît une critique signée Kantorowits dans laquelle il s'insurge contre la présentation des mannequins de Henein : « Il n'a qu'à se déclarer être le pape du surréalisme en Égypte et sonner la cloche de la revanche à l'horloge du charlatanisme[43] ».

En 1944, à l'occasion d'une « Conférence sur le Rayonnement de l'esprit poétique moderne parti de Paris », publiée dans *La Revue des conférences françaises en Orient* (ill. 7), Henein souligne la densité du maillage surréaliste parisien et l'internationalisme du mouvement :

> À Paris, aucun sillage ne se perd ; par un vague miracle dont tout le monde se fait complice, une idée, une image, une boutade, une gifle, jaillies à une table de bistrot, s'insinuent le lendemain dans l'atelier d'un peintre, s'étalent sur un chevalet, rebondissent dans une salle de rédaction improvisée [...] différents poèmes écrits à Prague, à Londres, à Santiago, à New York, peuvent passer pour représenter un seul et même foyer d'inspiration[44].

La même année, *La Semaine égyptienne* publie son compte rendu de l'Exposition de l'art indépendant :

> Ce qu'il convient pourtant de rappeler, c'est que la guerre qui, en se prolongeant, marque presque tous les esprits d'un conformisme stérilisant, engendre à tous les carrefours un art de redites et de platitudes, finit même par avoir raison de toute spontanéité de jugement ou de comportement, n'a pas entamé la source libertaire d'inspiration dont procède l'art indépendant[45].

Dans son compte rendu du Salon des Indépendants pour *Images*, Moscatelli relate le fait suivant : « De l'avis unanime, ce Ve Salon des Indépendants, dont la

---

41 Mohamed Saddik (dates inconnues), critique. Mohamed Saddik, « La IIe Exposition de l'art indépendant, Le Caire, 10 mars 1941 », archives Ramsès Younane, Bibliothèque Kandinsky, Paris.

42 *Le Journal d'Égypte*, 16 mars 1941.

43 Samuel Kantorowits (dates inconnues), journaliste. « Sur la cimaise : chez les indépendants », dans *L'Égypte nouvelle*, 18 mars 1941.

44 Georges Henein, « Conférence prononcée au Caire, en 1944, aux Amis de la Culture Française en Egypte sur le Rayonnement de l'esprit poétique moderne parti de Paris », dans *La Revue des conférences françaises en Orient*, mai 1945.

45 Georges Henein, « Exposition de l'art indépendant », dans *La Semaine égyptienne*, mai 1944.

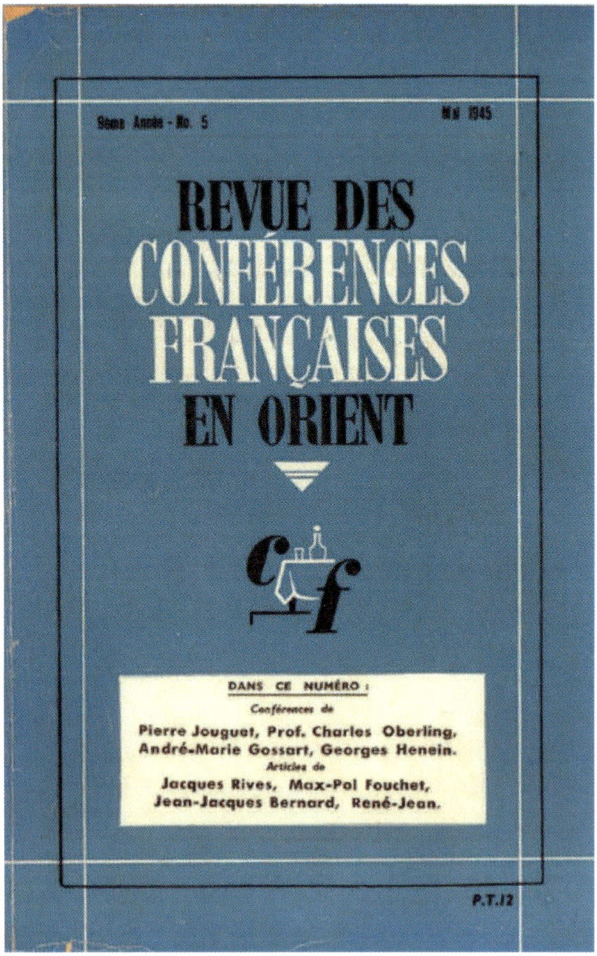

Illustration 7 : *La Revue des conférences françaises en Orient*, mai 1945. © Archives CEAlex/CNRS.

continuité place à l'improviste Le Caire parmi les métropoles les plus à jour quant à l'art pur et libre, est d'une cohésion, partant d'une qualité jamais égalée jusqu'ici ». À propos de Ramsès Younane, il souligne : « Ramsès Younane qui se place à l'avant-garde du mouvement pictural égyptien, procède d'un surréalisme de la meilleure veine[46] ».

Si la presse francophone se fait régulièrement l'écho des interventions des membres d'Art et Liberté, soulignant les liens entre Paris et l'Égypte, les sources tarissent aux lendemains de la guerre. Dès 1946, certains membres d'Art et Liberté se sont associés au sein d'un collectif appelé Groupe de l'art contemporain qui restera actif jusqu'au milieu des années 1950, et se détachera progressivement du

46 Jean Moscatelli, « Les Expositions », dans *Images*, 15 avril 1945.

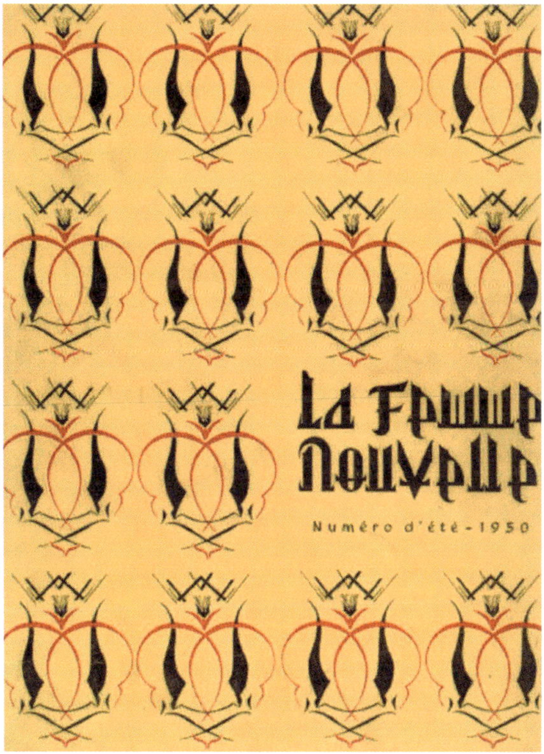

Illustration 8 : *La Femme nouvelle*, été 1950. © Archives CEAlex/CNRS.

surréalisme pour lui préférer un langage vernaculaire nourri d'un répertoire de symboles emprunté à la tradition populaire.

« N'êtes-vous pas frappé de constater que ce qui a maintenu le surréalisme depuis la fin de la guerre, ce sont les actes et les œuvres individuels, tandis que tout ce qui tendait à l'expression collective aboutissait au plus cruel échec, quand il ne minait pas l'édifice patiemment élevé ? » – c'est par ces mots que Georges Henein rompit avec Breton à l'été 1948[47]. L'écart opposant les surréalistes autour de Breton et les membres d'Art et Liberté s'était en effet creusé au point d'aboutir à une rupture définitive.

Malgré les efforts déployés par Georges Henein pour répandre le message du groupe, notamment à travers la création de *al-Taṭawwor* destiné au public lettré arabe, force est de constater le revers qu'a connu son initiative. Avec le groupe Art et Liberté, Le Caire était pourtant enfin à l'heure de Paris. Dans un texte intitulé « La Littérature écartelée » publié dans *La Femme nouvelle* à l'été 1950 (ill. 8), Henein écrivait :

[47] Lettre de Georges Henein à André Breton, 26 juillet 1948, archives André Breton, Bibliothèque littéraire Jacques Doucet, Paris.

> Depuis 1919, année de Versailles et de Dada, fin de l'Europe et fin de l'écrivain à conscience homogène, la littérature vit en état d'écartèlement. On pouvait attendre de la seconde guerre mondiale qu'elle constituât un orage décisif d'où la littérature fut [sic] sortie réconciliée avec elle-même. Il n'en a rien été et les écrivains soucieux d'avenir en sont réduits à interroger les voyantes sur ce qui sera leur ligne de vie[48].

Pressentant l'exil de son sujet, le poète Foulad Yeghen écrivait dans un essai épitaphe daté de 1942 et publié en 1953 dans *La Bourse égyptienne* :

> Que vont devenir le témoignage pathétique d'un Georges Henein (30 ans), le style un peu court mais violent et continu d'un Albert Cossery (30 ans) ? On les entend de moins en moins, ils ne parlent pas notre langue. Il a manqué aux écrivains de 1900 à 1940, exception faite de quelques-uns, l'amour du pays qui donne le suc et la moelle. Ces observateurs de l'extérieur ont payé leur tribut et disparaissent[49].

En 1951, le Comte d'Arschot, écrivait dans un ouvrage intitulé *Peintres et sculpteurs de l'Égypte contemporaine* :

> Dans les arts plastiques, le surréalisme n'a pas ouvert de nouvelles perspectives pour les artistes égyptiens. Ceux qui se sont laissés séduire par cette école n'y ont adhéré que de manière superficielle, leur subconscient ayant certaines complexités auxquelles le surréalisme ne peut pas répondre de la même manière qu'il a pu le faire en occident. Le fait est qu'il y a entre les sentiments orientaux et les nôtres une frontière que seul quelqu'un ayant une profonde connaissance des deux sensibilités peut franchir avec facilité. Par conséquent, pour éviter de courir le danger d'être imprécis, nous ne pouvons pas qualifier de surréalistes toutes les formes d'expression qui s'y attachent de près ou de loin[50].

En 1943, Henein écrivait dans un article consacré à Éluard publié par *L'Égypte nouvelle* : « On écrit comme on marche, comme on souffre, comme on se bat[51] ». Ces quelques mots semblent résumer la contribution d'Art et Liberté au surréalisme international, l'étude de la presse francophone d'Égypte permettant de souligner l'importance des bouleversements artistiques, politiques et sociaux provoqués par le groupe surréaliste égyptien, tant à travers ses liens avec Paris que par les conditions de sa réception. Simultanément, la révolution de 1952 et son projet nationaliste ont eu pour effet de stopper la diffusion de la francophonie et de remettre au goût du jour la question d'un « art authentiquement égyptien ». En lien avec la *nahḍah*, cette préoccupation majeure de la création artistique et littéraire égyptienne a achevé de reléguer au second plan les combats d'Art et Liberté et de plonger le mouvement dans l'agonie.

L'appropriation et la mise en œuvre du surréalisme par Art et Liberté, telle que transcrite par la presse francophone d'Égypte, a permis de mettre en évidence l'importance des réseaux littéraires et artistiques nationaux et internationaux liés aux

48 Georges Henein, « La Littérature écartelée », dans *La Femme nouvelle*, été 1950.

49 Foulad Yeghen (1901–1947), auteur, poète. *La Bourse égyptienne*, 8 juin 1953. L'étude paraît de manière posthume.

50 Philippe d'Arschot, *Peintres et sculpteurs de l'Égypte contemporaine*, Bruxelles : Éditions des Arts Plastiques 1951, 19–20.

51 George Henein, « Paul Éluard et le surréalisme », dans *L'Égypte nouvelle*, 23 janvier 1943.

répercussions notamment politiques et diasporiques de la Seconde Guerre mondiale. La diversité des acteurs médiatiques, institutionnels et particuliers, qu'ils aient été conservateurs ou avant-gardistes, a permis de contribuer à une très large diffusion du surréalisme égyptien, et ce malgré le constat d'échec qu'a connu le mouvement à l'aube des années 1950.

Chapter 9
Joyce Mansour et le surréalisme. Un bestiaire partagé

Fabrice Flahutez

Le présent texte tente de montrer la façon dont André Breton (1896–1966) reconstitue le surréalisme en tant que groupe après l'exil américain. Les surréalistes ayant été très largement dispersés pendant plus de cinq années, vont essayer de se retrouver à partir de 1946 à Paris, mais aussi d'accueillir de nouveaux poètes et artistes venant d'horizons et de contrées les plus diverses et aussi lointaines qu'inattendues. Ce fut le cas de Joyce Mansour (1928–1986), poétesse égyptienne d'expression française célébrée par André Breton à son retour d'exil, ce qui lui permettra d'entretenir des liens étroits avec nombre de surréalistes dans une atmosphère d'intense activité créatrice[1]. Le bestiaire et le vocabulaire des formes dans l'œuvre de Joyce Mansour sont en grande partie liés au surréalisme de l'entre-deux-guerres, mais trouvent dans le contexte des années 1950 un moyen de renforcer une certaine idée du surréalisme international. Joyce Mansour sera également l'une des collectionneuses les plus affirmées de l'univers surréaliste, fréquentant avec Breton le marché aux puces à Paris et cultivant un tropisme pour les primitivismes[2]. De nombreuses photographies et même un court film montrent la poétesse dans son appartement parisien entourée des artistes surréalistes, d'objets hétéroclites trouvés au hasard des rencontres, et de toute une statuaire en provenance d'Océanie conforme au goût des surréalistes pour ces objets[3].

Quelles ont été les modalités de rapprochement de milieux littéraires lointains comme ceux de Mansour et des surréalistes parisiens dans un contexte de refondation du surréalisme après 1945 ? C'est à cette question que nous tenterons de répondre en montrant à la fois la complexité d'une telle tentative sur le plan théorique et la facilité avec laquelle le surréalisme s'est distingué dans l'appropriation d'univers exogènes. Il faut dire qu'après 1945 André Breton s'active à renouveler le surréalisme après tant de défections dans ses rangs et de trahisons accentuées

1 Marie-Francine Mansour, *Une vie surréaliste : Joyce Mansour, complice d'André Breton*, Chaintreaux : Éditions France-Empire monde 2015.

2 Marie-Francine Mansour, *Une vie surréaliste.*

3 Voir par exemple Robert Benayoun, réalisateur, « Joyce Mansour présente à Georges Benayoun sa collection d'œuvres d'art rassemblée avec Breton », film de 9 min 38, Office national de radiodiffusion télévision française, 19 avril 1970, http://www.ina.fr/video/I0513 2588.

par l'éclatement du groupe pendant l'exil américain[4]. Ce renouvellement théorique passera par la préemption de nombreuses nouvelles recrues dont Mansour, mais aussi par la mise en place d'un discours assimilateur très sophistiqué. Le cas étudié ici montre de façon exemplaire cette appropriation au profit d'une ligne très surréaliste de la création contemporaine.

Le surréalisme ou la fabrique des affinités électives

Dans le milieu des années 1950, un manuscrit de Joyce Mansour écrit en Égypte retient particulièrement l'attention de Breton au point qu'il propose Pierre Molinier (1900–1976) pour en illustrer l'édition française. Il faut dire que Pierre Molinier est alors quasiment inconnu dans les milieux littéraires parisiens, malgré une activité de peintre dans les cercles conservateurs de Bordeaux et de sa région[5]. Molinier, alors connu essentiellement pour ses tableaux et photomontages érotiques mettant en scène son propre corps travesti et masqué, dans des propositions d'inversement de genre, avait envoyé à André Breton des pièces qui l'avaient surpris de sorte que cette prise de contact fut aussitôt suivie d'une intégration aussi fulgurante qu'imprévue de l'artiste dans le groupe surréaliste en reconstruction. L'ouverture d'esprit du surréalisme pour accueillir un sang nouveau aura donc profité au même moment à la fois à Mansour et à Molinier. La collaboration que Breton souhaite pour Mansour devait s'articuler autour de son petit livre autobiographique et fictionnel intitulé *Jules César*. Pourtant, *Jules César* sera finalement illustré par un autre artiste, Hans Bellmer (1902–1975) dont la vie personnelle trouve un écho inattendu dans le texte de Joyce Mansour (ill. 1).

La collaboration entre Mansour et Bellmer est le fruit d'une rencontre particulièrement fertile, mais c'est aussi un événement propre à développer les liens qui se tissaient entre Paris et un « pôle » surréaliste au Moyen-Orient. Il s'agit donc de revenir sur cette aventure éditoriale qui manifeste la fraternité des exilés (Breton–Mansour–Bellmer) dans le travail poétique. Il faut rappeler la personnalité de Joyce Mansour pour comprendre l'attrait que le surréalisme a pu exercer sur toute une génération coincée dans l'émergence des nationalismes au-delà de la mer Méditerranée.

Joyce Mansour n'est pas égyptienne mais anglaise. Elle est née Joyce Patrice Adès le 25 juillet 1928, à Bowden en Angleterre, mais va grandir en Égypte dans la haute société bourgeoise du Caire. Sa mère décède alors qu'elle est encore adolescente, et son premier mari Henri Naggar, rencontré peu après, décède à son

---

4 Voir Fabrice Flahutez, *Nouveau Monde et nouveau mythe. Mutations du surréalisme de l'exil américain à l'Écart absolu*, Dijon : Les Presses du réel 2007.

5 L'ouvrage le plus complet sur l'œuvre et la vie de Pierre Molinier est Jean-Luc Mercié, *Pierre Molinier*, Dijon : Les Presses du réel ; Paris : K. Mennour 2010.

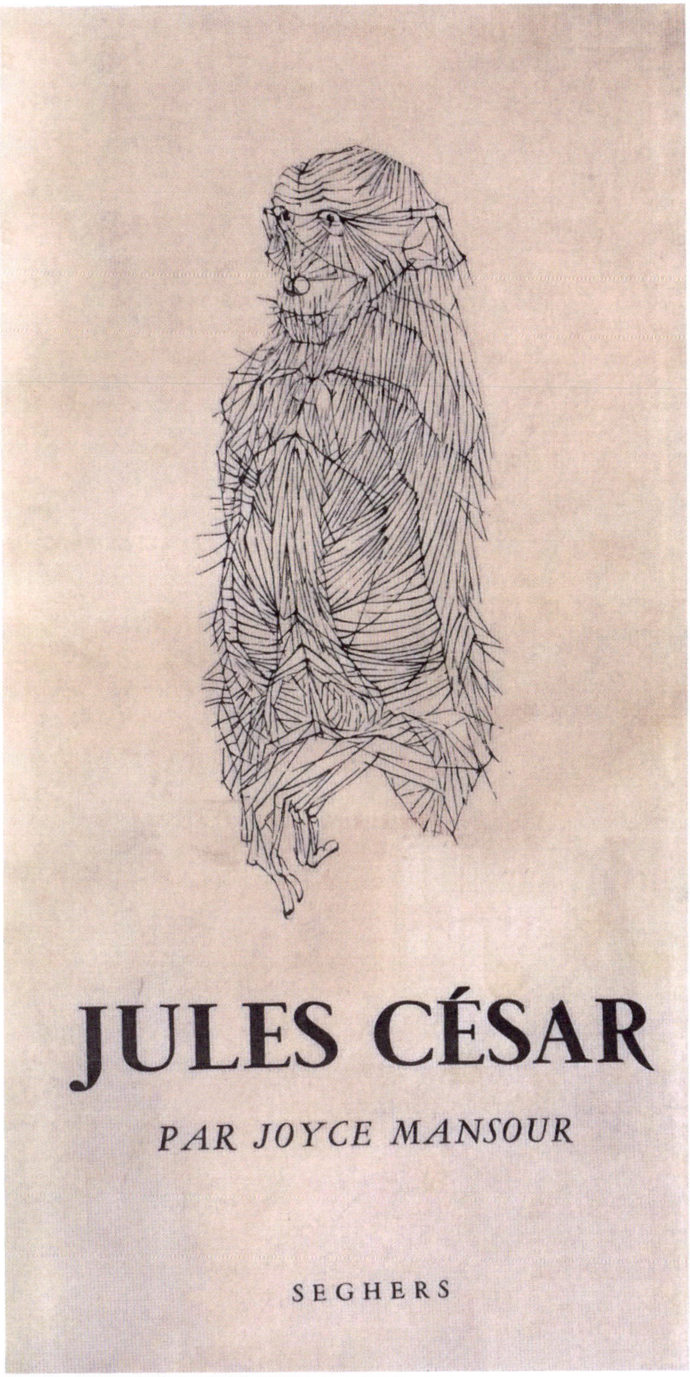

Illustration 1 : Couverture du livre : Joyce Mansour, *Jules César*, avec cinq cuivres gravés à la pointe et au burin par Hans Bellmer, Paris : Pierre Seghers 1955. © Éditions Robert Laffont.

tour trois ans plus tard, ce qui marquera profondément sa vie[6]. En 1949, elle se marie avec Samir Mansour, un francophone, et ils achètent trois ans plus tard un appartement dans les quartiers chic du XVIe arrondissement de Paris. C'est par cette rencontre amoureuse que le français va devenir la langue véhicule dans le couple, mais va aussi permettre à Joyce Mansour de commencer à écrire en français avant leur installation définitive à Paris en 1956. Joyce Mansour n'a jamais rien publié en Égypte avant de venir s'installer à Paris. Elle n'a pas non plus écrit en anglais ou en arabe puisque sa langue d'écriture sera le français. On peut dire que le contexte arabe ou même égyptien n'a pas la résonance escomptée dans les textes de la poétesse.

Le groupe surréaliste à Paris avait donc une vision très lointaine de celle qui allait devenir l'une des protagonistes de premier plan des échanges au sein du groupe dans les années 1950. Dès la publication en 1953 de son premier recueil chez Pierre Seghers de son premier recueil en français intitulé *Cris*[7] en 1953 où la violence poétique et l'automatisme sont poussés à l'extrême et bien avant son installation en France, les surréalistes ont donc dû fantasmer la poétesse vivant au Moyen-Orient. Cette publication a pu se faire grâce à l'intervention de l'artiste et poète Georges Hugnet (1906–1974) et sera suivie de deux autres titres, *Jules César*[8] en 1955 toujours chez Seghers, et *Déchirures* aux Éditions de Minuit[9]. Les textes de Joyce Mansour font se télescoper des univers très dissemblables, l'Orient et l'Occident, dans une volonté de déflagration poétique telle que la voulait « la croyance à la réalité supérieure de certaines formes d'associations » mise en avant par le surréalisme dès 1924[10].

Comme l'analyse Jean-Jacques Luthi dans l'un des premiers articles sur le surréalisme en Égypte qui paraît dans une revue universitaire française :

> Joyce Mansour représente, en fait, la nouvelle génération de poètes surréalistes égyptiens. Les sciences occultes, la Kabbale et les rituels de magie lui semblent familiers puisque leurs expressions sibyllines reviennent constamment sous sa plume. Sa violence provocatrice, où sang, sueurs et larmes s'accordent avec le thème de l'amour et de la mort – si proche l'un de l'autre – ne peuvent que surprendre le lecteur[11].

En tout cas, la réception des écrits de Joyce Mansour à Paris devance l'arrivée de celle qui vient en France en cette année 1956 pour échapper à la révolution qui

---

6 Pour les détails biographiques de la jeunesse de Joyce Mansour, nous renvoyons à Marie-France Desvaux-Mansour, « Le Surréalisme à travers Joyce Mansour. Peinture et poésie, le miroir du désir », thèse de doctorat, Université Paris 1 Panthéon-Sorbonne, https://www.theses.fr/2014PA010520 ; mais aussi à Marie-France Mansour, *Une vie surréaliste.*

7 Joyce Mansour, *Cris*, Paris : Pierre Seghers 1953.

8 Joyce Mansour, *Jules César* [1955], Paris : Pierre Seghers 1958.

9 Joyce Mansour, *Déchirures*, Paris : Éditions de Minuit 1955.

10 André Breton, « Le manifeste du surréalisme » (1924), dans *Œuvres complètes*, dir. Marguerite Bonnet, Paris : Gallimard/Pléiade 1988–2008, 1: 328.

11 Jean-Jacques Luthi, « Le Mouvement surréaliste en Égypte », dans *Mélusine 3. Marges non-frontières*, Henri Béhar, dir., Lausanne : L'Age d'homme 1982, 26.

chasse d'Égypte l'oligarchie des grands propriétaires et du grand capital à laquelle sa famille appartenait. La condition d'exilée de Joyce Mansour cristallisera sans doute un point de ralliement supplémentaire pour André Breton qui, à peine dix ans auparavant, revenait d'un exil de plus de cinq ans aux États-Unis[12]. L'amitié de Joyce Mansour et d'André Breton durera jusqu'à la mort du poète fin septembre 1966. Au regard de ces repères biographiques, Joyce Mansour a donc traversé la constellation surréaliste avant d'arriver à Paris et ce qui paraît intéressant, c'est la façon dont les surréalistes ont intégré l'héritage de la poétesse dans leur panthéon.

Jules César *et le surréalisme*

Comment les écrits de Joyce Mansour, anglaise de culture juive élevée en Égypte, ont pu rencontrer la poésie surréaliste ? Les ouvrages de Joyce Mansour ont même été illustrés par des artistes surréalistes, ses textes manifestant ainsi un rapport à l'image pour le moins étonnant. L'exemple de *Jules César* est particulièrement éclairant et permet de comprendre à la fois le travail collectif qui était de mise dans le groupe, et aussi les points de jonction que les artistes inventent pour rendre l'œuvre cohérente sur le plan poétique. Quelle a été la trajectoire de ce livre dont le texte va être coloré par une imagerie provenant des plus inavouables labyrinthes de Hans Bellmer ? Que signifient pour le lecteur d'aujourd'hui ces rapports incongrus entre les images d'un artiste allemand en exil en France et le texte largement autobiographique d'une exilée anglo-égyptienne au cœur des années 1950 ? Le surréalisme est un internationalisme assumé et il participe de son rapport à l'histoire contre les nationalismes en tout genre, la collaboration de Joyce Mansour et de Bellmer en est un exemple symptomatique.

Jules César est donc le premier texte de Mansour comportant des illustrations et notamment des gravures de Hans Bellmer à la toute fin de l'année 1955. Il sera réédité par Pierre Seghers en 1958 dans une édition moins confidentielle et avec seulement une couverture réalisée par Hans Bellmer. L'histoire de la composition de cet ouvrage est intéressante car Breton entreprend pour le réaliser de mettre en contact des univers hétérogènes avec pour souci principal de susciter une œuvre poétique collective où l'étrangeté surréaliste résidera dans la confrontation d'images et de textes.

Depuis son premier envoi à André Breton en 1954, *Cris*, on peut affirmer que Joyce Mansour est l'une des membres les plus remarquées du groupe surréaliste, ce qui sera confirmé par sa présence aux réunions dès son arrivée à Paris en 1956[13]. La présence de Mansour est donc importante et tout va être fait pour qu'elle croise

12 Sur l'exil des surréalistes, voir notamment Flahutez, *Nouveau Monde et nouveau mythe*, et Martica Sawin, *Surrealism in Exile and the Beginning of the New York School*, Cambridge, MA : MIT Press 1995.

13 Joyce Mansour signe les tracts et les déclarations collectives du groupe.

son œuvre avec celles d'autres artistes. Le texte, rédigé sans penser à un quelconque illustrateur, va susciter chez Breton la volonté de le soumettre à des images venues d'ailleurs. Plusieurs questions se posent dans cette collaboration. Était-il nécessaire que ce texte fasse l'objet d'une telle mise en images ? N'était-ce là qu'un moyen de rendre compte de la cohésion du groupe ? Était-ce une volonté de mieux vendre au public le fantasme de la rencontre d'une poétesse égyptienne avec un artiste surréaliste à Paris et conforter l'internationalisme inhérent au groupe ? La collaboration poétique n'allait-elle pas recouvrir une certaine histoire de la décolonisation alors que se développait le conflit algérien qui, bien que lointain, plaçait l'Afrique du Nord sur la sellette aux yeux d'une certaine bourgeoisie ? La rencontre de Mansour et de Bellmer (ou de Molinier) n'était-elle pas une métaphore sur le plan poétique de *L'Amour fou* et de *Nadja* ?

Toutes ces questions restent sous-jacentes et montrent que *Jules César* a une portée plus large que le problème purement poétique. Revenons à l'historique de cette collaboration. André Breton demande donc à Pierre Molinier nouvellement rencontré d'illustrer de quelques dessins *Jules César* de Mansour[14]. « C'est d'un humour et, comme toujours, d'une liberté de dire extraordinaires », écrit André Breton le 8 juin 1955 à Pierre Molinier. « Je suis obsédé du désir que cela paraisse [...] avec des dessins de vous, de l'ordre de ceux dont vous ornez vos poèmes[15]. » Breton fait un lien analogique entre deux univers, celui de Pierre Molinier où l'ambiguïté du genre est manifeste faisant une place totem à l'androgyne primordial et l'univers de Joyce Mansour qui est, lui, imprégné d'ésotérisme et de mythes et légendes égyptiennes. Il faut préciser que le surréalisme après 1945 vouait un culte aux ésotérismes comme moyens poétiques insoupçonnés. L'alchimie, l'occultisme et les ésotérismes les plus exotiques étaient des univers où l'explication échoue au profit d'une quête poétique du merveilleux. *Jules César* de Mansour tout comme les *Succubes*[16] de Pierre Molinier ont sans doute déclenché chez Breton des ponts analogiques renvoyant à ces corpus ésotériques qui, depuis le retour d'exil de Breton, se trouvaient au cœur du surréalisme. André Breton ne cache d'ailleurs pas son ambition de rendre conforme les œuvres des artistes à la nouvelle évolution du surréalisme après la guerre. Le meilleur exemple, et peut-être le plus célèbre, en est la collaboration qui s'instaure entre Joan Miró et Breton autour des *Constellations*[17].

---

14 Le premier contact d'André Breton avec Molinier est établi en avril 1955 lorsque Breton répond à la lettre que Molinier lui avait adressée.

15 Pierre Petit, *Pierre Molinier, une vie d'enfer*, Paris : Ramsay/Jean-Jacques Pauvert 1992, 102.

16 Voir : https://fr.wikipedia.org/wiki/Succube (version du 11 avril 2018) : « Un succube (le nom est masculin) est un personnage de légende. Ce sont des démons qui prennent la forme d'une femme pour séduire un homme durant son sommeil et ses rêves. Les succubes servent Lilith et ont pour mode d'action la séduction des hommes. Leur pendant masculin est l'incube. »

17 Voir à ce sujet : Fabrice Flahutez, « La Genèse des *Constellations*. Une circulation de sens entre Breton et Miró de 1940 à 1959 », dans : *La Fabrique du titre*, Nadeije Laneyrie-Dagen, Pierre-Marc de Biasi et Marianne Jakobi, dir., Paris : CNRS Éditions 2012, 253-264.

Les *Constellations* réunissent une série de gouaches auxquelles Breton associe des poèmes afin de montrer que le surréalisme n'a été affecté ni par la guerre et l'exil ni par l'éclatement du groupe. Bien que les *Constellations* aient été réalisées pendant la Seconde Guerre mondiale en Europe et que Breton ait été en Amérique à cette époque, la réunion de cette série de gouaches avec des poèmes de Breton a pour effet de créer un corpus homogène qui résonne avec le surréalisme tel qu'il se développe après 1945. Il en est de même pour le texte de Mansour et les images de Bellmer. Une façon pour le poète de donner une cohérence à des démarches parfois très éloignées les unes des autres. L'exemple des *Constellations* permet de voir que le livre de Mansour n'échappe pas à cette volonté unificatrice de Breton.

Jules César est un personnage à la fois fictionnel et autobiographique qui se présente dans une inversion de genre puisqu'il s'agit d'une femme, et parfois aussi d'un homme, dans le texte en prose de Mansour. Il y a comme une condensation des genres des personnages au sens freudien du terme et le lecteur est dans une situation d'indécision. *Jules César* est une nourrice, mais peut-être l'empereur, aux traits extraordinairement exacerbés, elle est une créature du rêve, violente, fuyante. Elle allaite des jumeaux

> nés ensemble à Sodome d'une vache et d'un fossoyeur après deux heures de travaux bien arrosées à la bière [… les deux jumeaux étaient] cramponnés aux mamelles gorgées de miel de leur nourrice Jules César, ils se jurèrent avec des babillements sucrés de boire tout le sang du monde[18].

L'inversion de genre est également consubstantielle à l'œuvre de Pierre Molinier puisque ses montages photographiques mettent en scène le travestissement de l'artiste en cette femme improbable, androgyne qu'on ne rencontre que dans le rêve. Pierre Molinier se travestissait en la femme désirée en portant un masque et des collants qui faisaient disparaître progressivement son apparence masculine. C'est la raison pour laquelle André Breton a tout de suite pensé à la parenté unissant l'univers de Joyce Mansour à celui de Pierre Molinier. L'artiste et la poétesse rencontraient sans même le savoir l'évolution que Breton voulait insuffler au surréalisme de cette époque. C'est-à-dire une investigation de l'hybridation, de l'androgyne primordial à l'origine de bien des mythes et répondant au désir de concilier les contraires comme le souhaitaient tant la psychanalyse freudienne, l'alchimie que le surréalisme. La figure androgyne répond aux fondements de l'occultisme qui place l'être primordial et hermaphrodite au sommet de l'élaboration du Grand Œuvre. Au-delà de cette quête théorique souvent considérée comme absconse de la part des exégètes du surréalisme, Breton essaie de théoriser après 1945 la nécessité d'un nouveau mythe collectif propre à transformer le monde et changer la vie.

Dans la préface qu'écrit Breton pour l'exposition Pierre Molinier à la galerie de l'Étoile scellée en janvier 1956, on retrouve toujours la volonté du poète de

---

18 Mansour, *Jules César*, 9.

rapprocher les silhouettes de l'artiste de la « petite folle des bois[19] » du *Jules César* de Mansour et de tout un panthéon féminin allant de *Madame Edwarda* de Georges Bataille à *Histoire d'O* de Pauline Réage[20]. Pourtant *Jules César* ne sera pas illustré par Pierre Molinier malgré la volonté d'André Breton. Il faut dire qu'au début du mois de mai 1955, soit un mois avant que Breton n'écrive à Pierre Molinier, Joyce Mansour rencontre Hans Bellmer lors de sa seconde présentation de dessins chez Jean-Jacques Pauvert à Paris du 6 mai au 4 juin 1955[21]. La rencontre doit sans doute beaucoup à Georges Hugnet qui avait été l'entremetteur de Joyce Mansour auprès de son premier éditeur Pierre Seghers et qui était, par ailleurs, le collaborateur de Hans Bellmer pour la publication d'*Œillades ciselées en branche* en 1939 chez Jeanne Bucher[22]. C'est à l'occasion de cette exposition que Joyce Mansour remet le texte de *Jules César* à Hans Bellmer pour qu'il le lise et lui soumette un projet de mise en image. « Chère Madame », écrit Bellmer,

> Je vous remercie d'être venue avec votre mari me voir chez Jean-Jacques Pauvert. En faisant l'addition de cette rencontre, des deux volumes de prévus, de l'enthousiasme que j'en ai éprouvé et du manuscrit que j'ai pu lire en partie chez Pauvert (*Jules César*) : je serais heureux d'être à votre disposition, de collaborer avec vous si l'occasion se présente[23].

L'éditeur Pierre Seghers écrit à Joyce Mansour pour la tenir au courant de l'avancée du projet d'illustration de son livre :

> [...] Dans l'intervalle, Bellmer a fini les gravures : absolument magnifiques. D'une audace et d'une finesse tout à fait exceptionnelles. Nous serons très fiers de cet ouvrage. Nous nous occupons très activement de la fabrication en ce moment. La composition est terminée. Nous allons commencer le tirage des gravures chez le taille-doucier. Nous vous adresserons dans deux ou trois jours les cinq gravures – le nécessaire a été fait bien entendu, pour la révision minutieuse du texte. Nous travaillons également à la couverture. Bellmer assure ce travail avec moi [...][24].

---

19 André Breton, « Préface », dans *Pierre Molinier*, cat. exp. galerie de L'Étoile scellée, Paris, 27 janvier–17 février 1956.

20 Il est d'ailleurs étonnant que ces deux derniers ouvrages aient été également illustrés par Hans Bellmer : douze cuivres gravés à la pointe sèche et au burin par Hans Bellmer, datant de février–mars 1955 dans Pierre Angélique (pseudonyme de Georges Bataille), *Madame Edwarda*, Paris : Éditions Georges Visat 1965 ; et gravure au burin de couleur bistre pour la page de titre de Pauline Réage, *Histoire d'O*, Sceaux : Éditions Jean-Jacques Pauvert 1954.

21 *Hans Bellmer. Exposition de portraits*, du 6 mai au 4 juin avec un texte de Jean Cocteau, cat. exp., Paris : Librairie Jean-Jacques Pauvert 1955.

22 Hans Bellmer et Georges Hugnet, *Œillades ciselées en branche*, petit ouvrage illustré par 25 dessins de Hans Bellmer (6 pleine page) reproduits en héliogravure avec des retouches au burin et encrés en couleur sur le cuivre, Paris : Jeanne Bucher 1939.

23 Lettre de Hans Bellmer à Joyce Mansour, Paris le 14 mars 1955, cit. dans Desvaux-Mansour, « Le Surréalisme » (voir notamment cette référence dans les archives Mansour reproduites dans la thèse, cf. corr. n° 29), 273.

24 Lettre de Pierre Seghers à Joyce Mansour, Paris, le 11 octobre 1955, citée dans Desvaux-Mansour, « Le Surréalisme » (voir notamment cette référence dans les archives Mansour reproduites dans la thèse, cf. corr. n° 31), 281.

A ce stade d'achèvement du projet, André Breton, qui a sans doute été mis au courant, écrit à Pierre Molinier pour l'avertir que le projet qu'il avait fomenté au mois de mai de lui confier l'illustration de *Jules César* n'est plus d'actualité. « Il n'a pu être donné suite au projet d'illustration pour *Jules César* », écrit Breton le 1er octobre 1955 :

> Comme, presque en vous pressentant, j'avais écrit à Joyce Mansour pour la disposer tout en ce sens, j'ai appris d'elle qu'elle s'était déjà engagée, par l'intermédiaire de l'éditeur, Pierre Seghers, pour que le conte paraisse avec plusieurs eaux fortes ou pointes sèches de Bellmer. Rien ne pouvait plus se rattraper et je puis vous assurer qu'elle en était très malheureuse. J'espère bien que ce sera pour la prochaine fois. Cela m'a tellement contrarié, pour ma part, que j'ai remis de jour en jour de vous le dire[25].

Bien que Breton ait souhaité que ce soit Pierre Molinier qui illustre *Jules César,* il semble que Joyce Mansour ait préféré le travail et l'univers de Hans Bellmer. Une hypothèse apparaît à la lumière de la biographie de Hans Bellmer. Au printemps 1941, Hans Bellmer rencontre Marcelle Sutter avec qui il se mariera le 15 mai 1942, une union dont naîtront le 13 avril 1943 deux jumelles : Doriane et Béatrice. Bellmer écrit : « Doriane est tout ce que j'ai pu rêver depuis toujours de ma réincarnation sous forme de petite fille. Elle est à moi[26]. » Le couple Bellmer-Sutter sera un échec, et de nombreuses lettres témoignent d'un naufrage sentimental. La procédure judiciaire intentée par Marcelle Sutter lui attribuera la garde exclusive des jumelles. La biographie personnelle de Hans Bellmer semble donc rencontrer précisément la trame narrative de *Jules César.*

Hans Bellmer propose des images pour le texte de Joyce Mansour

Une des planches proposées par Hans Bellmer pour illustrer la naissance des jumeaux monstrueux dans *Jules César* montre précisément un corps écorché laissant entrevoir l'intérieur d'un utérus où se débattent deux fœtus. La gémellité renvoie ici à la fois à la biographie de Hans Bellmer mais aussi au texte de Joyce Mansour. Ce thème se retrouvera d'ailleurs aussi dans d'autres travaux de Hans Bellmer. Une autre planche représente un singe au phallus démesuré à la manière également d'un écorché de planche anatomique. Et on peut lire dans *Jules César* : « Le père pencha sa tête simiesque sur le champ de bataille où sa femme se débattait contre les jumeaux[27] », ou plus loin :

> Elle savait que le grand singe apparaîtrait mais il lui semblait que l'impatience la rendait folle. Elle se promettait mille séduisantes félicités quand, après sa vengeance, les jumeaux

---

[25] Lettre d'André Breton à Pierre Molinier, 1er octobre 1955, cit. dans Petit, *Pierre Molinier,* 102–103.

[26] Notes biographiques inédites, janvier 1946, collection particulière Didier Deroeux, galerie Solstices, Lille, cit. dans *Hans Bellmer. Anatomie du désir,* cat. exp. Musée national d'art moderne, Paris : Gallimard/Centre Pompidou 2006, 227–228.

[27] Mansour, *Jules César,* 9.

> lui reviendraient, petits comme des nains et combien caressants [...] Soudain le singe fut là. Immense, il dominait Jules César ; la beauté de son sexe illumina son regard[28].

Le singe est par ailleurs un dieu de la fertilité connu sous le nom de Babi dans la mythologie de l'Égypte antique. Le visage déformé d'une des planches montre la face de l'homme fusionnant avec ses parties génitales. Cette image précède de près de six ans le portrait que Bellmer fait de Sade. L'originalité réside dans la façon dont les auteurs interprètent la recomposition du corps à partir d'éléments disjoints. D'un côté, chez Joyce Mansour, on a une fragmentation des corps comme autant de particules autonomes et de l'autre, *La Poupée* de Hans Bellmer permet de recomposer à l'infini, comme des phrases, les parties de ce corps signifiant. Tous ces motifs littéraires ou plastiques composent des sortes de collages qui rejoignent le collage surréaliste. Les motifs littéraires qui apparaissent dans *Jules César* de Joyce Mansour sont en lien avec les motifs picturaux de Hans Bellmer[29]. Il faut souligner que chez les deux auteurs, la dimension biographique est omniprésente. Par ailleurs, l'amour et la mort se trouvent encore une fois inextricablement mêlés dans le texte et dans les images, comme pour concilier les contraires Éros et Thanatos comme le veut le surréalisme.

Il est à noter que c'est Joyce Mansour qui définira le mot *viol* dans le *Lexique succinct de l'érotisme* du catalogue de l'exposition *EROS* à la galerie Cordier en 1959. De la même manière, la réponse de Joyce Mansour à l'enquête sur un tableau anonyme qui paraît dans le troisième numéro de la revue *Le surréalisme, même*, met en avant l'amour et la mort comme les deux faces d'une même pièce. Elle écrit : « Tout doit être rituel pour mener à l'accomplissement d'une scène d'amour et de carnage ; les gestes des participants échelonnent la marche de la procession vers l'extase ; même l'atmosphère respire le sang du désir[30]. »

Au-delà de l'illustration de *Jules César*, l'univers de Joyce Mansour rencontrera par la suite celui d'autres artistes surréalistes comme Roberto Matta qui aura d'ailleurs lui aussi deux jumeaux en 1943, Gordon et Batan. Il s'agira alors de mettre en exergue les visions oniriques, la gémellité, l'érotisme et la mort dans des compositions complexes et ce, au-delà de toute identité géographique ou nationale, conformément au surréalisme international.

Conclusion

L'illustration du texte de Mansour par Bellmer, loin d'être anecdotique, est intéressante parce qu'elle montre une commune attention à l'égard des figures d'hybridation de genre. La figure de l'androgyne primordial est un motif au cœur du

---

28 Mansour, *Jules César*, 60–61.

29 Voir aussi Marie-Laure Missir, « De Jules César à Jeux de la Poupée. Récit d'une rencontre "à facettes mobiles" entre Joyce Mansour et Hans Bellmer », dans *Pleine marge* 37 (2003).

30 Joyce Mansour, « Réponse à l'enquête sur un tableau anonyme », dans *Le Surréalisme, même* 3 (1957), 82.

surréalisme de l'après-guerre, car elle est la quintessence de la conciliation des contraires. Le simple attrait de Breton pour le culte Uli, sorte de divinité océanienne hermaphrodite, permet de s'en convaincre, tout comme les corpus d'images ésotériques et alchimiques qui peuplent les textes surréalistes jusqu'aux années 1960[31]. L'œuvre de Joyce Mansour a donc apporté au surréalisme un bestiaire et une forme littéraire qui, bien que faiblement nourri d'un contexte oriental, était compatible avec les concepts et les développements du surréalisme après 1945. Le surréalisme comme « machine » à fabriquer du collectif a donc parfaitement fonctionné, per mettant au groupe de se reconstituer avec des personnalités venant des pays les plus inattendus. La volonté internationaliste du surréalisme est une fois de plus mise en avant par André Breton qui considérait les nationalismes comme le terreau d'une sclérose de l'esprit. Les années qui suivent la fin de la Seconde Guerre mondiale sont toutefois porteuses d'une autre menace, celle de la guerre froide qui construit un monde polarisé entre deux blocs inconciliables. Le décentrement du groupe surréaliste à la recherche d'interlocuteurs venant de pays jugés périphériques montre à quel point Breton aura toujours privilégié la quête poétique audelà des frontières de papier.

31 Pour toute cette iconographie, nous renvoyons, entre autres, à notre ouvrage *Nouveau Monde et nouveau mythe*.

Chapter 10

Surrealism, quarantine, Mediterranean plague: Artaud, Tengour, Abdel-Jaouad

Megan C. MacDonald

> I, over and above everything else, am a colonizer, I am the intruder whose fate must be decided. When Mahmoud Wad Ahmed was brought in shackles to Kitchener after his defeat at the Battle of Atbara, Kitchener said to him, "Why have you come to my country to lay waste and plunder?" It was the intruder who said this to the person whose land it was, and the owner of the land bowed his head and said nothing. So let it be with me. In that court I hear the rattle of swords in Carthage and the clatter of the hooves of Allenby's horses desecrating the ground of Jerusalem. The ships at first sailed down the Nile carrying guns not bread, and the railways were originally set up to transport troops; the schools were started so as to teach us how to say "Yes" in their language. They imported to us the germ of the greatest European violence, as seen on the Somme and at Verdun, the like of which the world has never previously known, the germ of a deadly disease that struck them more than a thousand years ago. Yes, my dear sirs, I came as an invader into your very homes: a drop of the poison which you have injected into the veins of history. "I am no Othello. Othello was a lie."
>
> Mustafa Sa'eed in Tayeb Salih's *Season of Migration to the North*[1]

In this contribution, the plague is reassessed in a Mediterranean frame, in order to establish alternative kinships and genealogies between surrealisms which inhabit and cross the Mediterranean.[2] The plague is a "crisis" which "puts a special pressure on personhood" as well as a "catalyst" that makes us "rethink the idea of what it

---

1 Tayeb Salih, *Season of Migration to the North*, trans. Denys Johnson-Davies, London: Penguin Classics 2003, 94–95.

2 Earlier versions of this paper were presented at the Just Theory lecture series at SUNY Buffalo (September 2016) at the invitation of Rodolphe Gasché, and at "The Avant-Garde and its Networks: Surrealism in Paris, North Africa and the Middle East from the 1930s" at the Orient-Institut Beirut (November 2016). This paper is in homage to Rodolphe Gasché's "Autogeneous Engenderment: Antonin Artaud's Phonetic Body", originally published in 1978, whose afterlives I was exposed to in *The Stelliferous Fold: Toward a Virtual Law of Literature's Self-Formation* (2011). A more substantial version of this paper is included in my forthcoming monograph on Mediterranean literatures and the postcolonial *navette* (Liverpool University Press).

means to be human".[3] The modern subject is constituted by and travels via plague vectors, and connects the work of Antonin Artaud (1870–1952) and Habib Tengour (b. 1947), offering another avenue towards the relationship France–Algeria in and across the Mediterranean. Surrealism and the plague come together in the figure and the writing of Antonin Artaud as a disruption. Richard Barney and Helene Scheck consider the plague in the early modern context as "a disruption in apparently continuous temporal experience of historicity".[4] If the present volume addresses the avant-garde and its "networks", how are these networks constituted and measured? What is their temporality? If surrealism erupted as an avant-garde practice in early twentieth-century European spaces, what can we make of a resurgence or reappearance in the figure of Habib Tengour's French-Algerian surrealist manifesto written in 1981? What is it disrupting? And how might this contribute to discussions of modernity and the modern in the Mediterranean basin?

Noar Ben-Yehoyada draws a line between the pre-modern Mediterranean and "the current Mediterranean moment" in order to "show the role of Mediterraneanist imaginaries" across space and time.[5] As yasser elhariry and Edwige Tamalet Talbayev convincingly argue: "The modern Mediterranean's unique texture renders it a privileged site for its reconsideration as a discursive space marked by multiple concurrent temporalities."[6] Their "discursive" Mediterranean "reorients the conversation" around the Mediterranean, considering it through multiple and overlapping temporalities that results in "plural Mediterranean times".[7] Artaud's Mediterranean, established via the plague in transit, connects multiple Mediterranean times and ports discursively and imaginatively through a theory of the theatre, which reads like a manifesto.

Translation, transmission and the germ

Reading these connections through the dream and the plague, and their Mediterranean genealogies, brings multiple spaces and artistic practices together. This is a citational piece, one which puts multiple Mediterranean thinkers out to sea, in order

3 Ernest B. Gilman, "The Subject of the Plague", *Journal for Early Modern Cultural Studies* 10, no. 2 (2010), 24–25.

4 Richard A. Barney and Helene Scheck, "Introduction: Early and Modern Biospheres, Politics, and the Rhetorics of Plague", *Journal for Early Modern Cultural Studies* 10, no. 2 (2010), 10.

5 Naor Ben-Yehoyada, "Heritage Washed Ashore: Underwater Archaeology and Regionalist Imaginaries in the Central Mediterranean", in: *Critically Mediterranean: Temporalities, Aesthetics, and Deployments of a Sea in Crisis*, yasser elhariry and Edwige Tamalet Talbayev, eds., New York: Palgrave Macmillan 2018, 221.

6 yasser elhariry and Edwige Tamalet Talbayev, "Critically Mediterranean: An Introduction", in: *Critically Mediterranean: Temporalities, Aesthetics, and Deployments of a Sea in Crisis*, yasser elhariry and Edwige Tamalet Talbayev, eds., New York: Palgrave Macmillan 2018, 8.

7 elhariry and Talbayev, "Critically Mediterranean", 8–9.

to think the drifts, wakes, and shipwrecks of Artaud's "oriental germ".[8] James Clifford pairs the terms "transmission" and "translation" in *Returns*, preferring the latter to the former, as it "brings out the bumps, losses, and makeshift solutions of social life" where what he calls cultural translation "is always uneven, always betrayed".[9] Since surrealism and its Mediterranean translation are also bound up with the plague and plague logic, the term transmission plays just as important a role. Keeping translation and transmission in one space mobilizes both across land and sea. One organizing principle of this discussion is the *germ* – both a kernel and an organism capable of turning into something else, of sprouting and contaminating – as an initial stage for future developments. These germs connect the early modern subject, modernity and subjectivity, Mediterranean temporalities, and the postcolonial *navette* (shuttle) constantly in motion between Mediterranean shores, where the southern shore is often marked as belated at best and civilisationally inferior at worst. In short, surrealism in the Mediterranean is a literature of the plague, and its afterlives speak to contemporary *perceived infections* between Europe and North Africa.

The transmissions and translations in question are transported via and on the body, as well as in dreams, in fever and through text, connecting the artistic practices of surrealism to the spreading of disease. Michel Foucault claims that there is "a literature of plague that is a literature of the decomposition of individuality"[10] which begins with Thucydides and Lucretius, and hurdling centuries "continues with" Antonin Artaud and Albert Camus.[11] These are Mediterranean thinkers. For Foucault, the plague inaugurates two dreams – the political and the literary (*rêve politique* and *rêve littéraire*). In this "extremely interesting body of literature" the plague "appears as the moment of panic and confusion in which individuals, threatened by visitations of death, abandon their identities, throw off their masks, forget their status and abandon themselves to the great debauchery of those who know they are going to die". It is "a kind of orgiastic dream" where "the law is forgotten".[12] This is what he describes as the "literary dream". Foucault reads the plague in a continuum of abnormality, illness and associated medico-judicial control mechanisms. If leprosy in the seventeenth century demanded expulsion from the community, Foucault reads the plague which follows it, and its quarantine practices, as "a model of political control, and [...] one of the great inventions of the eighteenth century".[13] The plague is "vector-borne", as Robert Sallares notes, and it is the "most dangerous

8 Antonin Artaud, "The Theatre and the Plague", in: *The Theatre and Its Double*, trans. Victor Corti, London: Alma Classics 2014, 10.

9 James Clifford, *Returns: Becoming Indigenous in the Twenty-First Century*, Cambridge, MA: Harvard University Press 2013, 48.

10 Michel Foucault, *Abnormal: Lectures at the Collège de France, 1974–1975*, trans. Graham Burchell, New York: Picador 2004, 47.

11 Foucault, *Abnormal*, 54n15.

12 Foucault, *Abnormal*, 47.

13 Foucault, *Abnormal*, 48.

traveler in the medieval period".[14] While the rat or flea is necessary for plague transmission to humans, the disease only travels long distances via humans themselves, "because in general the vectors and other hosts will not move very far on their own".[15] It is for this reason that "quarantine worked as a control method", as "it stopped human movement and human trade transporting infected fleas around".[16] Foucault's connections between the plague and dreaming allow for an examination of how these dreams cross the Mediterranean via bodies that are either plague-infested, or marked as foreign, and thus undesirable.[17] The question of the historical *reliability* of the documents in question does not present much of a concern for this specific discussion. Rather, tracing the way these documents travel physically and discursively – and, as paper *navettes* (shuttles), transmit histories within them – adheres more to what Ben-Yehoyada calls "canons of probability".[18] In other words: who can travel and who is under quarantine?

The word *quarantine* refers to the number forty: a period of forty days, the time a ship must stay at anchor, held in isolation from the shore. Quarantine is also the regulation that puts the ship in quarantine, and the place where the ship is held, or the place where people are held apart. It is restraint for contagion, a term that is currently travelling worldwide like gossip, like fear, in the wake of a new pandemic, a plague whose origin is blamed on "the East" that has resulted in racist incidents and violence toward Asians in many countries. Before the science was discovered to understand the origins of plague, the plague often created scapegoats in early modern Europe – lepers and Jews, amongst others. Fear of the other is an ongoing contagious disease.

The central thread of this discussion will meander across and around the Mediterranean, in order to put Antonin Artaud in service of connecting the Mediterranean and bringing Algeria – more specifically contemporary writer Habib Tengour, as well as Hédi Abdel-Jaouad's work on surrealism in North African literatures – into the germination of surrealism (its transmission and translation), even if after the fact.[19] Alexandre Dumas also makes a brief appearance, as his

---

14 Robert Sallares, "Disease", in: *A Companion to Mediterranean History*, Peregrine Horden and Sharon Kinoshita, eds., Chichester: Wiley-Blackwell 2014, 253–254.

15 Sallares, "Disease", 254.

16 Sallares, "Disease", 255.

17 For Foucault, the discussion of the plague marks the distinction between the way lepers were treated (excluded from society and marked as dead/death) and how the plague functioned: with the plague, containment and surveillance replace the exclusion of lepers: "While leprosy calls for distance, the plague implies an always finer approximation of power to individuals, an ever more constant and insistent observation" (Foucault, *Abnormal*, 47).

18 Ben-Yehoyada, "Heritage Washed Ashore", 229.

19 *Meander* itself has Mediterranean connections, as the word comes etymologically from the winding Turkish river of the same name (today called Menderes), which empties into the Aegean. "Meander, *n.*", *OED Online*, Oxford University Press, June 2020, http://www.oed.com/view/Entry/115444.

treatment of Marseille, disease, dreams, archives and bones strengthens the links between Artaud, the plague and Tengour.

Tengour is a writer and trained ethnologist born in Algeria in 1947.[20] He moved to France at a young age with his father and now lives between France and Algeria. Tengour's trajectory allows for movement through archival space, geographies, genealogies, Mediterranean ports and pasts. Artaud's and Tengour's literary and physical journeys form a network of border conditions, shadows and doubles, bodies, antibodies, relics and bones, as well as ships that arrive in Marseille.

What is the relationship between surrealism and North Africa, or the Maghreb? Hédi Abdel-Jaouad sees explicit connections between North African writers and their surrealist counterparts and antecedents, and locates encounters between present-day Maghrebi writers and their surrealist precursors as continuities that mark a relationship to the past, rather than limiting them to European surrealism's 20th century heyday.[21] He argues that surrealist influence was "assimilated" into the work of North African writers, and touches "several aspects of Maghrebi literature".[22] The most fruitful surrealist influence is the notion of "a total man" which requires "the creation of a new language capable of expressing a wider humanity". Of all the avant-garde movements, he considers surrealism as offering "the most ambitious and radical project: a total remaking of man". And it is this very possibility for a radical break and recreation "which best responds to the aspirations of Third World writers".[23]

James Clifford in his article "On Ethnographic Surrealism", considers surrealism to be an ethnographic practice, calling it "ethnography's secret sharer – for better or worse".[24] Reading Artaud's account of the plague coming to Marseille via Beirut and Sardinia as a kind of Mediterranean biography is also a way of reading secrets and their transmission between East and West, between the surreal and the ethnographic. It situates Artaud's Marseille background as one which arrived by boat from multiple Mediterranean ports, connecting the eastern Mediterranean (through his mother's family) to Marseille, via Greek, Ottoman and Levantine roots. Artaud's convictions and identifications – his germs in transit – make for a surreal narrative which *lands* in France from elsewhere: France is a place where Mediterranean shuttles (*les navettes*) arrive, where surrealism itself is Mediterranean, water-born and waterborne. This *peste* renders André Breton's "pure state" of surrealism an infection from multiple

20 The intersection of these two disciplines – surrealism-tinged poetry and ethnography – in a postcolonial context supports and complicates James Clifford's remarks on ethnography and surrealism, which will be discussed below.

21 Hédi Abdel-Jaouad, "Tendances surréalistes dans la littérature maghrébine d'expression française", PhD thesis, Temple University, Philadelphia 1983, http://www.limag.com/new/index.php?inc=dspliv&liv=00000141.

22 Abdel-Jaouad, "Tendances surréalistes", 298.

23 Abdel-Jaouad, "Tendances surréalistes", 290.

24 James Clifford, "On Ethnographic Surrealism", *Comparative Studies in Society and History* 23, no. 4 (1981), 543.

ports. This Mediterranean birth/berth and bath, Artaud's ship, the *Grand-Saint-Antoine* collides with and crosses Tengour's ships from his poem "Traverser…" – the *Kairouan* and *Tassili, Hoggar*, solidly inland names tracing the sea, ones which do not "conjure up the blue-white dampness of the inhabited mirage".[25] The ports are cordoned off – more lines, surveillance, quarantine – to discourage "clandestine [migrants] on foot, potential harlequins".[26]

Bodies do not always travel, but if we follow Tengour, surrealisms do travel, and do so in such a way that earlier notions of centre and periphery are at least flipped on their head, and at most, obliterated. We can certainly make connections between plague, quarantine, surveillance, surrealist infections and contemporary critiques of the European Union as Fortress Europe, where refugees and economic migrants are contained and sometimes discarded, sometimes put in camps, other times dead at sea. A surrealist network as plague network includes Gilman's future plagues – "the projected coming plague" – which "may reveal the little world of man as a pathogenic reservoir, and the greater world as that of the global biosphere in which we maintain a precarious perch".[27] The refugee crisis in the Mediterranean and beyond creates a pathogenic reservoir where bare life has become the norm – bare life at sea – and necropolitics the rule. Crossing is precarious. Northern shores *continue* to look upon southern shores as if they are diseased.[28]

Perdre le nord / S'orienter

Three citations orient and frame the discussion of texts that travel and surrealism's past encounters. The first is from John Westbrook's "Reorienting Surrealism": "In French, to lose one's bearings means to lose sight of the North, '*perdre le nord*.' Yet to find one's way again requires heading East, '*s'orienter*'."[29] Further on he notes, reflecting on André Breton's considerations of the Orient: "Beyond a purely political theme or a literary issue, the Orient questioned surrealism at a level that

---

25 "Conjurer la moiteur bleue-blanche du mirage habité". Habib Tengour, "Traverser…", in: "Itinéraires d'écritures", special issue, *Peuples méditerranéens/Mediterranean Peoples* 30 (1985), 69–72. The Tassili ferry referenced by Tengour also appears in and is almost a character in Sarah Maldoror's 1986 film *Le Passager du Tassili* (based on the eponymous novel by Akli Tadjer), about a French-Algerian character stuck in between France and Algeria. The second half of the film concerns him misplacing his French passport and fearing being stuck at sea. Director Sarah Maldoror died from COVID-19 in April 2020 at the age of 91.

26 Tengour, "Traverser…", 70.

27 Gilman, "Subject of the Plague", 30.

28 See Megan C. MacDonald, "Bare Life at Sea (The Leper and the Plague)", in: *Biotheory: Life and Death under Capitalism*, Jeffrey R. Di Leo and Peter Hitchcock, eds., London: Routledge 2020.

29 John Westbrook, "Reorienting Surrealism", *The French Review* 81, no. 4 (2008), 707. *Orienter* acts as a kind of keyword: see Abdel-Jaouad's use of *orienter* in "Tendances surréalistes", 37; and James Clifford also uses the term on the first page of his "On Ethnographic Surrealism".

subtends aesthetics and politics – the level of knowledge."[30] Surrealism, argues Westbrook, "is beholden to [the] intertext [of the 'Oriental myth'], but also undermines the binary opposition governing both Orientalist desire and the desire for the Orient by delocalizing the Orient's otherness. *The Oriental Other is within the West.*"[31] This final claim will be important when considering the Oriental-Occidental figure of Antonin Artaud and his "oriental germ", as well as locating the French language in colonial and postcolonial North African literary and cultural productions, which will be addressed below.

The second quote is from Walter Benjamin's take on surrealism in 1929, when he writes, in reference to André Breton's *Nadja*: "And all the parts of Paris that appear here are places where what is between these people turns like a revolving door."[32] If surrealism began "as an inspiring dream wave", he diagnoses it as feeding on "the damp boredom of postwar Europe and the last trickle of French decadence".[33] He continues:

> The Surrealists' Paris, too, is a "little universe". That is to say, in the larger one, the cosmos, things look no different. There, too, are crossroads where ghostly signals flash from the traffic, and inconceivable analogies and connections between events are the order of the day. It is the region from which the lyric poetry of Surrealism reports. And this must be noted if only to counter the obligatory misunderstanding of *l'art pour l'art.* For art's sake was scarcely ever to be taken literally; it was almost always a flag under which sailed a cargo that could not be declared because it lacked a name.[34]

In Benjamin's text, Paris constitutes a universe, however little, and a crossroads: the ghosts, the traffic, the ship without a name, transit and crossings, legal or otherwise. Can this little universe travel? Was it infected in Marseille and transmitted to Paris?

Tengour asks in his 1981 surrealist manifesto: "Isn't the Maghreb the beginning and the end of the world? It is said that Atlas is wearying under his load. It is also said that the world is a miniature Maghreb but that everyone does their best to ignore this fact".[35] This same Mediterranean focus, with the microbial addition of the plague, supports an exploration of Habib Tengour's three pieces published in

---

30 Westbrook, "Reorienting Surrealism", 714.

31 Westbrook, "Reorienting Surrealism", 715; my emphasis.

32 Walter Benjamin, "Surrealism: The Last Snapshot of the European Intelligentsia (1929)", trans. Edmond Jephcott, *New Left Review* 108 (1978), 51. Foucault also uses the image of the revolving door in his chapter on plague and leprosy, writing: "Madness cannot be crime, just as crime cannot be, in itself, an act rooted in madness. It is the principle of the revolving door: In terms of the law, when pathology comes in, criminality must go out" (Foucault, *Abnormal*, 32).

33 Benjamin, "Surrealism", 47.

34 Benjamin, "Surrealism", 51.

35 Habib Tengour, "Le Surréalisme maghrébin, le surréalisme au Maghreb, le Maghreb surréaliste, les surréalistes maghrébins, surréalité maghrébine, la révolution surréaliste au Maghreb, Maghreb surréaliste Presse Service, le surréalisme au service du Maghreb, etc.", *Peuples méditerranéens/Mediterranean Peoples* 17 (1981), 77–81.

the journal *Peuples méditerranéens* between 1981 and 1985: "Le surréalisme maghrébin", "L'ancêtre fondateur dans la tradition orale maghrébine" and the poem "Traverser…". Tengour's timing is striking: why create a surrealist manifesto in the 1980s? The manifesto is signed "Constantine". Constantine (*Qusanṭīnah*) is considered Algeria's third city after Algiers and Oran, and was named after the Emperor Constantine, like Constantinople (today's Istanbul), a name kept by the French colonizers in Algeria. The Romans called it Cirta. It is slightly inland from the Mediterranean, a city suspended and connected by a series of bridges, made up of *passages* and *passerelles* (gangways). In a letter to Abdel-Jaouad, Tengour writes that he owes Breton a lot, as he is trying to "open up" a path for manifesto writing in the Maghreb. He signs the path with one of the places he lives. Does this city of bridges connect to his other home in Paris?

Moving to another namer of ships, the third citation is from dramatist, theorist, poet and artist Antonin Marie Joseph Artaud, son of Antoine-Roi (king) Artaud (of Marseille) and Euphrasie Nalpas (of Ottoman Smyrna, now the Turkish city of Izmir). Artaud was born in Marseille in 1896 and died in Paris in 1948. He has a worldly outlook, claiming:

> I am Mr Antonin Artaud of the Himalaya but I passed through Marseille, 4 rue Jardin des Plantes, Smyrna, Switzerland, Saint-Malo, Procida, Rome, Paris, Lyon, Berlin, Brussels, Brussels, Mexico, Ireland.[36]

This planetary jaunt, at first glance, is without obvious organization. From up high in the Himalayas (and inspired by Buddhism and Eastern mysticism), he holds the thread of Marseille. On 6 April 1933, Artaud performed his text "Le Théâtre et la peste" (The Theatre and the Plague or The Theatre and Pestilence) at the Sorbonne in Paris. Artaud's friend Anaïs Nin (1903–1977), the French-born Cuban American diarist and novelist, was in the audience, instructed by Artaud to sit in the front row. As she listened to his talk begin to morph into something else, she wrote in her *Diary*: "he let go of the thread we were following and began to act out dying by plague. No one quite knew when it began."[37] The performance continues its germination: "His face was contorted with anguish […]. He made one feel the parched and burning throat, the pains, the fever, the fire in the guts. He was in agony. He was screaming. He was delirious. He was enacting his own death, his own crucifixion."[38] Artaud was in search of new languages, total artworks and levels of experimentation that would undo all previously cemented notions of art, theatre, poetry, drawing. A kind of essence that is always searching for the antecedent,

36 Antonin Artaud, *Œuvres complètes*, vol. 20. Paris: Gallimard 1985, 361. Firebrace also cites this itinerary; see William Firebrace, "Mômo in Marseille", *AA Files* 59 (2009), 4.

37 Anaïs Nin, *The Diary of Anaïs Nin*, vol. 1, *1931–1934*, New York: Mariner Books 1969, 191. Jason Groves revisits Nin's recollection of Artaud's performance in light of contagion and influence, but ultimately goes in a different direction, in "Writing under the Influence", *MLN* 122 (2007).

38 Nin, *Diary of Anaïs Nin*, 192.

a previous, older, more original form. This quest connects him to Tengour. Temporally, Tengour is both in the present, looking back at surrealism's past (after the fact), and yet also *avant la lettre*, as he declares in his manifesto: "Le Maghrébin a longtemps été surréaliste sans le savoir".[39] Abdel-Jaouad calls this manifesto one of "equivalences", wherein Tengour looks for major aspects of themes of surrealist writing and artistic production, and then connects these elements to pre-existing Maghrebi artistic practices.[40] A strange double bind, but not if we follow Artaud's timelines, like lines securing boats.

Ships from the East: "Marseille – L'Arrivée"[41]

Artaud begins "The Theatre and the Plague" in the archives found on an island in the Mediterranean. The first page of this text – a historical fairy tale and plague warning – is the keystone for my argument:

> In the archives of the small town of Cagliari, Sardinia, lies an account of an astonishing historic occurrence. One night, about the end of April or the beginning of May 1720, some twenty days before the ship Grand-Saint-Antoine reached Marseille, where its landing coincided with the most wondrous outbreak of plague to be recorded in that city's history, Saint-Rémy, the Sardinian Viceroy, perhaps rendered more sensitive to that most baleful virus by his restricted monarchical duties, had a particularly agonizing dream. He saw himself plague-ridden and saw the disease ravage his tiny state. Society's barriers became fluid with the effects of the scourge. Order disappeared. He witnessed the subversion of all morality, a total psychological breakdown, heard his lacerated, utterly routed bodily fluids murmur within him in a giddy wasting-away of matter, growing heavy and then gradually being transformed into carbon. Was it too late to ward off the scourge? Although organically destroyed, crushed, extirpated, *his very bones consumed,* he knew one does not die in dreams, that our will-power even operates ad absurdum, even denying what is possible, in a kind of metamorphosis of lies reborn as truth. He awoke. He would show himself able to drive away *these plague rumours and the miasmas of the oriental virus.* The Grand-Saint-Antoine, a month out of Beirut, requested permission to enter the harbour and dock there. At this point the Viceroy gave an insane order, an order thought raving mad, absurd, stupid and despotic both by his subjects and his suite. He hastily dispatched a pilot's boat and men to the supposedly infected vessel with orders for the Grand-Saint-Antoine to tack about that instant and make full sail away from the town or be sunk by cannon shot. War on the plague. The autocrat did not do things by halves.[42]

Due to the Viceroy's dream or premonition, the ship avoids his island, and instead ends up in Marseille harbour.[43] Marseille's archives, according to Artaud, do not

39 Tengour, "Le Surréalisme maghrébin".
40 Abdel-Jaouad, "Tendances surréalistes".
41 Alexandre Dumas, *Le Comte de Monte-Cristo*, vol. 1, ed. Gilbert Sigaux, Paris: Gallimard 1998, 13.
42 Artaud, "Plague", 9; my emphasis.
43 Even though it appears on the first page of Artaud's text, the *Grand-Saint-Antoine* is not the first ship to be found in Artaud's *The Theatre and Its Double.* The first ship is a hypothetical

record what happened there, and it is only after those Caligari subjects see what happened in Marseille that they enter into their own archive the details of how they avoided the plague. This recording of the plague after the fact marks its absence, resulting in a close call rather than a port of call. Artaud notes that the members of the ship's crew "did not all die of the plague, but *were scattered over various countries*", a diasporic crew, embodying translation and transmission.[44] The ship, however, did not bring the plague to Marseille, because according to Artaud, "it was already there".[45] Artaud's description of the carnivalesque reversals that the plague deposits on the social order, where "barriers became fluid" and "[o]rder disappeared" are echoed in Foucault's theorization. Gilman sees the plague "as a biological catastrophe demanding a political response", and argues that it "can intervene in biopolitics" in such a way that it requires "a rethinking of sovereignty and 'biopower' in relation to the power of the plague subject".[46] Gilman's point in hindsight is seemingly obvious, but his "alternative biopolitics of the plague" connects sovereignty, surveillance, biopolitics and the plague-infested body in a radical way.[47] Modernity and the modern subject are coterminous with the plague, which allows us "to think finally about the configuration of a biopolitical plague subject, a process that would begin by reinstating the body as its anchor".[48] Considered in light of Artaud's reading of the plague and the role of sovereignty with the body as the "anchor", the body as anchor travels on a Mediterranean ship, and this will also have ramifications for the modern postcolonial subject in the former metropole. Historically, germ language has been weaponized to dehumanize populations. Rereading Artaud's Mediterranean plague next to and through Tengour is not a solution to this history. Rather, it reveals its continuity otherwise. Negative language around migration, refugees, racialized populations, disability, illness – to name but a few sites of continued discrimination – still employs germ logic and contamination in many European spaces.

The plague on the *Grand-Saint-Antoine* was "the original, oriental virus, hence the unusually horrible aspect" and thus *rejuvenated* an already existing and semi-

---

one, found in Artaud's preface. In the preface Artaud is concerned with the collapse of the living, writing that "confusion is a sign of the times", there is a "schism between things and words [...] between ideas and the signs that represent them" (p. 3). Language, life, the world, is out of joint. In other words, humans have lost sight of magic, and fear magic. Since humans have lost vivacity and culture, "our deep-rooted lack of culture is surprised at certain awe-inspiring anomalies; for example, on an island out of contact with present-day civilization, the mere passage of a ship carrying only healthy passengers can induce the outbreak of diseases unknown on that island but peculiar to our countries: shingles, influenza, grippe, rheumatism, sinusitis and polyneuritis" (pp. 4–5). Infection and contagion lie in wait in the preface, to be revived by an actual ship in Marseille.

44 Artaud, "Plague", 10; my emphasis.

45 Artaud, "Plague", 10.

46 Gilman, "Subject of the Plague", 35.

47 Gilman, "Subject of the Plague", 36.

48 Gilman, "Subject of the Plague", 40.

dormant plague that was specific to Marseille.[49] The ship's name, *Grand-Saint-Antoine*, refers to Saint Anthony of Egypt, patron saint of infectious diseases.[50] Artaud tells us that "the only genuine plague comes from Egypt, arising from the cemeteries uncovered by the subsiding Nile", according to old medical journals, as well as Herodotus.[51] The term *plague ship* has two meanings in English: a ship whose crew is infected with plague;[52] and *plagueship*, a seventeenth-century "title of mock respect for a tiresome person".[53] An alternative reading of this word, with the suffix *-ship* referring to the state or condition of having the plague, would support the concept of the body as anchor, carrying the plague around, embodying it. A plague/ship is a shipwreck within a ship. In terms of surrealist shipwrecks, Abdel-Jaouad considers the Moroccan writer Mohammed Khaïr-Eddine (1941–1995) "a good illustration of the surrealist shipwreck and the wanderer".[54] Khaïr-Eddine connects surrealism, the plague, and the biopolitical subject, writing: "I have become a pond of microbes."[55] Can this be contained?

Ottoman origins / Lingua franca

For Artaud even the source of the plague is up for discussion, as its origins are not clear. He is sceptical about the science of plague transmission: "During the 1880s, a French doctor called Yersin, working on the corpses of Indo-Chinese [colonial bodies] who had died of the plague" isolated the virus/microbe. Artaud contends: "In my eyes, this [thing 'only visible under a microscope'] is only a much smaller, infinitely smaller material factor [...] but does not help to explain the plague at all."[56] He continues:

49 Artaud, "Plague", 10.

50 Anthony of Egypt is considered the father of monasticism as he was the first monk to go into the wilderness, the subject of the "temptation of Saint Anthony", and patron of infectious diseases, especially of the skin (shingles, in particular, which Artaud mentions in his preface, and which is also known as St Anthony's fire). Other contenders include Anthony of Padua, patron saint of lost things and people, and Anthony of Athens, whose throat was slit in Constantinople. Smallpox was referred to as the "the so-called Antonine plague"; see Sallares, "Disease", 253.

51 Artaud, "Plague", 11.

52 "Plague ship, *n.2*", *OED Online*, Oxford University Press, June 2020, http://www.oed.com/view/Entry/267215. Gilman, "Subject of the Plague", 40, asks: "But what would be the response today to the modern counterpart of the plague ship – an airliner en route to a major city, transporting a passenger who was discovered to have been exposed to the Ebola virus or to be a carrier of dengue fever?"

53 "Plagueship, *n.1*", *OED Online*, Oxford University Press, June 2020, http://www.oed.com/view/Entry/144962.

54 Abdel-Jaouad, "Tendances surréalistes", 262fn50.

55 "Je suis devenu un étang de microbes." Cited in Abdel-Jaouad, "Tendances surréalistes", 262fn50.

56 Artaud, "Plague", 14.

> I would rather this doctor had told me why all great plagues last five months, with or without a virus [...] and how the Turkish Ambassador, passing through Languedoc towards the end of 1720, could draw an imaginary line from Nice to Bordeaux passing through Avignon and Toulouse, as the outer geographic limit of the scourge's spread, events proving him correct.[57]

For Artaud, these mysterious events reveal that "the disease has an inner nature whose laws cannot be scientifically specified and it would be useless to try and fix its geographic source".[58] Gilbert Buti attempts to "fix" the "source" of the eighteenth-century plague, recalling the following to the reader, as if this is common knowledge, or what passes for it:

> Avant d'ouvrir le registre, il me paraît souhaitable de rappeler à grands traits le cheminement de la contagion depuis le Levant, entendez le Proche-Orient et plus généralement le bassin oriental de la Méditerranée, jusqu'aux portes de la Valette. Comme la funeste peste noire, la contagion a été, en 1720, introduite par voie maritime à partir du monde ottoman, "terre d'élection de la peste".[59]

The plague is introduced through marine channels from the Ottoman world, "the land of the plague". One source says the plague was discovered on the *Grand-Saint-Antoine* after the death of a Turkish passenger on the ship.[60]

Back in Marseille, Artaud remarks that the captain of the ship *Grand-Saint-Antoine* is the only one who does not catch the plague. This recalls another fabled ship landing in Marseille, one which, as Rodolphe Gasché and William Firebrace have noted, makes the same journey as Artaud's *Grand-Saint-Antoine*. The ship *Pharaon* (Pharaoh, or King) is both a literary device and a character in Alexandre Dumas *père*'s well-travelled nineteenth-century novel *Le Comte de Monte-Cristo* (The Count of Monte Cristo). In Dumas's opening ship, it is only the captain who perishes, a mirrored reversal of Artaud. Both Artaud's and Dumas's ships come from the East. Chapter

57 Artaud, "Plague", 14.

58 Artaud, "Plague", 14.

59 Gilbert Buti, *La Peste à La Valette: La peste au village, 1720–1721*, Marseille: Editions Autres Temps 1996, 22. Buti's citation of "terre d'élection de la peste" comes from Daniel Panzac, *La Peste dans l'empire Ottoman, 1700–1850*, Leuven: Peeters 1985.

60 We can read this dead passenger – Turkish plague-carrier from the land of the plague – next to the first (and famous) Ottoman ambassador to France, referenced by Artaud, who was under quarantine during his 1720 visit to France: Yirmisekiz Mehmed Celebi Efendi (d. 1732). Yirmisekiz was ambassador to Louis XV's France under Sultan Ahmed III. His diplomatic memoirs, called an "Embassy Book" or *Sefâretnâme*, are based on his impressions of his time in the West, and are credited with slightly influencing a relatively closed eighteenth-century Ottoman universe, opening up a path, like Tengour on Breton. The plague and the Ottoman ambassador arrive on French soil together. For eighteenth-century French coverage of the event, see "L'Ambassade solemnelle de la porte ottomane à la cour de France", *Mercure de France*, December 1743 (Kateb Yacine's surrealist piece "Un Ancêtre en voyage" will appear in this same publication almost two hundred years later, in 1962). For a contemporary account of the Turkish ambassador's visit, see Paul Lunde, "A Turk at Versailles", *Saudi Aramco World* 44, no. 3 (1993), http://archive.aramcoworld.com/issue/199306/a.turk.at.versailles.htm.

1 of *Le Comte de Monte-Cristo* is titled "Marseille – L'Arrivée". Habib Tengour's ancestral considerations in "Ancêtre fondateur et tradition orale" are *signed* Marseille.[61] His poem "Traverser…" looks at those who have made the journey from North Africa (specifically Algeria) to France, and what awaits them there.

Abdel-Jaouad remarks that one thing linking what he calls "historical surrealism" and "ontological surrealism" in the Maghreb and the metropole is the French language.[62] One might look at French itself as another plague, or fever.[63] And of course, curriculums travel. Artaud probably read Dumas, and *The Count of Monte Cristo*, just as those Algerians educated in French may have had surrealism transmitted at some point through assigned texts, though it is a question of degrees. Abdel-Jaouad argues that for Maghrebi writers, especially the Algerian writer Kateb Yacine (1929–1989), "the beckoning of Apollinaire and the Avant-garde to draw from sources broader than their own is more than an opening on the world, it is an historical exigency: for the writer educated in the French system, the Other is within himself".[64] This echoes Westbrook at an angle, moving the direction of the vector: "*The Oriental Other is within the West.*"[65]

Abdel-Jaouad employs Edward Said's distinction between filiation and affiliation, which allows for Maghrebi writers to take what is useful from the past (colonial, pre-colonial or otherwise) in order to rewrite texts in their own way.[66] This rewriting also takes account of the well-trod path of *writing back* that many postcolonial writers engage in: "Because it is the locus of an historically conflictual situation *in which the I and the world are opposed*, Maghrebi writing in French involves rewriting the texts about them that the Other has produced over time."[67] It is filiation and affiliation, genealogies searching, like Artaud, for an "authentic language which is rooted in patrimony (Africa in the larger sense) and at the same time reconciled with the requirements of modernity (the West)".[68]

---

61 Habib Tengour, "L'Ancêtre fondateur dans la tradition orale maghrébine", *Peuples méditerranéens/Mediterranean Peoples* 18–21 (1982), 67–75.

62 Abdel-Jaouad, "Tendances surréalistes".

63 Alain Mabanckou was recently asked by the French president Emmanuel Macron to reflect (positively) on *la Francophonie*. He responded in an open letter to the president, outlining the neocolonial designs of France's promotion of the Francophonie in the world, as well as its colonial past. Alain Mabanckou, "Francophonie, langue française: Lettre ouverte à Emmanuel Macron", BibliObs, *L'Obs*, 15 January 2018, https://bibliobs.nouvelobs.com/actualites/20180115.OBS0631/francophonie-langue-francaise-lettre-ouverte-a-emmanuel-macron.html. Macron subsequently found a willing ambassador for his promotion of Francophonie in the French-Moroccan novelist Leila Slimani.

64 Hédi Abdel-Jaouad, "Kateb Yacine's Modernity: Rewriting Surrealism", *SubStance* 21, no. 3 (1992), 11.

65 Westbrook, "Reorienting Surrealism", 715; my emphasis.

66 Abdel-Jaouad, "Kateb Yacine's Modernity", 12.

67 Abdel-Jaouad, "Kateb Yacine's Modernity", 12; my emphasis.

68 Abdel-Jaouad, "Tendances surréalistes", 289.

In a Mediterranean context, this resembles a modern form of lingua franca, which Karla Mallette describes as "both language and a negation of meaningful speech – a 'barbarous jargon'; both culturally or ethnically specific – identified most often as Italian – and transnational. [...] a professional jargon."[69] The reference to "barbarous jargon" would be ironic, playful or weaponized in the land formerly known as Barbary, resembling Khaïr-Eddine's exhortation and practice of "la guérilla linguistique" in a postcolonial context.[70] Lingua franca as a historical object is more ghostly than archival, more gossip and hearsay than standardized, "an extraordinarily ephemeral and fleeting object of historical analysis, yet one that paradoxically endured for centuries and far beyond the Mediterranean environment that generated it".[71] Though hard to locate in the archives, there would have been no Mediterranean trade or transit without it.[72]

In *The Count of Monte Cristo*, the captain is the only one who "catches" brain fever. In Artaud's relaying of the plague's arrival in Marseille, the captain is a curious character in that he drives the plague to Marseille, but does not carry it. What is the difference between the plague and a virus, Artaud wonders? How does this new plague (which is the old plague) awaken in Marseille's inhabitants a dormant plague? Rodolphe Gasché notes in his treatment of Artaud's text, that "'the original virus', the virus of origin, upsets the already localized plague to which it adds itself as its double".[73] And yet, this is after the fact. Today, Marseille itself is seen by some as an oriental virus, rather than a city in France: an island apart, the first stop in or on the way to Africa (the other side of the Mediterranean), or a city that faces outward towards the Mediterranean, and is said to "turn its back" on France.[74]

Marseille at the time of Artaud's 1720 plague was already under quarantine. Saint-Rémy, a proto-surrealist, staves off the plague's arrival in Sardinia through dreaming (a practice Tengour will connect with North African Surrealism). Artaud writes:

> One cannot deny that a substantial though subtle communication was established between the plague and [Saint-Rémy]. It is too easy to lay the blame for communication of such a disease on infection by contact alone.
> But this communication between Saint-Rémy and the plague, though of sufficient intensity to release imagery in his dreams, was after all not powerful enough to infect him with the disease.[75]

69 Karla Mallette, "Lingua Franca", in: *A Companion to Mediterranean History*, Peregrine Horden and Sharon Kinoshita, eds., Chichester: Wiley-Blackwell 2014, 340.

70 Cited in Abdel-Jaouad, "Tendances surréalistes", 240.

71 Mallette, "Lingua Franca", 340–341.

72 Mallette, "Lingua Franca", ibid.

73 Rodolphe Gasché, "Autogeneous Engenderment: Antonin Artaud's Phonetic Body", in: *The Stelliferous Fold: Toward a Virtual Law of Literature's Self-Formation*, New York: Fordham University Press 2011, 57.

74 See Firebrace, "Mômo in Marseille", for a particularly poignant discussion of this.

75 Artaud, "Plague", 10.

If physical contact is not vital for transmission, dreams and language offer another vector. The plague, notes Artaud, affects the brain and the lungs, two things, he argues, that can be controlled. You can stop your breathing, or you can stop thinking. Is the plague similar to brain fever?[76] They come together in Mediterranean surrealisms.

Surrealism as patrimoine: *"Archéologie du savoir"*

> It is therefore strictly correct to say that without Mohammed Charlemagne would have been inconceivable.
>
> Henri Pirenne, *Mohammed and Charlemagne*[77]

We might read these Mediterranean ports and islands en route to the Maghreb. For it was not only that some North African writers and surrealists shared the French language, it was also that surrealist art and literature became part of what Abdel-Jaouad calls "du patrimoine de tout poète d'expression française" going so far to label it an "Archéologie du savoir", *pace* Foucault.[78] This is doubly interesting:

---

76 Dumas's Captain Leclère is not the only one to suffer from brain fever. The malady makes an appearance in another Mediterranean tale of centre and periphery, Dumas's *Les Frères corses* (The Corsican Brothers), also published in 1844. After the novella's publication, "Corsican syndrome" would be known as a syndrome connecting brothers who can feel one another's pain, as if through the transmission of dreams. Dumas stages his fantastic novella between Corsica and Paris, a centre–periphery shuttle that illustrates the difference between a Mediterranean island that does not "feel" French, and its overlords. Dumas writes: "Corsica is a French Department certainly, but Corsica is very far from being France"; see Alexandre Dumas, *The Corsican Brothers*, trans. Henry Frith, London: Routledge 1880, 7, https://www.gutenberg.org/ebooks/41881. Brain fever is a nineteenth-century specialty – a male malady analogous to the nervous condition of hysteria, gendered feminine – and also appears in Bram Stoker's 1897 novel *Dracula*, as well as in a twentieth-century Ottoman version of Stoker's text, Ali Rıza Seyfioğlu's *Kazıklı Voyvoda*, recently translated into English; see Ali Rıza Seyfioğlu and Bram Stoker, *Dracula in Istanbul: The Unauthorized Version of the Gothic Classic*, trans. Necip Ateş, ed. Ed Glaser, n.p.: Neon Harbor Entertainment 2017. It is not clear if "brain fever" is contagious, but the figure of Dracula is connected to disease in other ways. The historical Vlad the Impaler (also known as Vlad III Dracula and Vlad Tepes), one of the inspirations for *Dracula*, was rumoured to have used germ warfare against the Ottomans in the fifteenth century, in an instance of masking and doubling: "There is a theory that Tepes in effect used germ warfare against the Turks by paying infected Wallachians, disguised as Ottomans, to mingle with the invaders and spread disease among them; suitably high wages were paid to these men. Such tactics sound rather unlikely. Lepers were visibly ill and everyone, Turks and Christians alike, shunned them, stoning them in their bleeding rags and kicking them out of civilized society." M.J. Trow, *Vlad the Impaler: In Search of the Real Dracula*, Stroud: History Press 2003, 209. In Murnau's famous 1922 silent film *Nosferatu*, inspired by Stoker's *Dracula*, the figure of Nosferatu arrives in Germany with his dirt-filled coffins thought to be filled with plague from the East. His murders are conflated with plague that runs through the town until Nosferatu's death.

77 Henri Pirenne, *Mohammed and Charlemagne*, trans. Bernard Miall, New York: Barnes & Noble Books 1992, 234.

78 Abdel-Jaouad, "Tendances surréalistes", 15.

first, this mélange of inheritance and influence does not allow for an origin to be disentangled. And second, in the case of Tengour's ethnology practice – and the intersections between the rise of French ethnography and the surrealist movement, also discussed by Clifford – it covers the Mediterranean. As the recently deceased Algerian writer Nabile Farès (1940–2016) argues, ethnography, no matter its qualities, is always resented in a colonized country, because it comes only with political, social, economic and cultural violence.[79] It is well known that surrealists turned to exotic elsewheres for influence, but Clifford notes that this exotic turn also "included a certain Paris".[80] Benjamin's "little universe" of Paris devours the external exotic. Tengour's ethnographic training is another form of writing back and against colonization and French colonial knowledge production.

Clifford argues in "On Ethnographic Surrealism" that the year 1925 inaugurates the French ethnographic-surrealist knot via three events. First, the *Revue nègre* in Paris "enjoys a smash season", as jazz and black spirituals enchant a French bourgeoisie looking for something "primitive, *sauvage* ... and completely modern".[81] Second, Paul Rivet, Lucien Lévy-Bruhl and Marcel Mauss establish the Institut d'ethnologie in Paris, an "organization whose primary concern is the training of professional field workers and the publication of ethnographic scholarship";[82] later on Rivet will create the Musée de l'homme. Finally, in 1925, Breton and company "make [themselves] notorious" by supporting anti-colonial rebels in Morocco.[83]

The anti-colonial rebels in Morocco were led by Abd el-Krim in what is known as the Rif War (1920–1926), against both the Spanish and the French. This anti-bourgeois pro-rebel gesture was an excuse for the nascent French Communist Party (PCF) and intellectuals (including surrealists) to come together. Various stances were taken, with letters and manifestos published.[84] Abd el-Krim had both a

79 Cited in Abdel-Jaouad, "Tendances surréalistes", 17.

80 Clifford, "On Ethnographic Surrealism", 542.

81 Clifford, "On Ethnographic Surrealism", 555. In contemporary terms, the word *nègre* is offensive, and, bizarrely, still the term used for "ghostwriter" in French. Clifford writes: "During the twenties the term *nègre* could embrace modern American jazz, African tribal masks, voodoo ritual, Oceanian sculpture, and even pre-Columbian artefacts. It had attained the proportions of what Edward Said has called an 'orientalism' – a knitted-together collective representation figuring a geographically and historically vague, but symbolically sharp, exotic world."

82 Clifford, "On Ethnographic Surrealism", 543.

83 Clifford gestures even further than simple continuity between surrealism and ethnography: "The logic developed by Bataille, which I cannot pursue here, has provided an important continuity in the ongoing relation of cultural analysis and surrealism in France. It links the twenties context of surrealism proper to a later generation of radical critics, including Michel Foucault (editor of Bataille's *Complete Works*), Roland Barthes, Jacques Derrida, and the Tel Quel group" ("On Ethnographic Surrealism", 546). Surrealism infects the entire twentieth century of French intellectual thought.

84 These stances were not always legible, or, in fact, were *too* legible. David Drake writes of a letter of support for the rebels signed by many intellectuals, including Artaud and Breton. But Artaud claims he did not support it, so names may have been added without consent.

religious and a Spanish secular education; he worked as an interpreter, translator and go between, before rebelling against the Spanish and French military, a hybrid of dragoman and lingua franca. He makes an appearance in Tengour's manifesto, in a North African genealogy that adds to and rewrites Breton's: "Abd el Krim correspondait avec la Troisième Internationale".[85] And after a line break, a critique, turning away from history and the sea itself: "Un goût immodéré de l'histoire et de la dispute l'enchaîne ironiquement à une hagiographie sommairement exploitée. [...] Il tourne le dos à la mer et se méfie du soleil pour en connaître les coups terribles."[86] Abd el-Krim's rebellion eventually fails, and he is exiled to the island of Réunion in the Indian Ocean, a form of house arrest in the outer colonies. He escapes after twenty years and makes his way to Egypt, where he dies at the age of eighty after living to see Algerian independence.

Abdel-Jaouad links ethnography to North African surrealists through a *style* of writing, where the refusal of the colonizer's ethnographic gaze results in refusing "imposed reality", creating "surréalité", that is, "establishing one's own 'ethnographic presence' for oneself".[87] Tengour does this both in his surrealist manifesto and his poem "Traverser...". Even if Abdel-Jaouad is somewhat concerned, again, with direct transmission (i.e. there is little evidence of historical contact between North African writers and surrealists in the metropole), we might think about imaginary kinship, since North African participation could have happened by sheer virtue of Maghreb existence in the metropole (whether direct or indirect on the level of the individual). It was always already a kernel – at least since the nineteenth century, there is no such thing as an *absence* of contact between colonized Algeria and the metropole/Paris producing surrealists and surrealism. It may take the form of rewriting, as Abdel-Jaouad's claims on Kateb Yacine's *œuvre* make manifest. For Clifford, ethnography "suggests a characteristic attitude of participant observation among the artefacts of a defamiliarized cultural reality".[88] He continues: "The surrealists were intensely interested by exotic worlds, among which they included *a certain Paris*."[89] By the time Tengour makes it to France with his father in the 1950s, the potentially

See David Drake, "The PCF, the Surrealists, *Clarté* and the Rif War", *French Cultural Studies* 17, no. 2 (2006). Abd el-Krim's more recent afterlives include posters of his face in Marseille in 2019 in solidarity with protests in Morocco – see Megan C. MacDonald, "Algeria Time and Water Logic: Image, Archive, Mediterranean Futurity", in: *Languages of Resistance, Transformation, and Futurity in Mediterranean Crisis-Scapes: From Crisis to Critique*, Maria Boletsi, Janna Houwen and Liesbeth Minnaard, eds., London: Palgrave 2020 – and a recent appearance on the ARTE documentary *Décolonisations* (2019) directed by Karim Miské and Marc Ball. For more on the surrealists and the Rif War, see Hassan Banhakeia, "L'Histoire oubliée des surréalistes et la guerre du Rif", May 2005, http://emsomipy.free.fr/Documents/Art.Maroc128.Rif.Surrealistes.htm.

85 Tengour, "Le Surréalisme maghrébin", 78.

86 Tengour, "Le Surréalisme maghrébin", 78.

87 Abdel-Jaouad, "Tendances surréalistes", 18.

88 Clifford, "On Ethnographic Surrealism", 542.

89 Clifford, "On Ethnographic Surrealism", 542; emphasis added.

exotic other for inspiration has become the revolutionary rebel, danger to the colonial project ("mission civilisatrice"), and the to-be-contained. And this lens, too, is the product of colonial ethnography. If, as Westbrook has it, the "Orient" is both inspiration for surrealists as well as something they cannot quite *contain*, is Tengour playfully suggesting surrealism was already in "the Orient" a case of reversing the gaze but keeping the logic, or claiming a root?

The post-World War I malaise in Europe – which helped produce the surrealist mentality, the aesthetic of the fragment, modernist works and so on – happened in the wake of six million French war casualties. In order to replace workers in the metropole who had died in WWI, workers were imported from the colonies. By 1930, Paris and its outskirts were home to a North African population of 70 000. The period following World War II also saw a huge increase in workers imported from France's southern shore of the Mediterranean, French subjects all, though not considered citizens, a surreal conceit. When the Algerian War of Independence began in 1954, there were already 200 000 Algerians in France. By the 1980s, almost twenty years after Algerian Independence, when Tengour is writing his manifesto and poetry between Algeria and France, French youth of North African background were fighting for rights, recognition and equality. In 1981 there were riots outside of Lyon, widely covered by the media and inaugurating what would become a long series of instances of public unrest in the *banlieues*, or urban outskirts. It was also thought to be the first time that cars were burned in protest. A march against racism and for equality in 1983 began with seventeen people deciding to walk from Marseille to Paris. They picked up more marchers along the way, arriving in Paris fifty days later with 100 000 people attending the event.[90] This corresponds and coincides with the so-called *beur* novel's appearance in France.[91] Tengour writes in his manifesto: "Il existe en effet un espace divisé appelé Maghreb mais le Maghrébin est toujours ailleurs. Et c'est là qu'il se réalise."[92] If, following Etienne Balibar's suggestive question "Algérie, France: une ou deux nations?",[93] we claim that – surreally – perhaps after centuries of resentment, transmissions, translation and transit, Algeria and France are "still" one country, is the "ailleurs" of "le Maghrébin" found in France, and thus in Algeria at the same time?[94] Is to be French necessarily to be Mediterranean?

---

90 See the Al Jazeera documentary *Muslims of France* (2014), directed by Karim Miské, for interviews with those involved with the march.

91 *Beur* is French slang (known as *verlan*, where the end of a word is put at the beginning, making it "backwards") for "Arab". This term, too, has changed with time. Slang of slang, now the term *rebeu* is used, the backward term itself made backward again. See Hakim Abderrezak, *Ex-Centric Migrations: Europe and the Maghreb in Mediterranean Cinema, Literature, and Music*, Bloomington: Indiana University Press 2016, 225n1, where he notes that *rabza* is an "up-and-coming" term to replace *rebeu*.

92 Tengour, "Le Surréalisme maghrébin", 78.

93 Étienne Balibar, "Algérie, France: Une ou deux nations?", *Lignes* 1, no. 30 (1997), 5–22.

94 A version of this argument, but in the colonial context, to support claims of surrealism's influence in Algeria, was made by Gérard-Georges Lemaire in his review of the special issue

Plague transmission and the world, print culture and the word

The plague represents the other side of the miracle.
Graham Hammill, "Miracles and Plagues"[95]

Connecting other "elsewheres", we move back to Artaud, and further out from the Mediterranean. In *Artaud le Moma* – the title of this work coincides with an Artaud exhibition at the Museum of Modern Art (MoMA) in New York, and plays on Artaud's text "Artaud le Mômo" – Jacques Derrida describes Artaud as "celui qui se présentait souvent lui-même comme un revenant".[96] Where or what is this ghostly Artaud returning from? The "Mômo" in Artaud's text "Artaud le Mômo" is often read as referring to "kid", *le môme* in Marseille slang, or the fool. Gasché notes that Artaud describes the plague virus as a "têtard" (tadpole) a French word "also meaning child or tot".[97] In light of the readings at hand, Mômo, a common French nickname for Mohammed, could also be read as another reference "from the East". Artaud the man became like a puppet or a doll when he was in psychiatric hospitals undergoing electroshock therapy. On Artaud's prolonged electrocutions, Derrida writes: "je n'ose pas dire ce martyr par crainte de re-christianiser son insurrection contre le christianisme qui dévorait et parasitait son corps".[98] For Derrida, Christianity is like the plague for Artaud, devouring him. Artaud himself writes in his preface to *The Theatre and Its Double*: "All true effigies have a double, a shadowed self."[99]

Artaud was the son of East and West, revolting against the West and its holy ghosts. His middle names are Mary and Joseph, mother-father. Considering himself self-fashioned, he wrote: "Me, Antonin Artaud, I am my son, my father, my mother and me; […] from the grandmother much more than mother-father."[100] How

---

of *Algérie Littérature/Action*; Gérard-Georges Lemaire, "Algérie Littérature/Action: André Breton, le surréalisme et l'Algérie", *Ent'revues*, 16 January 2017, https://www.entrevues.org/aufildeslivraisons/14112-2/.

95 Graham Hammill, "Miracles and Plagues: Plague Discourse as Political Thought", *Journal for Early Modern Cultural Studies* 10, no. 2 (2010), 86.

96 Jacques Derrida, *Artaud le Moma*, Paris: Galilée 2002, 17. Derrida, too, arrived in France from Algeria (like Tengour, but earlier), inhabiting, but not fully, the hyphen (*trait d'union*) in the term *Franco-Maghrébin*. See Jacques Derrida, *Monolingualism of the Other: Or, The Prosthesis of Origin*, trans. Patrick Mensah, Stanford: Stanford University Press 1998; and Megan C. MacDonald, "Haunting Correspondences and Elemental Scenes: Weaving Cixous after Derrida", in: *Cixous after / depuis 2000*, Elizabeth Berglund Hall, Frédérique Chevillot, Eilene Hoft-March and Maribel Penalver Vicea, eds., Amsterdam: Brill Rodopi 2017.

97 Gasché, "Autogeneous", 54.

98 Derrida, *Artaud*, 20.

99 Artaud, *The Theatre and Its Double*, 6.

100 Dumas *père* is also an effigy with a shadow. Here, antecedents have borders that are both blurred and transcolonial. His father, General Thomas-Alexandre Davy de la Pailleterie, was born in Haiti in 1762 to a French nobleman and a black slave. He was taken to France by his father at age 14, entered the military academy, and went on to have a successful military career. He was thus born into slavery and nobility. His slave status was removed upon reaching the metropole, revealing the borders of what happens in the colony and not in the

ancient or original are his antecedents? They speak in many languages. If every effigy has a shadow, what is the shadow of the oriental germ, or the eastern virus?

The viceroy in Artaud's tale, Saint-Rémy, did exist historically, but his name comes from further back, Sardinia wrapped back into France.[101] Saint Remigius, known in French as Saint Remi or Saint Remy, is the saint from whom the city of Reims in France derives its name. An oriental germ of a different flavour, Bishop Remy baptized the first king of the Franks, Clovis, as a Catholic on Christmas Day in 508 (after Clovis was convinced by his wife Clotilde to convert), and thus ushered in the French monarchy as a Catholic one, rendering the city of Reims as an archive: Clovis is considered to be the first king of France. Centuries later, Pirenne calls the result of Islam's advance towards the western Mediterranean "the final separation of East from West, and the end of Mediterranean unity".[102] From here on, the western Mediterranean can be considered "a Musulman lake".[103]

The plague, writes Artaud, is "the revelation".[104] We might read Catholicism's arrival in the monarchy, thus founding what is called France, as a plague of Catholicism, a germ from the Orient, with a shadow that became occidental. Artaud remains (and yet continues to come back, *revenant*) as a kind of uncanny martyr. But a martyr for whom? Or what? Artaud died in a hospital in Paris in 1948, and was initially buried there. In 1975, at the request of his family, his remains were transferred to the family burial plot in Marseille. When what remained of his body got to Marseille, the tomb was already full.[105] As Gasché offers, on Saint-Rémy's dream and the social: "His dream as well as the circulating rumors in the social body of the town are already the first signs of the plague".[106] The madness of the plague is already there, embodied in speech. This oral contagion, dreams, gossip and the plague, can be compared to the rise of print culture itself as a plague. Where lingua franca is difficult to find in print, Gilman writes of the "dark side of the first Gutenberg revolution [...] glimpsed by those who, during the era of early

metropole. Dumas *père*'s father chose the name of his mother, Dumas, and passed it along to his son Alexandre. Alexandre kept this name, like Artaud, more grandmother than mother-father. Another question of burial and archives arose when, in 2002, Alexandre Dumas's ashes were reinterred in the Pantheon. These transferred bones and ashes are doubled graves from potentially destabilizing roots.

101 Rodolphe Gasché reads Artaud's archives as a space which "not unlike Saint-Remy in his dream [...] gather and record the emanations of the plague"; see "Autogeneous Engenderment", 61. Reims itself is an archive to monarchs, holding the bones of the *original* Saint-Rémy. The real bones are in a reliquary, having become the dead doubles that stand in for, or previously formed part of the living. We might call this biomorphic art if the bones were not real, or even organic surrealism.

102 Pirenne, *Mohammed and Charlemagne*, 284.

103 Pirenne, *Mohammed and Charlemagne*, 284.

104 Artaud, "Plague", 20.

105 See Firebrace's account for more details on Artaud's final unmarked resting place.

106 Gasché, "Autogeneous Engenderment", 56.

modern plagues, saw in print a monster of uncontrolled replication".[107] Artaud's stuttering body and logorrhea split the difference.

Tengour offers a Maghrebi response to surrealist concerns, sometimes with a Sufi twist, but also uses the manifesto to answer back to those who would define him, invoking print culture, and the missive, as a way to transmit a twentieth-century Mediterranean plague in a rewriting of oral traditions. One of the equivalences involves madness. Tengour writes in an ethnographic spirit that North Africans are in touch with madness, but their artists less so (reclaiming it from a colonizing or ethnographic lens, specifically the colonial postcard – "des fous de cartes postales"[108]). The madman inhabits a liminal position, which Ferda Keskin compares to the movement of immigrants and refugees across bodies of water, "reminiscent of the medieval madman who was forced to wander through European rivers in the *Narrenschiff*, the Ship of Fools", which Foucault explores in *Folie et déraison*.[109] Like the madman, the migrant or refugee inhabits a "liminal position unique to the threshold itself, the very point of passage with no behind or beyond, [which] constitutes a space which includes the madman, but also the exiled, the immigrant, the refugee, and excludes the same figures by the very act of including them".[110] Madness and migration in one body, constantly on the threshold, suspend surrealism in the Mediterranean and do not guarantee arrival for those attempting to cross it in the present day. A modern form of the plague outnumbers attempts at quarantine, and various European countries turn away boats of migrants and refugees, always claiming that they are the responsibility of another country.[111]

Stefania Pandolfo offers a sensitive discussion of madness, ethnography, psychoanalysis, Quranic cures and the legacy of the French Protectorate in Morocco in *Knot of the Soul: Madness, Psychoanalysis, Islam*. She notes that the French introduced vaccines in Morocco at the same time that they tried to wipe out traditional forms of medicine, while quarantines were put in place in the name of public health, in a kind of double germ-work.[112] Pandolfo turns to Frantz Fanon's notion of "deculturation" to consider colonial trauma and ethnography, what Fanon calls "the negative of a more gigantic work of economic, and even *biological*, enslavement".[113] Fanon's use of *biological* connects the germ to racial exclusion – or pushed forward,

107 Gilman, "Subject of the Plague", 33.
108 Tengour, "Le Surréalisme maghrébin", 78.
109 Ferda Keskin, "On the Melancholy Shore", in: *Kalliopi Lemos: Round Voyage*, exhibition catalogue, Istanbul: santralistanbul 2008, 59.
110 Keskin, "On the Melancholy Shore", 59.
111 The *Aquarius* crisis is only a single recent example of this; see Ramzy Baroud and Romana Rubeo, "What Is behind the Aquarius Refugee Ship Crisis?", *Al Jazeera*, 17 June 2018, https://www.aljazeera.com/indepth/opinion/aquarius-refugee-ship-crisis-180617091028528.html.
112 Stefania Pandolfo, *Knot of the Soul: Madness, Psychoanalysis, Islam*, Chicago: University of Chicago Press 2018, 43.
113 Fanon cited in Pandolfo, *Knot of the Soul*, 6; my emphasis.

the germ and the postcolonial condition of non-recognition or always othering, what Pandolfo describes as follows: "the unending war is also the unending temporalities of trauma".[114] Pandolfo cites Ibn Khaldun's *Muqaddima*, where he writes of a fourteenth-century plague that "swallowed up many of the good things of civilization and wiped them out [...] both in the East and the West", and connects this plague-writing to the post-temporal space of the Arab Spring in the SWANA (South-West Asia and North Africa) region, where increased migration and stuckness and despair at home result in a "slow death".[115] What is the *post* in post–Arab Spring? (Abdel-Jaouad hears echoes of Frantz Fanon's project and national prescriptions for postcolonial men and women in Artaud's call for a new man, though he does not go so far as to call Fanon a surrealist.[116]) Pandolfo writes of Moroccan youth "thrown into an Elsewhere that is also a different time, a temporality that is not of this world, and, at the same time, is the bodily record of a zone of exclusion".[117] Contemporary madness, colonial quarantine and contemporary bodies in transit and those stuck on the other side all embody this "biopolitical suffering".[118]

In addition to madness, Tengour's other equivalence involves dreaming. Ibn Arabi, Tengour claims, was a surrealist without knowing it. Connecting all of these dreams results in a trans-Mediterranean dreaming, a fever spanning centuries. Tengour cites Ibn Arabi's views on writing:

> In what I have written I have never had a deliberate purpose, like other writers. Glimmers of divine inspiration illuminated me and nearly overcame me, so that I couldn't free my mind of them except by writing down what they revealed to me. If my works show any kind of formal composition, this form is not intentional. I have written some of my works on the behest of Allah, sent to me during my sleep or through revelation.[119]

---

114 Pandolfo, *Knot of the Soul*, 24.

115 Pandolfo, *Knot of the Soul*, 27.

116 Abdel-Jaouad, "Tendances surréalistes", 290, 25. Abdel-Jaouad sees the political and artistic vision of the Souffles group as continuing the legacy of surrealism through their radical politics and dedication to the manifesto form. *Souffles* (1966–1972) was an Arabic- and French-language quarterly based in Rabat, Morocco. Contributors that Abdel-Jaouad considers as working in the surrealist vein include: Abdellatif Laâbi, Mohammed Khaïr-Eddine, Mostafa Nissaboury, Abdelkébir Khatibi, Abdelaziz Monsouri, Bernard Jakobiak and Tahar Ben Jelloun. Abdel-Jaouad calls Laâbi "a kind of André Breton" (p. 204). Olivia C. Harrison and Teresa Villa-Ignacio recently published a critical anthology and translation of the journal, calling it "one of the most fascinating and varied repositories of postcolonial Moroccan poetry and cultural criticism" (p. 3). The first issue began with a manifesto which "declares a decisive break with literary forms and idioms derived from the French and Arabic literary canons and calls for writers to establish a new Moroccan literature in both French and Arabic" (p. 4). See Olivia C. Harrison and Teresa Villa-Ignacio, "Introduction: Souffles-Anfas for the New Millennium", in: *Souffles-Anfas: A Critical Anthology from the Moroccan Journal of Culture and Politics*, Olivia C. Harrison and Teresa Villa-Ignacio, eds., Stanford: Stanford University Press 2015.

117 Pandolfo, *Knot of the Soul*, 209.

118 Pandolfo, *Knot of the Soul*, 101. Here Pandolfo is reflecting on Didier Fassin's work on "bio-legitimisation".

119 Habib Tengour, "Maghrebian Surrealism [Essay & Manifesto]", trans. Pierre Joris, 2017, https://jacket2.org/commentary/habib-tengour-maghrebian-Surrealism-essay-manifesto.

Like a dreaming surrealist poet, Ibn Arabi gets his written inspiration while sleeping. In some ways, Tengour's manifesto is a lament, a text of mourning. Tengour writes of Breton's definition of absolute surrealism, and speaks of the Maghreb case of "SURREALISME Relatif" during the 1920s (in *Relatif* we see the word *Rif*). He writes, on the relative nature: "Il leur était difficile de faire autrement: la famille était un manque qu'ils pleuraient devant un guichet de poste, la patrie une identité confisquée et la religion une reconnaissance."[120] The periphery's arrival in the centre comes up against what is available to the colonized in the metropole: the ethnographers moving south from Paris, and Tengour's Algerian families crying at the French post office, defined by a lack, might cross one another at sea. Letters that cannot travel transform into paper *navettes en panne*. Tengour is ambivalent about genealogies, yet still uses this manifesto to write North African writers and historical figures into an archive of surrealism on the southern shore:

Le Maghrébin de passage est surréaliste dans Djeha.
Nafzawi est surréaliste dans la révélation sexuelle.
Ibn Khaldoun est surréaliste dans l'intrigue.
Sidi Ahmed ben Youssef est surréaliste dans l'imprécation.
Mejdoub est surréaliste dans la détresse.
Feraoun est surréaliste dans Si Mohand.
Kateb est surréaliste dans la tradition.
Dib est surréaliste dans la dérive.
Mrabet est surréaliste dans ses joints.
Sénac est surréaliste dans la rue.
Kheir eddine est surréaliste dans le délire éthylique.
Je suis surréaliste quand je ne suis pas là.
Tibouchi est surréaliste dans certains vers.
Baya n'est pas surréaliste malgré la sympathie de Breton.
Etc.[121]

The one woman on the list – the Algerian artist Baya – was claimed by surrealists, though Tengour rejects this categorization.[122] If the "Je" (I) in Tengour's list is read

---

Original French: "Dans ce que j'ai écrit, je n'ai jamais eu de propos délibéré, comme d'autres auteurs. Des lueurs d'inspiration divine m'illuminaient et me submergeaient presque, de sorte que je ne pouvais en libérer mon esprit qu'en mettant par écrit ce qu'elles me révélaient. Si mes œuvres témoignent d'une quelconque forme de composition, cette forme n'est pas intentionnelle. J'ai écrit certains ouvrages sur le commandement d'Allah, qui m'était envoyé pendant le sommeil ou par une révélation." See Tengour, "Le Surréalisme maghrébin", 79.

120 Tengour, "Le Surréalisme maghrébin", 79. A contemporary surreal version of this can be found in Coline Serreau's 2005 film "Saint-Jacques… La Mecque", connecting the French post office, Catholic pilgrimages and Islam in Europe. The ellipses in the film's title are both journey and non sequitur, where a journey to Mecca happens *in* Europe on a Catholic pilgrimage site, and Spain (site of inquisition) becomes Mecca for the illiterate protagonist, who will learn how to read (a Quranic injunction) on the journey.

121 Tengour, "Le Surréalisme maghrébin", 80. For more on manifestos, see Monique Bellan's contribution to this volume.

122 Abdel-Jaouad remarks that for Breton and Jean Sénac, Baya was "the very incarnation of the '*femme-enfant*'" which obsessed surrealists; see "Tendances surréalistes", 160. In the catalogue

as the poet speaking, what does it mean for him to claim he is surrealist when he "[is] not there" (*ne suis pas là*)? He is surrealist when and because he is between France and Algeria.

Crossing on fire: Migrants, refugees and the plague

Tengour's crossing in "Traverser..." is described as "la traversée décisive / étranger en amnésie", echoing Stuart Hall's claims about migration being a one-way trip.[123] Things, people, roots get lost in the crossing – is the Mediterranean one long shore or many? – but not without infecting one another. Tengour, like Dumas, references the pharaoh with his water crossing, reaching back to Moses and Abrahamic genealogies. All *real* plagues, Artaud reminds us, come from the Nile. The sea itself becomes a kind of germ, as Tengour writes in "Traverser...": "La mer caresse mais n'est pas tendre".[124] The six-page poem written in Constantine, laments landing in France. Constantine is a palimpsest, witness to history. "Traverser..." creates its own genealogies, reading religious heritage ("Pharaon tyrannisait la terre entière alors Dieu sauva Moïse de la noyade pour servir d'instrument à sa vengeance"[125]) as well as archaeological traces of pre-Islamic North Africa ("Les sites maritimes ont d'abord été colonies métèques / il reste du vin fossile en amphore [...] nous arrivâmes plus tard par la piste"[126]). The sea will become even less "tender": this poem is written in 1985, around the time the sea will start bearing witness to large numbers of clandestine migrants and refugees attempting to cross the Mediterranean and the Strait of

for Baya's 1947 exhibition *Derrière le miroir*, Breton called her "a sparkling ghost" who embodied "the contemporary Berber imagination while keeping alive the tradition of Ancient Egypt"; cited in Abdel-Jaouad, "Tendances surréalistes", 160–161. Abdel-Jaouad notes that for the surrealists, the Middle Ages was a time of magic and science, a "privileged space" (p. 162), and that the surrealists wanted to recapture that energy. Breton projects this notion of an earlier, simpler time, in a philo-Orientalist gesture which makes Baya the exciting noble savage, writing in the same catalogue: "Dans une époque comme celle que traverse le monde musulman, il est peut-être naturel que le geste de Baya reproduise dans l'ombre celui de la jeune bergère du Moyen-Age européen, mais surtout il est hautement significatif, au point de vue sociologique, qu'elle recoure au moyen d'intervention sur la vie extérieure qu'à tout prix il s'agit pour elle de se concilier"; cited in Abdel-Jaouad, "Tendances surréalistes", 162. For Tengour, Baya is a "pre-Surrealist, or Surrealist *avant la lettre*" who, for the surrealists, fills a "nostalgic and tragic lack"; see Abdel-Jaouad, "Tendances surréalistes", 161. Martine Antle sees Breton's Orientalist projection onto Baya as a "fantastic *Thousand and One Nights* perspective". The Parisian avant-garde, argues Antle following Sara Makhoul's claims, may have even "seized on Baya to protest colonization in Algeria and to free themselves from the unease and sense of guilt experienced by intellectuals of the period". See Martine Antle, "Surrealism and the Orient", *Yale French Studies* 109 (2006), 11.

123 Tengour, "Traverser...", 70. Stuart Hall, "Minimal Selves", in: *The Real Me: Postmodernism and the Question of Identity*, ICA Documents 6, Lisa Appignanesi, ed., London: The Institute of Contemporary Arts 1987, 44.

124 Tengour, "Traverser...", 70.

125 Tengour, "Traverser...", 71.

126 Tengour, "Traverser...", 72.

Gibraltar from the Maghreb to Europe (Spain and France). Hakim Abderrezak summarizes the phenomenon succinctly:

> Maghrebi clandestine migration has come to be known in the Maghreb as *hrig* and *harga*, or "burning," in Arabic. These terms come from the Arabic triliteral root (*ha-ra-qaf*) [ح.ر.ق], which refers to the act of burning. Transcriptions include *lahrig, l'hrig, el hrig, h'rig, harq,* and *hrague.* Hrig covers the clandestine migrant's (1) burning desire to leave, (2) burning of kilometers to the final destination, and (3) burning identification papers in hopes to make repatriation more difficult for authorities.[127]

In a rejection of surveillance (burning their identity markers) the *harraga* risk death and quarantine. This further connects the plague to the modern subject and biopolitics, following Gilman, who asks: "How can the subject of the plague – and the plague subject – be factored into a theory of biopolitics? How, from the opposite perspective, can a theory of biopolitics accommodate, or be accommodated to, a history of the plague?"[128] Taking the negative rhetoric around refugees and migrants to its limit brings liquid metaphors into contact with disease: flood, invasion, swamp, virus, plague.

Tengour reflects on those who make the crossing from Algeria through more official networks, then send for wife and children, only "to end up stifled in a *banlieue* on lockdown [*quadrillée*], impotent / nostalgic", leaving a landscape of one country without economic opportunity in exchange for confinement in the next.[129] Are they nostalgic for a pre-colonial past? What did that look like? How is it remembered? Nostalgia is a form of home fever, and in the case of Breton, his nostalgia connects something that was never his to a time that never was, through artefacts and artists from the Mediterranean's southern shores (such as Baya), and beyond. People and air are portioned out in the poem. Foucault uses the term *quadrillé* (both "divide into squares" and "lock down") to theorize the plague town under surveillance: the diseased are kept *from* (but still *with*) the healthy.[130] Artaud follows the plague as it moves from the body of the individual to the society of bodies: "Once the plague is established in a city, normal social order collapses. [...] Each family wants its own [pyre to burn the dead]."[131] The *banlieue* reconsidered, or rewritten through plague

---

127 Abderrezak, *Ex-Centric Migrations*, 7–9. There is an entire literature and cinematic tradition of clandestine crossings from the Maghreb; see Abderrezak, *Ex-Centric Migrations*, and Stefania Pandolfo, "'The Burning': Finitude and the Politico-Theological Imagination of Illegal Migration", *Anthropological Theory* 7, no. 3 (2007).

128 Gilman, "Subject of the Plague", 34.

129 Tengour, "Traverser...", 70. Original French: "se retrouver dans une banlieue à air comprimé quadrillée impotent/nostalgique".

130 Foucault, *Abnormal.*

131 Artaud, "Plague", 15. You do not need to read Artaud for this kind of detail on the level of the social regarding the plague, you could also read Daniel Defoe's *Diary of the Plague Year*, published two years after the Marseille plague of 1720, and referencing the London plague of 1665. Gilman notes that it was "the fear that an outbreak in Marseille might cross the Channel" which led to Defoe's writing of the *Diary*; see "Subject of the Plague", 25. Both Defoe and Artaud mention looting – Artaud describes "the scum of the populace,

logic and a Mediterranean continuum, is a space of quarantine, one sometimes reached through *burning* across the Mediterranean: a pyre in flames. Artaud was both inside and outside the social order, individual and part of the family – "insider (the son of a wealthy Marseille family) and also the self-created outsider (the sick man, the excluded, the deluded, the foreigner). It was a dual role he loved to play".[132] For Tengour, insider status is physical: sequestration in the metropole.[133]

Smyrna and the archive as shipwreck: An appeal from the old metropole

> As a child Artaud would be taken down to the quayside of La Joliette to watch his father's ships arrive, bringing goods from the eastern Mediterranean. On occasion he travelled out by boat to visit his extended family in the Levant. His mother, Ephrasie Nalpas, was of Levantine origin, her Greek family mixed with Italian, Maltese and Armenian elements. She came from Smyrna, not far from the site of Phocea, the original town of the Phoceans, the Greek traders who had founded Marseille back in the sixth century BC. Her family traded in dried fruits, cloth, carpets and other goods. Three of Artaud's four grandparents were from this same family in the Levant, now bordered by Turkey and Syria. Like many Greeks they were multilingual, speaking Greek at home, Turkish to the authorities and French and Italian for business. Artaud identified with this maternal side of the family and felt himself to be part of some exotic exterior Orient, part imagined, part real, set against the solid materialism of his Marseillais father.
>
> William Firebrace, "Mômo in Marseille"[134]

> Genealogical histories confirm and explain a present: how we got here from somewhere different; what from the past defines us now.
>
> James Clifford, *Returns*[135]

---

immunized so it seems by their frantic greed" who "enter the open houses and help themselves to riches they know will serve no purpose or profit" (p. 15). Genealogical reversals occur. Kinship is overturned – "The remaining survivors go berserk; the [up until that point] virtuous and obedient son kills his father, the continent sodomize their kin. The Lewd become chaste" (pp. 15–16). The plague, writes Artaud, is "the revelation" (p. 20).

132 Firebrace, "Mômo in Marseille", 4.

133 We might take this further to impose *quadrillé* on the camps set up for *les harkis*, Algerians who fought (often as a result of force or coercion) alongside French colonizers during the Algerian War of Independence. They and their families were rejected by independent Algeria, and subject to violence and death. The French were not thrilled about accommodating them, but many *harkis* were resettled in France, some living for many years in special camps, as if in quarantine from the rest of the population. And, of course, Le Corbusier's Marseille project also obeys the logic of *quadrillé* and aspires to the surrealist project of the new man.

134 Firebrace, "Mômo in Marseille", 4.

135 Clifford, *Returns*, 34.

Since Artaud left the surrealist group in 1929, he was most likely not involved with their counter-exhibit to the Colonial Exposition in 1931, called *La Verité sur les colonies*, but we do know that he was inspired by colonial expositions themselves. Susan Sontag tells us that Artaud saw and was inspired by a Cambodian theatre performance in Marseille in 1922 and the Balinese theatre in Paris in 1931, both features of colonial expositions. But it was not the specificity of Cambodia or Bali which so moved him: "What counts [for Artaud] is that the other culture be genuinely other; that is, non-Western and non-contemporary."[136] Artaud's affiliation with Breton and the surrealists for a time involved what Sontag calls "the Turn to the East". After this turn, there came another: the "interest in a suppressed part of the Western past – heterodox spiritual or outright magical traditions".[137] Artaud's "turn" to the East is multiple, at the intersection of brain fever and the unconscious where some "easts" are closer than others, and often a return to roots and routes (real and imagined).

The Mediterranean is a body of water that unites elsewheres: Smyrna, Marseille, Sardinia, the small island of Monte Cristo, Alexandria, Beirut, Constantine, through the Dardanelles, Istanbul, and again up the Bosphorus all the way to the Black Sea (which Braudel refers to as only "partly Mediterranean"[138]). Smyrna is in the municipal archives in Marseille, even if Artaud's plague story is not. In 1914 – on the heels of the Balkan Wars in 1912–1913, which signalled the end of five hundred years of Ottoman rule in the Balkans – the mayor of Smyrna wrote a desperate letter to the mayor of Marseille. Purges of Greeks had begun in Smyrna. The mayor of Smyrna (is he a Greek and a Turk?) asks the mayor of Marseille to send able-bodied Marseille men to aid the Greeks, since Greece (Phocée) founded Marseille (known to the Ancient Greeks as Massalia, and today referred to as a "cité phocéenne"); Phocée in the sixth century BC was the metropole of Greek colonization in the western Mediterranean. The mayor's description of the violence sounds not unlike the plague: villages "exposed to outrageous violence, fires, and massacres" from the "ravishing Turks".[139] He claims that some in Phocée/Smyrna "recognize France as their second *patrie*" or homeland. The mayor appeals to what he calls the "rich colony", and claims that Marseille cannot remain "insensitive to this appeal from the old metropole, powerful and rich too, in the past, but which suffers today". And in case the mayor of Marseille should lose his bearings, his Phocéen counterpart included a map of the area with the letter

136 Susan Sontag, "Approaching Artaud", in: *Under the Sign of Saturn*, New York: Vintage Books 1981, 44.

137 Sontag, "Approaching Artaud", 44.

138 Fernand Braudel, *The Mediterranean and the Mediterranean World in the Age of Philip II*, vol. 1, Berkeley: University of California Press 1996, 109.

139 Letter from the mayor of Smyrna to the mayor of Marseille, Archives municipales, Marseille, 30II.99, http://archivesenligne.marseille.fr/4DCGI/Web_VoirLaNotice/03_06/30II99/ILU MP24437. All translations from the letter into English are my own.

defined by the blue of the sea, as well as a kind of manifesto in the form of a typewritten poem, titled "À Marseille!" (To Marseille!).[140]

Smyrna remains in the Artaud archive, with the attempted burial in Marseille, even though the tomb, the crypt, is full to bursting. Smyrna in the Marseille archive is an "East" appealing to a "West" (Marseille) founded in the East for help from the Turks (even further East). It is Artaud across the Mediterranean, with his mother's roots in Smyrna and his father's in Marseille. There may be no mention of the *Grand-Saint-Antoine* in Marseille's archives (Artaud claims that record is in Sardinia), but there is a record of Marseille–Smyrna erasures and appeals. Smyrna – appealing to ancient brotherhood, roots and routes, foundations and origins – handing parchment across telegraph wires (as if through the magic of dreams) and mail sent by ships across the Mediterranean. Plague as brain fever is an alternative germ transmission. Even though Henri Pirenne argues that the arrival of Islam in North Africa shattered a previous Mediterranean unity, Nükhet Varlık contends that Mediterranean unity was retained with the experience of the plague:

> As far as the broader Mediterranean world is concerned, the traditional scholarship seems to suffer from assumptions of differences between Christian and Muslim (or Oriental and Occidental) societies with respect to their experiences of plague. [...] In fact, there is compelling evidence in support of the Mediterranean as a unified disease zone, with shared epidemiological experiences, as well as a common heritage of medical traditions.[141]

Pirenne's broken Mediterranean is reunited through plague: the Mediterranean itself morphing from lasso into *cordon sanitaire*, a single shore.[142]

---

140 Like so many archival finds, this was random and felicitous. I found the letter in the Marseille municipal archives while looking for traces of locals' responses to Le Corbusier's controversial, but now celebrated, Unité d'habitation/Cité radieuse. William Firebrace convincingly argues that the "finest" buildings in Marseille are those built with the intention of keeping populations separated from one another, "the insiders from various kinds of outsiders"; see "Mômo in Marseille", 4. He cites Le Corbusier's Cité as an example, as well as the ruined Hôpital Caroline and the Vieille Charité. Le Corbusier once wrote: "The cities are sick with the plague"; cited in Firebrace, "Mômo in Marseille", 8.

141 Nükhet Varlik, *Plague and Empire in the Early Modern Mediterranean World: The Ottoman Experience, 1347–1600*, New York: Cambridge University Press 2015, 2–3.

142 Pirenne's theories, presented in what Theofilo Ruiz calls "his rightly famous though incorrect great book", have been disproved by multiple historians, but the claims may have just been too early. Pirenne's thesis was a temporal problem, literally ahead of its time, since, as Ruiz claims: "What Pirenne (1960) had claimed had taken place with the coming of Islam into the western Mediterranean in the seventh and eighth centuries [...] really did take place in the early modern period. The opening of Atlantic, African, and Asian markets represented a watershed in Mediterranean history, as the Sea and the lands around the western Sea would not begin to play a significant role in world affairs again until the present period." See Theofilo F. Ruiz, "The Mediterranean and the Atlantic", in: *A Companion to Mediterranean History*, Peregrine Horden and Sharon Kinoshita, eds., Chichester: Wiley-Blackwell 2014, 422.

Postscript: Rattle/revenant

> Talk about Mediterraneans can be serious or ironic: how they became city dwellers, fishermen, and navigators or how they remained peasants, shepherds, and landlubbers. Mediterraneans feel closer to their cities than to their states or nations; indeed, cities are their states and nations and more. City dwellers – nobles and commoners alike – aspire to a patrician rather than republican order; they communicate more with one another than with the provincials, whom they despise and mock. Mediterraneans assign newcomers the most menial chores in the city, the coarsest in the port.
>
> Predrag Matvejević, *Mediterranean*[143]

At the end of Dumas's *The Count of Monte Cristo*, the count decides it may finally be time to die. He says to Maximilian Morrel, a man he has saved in many ways, "You cannot take me for a commonplace man, a mere rattle, emitting a vague and senseless noise."[144] I have hoped to show in this paper that Artaud, too, is no commonplace man, a mere rattle, and that bringing him back (once again) from the dead serves to strengthen Mediterranean connections that predate him and that come after him. Even Artaud's seemingly nonsensical linguistic combinations gesture towards a Mediterranean lingua franca. Reading surrealism as trans-Mediterranean dreaming via plague logic creates an alternative genealogy, makes space for alternative dreams and reveals postcolonial nightmares that have yet to be worked through. Following Gilman's insistence that the biopolitical body is bound up with the history of the plague makes for modern subjects whose dreams are infectious and infected, host and carrier. It is a planetary Mediterranean, and Artaud is body and anti-body, relic and reliquary, the son of a king (Antoine-Roi) without a kingdom. And as for Tengour, he too makes a rattle, rewriting the literary and ethnographic scripts for himself and those Maghrebis here and elsewhere. He reminds us that in Mediterranean crossings, if we follow the vectors, there are always liquid traces – *sillages* – wakes.

---

143 Predrag Matvejević, *Mediterranean: A Cultural Landscape*, trans. Michael Heim, Berkeley: University of California Press 1999, 16.

144 Alexandre Dumas, *The Count of Monte Cristo*, London: Routledge 1888, https://www.gutenberg.org/ebooks/1184.

Cumulative bibliography

This bibliography has been compiled from the sources discussed and referred to in the chapters of this volume. It is divided into three sections: archival material; newspapers, magazines and reviews containing poems, essays, reviews, interviews and similar texts; and a general bibliography. Note that references are presented in the format corresponding to the language of the chapter in which they are cited.

Archives

The following archival material has been referred to in one or more chapters of this volume.

Arslan, Yüksel, "La Technique, ou comment on fabrique une Arture", 17 February 1981, Collection Arslan.

Arslan, Yüksel, to José Pierre, 12 November 1959, Archives of the Association Atelier André Breton.

Breton, André, à Georges Henein, 8 avril 1936, archives André Breton, Bibliothèque littéraire Jacques Doucet, Paris.

Henein, Georges, à André Breton, 26 juillet 1948, archives André Breton, Bibliothèque littéraire Jacques Doucet, Paris.

Mayor of Smyrna to the mayor of Marseille, Archives municipales, Marseille, 30II.99, http://archivesenligne.marseille.fr/4DCGI/Web_VoirLaNotice/03_06/30II99/ILUMP24437.

Morpurgo, Nelson, « Marinetti in Egitto », 1938, archives Nelson Morpurgo, Beinecke Rare Book and Manuscript Library, Yale University, New Haven.

Narkiss, Mordechai, to Georges Cyr, 20 October 1943, archives of the Bezalel National Museum, Jerusalem.

Roditi, Édouard, to André Breton, 3 September 1959, Archives of the Association Atelier André Breton.

Saddik, Mohamed, « La IIe Exposition de l'art indépendant, Le Caire, 10 mars 1941 », archives Ramsès Younane, Bibliothèque Kandinsky, Paris.

Schehadé, Georges, "Poésies 1930–1936", typescript, Jad Tabet Collection.

Schehadé, Georges, à André Breton, Beyrouth, 26 avril 1950, fonds André Breton, Bibliothèque littéraire Jacques Doucet, Paris.

Schehadé, Georges, à André Malraux, s.l., 15 décembre 1953, Bibliothèque littéraire Jacques Doucet, Paris (MLX, C. 734).

Schehadé, Georges, to Antoine Mourani, 21 June 1926, Collection Paul and Anne Mourani.

Schehadé, Georges, à Benjamin Péret, Beyrouth, 16 décembre 1958, fonds Benjamin Péret, Bibliothèque littéraire Jacques Doucet, Paris (Ms 34.712).

Newspapers, magazines, and reviews

Reference is made in this volume to poems, essays, reviews, interviews and other such texts published in the following newspapers, magazines and reviews. The individual texts appearing in these sources have not been entered separately in the general bibliography.

al-Ādāb (Lebanon): 9, no. 3 (1961), 9, no. 4 (1961), 9, no. 7 (1961).

al-Adīb (Lebanon): 12 (1954), 12 (1959), 9 (1965).

al-Akhbār (Lebanon): 11 November 2006, 20 February 2010, 25 September 2010, 26 November 2011.

Arsenal: Surrealist Subversion (USA): 3 (Spring 1976).

Art et Liberté (Égypte): 1 (mars 1939), 2 (mai 1939).

*al-Binā*ʾ (Syria): full date 1953.

La Bourse égyptienne (Égypte): 9 novembre 1927, 12 mars 1937, 22 mai 1942, 16 décembre 1944, 10 février 1948, 8 juin 1953.

Bulletin de l'Atelier d'Alexandrie (Égypte): 1985.

Les Cahiers d'Alexandrie (Égypte): 1967.

Clé (France): 2 février 1939.

Commerce (France): 26 (Winter 1930).

Cumhuriyet (Turkey): 5 January 1937, 27 March 1937, 19 May 1937, 20 August 1937, 23 December 1937.

Le Désir libertaire (France): 1 (5 décembre 1973), 2–3 (15 avril 1974), 4 (26 juillet 1974), 5 (1 novembre 1974), « L'Amnésie administrée » (1980), « L'Islam brûle » (25 décembre 1980), « SUBobJECTIVITÉS » (1981).

Don Quichotte (Égypte): 29 mars 1940.

L'Égypte nouvelle (Égypte): 22 mars 1924, 6 juin 1925, 18 mars 1941, 23 janvier 1943.

L'Égyptienne (Égypte): juillet 1927, février 1929, février 1930, février 1931, avril 1932, juin 1934.

La Femme nouvelle (Égypte): décembre 1949, été 1950, 1951.

La Gazette d'Orient (Égypte): mai 1937.

al-Ḥadīth (Syria): July 1933, September 1936, January 1948, January 1949, January 1950, January 1956, May 1958.

L'Illustration juive (Égypte): décembre 1929, mars 1930.

Images (Égypte): 5 janvier 1930, 11 décembre 1937, 11 mars 1938, 18 mars 1941, 11 mars 1945, 25 mars 1945, 15 avril 1945, juin 1945, 5 août 1945, 9 septembre 1945, 18 novembre 1945, Noël 1945.

Le Journal d'Égypte (Égypte): 15 juin 1937, 16 mars 1941, 9 janvier 1950.

Journal du commerce et de la marine (Égypte): 8 Décembre 1958.

Journal suisse d'Égypte et du Proche-Orient (Égypte): 25 mars 1942, 23 avril 1952, 30 avril 1952, 21 mars 1956.

Lignes (France): 30 (1997).
Loisirs (Égypte): printemps 1950.
London Bulletin (UK): 15 juin 1939, 15 avril 1939.
Mawāqif (Lebanon): 35 (1979), 32 (1978).
Mercure de France (France): December 1743.
Messages d'Orient (Égypte): avril 1926.
al-Mulḥaq (Lebanon): 4 October 1964, 20 June 2015.
al-Nahār (Lebanon): 23 January 1983.
La Nouvelle Revue française (France): avril 1929, février 1939.
La Part du sable (Égypte): 1 (1947).
Le Périscope (Égypte): 31 mars 1945.
Peuples méditerranéens/Mediterranean Peoples (France): 17 (1981), 18–21 (1982), 30 (1985).
Le Phare égyptien (Égypte): 9–10 mars 1926.
Le Progrès égyptien (Égypte): 4 avril 1947.
al-Qīthārah (Syria): 10 (1947).
La Réforme (Égypte): 9 mai 1945.
La Révolution surréaliste (France): 12 (15 décembre 1929).
La Revue des conférences françaises en Orient (Égypte): octobre 1937, janvier 1939, mars 1939, mai 1945, juin 1945, octobre 1945, octobre 1946, décembre 1946, octobre 1947, juin–août 1948, septembre 1948.
La Revue du Caire (Égypte): avril 1938, mai 1939, avril–juin 1939, novembre 1939, juin 1941, février 1942, juin 1942, août 1945, octobre 1948, novembre 1949, janvier 1950, septembre 1950, octobre 1950, avril 1951, septembre 1951, décembre 1951, janvier 1952, janvier 1953, février 1955, avril 1955.
La Semaine égyptienne (Égypte): Pâques 1927, juillet 1927, 1 octobre 1927, 30 novembre 1933, 11 février 1937, mars 1941, mai 1944.
Shiʿr (Lebanon): 1 (1957), 7-8 (1958), 9 (1959), 14 (1960), 15 (1960), 16 (1960), 18 (1961), 19 (1961), 24 (1962), 28 (1963), 33–34 (1967), 35 (1967).
Der Spiegel (Germany): 41 (1960).
Supérieur inconnu (France): 9 (1998).
Le Surréalisme, même (France): 3 (1957).
al-Taṭawwur (Egypt): 1 (1940), 3 (1940).
Le Temps (France): 4 October 1935.
Un effort (Égypte): Noël 1933, février 1935, octobre 1935.
Valeurs (Égypte): juillet 1945, avril 1945, octobre 1945, janvier 1946, avril 1946, juillet 1946, octobre 1946.
Variétés (Belgium): 1929.
Varlık (Turkey): 1 (1933).

Yaprak (Turkey): 8 (15 April 1949), 9 (1 May 1949), 13 (1 November 1949), 18 (15 January 1950), 20 (15 February 1950), *Son Yaprak* ("last *Yaprak*"; 1 February 1951).

Films

Benayoun, Robert, réalisateur, « Joyce Mansour présente à Georges Benayoun sa collection d'œuvres d'art rassemblée avec Breton », film de 9 min 38, Office national de radiodiffusion télévision française, 19 avril 1970, http://www.ina.fr/video/I05132588.

Maldoror, Sarah, director, *Le Passager du Tassili*, TV film, Antenne 2, 1986.

Miské, Karim, director, *Muslims of France*, TV series, Al Jazeera 2014.

Miské, Karim, and Marc Ball, directors, *Décolonisations*, TV series, Strasbourg: ARTE 2019.

Murnau, F.W., director, *Nosferatu*, Prana Film 1922.

Serreau, Coline, director, "Saint-Jacques... La Mecque", film, Téléma and France 2 Cinéma 2005.

General bibliography

Individual poems, manifestos, essays, reviews and similar texts that are found in larger collected works have not been entered separately into this general bibliography, with only the more inclusive work listed here; equally, if such texts appeared in newspapers, magazines or reviews, they have been included in the previous section of this bibliography.

Abdel-Jaouad, Hédi, "Kateb Yacine's Modernity: Rewriting Surrealism", *SubStance* 21, no. 3 (1992), 11–29.

Abdel-Jaouad, Hédi, "Tendances surréalistes dans la littérature maghrébine d'expression française", PhD thesis, Temple University, Philadelphia 1983, http://www.limag.com/new/index.php?inc=dspliv&liv=00000141.

Abderrezak, Hakim, *Ex-Centric Migrations: Europe and the Maghreb in Mediterranean Cinema, Literature, and Music*, Bloomington: Indiana University Press 2016.

Abū Shabakah, Ilyās, *Rawābiṭ al-fikr wa-l-rūḥ bayn al-ʿarab wa-l-faranjah*, 2nd ed., Beirut: Dār al-Makshūf 1945.

Ades, Dawn, Krzysztof Fijałkowski, Steven Harris, Michael Richardson and Georges Sebbag, eds., *The International Encyclopedia of Surrealism*, vol. 1, *Movements*, London: Bloomsbury 2019.

Adil, Fikret, *Asmalımescit 74: Bohem Hayatı*, Istanbul: Sel 2015.

Adonis [Adūnīs], *Sufism and Surrealism*, trans. Judith Cumberbatch, London: Saqi Books 2005.

Adūnīs, *al-Naṣṣ al-qurʾānī wa-āfāq al-kitābah*, Beirut: Dār al-Ādāb 2010.

Adūnīs, *al-Ṣufiyyah wa-l-sūriyāliyyah*, London: Dār al-Sāqī 1992.

Ahmad, Feroz, "Politics and Political Parties in Republican Turkey", in: *The Cambridge History of Turkey*, vol. 4, Reşat Kasaba, ed., Cambridge: Cambridge University Press 2008, 226–265.

Akbulut, Durmuş, *Türk Resminin Öncüleri*, Istanbul: Deffter 2009.

Akcan, Esra, "Channels and Items of Translation", in: *Art History in the Wake of the Global Turn*, Jill H. Casid and Aruna D'Souza, eds., Williamston, MA: Yale University Press 2014, 145–159.

Albach, Hester, *Léona, héroïne du surréalisme*, Paris: Actes Sud 2009.

Alexandrian, Sarane, *Georges Henein, 1914–73*, Paris: Seghers 1981.

Alquiè, Ferdinand, *Philosophie du surréalisme*, Paris: Flammarion 1955.

Althusser, Louis, and Étienne Balibar, *Reading Capital*, trans. Ben Brewster, London: Verso 1979.

And, Metin, *Karagöz: Turkish Shadow Theatre*, Istanbul: Dost Yayınları 1975.

Anday, Melih Cevdet, *Paris Yazıları*, Istanbul: Adam 1982.

Angélique, Pierre [Georges Bataille], *Madame Edwarda*, Paris : Éditions Georges Visat 1965.

Antle, Martine, "Surrealism and the Orient", *Yale French Studies* 109 (2006), 4–16.

Apollinaire, Guillaume, *Le Bestiaire, ou Cortège d'Orphée*, Paris: Deplanche 1911.

Apollinaire, Guillaume, *Calligrammes*, Paris: Gallimard 1925.

d'Arschot, Philippe, *Peintres et sculpteurs de l'Égypte contemporaine*, Bruxelles : Éditions des Arts Plastiques 1951.

Arslan, Yüksel, "Autobiography", in: *A Retrospective of Yüksel Arslan: Catalogue*, Levent Yilmaz, ed., Istanbul: Santral İstanbul 2010, 248–253.

Arslan, Yüksel, "Being a Loner is a Wonderful Thing", in: *Yüksel Arslan: Artures*, exhibition catalogue, Zurich: Hatje Cantz 2012, 177–179.

Arslan, Yüksel, and Ferit Edgü, *"Batı Kültürü önünde hiçbir saplantım yok", Mektuplar 1957–2008*, Istanbul: Kitap Yayınevi 2011.

Art et Liberté, *La Séance continue*, Le Caire : Éditions masses 1945.

Art et Liberté, « Vive l'art dégénéré », manifeste, 22 décembre 1938.

« L'Art indépendant en Égypte », catalogue de la IIe Exposition de l'art indépendant, Le Caire, 1941.

Artaud, Antonin, *Œuvres complètes*, vol. 20. Paris: Gallimard 1985.

Artaud, Antonin, *The Theatre and Its Double*, trans. Victor Corti, London: Alma Classics 2014.

Aspley, Keith, *Historical Dictionary of Surrealism*, Lanham: The Scarecrow Press 2010.

ʿAyyāsh, ʿAbd al-Qādir, *Muʿjam al-muʾallifīn al-sūriyyīn fī l-qarn al-ʿishrīn*, Damascus: Dār al-Fikr.

Ayyūb, Nabīl, "Unsī al-Ḥājj al-mukhtalif fī qirāʾah tafkīkiyyah nafsiyyah: al-Aṣl wa-l-muhammash; Aṭyāf al-Masīḥ/ashbāḥ Frūyd", in: *Naṣṣ al-qāriʾ al-mukhtalif (2) wa-sīmyāʾiyyat al-khiṭāb al-naqdī*, Beirut: Librairie du Liban 2011, 169–186.

Babaie, Sussan, "Voices of Authority: Locating the 'Modern' in 'Islamic' Arts", *Getty Research Journal* 3 (2011), 133–149.

Bağcı, Serpil, Filiz Çağman, Günsel Renda and Zeren Tanındı, *Osmanlı Resim Sanatı*, Ankara: T.C. Kültür ve Turizm Bakanlığı Yayınları 2006.

Baglione, Danielle, et Albert Dichy, *Georges Schehadé, poète des deux rives, 1905–1989*, Paris : Éditions de l'IMEC ; Beyrouth : Dār al-Nahār 1999.

al-Bahloly, Saleem, "History Regained: A Modern Artist in Baghdad Encounters a Lost Tradition of Painting", *Muqarnas* 35 (2018), 229–272.

Bakkalcioğlu, Ayfer, "Of Surrealism in Turkey", *Boğaziçi Üniversitesi Dergisi* 2 (1974), 1–5.

Balibar, Étienne, "Algérie, France: Une ou deux nations?", *Lignes* 1 no. 30 (1997), 5–22.

Baltacıoğlu, İsmail Hakkı, *Türklerde Yazı Sanatı: Türk Sanat Yazılarının Grafolojisi ve Estetiği Üzerine Sosyo-Psikolojik Deneme*, Ankara: S.A.Ş. Matbaası 1958.

Banhakeia, Hassan, "L'Histoire oubliée des surréalistes et la guerre du Rif", May 2005, http://emsomipy.free.fr/Documents/Art.Maroc128.Rif.Surrealistes.htm.

Baquey, Stéphane, « Georges Schehadé, Edmond Jabès et Kateb Yacine, une époque de la littérature de langue française en Méditerranée », *Med-Mem*, Marseille : INA Med-Mem 2013, http://www.medmem.eu/fr/folder/47/georges-schehada-edmond-jabas-kateb-yacine.

Barck, Karlheinz, "Latenter Surrealismus manifest: Manifeste des Surrealismus als Medien seiner Internationalisierung", in: *"Die ganze Welt ist eine Manifestation": Die europäische Avantgarde und ihre Manifeste*, Wolfgang Asholt and Walter Fähnders, eds., Darmstadt: Wissenschaftliche Buchgesellschaft 1997, 296–309.

Bardaouil, Sam, "'Dirty Dark Loud and Hysteric': The London and Paris Surrealist Exhibitions of the 1930s and the Exhibition Practices of the Art and Liberty Group in Cairo", *Dada/Surrealism* 19 (2013), 1–24.

Bardaouil, Sam, *Surrealism in Egypt: Modernism and the Art and Liberty Group*, London: I.B. Tauris 2017.

Bardaouil, Sam, et Till Fellrath, dir., *Art et Liberté. Rupture, guerre et surréalisme en Égypte, 1938–1948*, cat. exp., Paris : Skira/Centre Georges Pompidou 2016.

Bardaouil, Sam, and Till Fellrath, eds., *Art et Liberté: Rupture, War and Surrealism in Egypt (1938–1948)*, Paris: Skira/Centre Georges Pompidou 2016.

Barney, Richard A., and Helene Scheck, "Introduction: Early and Modern Biospheres, Politics, and the Rhetorics of Plague", *Journal for Early Modern Cultural Studies* 10, no. 2 (2010), 1–22.

Baroud, Ramzy, and Romana Rubeo, "What Is behind the Aquarius Refugee Ship Crisis?", *Al Jazeera*, 17 June 2018, https://www.aljazeera.com/indepth/opinion/aquarius-refugee-ship-crisis-180617091028528.html.

Bārūt, Muḥammad Jamāl, *al-Shiʿr yaktubu smahu: Dirāsah fī l-qaṣīdah al-nathriyyah fī Sūriyyah*, Damascus: Ittiḥād al-kuttāb al-ʿarab 1981.

Batur, Enis, *PARIS, Ecekent*, Istanbul: Remzi Kitabevi 2012.

Baxandall, Michael, *Patterns of Intention: On the Historical Explanation of Pictures*, New Haven: Yale University Press 1985, 58–62.

Baydoun, Abbas, "Culture and Arts; Re: The Actual", in: *Home Works: A Forum on Cultural Practices in the Region; Egypt, Iran, Iraq, Lebanon, Palestine and Syria*, Christine Tohme and Mona Abu Rayyan, eds., Beirut: Lebanese Association for Plastic Arts – Ashkal Alwan 2002, 22–31.

Bédouin, Jean-Louis, *Vingt ans de surréalisme 1939–1959*, Paris: Denoël 1961.

Bellan, Monique, "Defying the Order from Within: Art et Liberté and its Reordering of Visual Codes", in: *The Art Salon in the Arab Region: Politics of Taste Making*, Nadia von Maltzahn and Monique Bellan, eds., Beirut: Orient-Institut Beirut 2018, 135–164.

Bellmer, Hans, et Georges Hugnet, *Œillades ciselées en branche*, Paris : Jeanne Bucher 1939.

Benjamin, Walter, "Surrealism: The Last Snapshot of the European Intelligentsia (1929)", trans. Edmond Jephcott, *New Left Review* 108 (1978), 47–56.

Benk, Adnan, "A Painter of European Stature", in: *A Retrospective of Yüksel Arslan: Catalogue*, Levent Yilmaz, ed., Istanbul: Santral İstanbul 2010.

Ben-Yehoyada, Naor, "Heritage Washed Ashore: Underwater Archaeology and Regionalist Imaginaries in the Central Mediterranean", in: *Critically Mediterranean: Temporalities, Aesthetics, and Deployments of a Sea in Crisis*, yasser elhariry and Edwige Tamalet Talbayev, eds., New York: Palgrave Macmillan 2018, 217–240.

van den Berg, Hubert, and Walter Fähnders, eds., *Avantgarde*, Stuttgart: J.B. Metzler 2009.

Berk, İlhan, *Gerçeküstücülük: Antoloji*, Istanbul: Varlık 2004.

Berk, Nurullah, *Modern Painting and Sculpture in Turkey*, [Ankara]: Turkish Press 1958.

Berk, Nurullah, *Modern San'at*, Istanbul: Semih Lütfi Bitik ve Basım Evi 1935.

Berk, Nurullah and Orhan Koloğlu, *Fikret Muallâ: Hayatı, Sanatı, Eserleri*, Istanbul: Milliyet Yayınları 1971.

Berksoy, Semiha and Fikret Muallâ, *İki Aykırının Mektupları*, Istanbul: Kırmızı Kedi 2017.

Bernard, Suzanne, *Le Poème en prose de Baudelaire jusqu'à nos jours*, Paris: Librairie Nizet 1959.

Birsel, Salâh, *Fransız Resminde İzlenimcilik*, Ankara: Dost Yayınları 1967.

Birsel, Salâh, *İstanbul-Paris*, Istanbul: Türkiye İş Bankası Kültür Yayınları 1983.

Bocquet, Jérôme, "Francophonie et langue arabe dans la Syrie sous mandat: L'Exemple de l'enseignement missionnaire à Damas", in: *The British and French Mandates in Comparative Perspectives/Les Mandats français et anglais dans une perspective comparative*, Nadine Méouchy and Peter Sluglett, eds., Leiden: Brill 2004, 303–319.

Bonnet, Marguerite, « L'Orient dans le surréalisme. Mythe et réel », *Revue de littérature comparée* 54, fasc. 4 (1980), 411–424.

Bourdieu, Pierre, *Die Regeln der Kunst: Genese und Struktur des literarischen Feldes*, 7th ed., Frankfurt am Main: Suhrkamp 2016.

Bozdoğan, Sibel, "Art and Architecture in Modern Turkey: The Republican Period", in: *The Cambridge History of Turkey*, vol. 4, Reşat Kasaba, ed., Cambridge: Cambridge University Press 2008, 419–471.

Bozdoğan, Sibel, "Reading Ottoman Architecture through Modernist Lenses: Nationalist Historiography and the 'New Architecture' in the Early Republic", *Muqarnas* 24 (2007), 199–222.

Braudel, Fernand, *The Mediterranean and the Mediterranean World in the Age of Philip II*, vol. 1, Berkeley: University of California Press 1996.

Breton, André, *Almanach surréaliste du demi-siècle*, Paris : Éditions du Sagittaire, 1950.

Breton, André, *Free Rein = La Clé des Champs*, trans. Michel Parmentier and Jacqueline d'Amboise, Lincoln: University of Nebraska Press 1995, 7–18.

Breton, André, "Limites non-frontières du surréalisme", *La Nouvelle Revue française* 281 (February 1937), 200–215.

Breton, André, "Manifesto of Surrealism" [1924], 1999, http://www.exquisitecorpse.com/assets/manifesto_of_Surrealism.pdf.

Breton, André, « Préface », *Pierre Molinier*, catalogue de l'exposition à la galerie de L'Étoile scellée, Paris, 27 janvier–17 février 1956.

Breton, André, *Le Surréalisme et la peinture* [1928], Paris: Gallimard Folio essais 1965.

Breton, André, *Manifestes du surréalisme*, Paris: Gallimard 1981.

Breton, André, *Manifestoes of Surrealism*, trans. Richard Seaver and Helen R. Lane, Ann Arbor: University of Michigan Press 1969.

Breton, André, *Nadja*, Saint-Armand Cher: Folio 1964.

Breton, André, *Œuvres complètes*, dir. Marguerite Bonnet, 4 vol., Paris : Gallimard/Pléiade 1988–2008, 3.

Breton, André, *Position politique du surréalisme*, Paris: Éditions Pauvert 1971.

Breton, André, *Surrealism*, ed. Herbert Read, New York: Praeger Publishers 1971.

Buti, Gilbert, *La Peste à La Valette: La peste au village, 1720–1721*, Marseille: Editions Autres Temps 1996.

Camus, Albert, *Œuvres complètes*, vol. 2, *1944–1948*, Paris: Gallimard 2006.

Carrouges, Michel, *André Breton et les données fondamentales du surréalisme*, Paris: Gallimard 1950.

Cauvin, Jean-Pierre, « Petites histoires d'almanach : tour du monde des inventions tolérables », *Pleine marge* 12 (1990), 35–40.

Çelik, Zeynep, "Speaking Back to Orientalist Discourse", in: *Orientalism's Interlocutors: Painting, Architecture, Photography*, Jill Beaulieu and Mary Roberts, eds., Durham: Duke University Press 2002, 19–41.

The Centennial Tale of Turkish Painting, exhibition catalogue, Istanbul: Rezan Has Müzesi 2007.

Charbonnier, Georges, *Essai sur Antonin Artaud: Bibliographie, dessins, portraits et fac similes*, Paris: Seghers 1959.

de Chirico, Giorgio, *Hebdomeros* [1929], New York: PAJ Publications 1988.

Clifford, James, "On Ethnographic Surrealism", *Comparative Studies in Society and History* 23, no. 4 (1981), 539–564.

Clifford, James, *Returns: Becoming Indigenous in the Twenty-First Century*, Cambridge, MA: Harvard University Press 2013.

Corm, Georges Daoud, *Essai sur l'art et la civilisation de ce temps*, Beirut: Dār al-Nahār 1966.

Creswell, Robyn, *City of Beginnings: Poetic Modernism in Beirut*, Princeton: Princeton University Press 2019.

Daftari, Fereshteh, "Redefining Modernism: Pluralist Art before the 1979 Revolution", in: *Iran Modern*, Fereshteh Daftari and Layla S. Diba, eds., exhibition catalogue, New York: Asia Society 2013, 25–44.

Dauphin, Christophe, "'L'Éternité volante' de la messagère d'Ounsi el Hage", *K-Log Diffusion*, 7 October 2015, http://www.klogdiffusion.fr/leternite-volante-de-la-messagere-dounsi-el-hage/.

Deeb, Muhammad A., "The Critical Reception of al-Ḥājj and the *Poème en prose*", *Canadian Review of Comparative Literature* 12, no. 3 (1985), 371–393.

Deguilhem, Randi, "Impérialisme, colonisation intellectuelle et politique culturelle de la Mission laïque française en Syrie sous mandate", in: *The British and French Mandates in Comparative Perspectives/Les Mandats français et anglais dans une perspective comparative*, Nadine Méouchy and Peter Sluglett, eds., Leiden: Brill 2004, 321–344.

Deleuze, Gilles, and Felix Guattari, *A Thousand Plateaus: Capitalism and Schizophrenia*, trans. Brian Massumi, Minneapolis: University of Minnesota Press 1987.

Derrida, Jacques, *Artaud le Moma*, Paris: Galilée 2002.

Derrida, Jacques, *Monolingualism of the Other: Or, The Prosthesis of Origin*, trans. Patrick Mensah, Stanford: Stanford University Press 1998.

Desvaux-Mansour, Marie-France, « Le Surréalisme à travers Joyce Mansour. Peinture et poésie, le miroir du désir », thèse de doctorat, Université Paris 1 Panthéon-Sorbonne 2014, https://www.theses.fr/2014PA010520.

Diba, Layla S., "The Formation of Modern Iranian Art", in: *Iran Modern*, Fereshteh Daftari and Layla S. Diba, eds., exhibition catalogue, New York: Asia Society 2013, 45–65.

Dino, Abidin, *Gören Göz İçin Fikret Muallâ*, Istanbul: Kırmızı Kedi 2017.

Doğramacı, Burcu, « Objekte der Migration. Zeitgenössische künstlerische Strategien und produktive Aneignungen », in: *Dinge des Exils*, Doerte Bischoff and Joachim Schlör, eds., Munich : edition text und kritik 2013, 35–54.

D'Outreligne, Narjess, « Le surréalisme en Orient », *Arabica* 50, fasc. 2 (avril 2003), 248–251.

Drake, David, "The PCF, the Surrealists, *Clarté* and the Rif War", *French Cultural Studies* 17, no. 2 (2006), 173–188.

Drost, Julia, « "Caspar David Friedrich – peintre de l'angoisse romantique". Le Surréalisme et l'héritage romantique allemand », dans : *« Le Splendide XIXe Siècle » des surréalistes*, Julia Drost et Scarlett Reliquet, dir., Dijon : Les Presses du réel 2013, 207–228.

D'Souza, Aruna, "Introduction", in: *Art History in the Wake of the Global Turn*, Jill H. Casid and Aruna D'Souza, eds., Williamston, MA: Yale University Press 2014, vii–xxiii.

Dumas, Alexandre, *Le Comte de Monte-Cristo*, vol. 1, ed. Gilbert Sigaux, Paris: Gallimard 1998.

Dumas, Alexandre, *The Corsican Brothers*, trans. Henry Frith, London: Routledge 1880, https://www.gutenberg.org/ebooks/41881.

Dumas, Alexandre, *The Count of Monte Cristo*, London: Routledge 1888, https://www.gutenberg.org/ebooks/1184.

Duplessis, Yvonne, *Le Surréalisme*, Vendôme: Presses universitaires de France 1961.

Durozoi, Gérard, *Histoire du mouvement surréaliste*, Paris : Hazan 2004.

Dussert, Éric, « Notice biobibliographique », dans : Georges Schehadé, *Les Poésies* [1952], Paris : Gallimard 2001, 161–163.

Duyrat, Frédérique, et al., *Henri Seyrig (1895–1973)*, Beirut: IFPO Press 2016.

L'eau dans l'œuvre de Georges Cyr, catalogue d'exposition, Beyrouth : Centre culturel français 1997.

Edgü, Ferit, *Arslan*, Istanbul: Ada Yayınları 1982.

Edgü, Ferit, "Aşkın Resimleri", in: *"Sevmek Güzel Meslek Reis": B. Rahmi*, exhibition catalogue, İzmir: Folkart Gallery Publishing 2017, 155–157.

Edgü, Ferit, "Breton ve Nadja Üzerine Birkaç Söz", in: André Breton, *Nadja*, trans. Ismail Yerguz, Istanbul: Mitos Yayınları 1992, 5–6.

elhariry, yasser, and Edwige Tamalet Talbayev, "Critically Mediterranean: An Introduction", in: *Critically Mediterranean: Temporalities, Aesthetics, and Deployments of a Sea in Crisis*, yasser elhariry and Edwige Tamalet Talbayev, eds., New York: Palgrave Macmillan 2018, 1–22.

Eroğlu, Özkan, *Türkiye'de Resim Sanatı*, Istanbul: Tekhne 2015.

Ertürk, Nergis, "Surrealism and Turkish Script Arts", *Modernism/Modernity* 17 (2010), 47–60.

Eyüboğlu, Bedri Rahmi, *Dost Dost*, Istanbul: İş Bankası Kültür Yayınları 2004.

Eyüboğlu, Bedri Rahmi, *Gece Yarısı*, Istanbul: İş Bankası Kültür Yayınları 2002.

Eyüboğlu, Bedri Rahmi, *Mavi Yolculuk Defterleri*, Istanbul: Türkiye İş Bankası Kültür Yayınları 2008.

Eyüboğlu, Hughette, ed., *Biz Mektup Yazardık! Bedri Rahmi Eyüboğlu ve Çağdaşlarından Mektuplar: Biz Mektup Yazardık!*, Istanbul: Türkiye İş Bankası Kültür Yayınları 2015.

Fähnders, Walter, "'Vielleicht ein Manifest': Zur Entwicklung des avantgardistischen Manifestes", in: *"Die ganze Welt ist eine Manifestation": Die europäische Avantgarde und ihre Manifeste*, Wolfgang Asholt and Walter Fähnders, eds., Darmstadt: Wissenschaftliche Buchgesellschaft 1997, 18–38.

Fani, Michel, *Dictionnaire de la peinture au Liban*, Grenoble: Éditions de l'Escalier 1998.

Fenoglio, Irène, « Le choix d'une langue étrangère : enjeu non modique d'un mode de fonctionnement social : la "mode" du français en Égypte », *Transidis*, no. 1, décembre 1992, 77–89.

Fijałkowski, Krzysztof, and Michael Richardson, eds., *Surrealism: Key Concepts*, London: Routledge 2016.

Findley, Carter V., *Turkey, Islam, Nationalism, and Modernity: A History, 1789–2007*, New Haven: Yale University Press 2010.

Firebrace, William, "Mômo in Marseille", *AA Files* 59 (2009), 3–11.

Flahutez, Fabrice, « La Genèse des *Constellations*. Une circulation de sens entre Breton et Miró de 1940 à 1959 », dans : *La Fabrique du titre*, Nadeije Laneyrie-Dagen, Pierre-Marc de Biasi et Marianne Jakobi, dir., Paris : CNRS Éditions 2012, 253–246.

Flahutez, Fabrice, *Nouveau Monde et nouveau mythe. Mutations du surréalisme de l'exil américain à l'Écart absolu*, Dijon : Les Presses du réel 2007.

Flood, Finbarr Barry, "From the Prophet to Postmodernism? New World Orders at the End of Islamic Art", in: *Making Art History: A Changing Discipline and Its Institutions*, Elizabeth Mansfield, ed., London: Routledge 2007, 31–53.

Flood, Finbarr Barry, "Picasso the Muslim: or, How the Bilderverbot Became Modern, Part I", *Res* 67/68 (2016), 42–60.

Flusser, Vilém, *The Freedom of the Migrant. Objections to Nationalism*, dir. Anke K. Finger, Champaign : University of Illinois Press 2003.

Foster, Hal, *Compulsive Beauty*, Cambridge, MA: MIT Press 1993.

Foster, Stephen C., ed., "The Avant-Garde and the Text", special issue, *Visible Language* 21, nos. 3–4 (1987).

Foucault, Michel, *Abnormal: Lectures at the Collège de France, 1974–1975*, trans. Graham Burchell, New York: Picador 2004.

Freud, Sigmund, *The Standard Edition of the Complete Psychological Works of Sigmund Freud*, vol. 17, *1917–1919: An Infantile Neurosis and Other Works*, ed. James Strachey, London: Hogarth Press and Institute of Psychoanalysis 1955.

Gasché, Rodolphe, "Autogeneous Engenderment: Antonin Artaud's Phonetic Body", in: *The Stelliferous Fold: Toward a Virtual Law of Literature's Self-Formation*, New York: Fordham University Press 2011, 49–63.

Gelin, Mathilde, ed., *Daniel Schlumberger: L'Occident à la rencontre de l'Orient*, Beirut: IFPO Press 2010.

Gencer, Yasemin, "Pushing Out Islam: Cartoons of the Reform Period in Turkey (1923–1928)", in: *Visual Culture in the Modern Middle East: Rhetoric of the Image*, Christiane Gruber and Sune Haugbolle, eds., Bloomington: Indiana University Press 2013, 189–214.

Gharieb, Samir, *Surrealism in Egypt and Plastic Arts*, Cairo: Prism Publications Offices 1986.

Gille, Vincent, ed., *Trajectoires du rêve du romantisme au surréalisme*, Paris: Paris musées 2003

Gilman, Ernest B., "The Subject of the Plague", *Journal for Early Modern Cultural Studies* 10, no. 2 (2010), 23–44.

Giray, Muhteşem, *Müstakil Ressamlar ve Heykeltraşlar Birliği*, Istanbul: Akbank 1997.

Goer, Charis, et Michael Hofmann, dir., *Der Deutschen Morgenland. Bilder des Orients in der deutschen Literatur und Kultur von 1770 bis 1850*, Munich: Wilhelm Fink Verlag 2008.

Gökberk, Macit, "Dr. Robert Anhegger ve İstanbul Türk-Alman Kültür Merkezi", in: *Türkische Miszellen: Robert Anhegger, Festschrift, Armağani, Mélanges*, Gudrun Schubert, ed., Istanbul: Divit Press 1987, 5–10.

Görknar, Erdağ, "The Novel in Turkish", in: *The Cambridge History of Turkey*, vol. 4, Reşat Kasaba, ed., Cambridge: Cambridge University Press 2008, 472–503.

Groves, Jason, "Writing under the Influence", *MLN* 122 (2007), 1124–1137.

Güner, Kağan, *Modern Türk Sanatının Doğuşu: Konstrüktivist Türkiye Cumhuriyeti'nde Kültür ve İdeoloji*, Istanbul: Kaynak Yayınları 2014.

Günyol, Vedat, *Sanat ve Edebiyat Dergileri*, Istanbul: Alan Yayincilik 1986.

Haidar, Otared, *The Prose Poem and the Journal Shiʿr: A Comparative Study of Literature, Literary Theory and Journalism*, Reading: Ithaca Press 2008.

al-Ḥājj, Unsī [Ounsi El Hage], *Éternité volante*, ed. and trans. Abdul Kader El Janabi, Paris: Sindbad/Actes Sud 1997.

al-Ḥājj, Unsī, "Fī ghurfat Jāk Prīvīr", in: Jacques Prévert [Jāk Prīvīr], *Khamsūn qaṣīdah*, trans. ʿAbduh Wāzin, Beirut: Dār al-Nahār 1997, 25–31.

al-Ḥājj, Unsī [Ounsi El Hage], *La Messagère aux cheveux longs jusqu'aux sources et autres poèmes*, Paris: Sindbad/Actes Sud 2015.

al-Ḥājj, Unsī, *Kalimāt kalimāt kalimāt*, 3 vol., Beirut: Dār al-Nahār li-l-Nashr 1987.

al-Ḥājj, Unsī, *Lan*, Beirut: Dār Majallat Shiʿr 1960.

al-Ḥājj, Unsī, *Māḍī l-ayyām al-ātiyah*, Sidon: al-Maktabah al-ʿAṣriyyah 1965.

al-Ḥājj, Unsī, *al-Rasūlah bi-shaʿrihā l-ṭawīl ḥattā l-yanābīʿ*, Beirut: Dār al-Nahār li-l-Nashr 1975.

Hakim, Carol, *The Origins of the Lebanese National Idea: 1840–1920*, Berkeley: University of California Press 2013.

Hall, Stuart, "Minimal Selves", in: *The Real Me: Postmodernism and the Question of Identity*, ICA Documents 6, Lisa Appignanesi, ed., London: The Institute of Contemporary Arts 1987, 44–47.

Halman, Talat Sait, "I Am Listening to Istanbul: Orhan Veli Kanık", in: *Rapture and Revolution: Essays on Turkish Literature*, Jayne L. Warner, ed., Syracuse: Syracuse University Press 2007, 339–347.

Halman, Talat Sait, "Introduction", in: *I Am Listening to Istanbul: Selected Poems of Orhan Veli Kanık*, trans. Talat Sait Halman, New York: Corinth Books 1971, i–xxii.

Halman, Talat Sait, *A Millennium of Turkish Literature: A Concise History*, ed. Jayne L. Warner, Syracuse: Syracuse University Press 2011.

Halman, Talat Sait, *Türk Edebiyatı Tarihi*, Ankara: Kültür ve Turizm Bakanlığı 2006.

Hammill, Graham, "Miracles and Plagues: Plague Discourse as Political Thought", *Journal for Early Modern Cultural Studies* 10, no. 2 (2010), 85–104.

Hans Bellmer. Anatomie du désir, cat. exp., Musée national d'art moderne, Paris : Gallimard/Centre Pompidou 2006.

Hans Bellmer. Exposition de portraits, du 6 mai au 4 juin avec un texte de Jean Cocteau, cat. exp., Paris : Librairie Jean-Jacques Pauvert 1955.

Harrison, Olivia C., and Teresa Villa-Ignacio, "Introduction: Souffles-Anfas for the New Millennium", in: *Souffles-Anfas: A Critical Anthology from the Moroccan Journal of Culture and Politics*, Olivia C. Harrison and Teresa Villa-Ignacio, eds., Stanford: Stanford University Press 2015, 1–12.

Ḥasan, ʿAbd al-Karīm, *Qaṣīdat al-nathr wa-intāj al-dalālah: Unsī al-Ḥājj unmūdhaj*[an], Beirut: Dār al-Sāqī 2008.

Ḥāwī, Khalīl, *Khalīl Ḥāwī: Falsafat al-shiʿr wa-l-ḥaḍārah*, ed. Rītā ʿAwaḍ, Beirut: Dār al-Nahār 2002.

Hayot, Eric, and Rebecca L. Walkowitz, *A New Vocabulary for Global Modernism*, New York: Columbia University Press 2016.

Henein, Georges, et Jo Farna, « La Guerre qui revient » dans « Le Rappel à l'ordure », 1935, non paginé.

Henein, Georges, *Œuvres : poèmes, récits, essais, articles et pamphlets*, Paris: Denoël 2006.

Hilâv, Selahattin, *Edebiyat Yazıları*, Istanbul: Yapı Kredi Yayınları 2008.

Hilâv, Selahattin, "Yüksel Arslan Üzerine", in: *Yüksel Arslan: İlişki, Davraniş, Sıkıntılara Övgü'den Arture'lere (1955–1970)*, Mazhar Şevket İpşiroğlu, Orhan

Duru, Ferit Edgü and Selahattin Hilâv, eds., Istanbul: Yapı Kredi Yayınları 2016, 65–69.

Hilâv, Selahattin, Ergin Ertem and Onat Kutlar, eds., *Gerçeküstücülük*, Ankara: de 1962.

Hodges, Richard, and David Whitehouse, *Mohammed, Charlemagne, and the Origins of Europe: Archaeology and the Pirenne Thesis*, Ithaca, NY: Cornell University Press 1983.

Hourani, Albert, *The Emergence of the Modern Middle East*, Los Angeles: University of California Press 1981.

Hudson, Michael C., "Democracy and Social Mobilization in Lebanese Politics", in: *Analyzing the Third World: Essays from Comparative Politics*, Norman W. Provizer, ed., Cambridge: Schenkman 1978, 271–292.

al-Idlibī, Ulfat, "Ūrkhān Muyassar: Lamḥah min ḥayātihi al-khāṣṣah", *al-Maʿrifah* 160 (1975), 164-171.

İlhan, Attila, *Hangi Batı? (Anılar ve Acılar)*, Ankara: Bilgi Yayınevi 1972.

Ilyās, Jūsīf, *Taṭawwur al-ṣaḥāfah al-sūriyyah fī miʾat ʿām (1865–1965)*, Beirut: Dār al-Niḍāl 1983.

İpşiroğlu, Mazhar Şevket, "Önsöz", in: *Yüksel Arslan: İlişki, Davraniş, Sıkıntılara Övgü'den Arture'lere (1955–1970)*, Mazhar Şevket İpşiroğlu, Orhan Duru, Ferit Edgü and Selahattin Hilâv, eds., Istanbul: Yapı Kredi Yayınları 2016, 1–10.

İpşiroğlu, Mazhar Şevket, *Siyah Qalem*, Graz: Akademische Druck- u. Verlagsanstalt 1976.

İpşiroğlu, Mazhar Şevket, Selahattin Hilâv, Orhan Duru and Ferit Edgü, eds., *Yüksel Arslan (Bir Dönem: 1951–61)*, Istanbul: Ada 1977, 23–44.

İrepoğlu, Gül, *Zeki Faik İzer*, Istanbul: YKY 2005.

Jabrā, Jabrā Ibrāhīm [Jabra I. Jabra], "Modern Arabic Literature and the West", *Journal of Arabic Literature* 2 (1971), 76–91.

Jabrā, Jabrā Ibrāhīm, "Yūsuf al-Khāl: al-Mafāzah wa-l-biʾr wa-l-llāh" [1958], in: *al-Nār wa-l-jawhar: Dirāsāt fī l-shiʿr*, Beirut: Dār al-Quds 1975, 37–47.

Jacob, Preminda, "Between Modernism and Modernization: Locating Modernity in South Asian Art", *Art Journal* 58 (1999), 48–57.

al-Janābī, ʿAbdul Qādir [Abdul Kader El Janabi], ed., *Le Désir libertaire: Le Surréalisme arabe à Paris 1973–1975*, Toulouse: Éditions de l'Asymétrie 2018.

al-Janābī, ʿAbdul Qādir, *Tarbiyat ʿAbdul Qādir al-Janābī*, Beirut: Dār al-Jadīd 1995.

al-Janābī, ʿAbd al-Qādir, *Unsī al-Ḥājj: Min qaṣīdat al-nathr ilā shaqāʾiq al-nathr, mukhtārāt min ashʿārihi wa-khawātimihi*, Beirut: Jadāwil li-l-Nashr wa-l-Tarjamah wa-l-Tawzīʿ 2015.

al-Jayyūsī, Salmā al-Khaḍrāʾ, *Trends and Movements in Modern Arabic Poetry*, Leiden: Brill 1977.

Kane, Patrick M., *The Politics of Art in Modern Egypt: Aesthetics, Ideology and Nation-Building*, London: I.B. Tauris 2013.

Kaufman, Asher, *Reviving Phoenicia: The Search for Identity in Lebanon*, London: I.B. Tauris 2004.

Kemp, Robert, « Monsieur Bob'le », *Le Monde*, 3 février 1951, http://abonnes.lemonde.fr/archives/article/1951/02/03/monsieur-bob-le_2066305_1819218.html.

Keskin, Ferda, "On the Melancholy Shore", in: *Kalliopi Lemos: Round Voyage*, exhibition catalogue, Istanbul: santralistanbul 2008, 57–59.

el-Khoury, Alfred [Alfrād al-Khūrī], "Mulḥaq al-khamsīn ʿāman wa-ʿām", *al-Mulḥaq*, special issue, 20 June 2015, 19.

el-Khoury, Alfred [Alfrād al-Khūrī], "Unsī al-Ḥājj wa-l-suryāliyyah al-faransiyyah: Min al-jasad al-hādhī ilā l-ḥubb al-majnūn", MA thesis, American University of Beirut, Department of Arabic and Near Eastern Languages 2015.

Khoury, Gérard D., "Portrait de Gabriel Bounoure", in: *Dictionnaire des orientalistes*, François Pouillon, ed., Paris: Karthala 2008, 139–140.

Khoury, Gérard D., ed., *Vergers d'exil: Gabriel Bounoure*, Paris: Geuthner 2004.

Khoury-Ghata, Vénus, "La Poésie arabe au Moyen-Orient", *Europe* 609 (1980), 74–78.

Kober, Marc, « Le Démon de la perversité : à propos d'un échange entre André Breton et Georges Henein », dans : *André Breton*, Michel Murat, dir., Paris : L'Herne 1998, 377–382.

Kober, Marc, « Introduction », dans : *Le Désir libertaire. Le Surréalisme arabe à Paris, 1973–1975*, Abdul Kader El Janabi, dir., Toulouse : L'Asymétrie 2018, 9–28.

Kober, Marc, Irène Fenoglio et Daniel Lançon, dir., *Entre Nil et sable : écrivains d'Égypte d'expression française (1920–1960)*, Paris : Centre national de documentation pédagogique, 1999.

Köksal, Duygu, "Art and Power in Turkey: Culture, Aesthetics and Nationalism during the Single Party Era", *New Perspectives on Turkey* 31 (2004), 91–119.

Köksal, Duygu, "The Role of Art in Early Republican Modernization in Turkey", in: *La Multiplication des images en pays d'Islam*, Bernard Heyberger and Silvia Naef, eds., Würzburg: Orient-Institut Istanbul 2016, 154–167.

Krainick, Sibylla, *Arabischer Surrealismus im Exil: Der irakische Dichter und Publizist ʿAbd al-Qādir al-Ǧanābī*, Wiesbaden: Reichert 2001.

Kravagna, Christian, *Transmoderne: Eine Kunstgeschichte des Kontakts*, Berlin: b_books 2017.

Kushner, David, "Self-Perception and Identity in Contemporary Turkey", *Journal of Contemporary History* 32 (1997), 219–233.

Kutlar, Onat, *İshak*, Istanbul: A Dergisi Yayınları 1959.

Kutlar, Onat, *Sinema Bir Şenliktir*, Istanbul: Can 1991.

LaCoss, Don, "Egyptian Surrealism and 'Degenerate Art' in 1939", *Arab Studies Journal* 18, no. 1 (Spring 2010), 78–117.

Ladimer, Bethany, "Madness and the Irrational in the Work of André Breton: A Feminist Perspective", *Feminist Studies* 6, no. 1 (1980), 175–195.

Laffitte, Maryse, "L'Image de la femme chez Breton: Contradictions et virtualités", *Revue romane* 11, no. 2 (1976), 286–305.

Lançon, Daniel, *Jabès l'Égyptien*, Paris : Jean Michel Place 2009.

Lemaire, Gérard-Georges, "Algérie Littérature/Action: André Breton, le surréalisme et l'Algérie", *Ent'revues*, 16 January 2017, https://www.entrevues.org/aufildeslivraisons/14112-2/.

Lenssen, Anneka, "The Shape of the Support: Painting and Politics in Syria's Twentieth Century", PhD thesis, Massachusetts Institute of Technology 2014.

Lenssen, Anneka, Sarah Rogers and Nada Shabout, eds., *Modern Art in the Arab World: Primary Documents*, New York: Museum of Modern Art 2018.

Leoni, Francesca, and Mika Natif, eds., *Eros and Sexuality in Islamic Art*, Farnham: Ashgate 2013.

Lewis, Bernard, *The Emergence of Modern Turkey*, New York: Oxford University Press 2002.

Lunde, Paul, "A Turk at Versailles", *Saudi Aramco World* 44, no. 3 (1993), 30–39, http://archive.aramcoworld.com/issue/199306/a.turk.at.versailles.htm.

Luthi, Jean-Jacques, « Le Mouvement surréaliste en Égypte », *Mélusine 3. Marges non-frontières*, Henri Béhar, dir., Lausanne : L'Age d'homme 1982, 18–35.

Luthi, Jean-Jacques, *La Presse égyptienne d'expression française*, Alexandrie : Éditions de l'Atelier 1978.

Mabanckou, Alain, "Francophonie, langue française: Lettre ouverte à Emmanuel Macron", BibliObs, *L'Obs*, 15 January 2018, https://bibliobs.nouvelobs.com/actualites/20180115.OBS0631/francophonie-langue-francaise-lettre-ouverte-a-emmanuel-macron.html.

MacDonald, Megan C., "Algeria Time and Water Logic: Image, Archive, Mediterranean Futurity", in: *Languages of Resistance, Transformation, and Futurity in Mediterranean Crisis-Scapes: From Crisis to Critique*, Maria Boletsi, Janna Houwen and Liesbeth Minnaard, eds., London: Palgrave 2020.

MacDonald, Megan C., "Bare Life at Sea (The Leper and the Plague)", in: *Biotheory: Life and Death under Capitalism*, Jeffrey R. Di Leo and Peter Hitchcock, eds., London: Routledge 2020, 175–203.

MacDonald, Megan C., "Haunting Correspondences and Elemental Scenes: Weaving Cixous after Derrida", in: *Cixous after / depuis 2000*, Elizabeth Berglund Hall, Frédérique Chevillot, Eilene Hoft-March and Maribel Penalver Vicea, eds., Amsterdam: Brill Rodopi 2017, 36–54.

Maḥfūẓ, ʿIṣām, *al-Sūryāliyyah wa-tafāʿulātuhā l-ʿarabiyyah*, Beirut: al-Muʾassasah al-ʿArabiyyah li-l-Dirāsāt wa-l-Nashr 1987.

Maingon, Claire, "L'Académie Lhote – L'Atelier Léger: Enseignements comparés", in: *L'Éducation artistique en France du modèle académique et scolaire aux pratiques actuelles, XVIIIe–XIXe siècles*, Rennes: Presses universitaires de Rennes 2010, 219–229.

al-Malādhī, Suhayl, *al-Ṭibāʿah wa-l-ṣaḥāfah fī Ḥalab*, Damascus: Dār Yaʿrab li-l-Dirāsāt 1996.

Mallette, Karla, "Lingua Franca", in: *A Companion to Mediterranean History*, Peregrine Horden and Sharon Kinoshita, eds., Chichester: Wiley-Blackwell 2014, 330–344.

Manne, Robert, *The Petrov Affair: Politics and Espionage*, Sydney: Pergamon Press 1987.

Mansour, Joyce, *Cris*, Paris : Pierre Seghers 1953.

Mansour, Joyce, *Déchirures*, Paris : Éditions de Minuit 1955.

Mansour, Joyce, *Jules César* [1955], Paris : Pierre Seghers 1958.

Mansour, Marie-Francine, *Une vie surréaliste : Joyce Mansour, complice d'André Breton*, Chaintreaux : Éditions France-Empire monde 2015.

Mario Prassinos: In Pursuit of an Artist; Istanbul–Paris–Istanbul, exhibition catalogue, Istanbul: Pera Müzesi 2016.

Matvejević, Predrag, *Mediterranean: A Cultural Landscape*, trans. Michael Heim, Berkeley: University of California Press 1999.

Mercer, Kobena, "Introduction", in: *Cosmopolitan Modernisms*, Kobena Mercer, ed., Cambridge, MA: MIT Press 2015, 6-23.

Mercié, Jean-Luc, *Pierre Molinier*, Dijon : Les Presses du réel ; Paris : K. Mennour 2010.

Missir, Marie-Laure, « De Jules César à Jeux de la Poupée. Récit d'une rencontre "à facettes mobiles" entre Joyce Mansour et Hans Bellmer », *Pleine marge* 37 (2003), 155-167.

Mitter, Partha, "Decentering Modernism: Art History and Avant-Garde from the Periphery", *Art Bulletin* 90 (2008), 531–548.

Monaco, Arturo, "The Beginning of the New Age in Syro-Lebanese Poetry: The Case of the Revue *al-Qīthārah* (The Lyre, 1946–47)", in: *Qamariyyāt: Oltre ogni frontiera tra letteratura e traduzione; Studi in onore di Isabella Camera d'Afflitto*, Maria Avino, Ada Barbaro and Monica Ruocco, eds., Rome: Istituto per l'Oriente C.A. Nallino 2019, 391-405.

Monaco, Arturo, "Ispirazione romantica e sperimentalismo surrealista in due raccolte poetiche del siriano ʿAlī al-Nāṣir (1890–1970): *al-Ẓamāʾ* (1931) e *Suryāl* (1947)", *La Rivista di Arablit* 12 (2016), 29–50.

Monaco, Arturo, "Syria and the Reception of Surrealism: *Suryāl* 1947 vs. Radio Sūriyālī (SouriaLi) 2012", in: *New Geographies: Texts and Contexts in Modern Arabic Literature*, Roger Allen, Gonzalo Fernández Parrilla, Francisco Rodríguez Sierra and Tetz Rooke, eds., Madrid: Universidad Autónoma de Madrid 2018, 115–133.

Mualla, Fikret, *"Çakallar"*, Istanbul: Ada 1977.

Muhidine, Timour, "'Ce ciel postiche qui nous appartient à tous': Le Surréalisme en Turquie", in: *La Multiplication des images en pays d'Islam*, Bernard Heyberger and Silvia Naef, eds., Würzburg: Orient-Institut Istanbul 2016, 168–178.

al-Mūsā, Khalīl, "Khamsat udabāʾ muʾassisūn min Ḥalab al-Shahbāʾ", *al-Maʿrifah* 508 (2006), 204-217.

Muyassar, Ūrkhān, *Maʿa qawāfil al-fikr*, Damascus: Ittiḥād al-kuttāb al-ʿarab 1974.

Muyassar, Ūrkhān, *Suryāl wa-qaṣāʾid ukhrā*, Damascus: Ittiḥad al-kuttāb al-ʿarab 1979.

Nacentra, Raymond, ed., *Le Surréalisme: Sources, histoire, affinités*, exhibition catalogue, Paris: Galerie Charpentier 1964.

Nadeau, Maurice, *Histoire du surréalisme* [1945], Paris: Éditions du Seuil 1964.

Nantet, Jacques, *Pierre Gemayel*, Paris: J.C. Lattès 2001.

al-Nāṣir, ʿAlī, and Ūrkhān Muyassar, *Suryāl*, Aleppo: Maṭbaʿat al-salām 1947.

Nin, Anaïs, *The Diary of Anaïs Nin*, vol. 1, *1931–1934*, New York: Mariner Books 1969.

Nordbruch, Götz, *Nazism in Syria and Lebanon: The Ambivalence of the German Option 1933–1945*, New York: Routledge 2008.

Olgun, Tahir, *Edebiyati Lügati*, Istanbul: Âsâr-i lmiye Kütüphanesi Neşriyati 1936.

Özsezgin, Kaya, *Cumhuriyet'in 75. Yılında Türk Resmi*, Istanbul: Türkiye İş Bankası Kültür Yayınları 1998.

Öztoprak, Sema, *Adnan Turani: Yaşam Serüveni, Sanat Üzerine Düşünceleri ve Resimsel Birikimi*, Istanbul: Türkiye İş Bankası Yayınları 2005.

Özveren, Eyüp, "In Defiance of History: Liberal and National Attributes of the Ottoman-Turkish Path to Modernity", in: *Liberty and the Search for Identity: Liberal Nationalisms and the Legacy of Empires*, Iván Zoltán Dénes, ed., Budapest: Central European University Press 2006, 457–499.

Pandolfo, Stefania, "'The Burning': Finitude and the Politico-Theological Imagination of Illegal Migration", *Anthropological Theory* 7, no. 3 (2007), 329–363.

Pandolfo, Stefania, *Knot of the Soul: Madness, Psychoanalysis, Islam*, Chicago: University of Chicago Press 2018.

Panzac, Daniel, *La Peste dans l'empire Ottoman, 1700–1850*, Leuven: Peeters 1985.

Pelvanoğlu, Burcu, *Hale Asaf: Türk Resim Sanatında Bir Dönüm Noktası*, Istanbul: YKY 2007 [and 2018 for the second expanded edition].

Péret, Benjamin, "Le Surréalisme international", *Cahiers d'art* 5–6 (1935), 138.

Petit, Pierre, *Pierre Molinier, une vie d'enfer*, Paris : Ramsay/Jean-Jacques Pauvert 1992.

Peyre, Henri, "The Significance of Surrealism", *Yale French Studies* 2 (1948), 37–49.

Picon, Gaëtan, « Préface », dans : Georges Schehadé, *Les Poésies* [1952], Paris : Gallimard 2001.

Pierre, José, ed., *Investigating Sex: Surrealist Research 1928–1932*, trans. Malcolm Imrie, London: Verso 1992.

Pierre, José, ed., *Tracts surréalistes et déclarations collectives*, vol. 1, *1922–1939*, Paris: Terrain vague 1980.

Pierre, José, ed., *Tracts surréalistes et déclarations collectives*, vol. 2, *1940–1969*, Paris: Terrain vague 1982.

Pirenne, Henri, *Mohammed and Charlemagne*, trans. Bernard Miall, New York: Barnes & Noble Books 1992.

Ponnou-Delaffon, Erin Tremblay, "In and Out of Place: Geographies of Revolt in Camus's La Peste", *Studies in 20th & 21st Century Literature* 39, no. 1 (2015), article 8, https://doi.org/10.4148/2334-4415.1812.

Prassinos, Gisèle, *The Arthritic Grasshopper*, Adelaide: Wakefield Press 2017.

Prévert, Jacques, *Choses et autres*, Paris: Gallimard 1972

Prévert, Jacques, *Œuvres complètes*, Paris: Gallimard/Pléiade 1992–1996.

Prévert, Jacques, *Soleil de nuit*, Paris: Gallimard 1980.

Provence, Michael, *The Great Syrian Revolt and the Rise of Arab Nationalism*, Austin: University of Texas Press 2005.

Puchner, Martin, *Poetry of the Revolution: Marx, Manifestos and the Avant-Gardes*, Princeton: Princeton University Press 2006.

Qishta, Hisham, ed., *al-Taṭawwur*, 2nd ed., Cairo: Elias Publishing 2016.

Radwan, Nadia, "How a Ceramic Vase in the Art Salon Changed Artistic Discourse in Egypt", in: *The Art Salon in the Arab Region: Politics of Taste Making*, Nadia von Maltzahn and Monique Bellan, eds., Beirut: Orient-Institut Beirut 2018, 113–131.

Réage, Pauline, *Histoire d'O*, Sceaux : Éditions Jean-Jacques Pauvert 1954.

Record, Jean, « Un procès surréaliste : Abel Bessac contre André Breton », *La Dépêche*, 30 août 2017, https://www.ladepeche.fr/article/2017/08/30/2635946-un-proces-surrealiste-abel-bessac-contre-andre-breton.html.

Renda, Günsel, "Modern Trends in Turkish Painting", in: *The Transformation of Turkish Culture: The Atatürk Legacy*, Günsel Renda and Max C. Kortepeter, eds., Princeton: Kingston Press 1986, 229–248.

Richard, Anne, *La Bible surréaliste de Gisèle Prassinos*, Wavre: Éditions Mols 2016.

Richardson, Michael, "'Other' Surrealisms: Centre and Periphery in International Perspective", in: *A Companion to Dada and Surrealism*, David Hopkins, ed., Chichester: Wiley Blackwell 2016, 131–143.

Richardson, Michael, "Surrealism Faced with Cultural Difference", in: *Cosmopolitan Modernisms*, Kobena Mercer, ed., Cambridge, MA: MIT Press 2005, 68–85.

Richardson, Michael, and Krzysztof Fijałkowski, "Introduction: Surrealism as a Collective Adventure", in: *Surrealism Against the Current: Tracts and Declarations*, Michael Richardson and Krzysztof Fijałkowski, eds., London: Pluto Press 2001, 1–18.

Roberts, John, *Revolutionary Time and the Avant-Garde*, London: Verso 2015.

Rodinson, Maxime, *Marxisme et monde musulman*, Paris: Éditions du Seuil 1972.

Ruiz, Theofilo F., "The Mediterranean and the Atlantic", in: *A Companion to Mediterranean History*, Peregrine Horden and Sharon Kinoshita, eds., Chichester: Wiley-Blackwell 2014, 412–424.

Ṣā'ib, Saᶜad, "Ūrkhān Muyassar: Adīb wa nāqid", *al-Maᶜrifah* 160 (June 1975), 172-182.

Said, Edward W., *Orientalism*, New York: Pantheon Books 1978.

Said, Edward W., *Orientalismus*, Frankfurt am Main: Fischer 2009.

Saᶜīd, Khālidah, *Yūtūbiyā al-madīnah al-muthaqqafah*, Beirut: Dār al-Sāqī 2012.

Salih, Tayeb, *Season of Migration to the North*, trans. Denys Johnson-Davies, London: Penguin Classics 2003.

Sallares, Robert, "Disease", in: *A Companion to Mediterranean History*, Peregrine Horden and Sharon Kinoshita, eds., Chichester: Wiley-Blackwell 2014, 251–262.

al-Samṭī, ᶜAbd Allāh, "Tajārib awwaliyyah fī qaṣīdat al-nathr al-ᶜarabiyyah", *Nizwā*, 1 May 2011.

Şarman, Kansu, *Türk Promethe'ler: Cumhuriyet'in Öğrencileri Avrupa'da (1925–1945)*, Istanbul: T. İş Bankası Kültür Yayınları 2015.

Sawin, Martica, *Surrealism in Exile and the Beginning of the New York School*, Cambridge, MA : MIT Press 1995.

al-Sayyāb, Badr Shākir, *Poesie*, trans. P. Minganti, Rome: Istituto per l'Oriente 1968.

Sazyek, Hakan, *Cumhuriyet Dönemi Türk Şiirinde: Garip Hareketi*, Ankara: Akçağ Yayınları 2016.

Schehadé, Georges, *L'Écolier sultan* [1950], Paris: Gallimard 1973.

Schehadé, Georges, *Étincelles. Poèmes*, Paris : Éditions de la pensée latine 1927.

Georges Schehadé, *Monsieur Bob'le* [1951], in *Georges Schehadé, Œuvre complète, Le Théâtre, Tome 1*, Beirut : Dar an-Nahar 1989.

Schehadé, Georges, *Poésies*, Paris : G.L.M. 1938.

Schehadé, Georges, *Rodogune Sinne*, Paris : G.L.M. 1947.

Seggerman, Alex Dika, *Modernism on the Nile: Art in Egypt between the Islamic and the Contemporary*, Cairo: American University in Cairo Press 2019.

Seyfioğlu, Ali Rıza, and Bram Stoker, *Dracula in Istanbul: The Unauthorized Version of the Gothic Classic*, trans. Necip Ateş, ed. Ed Glaser, n.p.: Neon Harbor Entertainment 2017.

Shalem, Avinoam, "Exceeding Realism: Utopian Modern Art on the Nile and Abdel Hedi al-Gazzar's Surrealistic Drawings", *South Atlantic Quarterly* 109 (2010), 577–594.

Shattuck, Roger, "Love and Laughter: Surrealism Reappraised", in: Maurice Nadeau, *The History of Surrealism* [1945], trans. Richard Howard, Harmondsworth: Penguin Books 1978, 11–34.

Shaw, Wendy M.K., *Ottoman Painting: Reflections of Western Art from the Ottoman Empire to the Turkish Republic*, London: I.B. Tauris 2011.

Short, Robert S., "The Politics of Surrealism, 1920–1936", *Journal of Contemporary History* 1 (1966), 3-25.

Siyavuşgil, Sabri Esat, *Karagöz*, Istanbul: Milli Eğitim Basımevı 1951.

Sönmez, Necmi, "Formation – Conceptualisation – Emancipation", in: *A Retrospective of Yüksel Arslan: Catalogue*, Levent Yilmaz, ed., Istanbul: Santral İstanbul 2010, 61–74.

Sönmez, Necmi, *Paris Tecrübeleri; École de Paris – Çağdaş Türk Sanatı: 1945-1965*, Istanbul : Yapı Kredi Yayınları 2019.

Sontag, Susan, *Under the Sign of Saturn*, New York: Vintage Books 1981.

Sorin, Raphaël, « Georges Schehadé, le magicien », *Le Monde*, 8 mars 1985, http://abonnes.lemonde.fr/archives/article/1985/03/08/georges-schehade-le-magicien_2743197_1819218.html.

Stoker, Bram, *Dracula* [1897], Oxford: Oxford University Press 2011.

Stott, William, *Documentary Expression in Thirties America*, Chicago: University of Chicago Press 1986.

Suci, Hrant Melih, *Türk Resim Sanatında Gerçeküstücü Ressamlar*, Ankara: Pegem Akademi 2017.

Süreya, Cemal, *Şapkam Dolu Çiçekle: Toplu Yazılar I*, Istanbul: Yapı Kredi Yayınları 2006.

Tabet, Jad, "La Ville imparfaite: Le Concept de centralité urbaine dans les projets d'aménagement et de reconstruction de Beyrouth", in: *Reconstruire Beyrouth: Les Paris sur les possibles*, Nabil Beyhum, ed., Lyon: Maison de l'Orient 1991, 85–120.

Taminiaux, Pierre, "Breton and Trotsky: The Revolutionary Memory of Surrealism", *Yale French Studies* 109 (2006), 52–66.

Tansuğ, Sezer, *Türk Resminde Yeni Dönem*, Istanbul: Remzi Kitabevi 1995.

Tengour, Habib, "Maghrebian Surrealism [Essay & Manifesto]", trans. Pierre Joris, 2017, https://jacket2.org/commentary/habib-tengour-maghrebian-Surrealism-essay-manifesto.

Tietze, Andreas, *The Turkish Shadow Theatre and the Puppet Collection of the L.A. Mayer Memorial Foundation*, Berlin: Mann 1977.

Topuz, Hıfzı, "Bedri Rahmi in Paris", in: *"Sevmek Güzel Meslek Reis": B. Rahmi*, exhibition catalogue, İzmir: Folkart Gallery Publishing 2017, 26–57.

Topuz, Hıfzı, *Paris'te Bir Türk Ressam: Fikret Mualla'nın Yaşamı*, Istanbul: Remzi Kitabevi 2014.

Trow, M.J., *Vlad the Impaler: In Search of the Real Dracula*, Stroud: History Press 2003.

Unsī al-Ḥājj, al-mutamarrid, al-ḥālim, al-naqī: Shahādāt wa-aqwāl, unknown editor, Beirut: Muʾassasat Jūzīf Rʿaydī li-l-Ṭibāʿah and Dār al-Nahār 1995.

Varlık, Nükhet, *Plague and Empire in the Early Modern Mediterranean World: The Ottoman Experience, 1347–1600*, New York: Cambridge University Press 2015.

Veli, Orhan, Melih Cevdet Anday and Oktay Rifat, *Garip: Şiir Hakkında Düşünceler ve Melih Cevdet, Oktay Rıfat, Orhan Veli'den Seçilmiş Şiirler*, Istanbul: Yapı Kredi Yayınları 2014.

Veli, Orhan, *Garip* (2nd ed), Istanbul: Ölmez Eserler, 1945.

Westbrook, John, "Reorienting Surrealism", *The French Review* 81, no. 4 (2008), 707–718.

Wilson, Simon, *Surrealist Painting*, Oxford: Phaidon 1982.

Yağbasan, Eylem, "Ressam Halife Abdülmecid Efendi (1868–1944)", in: *Hanedandan Bir Ressam: Abdülmecid Efendi*, Ömer Faruk Şerifoğlu, ed., Istanbul: YKY 2004, 23–62.

Yaman, Zeynep Yaşa, *D Grubu 1933–1951*, Istanbul: Yapı Kredi Yayınları 2002.

Yıldız, Esra, "A Yüksel Arslan Biography", in: *A Retrospective of Yüksel Arslan: Catalogue*, Levent Yilmaz, ed., Istanbul: Santral İstanbul 2010, 567-580.

Yazar, Mehmet Behçet, *Genç Şairlerimiz ve Eserleri*, Istanbul: Kanaat Kitabevi 1936.

Yilmaz, Levent, "Without Following the Beaten Path", in: *A Retrospective of Yüksel Arslan: Catalogue*, Levent Yilmaz, ed., Istanbul: Santral İstanbul 2010, 11-30.

Yilmaz, Levent, ed., *A Retrospective of Yüksel Arslan: Catalogue*, Istanbul: Santral İstanbul 2010.

Young, Robert J.C., *White Mythologies*, London: Routledge 2004.

Ze'evi, Dror, *Producing Desire: Changing Sexual Discourse in the Ottoman Middle East, 1500–1900*, Berkeley: University of California Press 2006.

Ziadeh, May, "Something about Art", in: *Modern Art in the Arab World: Primary Documents*, Anneka Lenssen, Sarah Rogers and Nada Shabout, eds., New York: Museum of Modern Art 2018, 45–47.

Zürcher, Erik J., *Turkey: A Modern History*, London: I.B. Tauris 2004.

Index